Subjugate or Exterminate!

Subjugate or Exterminate!
A Memoir of Russia's Wars Against Chechnya

Akhmed Zakaev
Translated by Arch Tait

Academica Press
London~Washington D.C.

This English translation first published in the United States of America in 2018 by

Academica Press
1727 Massachusetts Avenue, NW, Suite 507
Washington, DC 20036

For orders call (978) 829-2577

Russian text © Akhmed Zakaev, 2018
English translation © Akhmed Zakaev, 2018
Introduction © Luke Harding, 2018

All rights reserved. Except for the quotation of short passages for the purpose of criticism and review, no part of this publication may be reproduced, stored in a retrieval system, or transmitted in any form or by any means, electronic, mechanical, photocopying, recording or otherwise, without the prior permission of the publishers.

ISBN 9781680530759

Library of Congress Cataloging-in-Publication Data

Names: Zakaev, Akhmed, author. | Tait, A. L., translator.
Title: Subjugate or exterminate! : a memoir of Russia's wars against Chechnya /Akhmed Zakaev ; translated by Arch Tait.
Description: London ; Washington, DC : Academica Press, [2018] | Includes bibliographical references and index.
Identifiers: LCCN 2018042252 | ISBN 9781680530759 [hardcover] ISBN 9781680530889 [paperback]
Subjects: LCSH: Zakaev, Akhmed. | Chechnëiìa (Russia)--History--Civil War, 1994---Biography. | Checheno-Ingushetia (Russia)--History--Biography.
Classification: LCC DK511.C37 Z337 2018 | DDC 947.086--dc23
LC record available at https://lccn.loc.gov/2018042252

The publishers have made every effort to ensure that the URLs for external websites referred to in this book are correct and active at the time of going to press. However, the publishers have no responsibility for the websites and can make no guarantee that a site will remain live or that the content is or will remain appropriate.

Every effort has been made to trace all copyright holders, but if any have been inadvertently overlooked the publishers will be pleased to include any necessary credits in any subsequent reprint or edition.

For further information on Academica Press, visit our website: academicapress.com

Designed by Nai Zakharia

Cover from an original illustration by Adam Guergarlo

Table of Contents

Map of the Chechen Republic of Ichkeria	x
Foreword by Luke Harding	xi

PART 1
Introduction 1

I. A Chechen Childhood and My Early Career 3

Zakaev's birth in exile in Kazakhstan, schooling in Chechnya. His acting career. The Checheno-Ingush Union of Theatre Workers. Meets Djohar Dudaev, future president of an independent Chechnya.

II. The Birth of the Chechen Republic of Ichkeria 13

The impact of Perestroika in Chechnya. The National Congress of the Chechen People in 1990. General Djohar Dudaev elected president of the independent Chechen Republic. Conduct of Ruslan Khasbulato. Zakaev appointed Chechen Republic minister of culture.

III. The First Russo-Chechen War 27

1994. Russia invades Chechnya to 'restore constitutional order.' Zakaev appointed commander of the Chechen government's Seventh Front. Hidden motives of the Russian 'War Party'.

**IV. Russia and the Organization
for Security and Cooperation in Europe** 45

Zakaev appointed to negotiate a ceasefire with Russia under the auspices of the Organization for Security and Cooperation in Europe. Shamil Basaev's Budyonnovsk Raid. Attempted assassination of Russia's General Romanov. Russian massacre of civilians in Samashki. Zakaev organizes disruption of Russian-sponsored 'new elections'.

V. Occupying Grozny 59

Hostage-taking in Kizlyar backfires, but Russia's military operation in Pervomaiskoye fails. CRI forces temporarily occupy Grozny. Zakaev commands Chechen forces in the battle for Goyskoye. Russia assassinates President Dudaev.

VI. Yeltsin's Phoney Victory   81

Russians begin 'Operation Iron Ring'. Assault on Goyskoye. Acting President Yandarbiev almost captured. Yandarbiev and Zakaev fly to Moscow for 'negotiations'. President Yeltsin claims the conflict has been ended.

VII. Reoccupying Grozny   105

Immediately the Russian presidential elections are over, war is resumed and it is claimed the Ichkerian government has been defeated. The Chechens reoccupy Grozny. American pressure prevents the Russian military from razing the city. A ceasefire is agreed with General Alexander Lebed. Most Russian troops withdraw from Chechnya.

VIII. After the Khasavyurt Accord   125

Zakaev leads the Chechen team negotiating with Lebed. Lebed's career. The Ichkerian government is in effective control of the country. After a smear campaign Yeltsin dismisses Lebed from all posts. Russian intelligence agencies prepare to take over the Russian state.

IX. Divide and Rule   147

The Russian intelligence agencies exacerbate divisions among the Chechen leaders in post-First War Chechnya. When Aslan Maskhadov is elected, Acting President Yandarbiev enacts Islamist reforms before Maskhadov's inauguration. Kidnappings of pro-Chechen westerners and journalists working in Chechnya, coordinated by the Russian intelligence agencies, inspire copycat kidnappings by Chechen criminals. A crime wave ensues.

X. Excluding the European Union   159

Ivan Rybkin, a moderate, replaces Lebed and negotiations resume. The Russians are determined to exclude the Organization for Security and Cooperation in Europe from mediation between Russia and Chechnya.

XI. Enter Berezovsky   173

In October 1996, Boris Berezovsky is appointed deputy to Security Council Secretary Rybkin. Zakaev negotiates removal of the last two remaining Russian brigades in Chechnya. An Intergovernmental Agreement is signed.

XII. Subverting Independence   187

The NKVD/KGB/FSB network in Chechnya. Russia's history of genocide in Chechnya. Extent of the destruction in the two recent wars. Russian airbrushing out of history of the role of Chechens in the defence of the Fortress of Brest in 1941. Negotiating with Berezovsky. Russian attempts to undermine Chechen independence. Outflanking General Kulikov over the continued presence of Russian troops in Chechnya.

XIII. A Chechen Crime Wave Made in Russia 211

Heads of other Caucasian republics move towards establishing diplomatic relations. Russia engineers the murder of six members of the Red Cross working in Chechnya. Yandarbiev does nothing to stop it. Journalists employed by Berezovsky are 'kidnapped', inaugurating a crime wave and seriously harming the CRI's international reputation. The CRI's second presidential election. Zakaev's manifesto for Chechen democracy

XIV. A False Dawn 229

Aslan Maskhadov is elected president, but alienates his opponents. Yandarbiev rushes through reforms to 'islamize' the republic before Maskhadov's inauguration. In May 1997, Maskhadov and Yeltsin sign a doctored peace treaty, which the Russians undermine as Yeltsin prepares for a second war. Chechens prematurely celebrate the end of conflict.

PART 2
I. Missed Opportunities in Europe 261

Chechen delegates behave crassly in The Hague and are never invited back. Opportunities to move towards international diplomatic recognition of Chechen independence are consistently missed. The role of the FSB in manipulating the muftiate in Chechnya. Akhmad-haddzhi Kadyrov. Antelope hunting in the Kazakh steppe.

II. Learning Statecraft 277

May 1997, diplomatic visit to Georgia to establish neighbourly relations. Prospective mediation in Georgian-Abkhazian relations. Improving life for Chechens living in Georgia. Meetings with Eduard Shevardnadze. Hostile Russian reaction. Inept Chechen ministers mar Georgian-Chechen relations. Official visit to Georgia by President Maskhadov.

III. Funding Fanaticism 297

Tripartite commercial agreement between Russia, Azerbaijan, and Chechnya. Rybkin and Berezovsky dismissed and replaced by Vladimir Putin in order to protect the Yeltsin 'family' from future criminal prosecution. Misrepresenting Russian aggression against Chechnya as part of George W. Bush's 'war on terror', Russia supports Islamist factions in Chechnya, and CRI law enforcement agencies cannot cope. Three British and one New Zealand telephone engineers are beheaded. Zakaev names the culprits. Putin funds detachments of Islamist fanatics.

IV. The Threat of Democracy 323

Yeltsin commends Wahhabi extremism just as the CRI government attempts to outlaw it. Saudi nationals in Chechnya call for assassination of Maskhadov as an apostate from Islam. Berezovsky warns that Russia fears Chechen independence will cause a chain reaction in other republics. Moscow decides to restart the war. The pretext is an incursion by Shamil Basaev into Dagestan. Russia considers Islamist extremism less dangerous than Western-style democracy. A new war with Chechnya will make the unknown Putin a credible presidential candidate.

V. Destabilization 339

President Maskhadov introduces 'full Sharia law' and rapidly loses credibility. Mufti Akhmad-haddzhi Kadyrov persuades Putin he is the real power in Chechnya, and willing to compromise on independence. Udugov plots with Berezovsky to overthrow Maskhadov. Shamil Basaev contributes to the destabilization.

VI. Gambling on Putin 359

Threats of criminal proceedings against Yeltsin's entourage lead him to 'gamble on Putin and declare him his successor'. The FSB blows up apartment buildings in Moscow, Buynaksk, and Volgodonsk, blaming 'Chechen terrorists', and presenting Putin as the only strong man capable of protecting Russian voters.

VII. The Second Russo-Chechen War 365

On 23 September 1999 missile strikes are launched against civilian targets across Chechnya. Subsequent military operations are genocidal. A secret Russian document states, 'We do not need to be squeamish.' Chechnya's Resistance forces are contaminated by externally funded Islamists not averse to collaborating with the FSB. The Russians retake Grozny.

VIII. With Friends Like These ... 389

The Chechen retreat from Grozny is mishandled, with absurd commands issued by Ruslan Gelaev which cause major loss of life. On the eve of the evacuation Zakaev is, for the second time in two days, involved in a car crash in the blackout and seriously injured. His surviving troops are demobilized and urged to find their way back to their homes.

IX. Hors de Combat 407

Refusing to be evacuated, Zakaev is eventually forced to recognize he is now endangering the lives of those entrusted with his security. A traitor tries to deliver him into the hands of the Russian army but his bodyguards enable him to escape to Urus-Martan. Eventually, by bribing Chechen police and FSB agents, he is spirited across the frontier to Ingushetia.

X. A New President for Russia 423

From Ingushetia Zakaev is moved, with highly placed help, to Georgia. A battle between those in the retreating Chechen column and a Russian paratroop brigade is demythologized. Retreating Chechen troops are not well protected by their commanders, and a massacre occurs at Saadi-Kotar (Komsomolskoye). A stage-managed 'capture' of Salman Raduev boosts Putin's ratings and, on 26 March 2000, he is elected president of Russia.

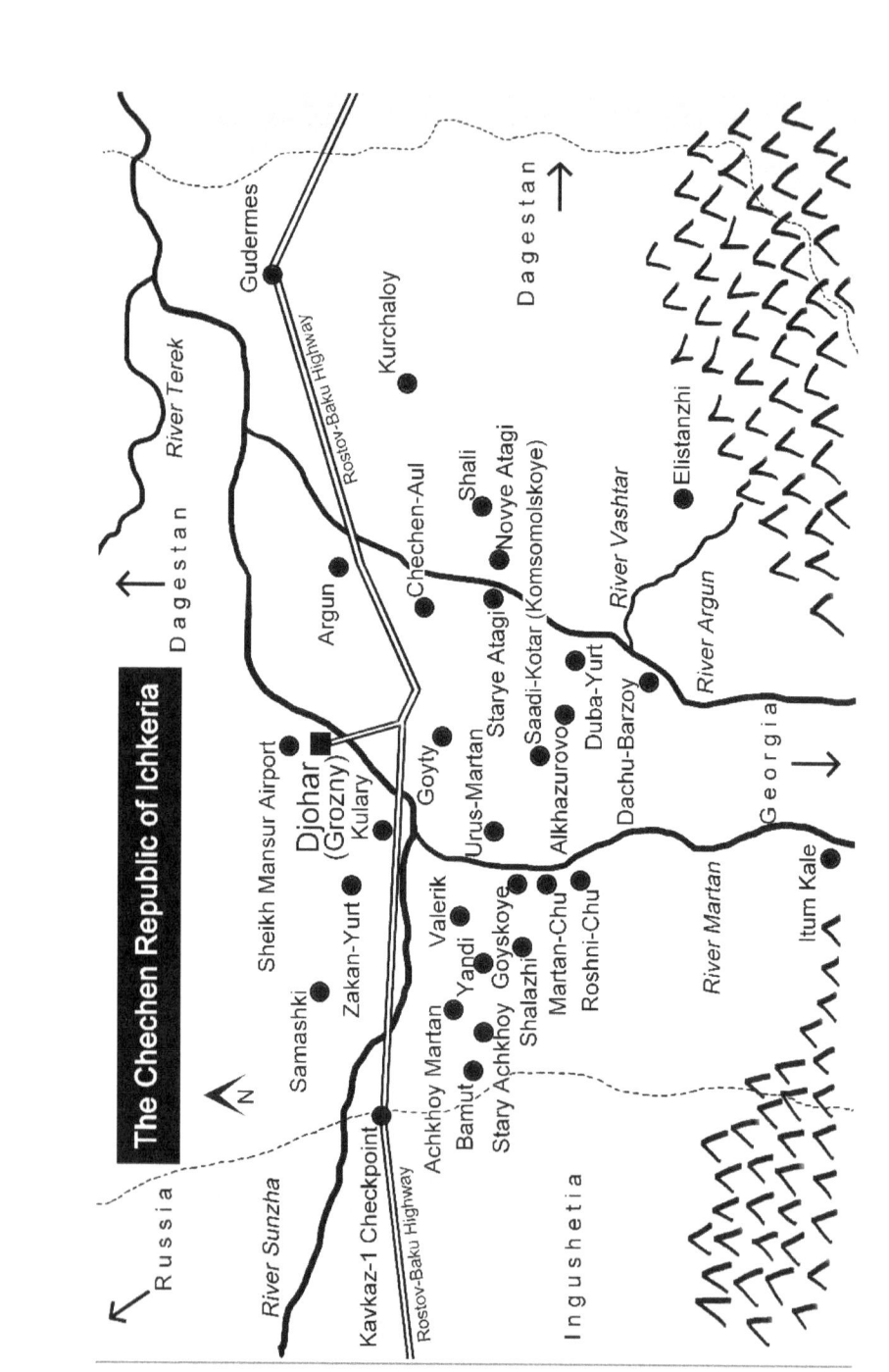

Foreword

Akhmed Zakaev is one of the late twentieth century's most important witnesses. He played a key role in Chechnya's struggle for independence. During Chechnya's two doomed wars with Russia – between 1994-1996 and 1999-2003 – Zakaev was at the heart of events. He was variously a minister, a military commander, a negotiator, and a presidential candidate. Most other senior Chechen figures from this period are dead. Many were wiped out by Moscow. Zakaev is almost the last survivor.

His memoir – 'Subjugate or Exterminate!' – is therefore a compelling historical document, and a unique one. It is a first-hand account of how after the collapse of the Soviet Union Chechens tried to build their own sovereign democratic state. This was never going to be easy. For 130 years imperial and Soviet Russia had sought to conquer and divide the Chechen people. During the Second World War, Stalin deported Chechnya's entire population, including the author's family.

Zakaev grew up in Soviet Chechnya. He spent the 1980s working as a modestly paid actor in the capital Grozny, often playing Shakespearean roles. He found himself drawn into politics following the tumultuous events of 1991. That summer the KGB staged a coup. It failed. Ethnic Soviet republics, led by the future Baltic states, rose up and demanded independence. So did Chechens. In November 1991 the charismatic general, Djohar Dudaev, was sworn in as their first president.

As Zakaev writes, this was a moment of collective optimism. Russian troops and officials exited from what was a precarious quasi-country: the Chechen Republic of Ichkeria. It seemed that Chechnya and possibly the wider North Caucasus were about to take their place in a new ascendancy of nations. For five generations, Chechens had been under Moscow rule. Now they were a colony no more.

Zakaev gives a clear-eyed and remarkably honest account of what happened next. The largest obstacle to Chechnya building a successful state was, of course, the Kremlin and its spy agencies. From the outset, the KGB did everything it could to wreck Chechnya's independence. It tried to divide

Chechen society, backed pro-Moscow Chechen groups, and created a multiplicity of rival political parties.

But Zakaev is scathing too about the weaknesses and disastrous errors of Chechnya's own leaders. They were, quite often, irresponsible, short-sighted and vain. Too frequently Chechen politicians put their own petty interests above national unity. This resulted in factionalism, conflict, enmity and religious division – all of which the 'enemy,' as Zakaev terms Russia, was able gleefully to exploit.

What makes Zakaev's personal story so important is that – unlike previous Russian accounts – it is written from the Chechen perspective. Zakaev was an insider, an intelligent and reflective one. In November 1994 Dudaev appointed him minister of culture. He accepted the job reluctantly, wrapped up his affairs in Moscow and moved back to Grozny.

Zakaev's writing is shot through with a radiant lyricism, in a wonderful translation from the Russian by Arch Tait. Here Zakaev describes the general mood of foreboding as he takes up his new post:

'I had a sense that something evil was in the air. It was rising eerily out of the dank earth that evening, taking form and fusing with the darkness which blanketed the city. It was tangible in the raw chill of autumn.'

A week later Russia attacked. This was the First Chechen War. The Russian air force began bombing. Much of it was indiscriminate. Zakaev used wire to close up his ministry's glass-blown offices and stepped into a new role as military commander. He describes the ensuing conflict – the bloodiest in Europe since the Second World War – as a 'vision of hell.'

The detail is haunting. Zakaev recalls bombardment, bodies in the streets, and the deaths of close comrades. Dogs roam the ruins. 'War has its own rules. There is no time off in war, no weekend, no slavish adherence to procedure and tidy timetables,' he writes. Zakaev turns out to be an innovative field officer. On the run from Russian troops, he uses phosphorescent logs to illuminate the paths around a forest camp.

When Russia decided to sue for peace Zakaev was part of the delegation that travelled to Moscow and held talks with President Boris Yeltsin. (It was a brave move: Zakaev wondered if he and the Chechen delegation might be poisoned. They weren't.) Yeltsin, in Zakaev's telling, was a brusque, bear-like figure who behaved like a tsar. The negotiations on the eve of presidential elections were little more than a PR stunt. Once Yeltsin was re-elected, the Russians resumed their offensive.

And yet in summer 1996 the 'rebels' – as Moscow called them – defeated one of the most powerful armies on the planet. Russian soldiers were demoralized. Chechen units, by contrast, had grown in strength. They acquired money, weapons and ammunition from Russia itself, rather than from shadowy outside powers, Zakaev explains. He watched as Russian military columns trundled back home, in their first egress from Chechnya in four centuries.

This was the high point of Chechen independence. That October Zakaev travelled to Moscow for further peace negotiations with General Alexander Lebed – an 'honest opponent,' in Zakaev's view. Lebed had political ambitions, however, and soon after was removed.

When Zakaev got back to Grozny he found it also in the grip of palace intrigue. From here on, the Chechen government's attempts to build a functioning country began to fall apart. Rival factions refused to agree a single candidate for president. Law and order got worse. Criminal gangs began kidnappings. Corruption and nepotism were rife. Reluctantly, Zakaev decided to stand for president himself – 'the biggest mistake of my life,' as he later realised.

Zakaev blames much of this on Moscow and its agents – arguing that the Chechens have, for centuries, been victims of Russian chauvinism. The murder of foreigners, including a group of Red Cross workers, dealt a disastrous blow to Chechnya's image abroad. Zakaev attributes these savage episodes to Russia's intelligence agencies working through 'complicit or unwitting' locals.

By the time Aslan Mashkadov was sworn in as president, Yeltsin was already preparing a second war against Chechnya. In May 1997 Zakaev – now deputy prime minister – went with Mashkadov to Moscow to sign a peace treaty. Mashkadov turned out to be a disappointing leader, who promoted cronies. Meanwhile, radical Islamists backed by Russian operatives grew in strength, bringing the republic to the brink of civil war.

Zakaev writes well about the rise of Vladimir Putin and the role played by the oligarch Boris Berezovsky at Yeltsin's court. Zakaev blamed the series of apartment bombings in Russia, which took place in autumn 1999, on the FSB. (So did Alexander Litvinenko, whom Zakaev later got to know in exile in London.) The bombings provided Putin, the prime minister, with a pretext. In September 1999 the war began when Russian military planes bombed Chechnya.

Putin's indiscriminate goal – Zakaev writes – was to 'flatten' everything. The struggle that winter for control of Grozny was bloody and grim. While driving in darkness to a meeting Zakaev's vehicle crashed – 'no pain, just a flash of light.' His injuries were so serious they prevented him from playing any further role in military operations. Paradoxically, they also saved his life. After a hair-raising period on the run, shifting from village to village, Zakaev was smuggled out of Chechnya and, a few months later, out of Russia.

He has yet to go back. The Putin who initiated the Second Chechen War would in 2000 become president. Two decades later he still has the same job. In the meantime, Chechnya has become a neo-Stalinist clandom, run by the murderous Ramzan Kadyrov. It is – formally – loyal to Moscow. Putin has crushed other rebellious ex-Soviet republics – Georgia in 2008 and Ukraine in 2014. In 2016 he helped elect Donald Trump.

Chechen independence seems more distant than ever. And yet 'Subjugate and Exterminate!' is a reminder that the idea of Chechen nationhood remains a potent one, not only for this generation of Chechens – many of them in exile – but for future generations too. The idea lives on. Zakaev's memoir is an essential document in an age of lies.

Luke Harding
December 2018

Part 1

Seeing the Chechens as our enemies, we tried by all measures to destroy them and even to turn their merits into flaws. We considered them fickle in the extreme, credulous, sly and perfidious because they would not carry out our demands, which offended against their concepts, morality, customs and way of life. We so vilified them only because they would not dance to our tune, the sounds of which were too harsh and raucous for their ears.

General Melentiy Olshevsky, *The Caucasus from 1841 to 1866*

Introduction

It has been the fate of Chechens for every generation to be scarred by national tragedy. For my parents' generation that tragedy was the deportation of the Vainakhs to Central Asia with massive loss of life. My grandfather's generation endured the dark years of Bolshevik terror, in danger at any moment of being declared an 'enemy of the people,' which in those times led to execution in the cellars of Russia's Cheka secret police, predecessor of the NKVD/ KGB/ FSB.

As we look back over our history, we see the Chechens in earlier centuries fighting with total dedication to defend their freedom. The real tragedy, however, is that each generation, after facing apocalyptic ordeals, has at the end of its days been forced to witness some new catastrophe inflicted on our people by the Russian state. My parents' generation, the tragedy of whose early years culminated in the deportation of the Chechens to Central Asia, in their declining years faced two devastating wars with Russia, the barbarity of which surpassed anything our people had previously suffered. Now it is the turn of my generation to live with the memory of those wars, and pray to the Almighty that deliverance of the Chechens from the Russian Empire may one day bring this succession of disasters to an end. These new wars have been the major occurrence in the lives of those drawn into them.

Years later, finding myself in the West, I saw conflict breaking out among Chechens who had been involved at the very beginning of these terrible events, and doubts assailed me that our struggle and the suffering of so many victims had been needless and futile: perhaps we really were not yet ready for nationhood? At such moments, however, I would remember those no longer among the living, alongside whom I fought, sharing privation and danger, and begin to think the Almighty had prolonged my days so that the memory of those who gave their lives for the freedom of the Chechen people should not suffer an ultimate betrayal. At such times I felt my duty was more to the fallen than to the living.

As I began writing these memoirs, I was determined also that we should not allow the imposition of only one version of recent history, the passing to future generations of a perverse account written by people who habitually bury their crimes under accretions of lies. My task is not to present our own deeds in a favourable light. If we pass in silence over our mistakes and failings, what we relate will have no value, because worthwhile experience can be derived only from truth and reality. If it seems at times to the families of our fallen leaders and military commanders that my descriptions are unflattering, they must understand that my purpose has not been to criticize those dear to them: I am trying only to give an objective political assessment of events on the stage of history in which those individuals played a leading part. It is the duty of those of us who were witnesses and participants in these events to pass to our descendants a truthful description of these decades of war, neither seeking to conceal our failings, nor allowing the adversary to slander the sacred memory of our heroes and belittle an unprecedentedly courageous achievement of our nation. Only then can we be certain that future generations of Chechens will not be rootless creatures bereft of the traditional values of their people and ignorant even of what those are. That is a prerequisite for the survival of the Chechens and their ultimate victory, because freedom is needed only by a people professing high moral values and mindful of their past. The alternative is a nation divided, and ultimately dispersed like dust by the storms of history.

All the dialogue reported in this book has been reconstituted from memory and such notes as I made at the time. I cannot claim it is a verbatim record, but do assert that I have conveyed its meaning without distortion.

I

A Chechen Childhood and My Early Career

Zakaev is born in exile in Kazakhstan but schooled back in Urus-Martan, Chechnya. His acting career. The Checheno-Ingush Union of Theatre Workers. Meets Djohar Dudaev, future president of the independent Chechen Republic.

I was born in Kazakhstan, and returned to Urus-Martan in my mother's arms when only a few weeks old. My parents had nine children: five sons and four daughters. All the grown-ups' stories I remember from my childhood related to Stalin's deportation of the Vainakhs, and I was familiar with the geography of Kazakhstan, reflected in such exotic-sounding place names as Semipalatinsk, Aktyubinsk, Kokchetav, and Taldykurgan, long before I knew the geography of Chechnya.

In 1966 I went to the local Urus-Martan school and became friends with another boy in my class, Aindi. My school memories are inextricably bound up with Aindi, because we were accomplices in all our boyhood pranks and adventures. The most ambitious of these were our joint secret expeditions to Grozny, which we began to undertake some time after second or third grade. Aindi and I knew the stop from which buses set off to the capital which, by our criteria, was unimaginably grand and crowded with people. Having saved up money for the tickets, we would set off. Sometimes, and this was definitely the preferred option, we even managed to save enough to go by taxi. The mistrustful drivers always insisted on seeing the money in advance and, with great aplomb and the mien of world-weary millionaires, we would show off our crumpled rubles.

For a little extra, the taxi drivers would take us straight to Grozny Central Market. It seemed to us a city within the city, and we studied it closely, knew the trading rows and pavilions, and gradually came to recognize many of the traders. Walking round the periphery, we gained a fair knowledge of the streets and alleys adjoining it. After a time we noticed that the further we moved from the market, the fewer people in Grozny were speaking Chechen.

At that time it was virtually a Russian town, almost out of bounds for Vainakhs.

Aindi and I sometimes summoned up the courage to make short trips by tram, a special adventure. We meticulously memorized the way back to 'our' market. The Russians probably regarded us Chechen village boys as little savages, but we in turn were amazed at their bad behaviour, the way they swore without compunction, threw litter down in the streets, and got drunk in public in the numerous beer bars and cafes near the market. What amazed us most of all was Russian men swearing in front of women and children. To us, they were the uncouth savages.

Some incidents recurred during our tram escapades. We had only to start talking Chechen for other passengers (who seemed always to be older Russian women) to rudely interrupt us with an injunction to 'Talk like human beings!' For Aindi and me that was our first lesson in inter-ethnic relations. I subsequently met not a few decent, educated, well-mannered Russians, but these early impressions are etched in my memory and were the foundation stone of my later certainty that our Chechen and Russian peoples are very different in culture, mentality, and everything else that qualifies as national characteristics.

Aindi and I were implacable rivals in every aspect of our young lives: in the marks we got at school, at sports, in the way we dressed, and as to which of us could save most money for the next expedition into town. Even the books we boys were given by girls on 23 February, Soviet Army Day (we learned only later of the other, tragic, significance of this date for Vainakhs, the beginning of the Stalin Deportation), served to fuel our rivalry: who had more pictures in their book, who had the longer dedication? This did not keep us from being great friends, and our friendship was cemented by the shared secret of our regular trips to Grozny.

I remember, at the beginning of the school year in which we moved up to second grade, we had a new teacher, a young Chechen woman, in charge of our class. She stood at the front, opened the class register, and got each pupil to stand up in alphabetical order and state their date of birth. When it was my turn, I said I was born on such-and-such a day of such-and-such a month in 1959. Hearing this, Aindi, who was sitting at the front desk, laughed out loud. He turned towards me to say something, but couldn't. He just sat there chortling, face down on the desk, his mirth so infectious that soon the whole class was in fits of laughter.

'What is wrong with you, Askhabov?' the teacher asked, trying not to smile. Still laughing, Aindi, looked in my direction and said, 'What an amazing boy Zakaev is! Last year he said he was born in 1959, the year before that he said the same, and now he's still saying he was born in 1959!'

'And how do matters stand with you, Askhabov, in respect of the year you were born?'

'In first grade my date of birth was 1958, and now it is 1959 of course,' Aindi replied.

The whole class fell about, and this time the teacher was laughing too. The hapless Aindi had supposed that every year added to his age added another year to his date of birth. In Chechen families, particularly in the countryside, birthdays were not celebrated, and that is why Aindi did not really understand the question put to him in Russian.

My first impressions of Grozny are inextricably linked with Aindi and those early years at school. Later, when I was actually living there, I would find places Aindi and I had visited long before. I would recognize old cafes and shops, and notice changes. These childhood memories were still strong and vivid in my mind when the First War began. I suppose everyone has a secret place in the land of childhood to which memory returns at difficult moments in life, and where under a hot, clear sun, surrounded by the carefree laughter of children, our friends and classmates, we find solace and renewed strength to continue the struggle.

I should mention here another aspect of what it meant to be a Chechen at that time. There were probably few people around me who had never gone off on *shabashka*. This was the slang name given to seasonal manual work outside the republic which native inhabitants of Checheno-Ingushetia, working in a great variety of professions including the arts, had no option but to engage in. I should explain what exactly shabashka was, and why for decades Chechens and Ingush had to leave in search of labour.

Checheno-Ingushetia was rich in mineral resources, especially oil. It was the largest industrial centre in the Caucasus, with highly developed industry and agriculture. The republic had an advanced oil extracting and refining industry, as well as gas, electric power and chemical sectors, mechanical engineering and metalworking, forestry and timber processing, and food industries. Throughout the republic there were several dozen large and medium-sized factories, including plants of national importance. Despite this abundance of factories, however, there were no jobs for Chechens or Ingush because, since the Vainakhs' return from exile, a secret Soviet directive forbade employing them in factories. It was standard practice in Checheno-Ingushetia for a new factory to be built and the workers and engineers then to be brought in from Russia. Not only that, but top officials of the republic would meet these newcomers with ceremonious speechifying and music and, right there on the station platform or in the hall at the airport, hand them keys to apartments and deeds to plots of land on which to build holiday dachas. All this at a time when Chechens and Ingush could not, even for huge amounts of money, legally buy an apartment in their own capital city or obtain a permit to live there. The Soviet regime did everything in its power to ensure that the city of Grozny was a Vainakh-free zone, to ensure that Chechens and Ingush remained agricultural labourers, and had no specialists working in high technology industries. The clear intention was to deprive us of the opportunity of developing, even in a hypothetical, distant future, a modern, civilized society or of living without the incessant care and attention of our 'great elder brother,' as official propaganda described the Russians. In order to avoid the policy of apartheid becoming manifestly scandalous, a few token Vainakhs, like Sazhi Umalatova, a welder at the gigantic Red Hammer factory, were permitted to live and work in Grozny.

Chechens and Ingush were allowed to work in the fields, grow sugar beet, and harvest it in the autumn. This was, without exaggeration, hard labour. Typically, the local administration of the village or regional centre would, at its discretion, allocate families one or two hectares of land sown with sugar beet, depending on the number of members of the family. In the blazing sun, the fields needed to be weeded by hand three times in the course of the summer. This is probably my worst childhood memory. From the age of eight or nine, all village children in the lowland part of the republic lived this nightmare. At four in the morning Mother would wake me, and in the chilly darkness before dawn we would climb up into the back of a truck which took us out to the field. After an hour or an hour and a half, the sun would rise and, at first, warm us but then begin mercilessly to scorch us.

There was nowhere in the fields to shelter from its blistering rays even during the lunch break, and this went on for some three weeks which, to me as a child, seemed like three years. Then, in late autumn, it was time to harvest the beet in rain and snow, in thick slush which sucked us in almost to our knees. We pulled up the crop, cleaning the mud and leaves from each root and, shivering in the icy wind, loaded it on to the trucks. For weeding we were paid 50-60 rubles, and for cleaning and loading the beet we received 40-50 kilograms of sugar, usually in the following January. The earnings were insufficient to feed an average Vainakh family with five or six children. Accordingly, it is no exaggeration to say that 70-80 per cent of the entire Vainakh population of working age were forced to seek work each year in Central Asia and the Russian heartland.

This seasonal work was very arduous. The working day was 12-14 hours, from dawn till nightfall. Nevertheless, you could earn 500 rubles a month on average. The gangmaster received the greater part of his remuneration at the end of the season. By agreement with those in charge of the local collective or state farm and, more particularly, with those directly negotiating the contracts, the amount of work reported as having been done could be exaggerated and the resulting extra pay allocated to 'dead souls,' a concept familiar from Gogol's eponymous novel, which meant notional workers who existed only on paper. Naturally, the gangmaster had to hand over a good 50 per cent of these fraudulent charges to those signing the work sheets, namely the director or chairman of the farm, various accountants, cost controllers, and the site supervisor. They shared out the spoils among themselves. In a good season, a gangmaster could make 10,000 rubles or more. As for the workers, unless they were direct family or close relatives of the gangmaster, they were paid an agreed fixed wage of 500-1,000 rubles a month, depending on their skills. A good bricklayer or carpenter would be paid about twice as much as an unskilled labourer. In addition, everybody had three free meals a day, as much as they could eat.

I took a brigade on shabashka for four seasons in succession. The first time I spent just over a month there before leaving to study at the Arts Institute in Voronezh. After that first experience, I vowed to avoid casual labour in future if at all possible.

I completed my diploma as a film and theatre actor, and in 1981 returned to the republic to work at the Checheno-Ingush Drama Theatre. My career went well. I acted in all the theatre's plays, in major roles, as a supporting actor, in walk-on parts. From the outset, I got on well with the other actors, the staff, producers and directors. The only problem was the money. Young, newly graduated actors were paid 85 rubles a month, irrespective of how many roles they played or how good they were. Only very patriotic people with a deep commitment to our language and culture were likely to be found working in the theatre.

Between 1981 and 1985 my salary rose to 120 rubles. There were no vacancies higher up and I had no prospect of earning more. I took on a half-time job as a scene-shifter, setting up the flats before a play and dismantling them afterwards. This brought in an extra 30-40 rubles.

In 1985, I was allocated a one-bedroomed apartment in the centre of Grozny. This was a major, and unusual, stroke of luck. By this time I had two children and my wife did not go out to work. While we were living in a family hostel and dreaming of an apartment, I thought that having a place of our own would be the end of all our problems, but when I was finally issued the warrant for an apartment, I faced the new problem of how to furnish it.

I tried negotiating with Mimolt Soltsaev, our theatre's principal director, to take unpaid leave for the 5-6 months between the end of one season and the beginning of the next. Theatres in the USSR gave repertory performances from autumn to spring, and then went on tour from spring until the following autumn. In the summer, our theatre usually toured in the republic. At first, Mimolt flatly refused. I said that in that case I would have no option but to leave the theatre, and he relented. In early May 1985, I and my wife went to Aktyubinsk province in Kazakhstan, leaving our children, Radima and Shamil, with my parents in Urus-Martan.

In the course of three years, always returning to the same Soviet farm, I and my team built 24 houses, a library, a school, and a cinema. Deep down, I always had a yen to be a builder and could happily spend hours on the site. My commendable attitude was noted by the farm administration, and in my third year there I was appointed site supervisor. It was unusual for an outsider to be appointed to a position of such responsibility. The farm's Party organization nominated me for membership of the Communist Party, which offered a good prospect of making a career as a builder, but I returned to Chechnya. Gorbachev's Perestroika was just beginning, and this set Soviet people free not only to engage in private enterprise but also to express themselves freely in the arts. The change came only gradually, because senior Party apparatchiks, especially in the provinces, resisted furiously, and had to be forced to accept the changes by periodically being put in their place from the very summit of the Party Olympus.

I had a good friend in Grozny, Khusein Guzuev. We were fellow students in the Faculty of Acting at the Voronezh Arts Institute, before Khusein went to study directing in Moscow at GITIS, the Institute of Dramatic Art. He was a true master of his craft.

In the spirit of the dizzying changes taking place, in 1989 Khusein and I and a number of like-minded friends founded the Daimokhk Association. This was to all intents and purposes an alternative Ministry of Culture, because our constitution allowed us to operate in all areas related to 'national culture.' I have to give due credit to Abdulla Kindarov, the minister of culture of the Checheno-Ingush Autonomous Soviet Socialist Republic at the time. We found him to be an extremely decent man who not only did not place obstacles in our path, but later defended us when we were under attack from the Party bosses at republican level. I gratefully remember him as a wise, honourable man and dedicated Chechen patriot.

We were able to start work unhindered, in no small measure because in 1990 I had been elected chairman of the Checheno-Ingush Union of Theatre Workers, the UTW, which represented all the republic's theatre companies. The election was attended by a delegation from Moscow. Although the UTW was officially a social organization, its administrative functions were closer to those of a government ministry. At the time of my election, our Union was a constituent part of the UTW of the Russian Soviet Federal Socialist Republic. This was headed by Mikhail Ulianov, a well known theatre and film actor. There was also a UTW of the USSR, with Kirill Lavrov in charge. When I took on the job, I nevertheless carried on working in the theatre, and was only too familiar with the needs and problems of theatre people.

I set about making contact with our sister unions in other parts of the USSR, and to that end went to Moscow and Tbilisi. Giga Lordkipanidze was chairman of the Georgian UTW, and we struck up a very good relationship in the best traditions of the Caucasus. At the same time, I met the famous Georgian film director, Buba Khotivari, and the Vice-Rector of the Rustaveli Theatre and Film University, Georgiy Dolidze, which enabled us to send five of our budding film-makers there to study film direction.

This was a major success, because the amazing achievements of Georgian cinema were renowned not only in the USSR but throughout the world. Unfortunately these joint endeavours were interrupted just as everything was getting going. There was a conflict between Georgia and Abkhazia, and Chechen volunteers intervened on the side of the Abkhazians. Their involvement had little popular or political support in Chechnya, and at a press briefing on the subject, Djohar Dudaev, the president of the Chechen Republic, stated that this was a war not for the independence of Abkhazia, but a ruse to prise off this wonderful part of the Caucasus for Russia. Despite Grozny's official position, Russian propaganda went to great lengths to stress that the Chechen volunteers were playing a decisive role in the victory of the Abkhazians. We remained on good terms with our Georgian colleagues, but it became impossible to continue our project in the context of a civil war in Georgia which had been instigated by Russia. The conflict has continued to flare up periodically ever since. We had to start all over again.

In 1992 I went to Moscow and met Mikhail Ulianov of the Russian UTW, in order to regularize the relationship between our two unions. With the Chechen Republic's declaration of independence in 1991, our union ceased to be a constituent part of the UTW of the Russian Federation, although Russo-Chechen cultural and artistic contacts continued. It was essential to re-align ourselves with political realities, so I proposed to Ulianov that we should conclude an agreement as equal partners. He agreed, and we signed an agreement in the presence of journalists and theatre people from both countries. I remember, as he signed, the inimitable Ulianov remarked, 'There, ladies and gentlemen, Akhmed and I are setting a good example for Djohar Dudaev and Boris Yeltsin to follow. Let us hope they will shortly end this whole nightmare, especially in the way people think, and conclude a similar agreement!'

It is time to say a few words about Chechnya's first president. Djohar Dudaev was born on 15 February 1944 in Yalkhori in the Galanchozh region of the Checheno-Ingush ASSR. Eight days later, his entire family was deported to Pavlodar province in the Kazakh Republic, along with thousands of other Chechens and Ingush.

In 1957, Djohar and his family returned to their homeland and lived in Grozny. In 1959 he graduated from Secondary School No. 45 and worked as an electrician at Building and Installation Division No. 5, while studying in tenth grade at Evening School No. 55, completing the course in just one year. In 1960 he matriculated in the Mathematics and Physics Faculty of the North Ossetian Pedagogical Institute and then, after a specialized one-year preparatory course, entered the Tambov Military Pilot Institute to train as a pilot and engineer. From 1962 he served in the Soviet Armed Forces as an officer and in administrative positions.

From 1966, he served in 52 Heavy Bomber Training Regiment, based at Shaikovka Aerodrome in Kaluga province, starting as deputy commander of a single aircraft. In 1971-4 he studied at the Command Training Faculty of the Gagarin Air Force Academy. From 1970 he served in 1225 Heavy Bomber Regiment near Irkutsk. In subsequent years he successively held the posts of air regiment deputy commander, chief of staff, wing commander and, from 1980, commander of the same regiment. In 1982 he was appointed chief of staff of 31 Heavy Bomber Division of 30 Air Army, and in 1985 transferred to a similar position in 13 Guards Heavy Bomber Division.

In 1987-91 he was the commander of the strategic 326 Ternopol Heavy Bomber Division of 46 Air Army, stationed in Tartu in the Estonian SSR, and was simultaneously head of the city's military garrison.

In the Soviet Air Force he rose by 1989 to the rank of major general.

I met Djohar in the early 1990s, immediately before the First National Congress of the Chechen People. A few days earlier I had read in the newspapers and heard on television of the appointment of the first Chechen general in our recent history. I knew, of course, that in the more distant past there had been no few Chechens who rose to become generals in the Russian and Turkish armies, and even, apparently, one generalissimo. In recent history, however, because of the acutely suspicious attitude of Moscow towards Chechens, no representative of our nation had succeeded in making a brilliant military career in the Soviet Army. Accordingly, this news of our first general caused something of a sensation among Chechens.

At that time I knew Musa, who worked in a car repair workshop. One day he came and told me, 'My uncle is back from Estonia. We are having a get-together to meet him and hear what he has to tell us. Duki would like to meet you and other people in the arts.'

I asked, 'Who is Duki?'

'Have you really not heard about the Chechen general?'

'Of course I have! That would be brilliant. I would like very much to meet him.'

'It would be good if you could try to bring Imam Alimsultanov along too,' Musa said. 'Djohar is a great admirer of his songs.'

So that evening a group of us, together with Imam Alimsultanov, met up and went to see Djohar. That was our first acquaintance with the future president of Chechnya. He was in civilian clothing.

After the introductions, when we had all settled ourselves, Djohar told us he was in charge of the military garrison in Tartu, and gave us all his visiting card, which was something of a novelty at the time. He told us briefly about himself, and about his service and career in the army. He had been the youngest colonel in the Soviet Armed Forces and was several times recommended for promotion to general, but the Communist Party's Central Committee, which had to approve the appointment of generals, invariably turned the proposal down. It was only under Gorbachev that he finally attained that rank. He shared his thoughts and memories with us, and told funny and sad tales about Chechens who had served under him.

Djohar told us that, throughout his service in the Air Force, the idea of liberating Chechnya had never been far from his thoughts. He had wondered how Chechens could regain their freedom, and when that time might come. What he had to say was extremely interesting, and some of it I will not publish even now to prevent its being misinterpreted. I will say only that Djohar was the embodiment of love of his country, and all his ideas, thoughts and words showed him to be a sincere and uncompromising Chechen patriot. He felt deeply all the calamities, the grief and misfortune which had befallen the Chechens in the past, and had no intention of forgiving our enemies or forgetting our tragic history.

Djohar was a baby when the Vainakhs were deported, so had no personal memory of the event, but he knew all the circumstances of this disaster from the tales of his parents and other exiled Vainakhs. At the time, his father and sister had been away in the city, so Djohar was carried into exile by his mother – the family were reunited only in Kazakhstan. He was told the details of their journey to Central Asia by his mother, how people were packed into goods wagons and died of hunger and the searing, icy cold of February. It was a miracle that an unaccompanied woman with an infant in her arms survived an appalling exodus which proved fatal for thousands of Vainakhs.

Djohar told us about the tragedy in Khaibakh with such emotion it was as if he had been an eyewitness of the atrocity committed there by Stalin's butchers, who locked more than 700 women, children, and old people in a stable and burned them alive. His mother came from those parts, and the ancient ancestral tower in the place where she was born and grew up is still standing. Djohar told us how the sick in the Urus-Martan regional Hospital were flung into a pit of burning coals. He told us about the hundreds of people drowned in the icy waters of Lake Galanchozh, and many similar episodes during the Deportation of the Chechens and Ingush. 'How can we forget that? How can we forgive such things?' he exclaimed, with pain and anger in his eyes. We could see why, if he had not concealed thoughts like these, there had been such reluctance to promote him to the rank of general.

II
The Birth of the Chechen Republic of Ichkeria

The impact of Perestroika in Chechnya. The National Congress of the Chechen People in 1990. General Djohar Dudaev persuaded to abandon his military career and elected president of the independent Chechen Republic. Conduct of Ruslan Khasbulatov, a Chechen, as chairman of the Supreme Soviet of the Russian Federation. Zakaev appointed minister of culture of the Chechen Republic.

In the late 1980s and early 1990s, a whole host of organizations and leaders unsanctioned by Soviet officialdom appeared in Chechnya. The most radical of these was the Vainakh Democratic Party, headed by Zelimkhan Yandarbiev. Its members included Said-Khasan Abumuslimov, Ruslan Takhaev, Visita Ibrakhimov, Sulim Yunusov, and Yusup Soslambekov. Spontaneous rallies were being held. The Supreme Soviet of the Checheno-Ingush ASSR, under the leadership of Doku Zavgaev, saw things were getting out of hand and decided to follow the tried and trusted principle of, 'If you can't beat them, lead them.' Zavgaev set up a steering committee to convene a national congress which would establish an executive committee to include the leaders of all the political movements. The idea was to have this committee under the chairmanship of Lecha Umkhaev, a member of the Checheno-Ingush Supreme Soviet and trusted supporter of Zavgaev. The National Congress of the Chechen People duly met for the first time on 26 November 1990. I was invited as the representative of the Union of Theatre Workers, and by chance found myself sitting next to Djohar in the section reserved for guests.

Everything was going well and the Congress had shown the Chechen people to be united, when Zelimkhan Yandarbiev came to the podium. At the end of his speech he read out an anonymous letter, supposedly written by a midwife at the National Maternity Hospital. The contrite lady wrote that she and the hospital medical staff had been murdering Chechen and Ingush baby boys under a secret policy directive from Moscow. The effect was explosive and the response of the Congress delegates highly emotional. From that moment the power of Zavgaev, whose election as leader of the republic had been greeted with delight by Chechens and Ingush only a few months earlier, was tainted by association with Moscow.

For the first time since the Vainakhs' return from exile, the KGB had suffered a defeat when, instead of Nikolai Semyonov, the candidate sent in from Moscow, the Bureau of the Party's Provincial Committee of the Checheno-Ingush ASSR, which by this time had a majority of Chechens and Ingush on it, elected an ethnic Chechen to the post of first secretary. The KGB saw this as a victory for the Vainakhs, whom it never trusted and considered likely at any time to turn against the regime. Garsolt Elmurzaev, a member of the Bureau, warned before the vote that, if the meeting did not elect a Chechen, information in his possession indicated that widespread rioting in the republic was likely. The Bureau members rejected Moscow's candidate in favour of Zavgaev.

Now, however, Zavgaev was suddenly held responsible for everything Russia had done to the Vainakh people, which was, of course, precisely the effect whoever had concocted the 'anonymous' letter was hoping for. The reaction was predictable, because many of those directly responsible for the past sufferings of the Chechens and Ingush were dead by this time, Moscow was far away, and Zavgaev was here in their midst. Henceforth he was viewed as a proxy of Russia.

Now, after many years have passed, when I consider all that was going on at the time, it seems increasingly obvious that the 'midwife's letter' was the KGB taking its revenge on Zavgaev and all Chechens. I see this as the beginning of a campaign to undermine Vainakh solidarity. The KGB's favoured technique for dividing a society is to create a multiplicity of political parties and movements, led by people who are either directly controlled by the KGB or hyper-emotional in temperament. The letter read out by Yandarbiev at the Congress was a provocative fake. It marked the beginning of a fragmentation of Chechen society. No author of the letter was ever identified.

Everybody who was present will also remember the brilliant speech Djohar made, directly from his place in the hall. He warned the delegates to beware of the occupants of two buildings in Grozny, those of the Ministry of the Interior and the KGB. He knew how malign was the power which these two organizations wielded. I had always imagined the evil in our land to emanate primarily from the offices of the Communist Party's Provincial

Committee. Subsequent events proved Djohar only too right when he said that the heart of Russia's colonial system in Chechnya was not the Communist Party, which vapourized as soon as the bright light of glasnost was shone on it, but those two other organizations the Communists had created as the 'armed detachments of the Party.' Djohar said then that we should fear, not Russia's artillery or tanks or aircraft, but the never-sleeping evil nested in those two grandiose buildings on Ordzhonikidze Prospect.

His words were prophetic. We were to succeed in setting fire to Russian tanks, in destroying their artillery, and we even learned to shoot down their aircraft, but the discord those two organizations, particularly the KGB, sowed among our people not only brought war to our land, but destroyed our very people before they could get to their feet and gain a sense of their own identity. Djohar's speech had a powerful impact, but if we had fully assimilated its message, not just emotionally but also rationally, much in our recent history might have worked out less tragically.

The Congress completed its work by setting up the proposed standing Executive Committee. The members elected were a mixture of officials and leaders of community organizations and were unable to agree on who should chair it. Some supported Lecha Umkhaev, while the leaders of several community organizations favoured Zelimkhan Yandarbiev. Neither could muster a sufficient majority. Some of the Chechen national activists, like Yandarbiev, Said-Khasan Abumuslimov, and Yusup Soslambekov, were in open opposition to Zavgaev's government but could see they lacked popular support. If the existing regime was to be opposed effectively, nation-wide support was essential. They decided to send a delegation to Estonia to ask Djohar Dudaev to return to the republic and become chairman. Lecha Umkhaev and other representatives of the Supreme Soviet agreed to his candidacy, confident, no doubt, that he would never give up a highly successful military career in order to come back to Chechnya to head a community association. They were wrong.

The delegation arrived in Estonia to urge Djohar to become chairman, and left him little choice by claiming that, if he refused, the Chechen people would curse him as a traitor to the nation. They assured him that 90 per cent of Chechens were behind them, that this was a historic opportunity to realize the dream of an independent state, and that at this crucial moment Djohar's place was with his people. Dudaev had lived and served for several years in the Baltic states. He had regular contact with Estonians and had a very different outlook from that of Soviet military personnel and even civilians who lived in other parts of the USSR.

The Baltic peoples had a fierce hatred of all things Russian and Soviet. Usman Balgaev and I had once been in Brest, and from Byelorussia had travelled to neighbouring Lithuania. Even at that time, when we spoke Russian in the shops and cafes the sales assistants and waiters made no attempt to conceal their hostility, assuming we were Russians. When we explained we were Chechens from the Caucasus their attitude changed immediately. Speaking Russian with a very heavy accent, they were happy to talk to us frankly and we could see that, one and all, they were staunchly anti-Soviet. They had never become reconciled to the occupation of their country and had forgotten none of the atrocities that accompanied the invasion and sovietization of the Baltic states. The dissident criticism of the Soviet system which, despite all obstacles, we heard from Vladimir Bukovsky and Abdurakhman Avtorkhanov on Voice of America and Radio Liberty, and which we discussed only among very close and trusted friends, was expressed openly by people in the Baltic states. It was part of their everyday life.

In the 1990s, during the Singing Revolution in Estonia, Djohar, as commander of the Soviet garrison in Tartu, refused to allow the armed forces to be used against the civilian population. After that he became a national hero in the Baltic states. It was a moment of truth, a time when, in the jargon of pilots, he passed the point of no return and became committed to taking action against the Soviet regime and leading the Chechen people in their struggle for freedom and independence from a colonial empire. The Baltic states were the first of the European countries to perpetuate the memory of Djohar Dudaev by naming streets and squares after him.

Djohar's years in Estonia freed him from the bonds of Communist dogma. As a patriot and a Chechen, he could not allow anyone to accuse him of cowardice and betrayal. He abandoned everything, his work, a brilliant career in the armed forces, and returned home. He had last been in Chechnya only three or four months previously, during the Congress, and the republic must have seemed to him much like the Baltic states, mindful of its tragic past and united in its striving for freedom. Djohar was well aware that Chechens had no prospect of achieving a bloodless victory and the freedom they longed for unless they remained united. Alas, when he returned, the republic had already changed. The earlier unity was gone. He tried to rally the nation but it was too late; the opposing sides were already entrenched as implacable enemies, fighting not for the future of our people but for power. Those currently in power and their supporters called the unofficial political groups riffraff, capable only of confiscating and sharing out booty, while the outsiders called their opponents bloodsuckers and stooges of Moscow.

I have not the slightest doubt that the men who persuaded Djohar to come back to Chechnya had already done everything they could to split Chechen society before he was elected president. Even while he was president, some of them led armed opposition to his government, under instructions from Moscow. Others who continued nominally to support Djohar made it impossible, by their irresponsible, populist sloganeering, for him to unite the Chechens. These same demagogues simultaneously made it impossible for him to negotiate with Russia. Needless to say, the Russian intelligence agencies, once they got over their shock at the rebellion, took every opportunity to use the internal strife and other negative developments against the 'rebel republic,' as the Russian media commonly called Chechnya. It would have been surprising if they had not. Those Chechens, however, who were the main culprits in detonating internecine strife should have understood the likely consequences of their actions. They should have recognized the obvious fact that Moscow would exploit the divisions in society, which they had aggravated, to the detriment of the Chechen people as a whole and to frustrate their desire to break free from centuries of colonial bondage. They should also have had the wits to know that the international law to which Said-Khasan Abumuslimov so eloquently referred was written by powerful nations not to liberate small nations but to maintain and secure the global status quo. They should have known that only national unity could ensure the success of the Chechen people on its chosen path of liberation. To preserve that fragile unity required more than just a willingness to compromise: it demanded a willingness to go out of your way to seek compromises and propose them to political opponents. Sadly, they not only failed to make any effort to promote unity but did everything in their power to aggravate the dissension and bickering. They issued irresponsible statements and branded as 'enemies of the Chechen people' all who disagreed with their strident and dogmatic interpretation of reality.

Djohar had spent nearly all his adult life away from Chechnya and was unfamiliar with the politics of the republic. These people succeeded in inculcating in him their own uncompromising attitude towards opposition. Chechens tend to perceive unfairness as a personal insult, and do not forgive those who offend them, a feature of the Chechen mentality which Moscow has always been adept at exploiting. After turning certain individuals into personal enemies of Djohar and binding them with bloodshed, the Russian intelligence agencies were able to use them against the entire Chechen people.

It was from the Congress of 26 November 1990 and the one which followed it, at which Djohar was elected chairman of the Executive

Committee of the NCCP, that I found myself being drawn into politics. It came to play a part, and a very important part at that, in my life as I found myself a participant in an ongoing rally many thousands strong, which continued throughout August 1991 when the putsch by old guard Communists against Gorbachev was organized in Moscow. The Chechen reaction to it was to knock down the statue of Lenin and overthrow Doku Zavgaev, the first secretary of the Chechen Republican Committee of the CPSU, who had supported the putsch. Speaking in Lenin Square (shortly to be renamed Sheikh Mansur Square), Abdulla Bugaev, a member of the Checheno-Ingush Supreme Soviet, assured the demonstrators that Zavgaev really opposed the putsch: 'I have spoken to Zavgaev, and his personal opinion is that we are under no obligation to swallow what is being brewed up in Moscow. I therefore urge you to disperse and return to your homes. We will not allow the putsch organizers into our republic.'

These were difficult and worrying times. Under the pretext of 'helping with the harvest,' Russian troops, heavy army trucks, and refrigerated units of 4-5 windowless railway wagons were sent into the republic. Eyewitnesses reported that all the tracks at Sernovodsk railway station were blocked with these units. Rumours spread that the putsch organizers were preparing a new deportation of the Vainakhs, and Gorbachev later stated on television that just such a proposal had been made to him. After the beginning of the First War, Yeltsin's Kremlin published documents showing that there were indeed plans to deport the Chechens to the Povolzhiye region, so there was nothing fanciful about the rumours.

Almost a year earlier, on 27 November 1990, the Checheno-Ingush Supreme Soviet chaired by Zavgaev had passed a Declaration of State Sovereignty of the Checheno-Ingush Republic. Frankly, that struck me as unwise. I could not see Moscow condoning such action by an autonomous republic. I remember somebody put that question to Abdulla Bugaev: 'How do you expect Moscow to react to what you have done? Do you think they are going to change the Constitution?' To this Bugaev replied, 'What a foreign state thinks about our status is of no interest to us. We are an independent sovereign state in accordance with a law adopted by the Supreme Soviet of the USSR in April 1990, which gave equal rights to all union and autonomous republics. In accordance with the Kremlin's directives, we have brought the legislation of the Checheno-Ingush Republic into line with laws adopted by the Supreme Soviet of the USSR.'

Zavgaev at that time tried skillfully to play off Gorbachev against Yeltsin. When a referendum was announced on whether to preserve the USSR with a revised Treaty of Union, Yeltsin's Supreme Soviet of the Russian Federation successfully insisted that the ballot slip should include an item on whether to create the post of president in Russia. When the officials in Grozny received instructions to include this item on the ballot slip, the Supreme Soviet retorted that the Checheno-Ingush Republic was not a constituent part of the Russian Federation, and that including the issue in a referendum in Chechnya would breach the law. Whether or not Russia introduced the post of president was a domestic matter for Russia itself. That was the answer forwarded to Moscow.

Before the putsch of August 1991, the Checheno-Ingush Republic had existed for a year or so as a sovereign state, recognized by the legislation of the USSR and of Russia as an equal constituent territory of the USSR. Alongside all the union republics (Russia, Ukraine, Byelorussia, and the others) it was preparing to sign a revised Treaty of Union.

That was the political and legal situation in Chechnya at the time of the Moscow putsch. Nobody really believed all these laws and declarations were worth a bag of beans. We had little doubt that Russia would, as always, favour force over the rule of law, and accordingly the Chechens gathering in Grozny's central square anticipated having to rely only on their own efforts. At these meetings and rallies, there was a palpable sense of unity and solidarity. It is deeply regrettable that hostile intelligence agencies and sundry religious sectarians were to succeed in sabotaging that unity and weakening our nation which, I firmly believe, would otherwise have been perfectly capable of rising to the challenges of the modern world.

Political passions ran high not only in the squares of Grozny. The whole of the Checheno-Ingush Republic was passionately discussing the rapidly changing political situation in Russia and our republic. When Chechen presidential elections were held on 27 October 1991, Djohar Dudaev won convincingly. The date set for his Inauguration was 9 November but, one day before that, Yeltsin declared a state of emergency in the Chechen Republic. To enforce this, elite Russian troops were sent to the military airfield in Khankala, where they were halted in their tracks by Chechen volunteers. Faced with Chechnya's determination to defend its independence, the commanders of the Russian special forces decided not to put the lives of those under their command at risk and accepted the terms of the Chechen side. The troops were given a very ample meal and driven in comfortable coaches back out of the republic. Seeing that the attempt to implement Yeltsin's decree had failed, the Supreme Soviet of the Russian Federation rescinded it.

The chairman of the Supreme Soviet of the Russian Federation at this time was Ruslan Khasbulatov, a Chechen, and he was a key figure behind all the provocations to which we were subjected. The most devastating blow was when, after Dudaev's election as president, he contrived to split the Chechen people along religious lines. Khasbulatov was behind the appointment of Akhmed Arsanov, the leader of the Naqshbandi Sufi Order, as representative of the president of Russia in Chechnya and acting head of the republic. The members of this order have a very strong sense of solidarity, and many who had initially supported Djohar's election, now turned against him.

I remember vividly the day Djohar took office as president, and one episode in particular. The inauguration was to take place in a new theatre building with a large auditorium. Before taking the presidential oath, Djohar went to the old building of the Provincial Committee of the Communist Party and gave a speech from its balcony to the assembled crowd. Never in my life have I seen such a huge throng of people as on that day. Not only the vast square, but the roofs of the houses around it, the trees in the square, everything was packed with people who had come to hear him. There must have been a full 200,000 people in Sheikh Mansur Square. For years afterwards, when some claimed Djohar had been responsible for bringing about the war, I would refute the allegation by reminding them of that speech.

Djohar said, 'If we are really serious about freedom, if we are serious about wanting to build our own, independent state, we must be fully aware of the great difficulties we shall face. We will be severely tested. We will have to endure privations, and Russia may try to crush our aspiration to freedom by force. If today we are not ready for these trials and privations, if we fear the possibility of war, it would be better for us to wait, not to embark on direct confrontation of Russia. But if we have truly chosen to establish our own state, if that is your conscious choice, and if you have the will and the courage to pass through all the trials which await us on this path, then I take upon myself the duty of being your leader. And I give you my word that I will travel this path with you to the end!'

The whole square erupted as one with cries of 'Allahu Akbar!' 'Liberty or death!' After that nobody could hear anything: we were all deafened by the unanimous response to Djohar's question of the vast crowd gathered in the square.

Djohar then went to the theatre to take the presidential oath. He said that from that day on he would be obedient to the will of the nation which had elected him. He never broke that oath and never deviated from the path of freedom before leaving us to face the Almighty Creator. Djohar had sincere respect for his fellow countrymen. His guiding principle in politics was the will of the Chechen people, and unstintingly he gave the people his strength, his ability, and his life itself. That is why, when today some Chechens are heard muttering that Djohar, Aslan Maskhadov, and our other leaders chose the wrong path, their talk is treasonous. It is a treason not only against these great Chechen leaders, but against our ancestors and our past history, a treason against the struggle for freedom which our nation has waged over so many centuries and at such incalculable cost.

There are generations and there is the nation. It is said the nation is all our generations: those who lived, those now living, and those who will live in times to come. Heroes are one of the indestructible bonds which join together all the generations of an ethnos into a national entity, obliging those living today to revere the values for which their forebears gave their lives. For the nation's destiny, that is not only the moral but the practical value of their acts of heroism. I know in my heart that Chechens, insha'Allah, will remember Djohar for as long as our people respect such values as honour, courage, integrity and duty. The memory of Djohar will nurture and strengthen these qualities in future generations of Chechens, and that is the most precious contribution of our first president to our history.

After these momentous events, I returned to my studies. Time passed, and in autumn 1994 I was in Moscow in search of opportunities to make our film, *The Black Horsemen*. The once gigantic All-Union MosFilm Studio had split into numerous privately owned studios, one of which was under the direction of Yevgeny Matveyev, a major film star and People's Actor of the USSR. I successfully negotiated with him to make the film and we went through all the practical aspects of location, deadlines, stages of the filming, and so on. Alas, it was as if the project was jinxed. Towards the end of October there was an alarming report on television that my home town of Urus-Martan had been shelled by our Chechen government artillery during an assault on the nearby Gekhi military unit. This unit had been taken over by pro-Russian extremists headed by Bislan Gantemirov. The report spoke of civilian casualties and, as was typical of Russian propaganda, put all the blame for the bloodshed on Djohar's government. That evening I bought a plane ticket, and flew home first thing the next day. Planes from Moscow were landing at Sleptsovskaya in Ingushetia, but I reached Urus-Martan, saw my parents, and was greatly relieved to find that fears for my relatives were unfounded. In the afternoon, I went on to Grozny where my own family lived.

That evening I met Khusein Guzuev in Grozny. He was very professionally running the national broadcasting company and, under his leadership, Chechen television changed out of all recognition. I told him I was bringing good news from Moscow. I had agreed the filming of *The Black Horsemen*.

'I have news for you too,' Khusein said, 'although I am not sure whether you will see it as good or bad. I was talking to Djohar recently. He would like to see you, but Zelimkhan asked you to meet him first.'

'What do they want to see me about?' I asked in some puzzlement.

'I can tell you in confidence, they want to appoint you minister of culture.'

I burst out laughing. 'This is the perfect time for me to become a minister! But,' I added, 'I can hardly refuse to meet the president.'

'Then I'll see you in Zelimkhan's office in two days' time,' Khusein said.

I knew Zelimkhan Yandarbiev well, from back in the days of the Prometheus (Phyarmat) arts association. It had many young members who went on to become well known writers and poets, like Musa Akhmadov and Apti Bisultanov, with both of whom I was on friendly terms. Zelimkhan and I worked together on the staging of his play, *Faceless*. He translated 'Eliso,' a story by Alexander Kazbegi, into Chechen, adapted it for the stage, and I acted the principal role of Vazha. Later, when Zelimkhan began working in the Writers' Union and I was chairman of the Union of Theatre Workers, both our organizations were housed in an old, beautiful villa in a leafy side street off Red Frontline Soldiers Road, and we saw each other every day. We were on good, professional terms.

At the agreed time, I went up to his office on the eighth floor of the building which had formerly housed the Republican Committee of the Soviet Communist Party and was now the Presidential Palace. Khusein was waiting for me, and as I went in I noticed a touch of domesticity, a parrot in a cage with a side table to itself. Books and newspapers were strewn over the desk and chairs. We exchanged greetings, and I said to Zelimkhan, 'Even now you are vice-president you haven't outgrown your revolutionary habits!'

'The revolution is just beginning, and you think you can relax?' he replied jokingly, before continuing more seriously, 'You need to take on this ministerial position and come to work with us. You are just the kind of person who should be in this field now.'

I said, 'Zelimkhan, since you and Djohar are asking me to take on this job I won't try to wriggle out of it. In the current situation that would look as if I were turning away from the path we have chosen, and I will never do that. I have my own views on the matter, but certainly consider it my duty to listen to Djohar.'

'Fine. We shall meet in his office this evening, then,' Zelimkhan said, 'at about eight o'clock. He asked us to see him together.'

It gets dark early in October. A cold, autumn drizzle was falling as I drove back to the Presidential Palace and saw the windows lit on the ninth floor where Djohar had his office. Walking from the car park to the palace entrance, I remembered this enormous grey building being erected in record time in the 1970s. Construction continued day and night, and the storeys were piled one on top of the other at breakneck speed. Already then I saw clearly that the building's grim pomposity was intended to proclaim the unchallengeable might of the Communist regime, and to impress upon the eternally rebellious Chechens that Russia would never withdraw from their country. I also knew, however, that a saintly Chechen *evliya* had predicted many years earlier that, 'round a table' Soviet power would 'cease to exist.' That prediction instilled hope in many Chechens who hated this ruthless regime, but watching the building go up my heart sank. It was only too clear that year by year the Russians were consolidating their position in our land.

Approaching the massive doors of the main entrance, I remembered those disconcerting thoughts. Even now, there was little enough to be cheerful about. Admittedly, Russian officials and troops had left Chechnya for the first time in 130 years. We were at last close to liberating our country, but there was plenty of evidence to suggest that Moscow was not inclined to acquiesce in this. There were clashes and pitched battles with gangs armed by Russia, and the Moscow newspapers were writing openly about large army groups moving towards our frontiers. Events in Ingushetia two years earlier were fresh in our memories, when Chechen and Russian troops had been within a single shot of all-out war. It is difficult to convey these nebulous feelings, but I had a sense that something evil was in the air. It was rising eerily out of the dank earth that evening, taking form and fusing with the darkness which blanketed the city. It was tangible in the raw chill of autumn.

I went up to Zelimkhan's office again. He had also invited Khusein Ferzauli, the deputy prime minister for social affairs, evidently concerned that Khusein might be offended if a new minister was appointed in his area without his knowledge and approval. I heard later that Khusein did indeed have someone else in mind for the job, a singer very well known in the republic, but Djohar for whatever reason had turned him down. Khusein and I ran into each other in the ante-room and went through to Zelimkhan together. After the usual courtesies, Khusein asked, softening his remark with a jocular tone,

'Zelimkhan, are you sure you wouldn't like to do my job too?' 'No,' Zelimkhan replied. 'Otherwise I would not have invited you to confirm Akhmed as minister of culture,' thereby diplomatically making clear that the matter was settled.

We went up to the ninth floor, where Djohar was waiting. We greeted each other and embraced in accordance with Chechen custom. Three years had passed since we last met, but I noticed the president was as energetic as ever. His words and gestures were definite, and if he did have doubts or misgivings he was not going to show them to outsiders. As many others have remarked, Djohar had a powerful presence which energized whoever he was talking to. I thought as we sat down at his desk, 'Here is a man called by destiny to lead his nation.'

Djohar began the discussion, as Chechen etiquette requires, by enquiring after my parents and family. Then he asked why I had been so little in evidence in the republic and what I was doing. I thought that, with all his cares and duties, Djohar would have forgotten many details of our meetings years earlier, but I was mistaken. He had a retentive memory, and an enviable ability to recall names and events. Finally, he said, 'Akhmed, if everybody who was there when this whole business began chooses to stand aside, the five or six people I have with me now will not be able to build a state. We need to work on this together, setting aside personal concerns. It has been suggested that you would make an ideal minister of culture. How about it?'

Zelimkhan and Khusein had left by this time, referring to other business. I said, 'Djohar, I have told Zelimkhan, and say now to you, that I have no intention of abandoning our path. I want you to know that I firmly believe we need an independent Chechen state and am certain this is the only right path for us. I am your comrade and supporter in all things connected with that. You know that war with Russia is inevitable, but I give you my word that when it begins I shall be here, at home, and it will make no difference to me then whether I am a foot soldier or a minister. I know that my place will be here and that I must fight in the war. That is why I want to decline this present offer.'

'No,' Djohar said firmly. 'There is not going to be a war! The world will not allow it. I will not allow it. Russia is just trying to frighten us with its bellicose grimacing. It does not have the strength to start a war against us now, but even if they did take that decision the entire world would be against them. Do not even think about war. Think about the future.'

I felt Djohar was relying on the political sanity of the Russian authorities, and how was he to know then that the Kremlin would choose, out of all the possible options, the very worst, the most lunatic? I quote his words here so that all who accuse him of having wanted and deliberately provoked war should be in no doubt that is a downright lie. At the end of our talk I said, 'At the very least, I need to go back to Moscow to finish off some business. I have friends there, business partners, who are expecting and relying on me. I need at least two weeks to tie up my personal business, but after that I shall come back home and everything will be as you see fit.' 'All right. You have two weeks, but it will be better if you can tie up your affairs before that. Let me know as soon as you are back home.'

With that agreement, I left Djohar's office that bleak October evening.

III

The First Russo-Chechen War

1994. Russia invades Chechnya to 'restore constitutional order.' Zakaev appointed commander of the Chechen government's Seventh Front. Motives of the Russian 'War Party,' who need an invasion to conceal their corrupt selling off of military equipment during the Soviet withdrawal from East Germany.

At the height of the stand-off between Russia and Chechnya, Professor Abdurakhman Avtorkhanov, an internationally renowned political scientist and dissident who lived in Germany, made this appeal to the Chechens:

'Save Checheno-Ingushetia from a new tragedy. Resolve the issues of this crisis within the Constitution. I do not doubt the idealism of Djohar Dudaev and the nobility of his nationalist motives, but I am opposed to a new Jihad; I am opposed to a repetition of the Caucasian War as in the era of Shamil. We live in modern times, in a new environment, and with a new Russia. On the basis of the Adats, the precepts of the highlanders under which the old have the right to give advice to the young, I appeal to you personally, dear Djohar Dudaev. Please stop thinking of Jihad. Seek your salvation and freedom in the same way these have been won by the republics on the periphery of the former Soviet Union. We must understand that the price of national independence will be too high if we go forward without Russia and against Russia. I believe that, with a democratic Russia, there is every chance we will be able to achieve our goal by peaceful means.'

Apart from Djohar, neither his supporters nor his opponents paid any attention to this appeal. They dismissed the warning from a great Chechen scholar about the need to preserve national unity on the grounds that 'the old man has lived abroad so long he has lost touch with reality.' Djohar Dudaev, on being elected president of the Chechen Republic, wrote to Yeltsin:

To the President of Russia, Mr Boris Yeltsin.

Esteemed Mr President,

As a result of historic events you and I have been witnesses to and participants in dramatic changes in the destinies of peoples and the state. Through the efforts of Russia's democratic forces under your leadership, Russia has embarked upon a new and dynamic path of development. Your efforts have been welcomed by all the countries of the civilized world. Your aspiration to move the economy towards the world of tomorrow has also found support. The Russian people and Russian democrats see in you a new kind of leader. For my part, I wish you and our friends, the people of Russia, success worthy of its glorious history. As you know, the people of the Chechen Republic have today embarked on the path of independent development having, for the first time in many decades, gained freedom and independence. There are many difficulties, but that is not the present issue. Everything is amenable to the power of human beings and their intellect, their wisdom and human magnanimity. An invisible, but sometimes palpable, borderline of confrontation can prevent political leaders from seeing the reality of the world, from being aware of what the times call for. The problems which today have become so acute do not deserve the needless spilling of a single drop of human blood. Karabakh, Georgia, South Ossetia, North Ossetia, Ingushetia and many local conflicts which are preventing our peoples from building their future should be the focus of attention at all levels. I am personally convinced that through joint efforts we can not only halt their further development, but also stop the senseless and pointless carnage between fraternal peoples. We have no moral, human right to leave unresolved any problem which could generate tension. Much in the world today depends on our shared wisdom and farsightedness. In accordance with the good traditions of our peoples and in the name of their peace and prosperity, I extend to you the hand of friendship and propose that we should meet in the very near future to deal with all contentious issues for the sake of a better future. With profound respect and sincere good wishes to you and to the people of Russia,

Djohar Dudaev

President of the Chechen Republic

III: The First Russo-Chechen War

That the proposed meeting between Djohar Dudaev and Boris Yeltsin never took place was largely the responsibility of Ruslan Khasbulatov.[1] Khasbulatov bears a heavy responsibility for what happened subsequently in Chechnya. A moment of truth had arrived, and for the first time in the history of the Russo-Chechen conflict, he, a Chechen, occupied such a high position that he could effectively change the entire situation.

I watched on television as Khasbulatov declared the newly elected Chechen government illegal. It was after the elections of our president and parliament, and at that moment how relations between Russia and Chechnya developed depended solely on Khasbulatov. There was live coverage of a meeting of the Supreme Soviet of the Russian Federation, chaired by Khasbulatov. He adjourned the session. Some of the deputies had already stood up and were making for the exit when Khasbulatov called them back:

'Oh, just a moment, comrade deputies, if you will. I do apologize for forgetting. There is one matter we have to decide. I have received a proposal that the so-called elections in the Chechen Republic of a president and parliament should be declared illegal. Those in favour, please show.'

Khasbulatov was the first to raise his hand. A minute later he declared, 'Motion carried. Thank you, everybody.'

---

[1] Here is some information from his official biography:
Ruslan Imranovich Khasbulatov, born 2 November 1942 in Grozny, shortly before the Deportation of the Chechens to Kazakhstan and Central Asia. Spent his childhood and was schooled in Kazakhstan.
Graduated in 1965 from the Law Faculty of Moscow State University. In 1970, became a postgraduate student of the Faculty of Economics, Department of Economies of Foreign Countries. In 1970, defended his candidate's dissertation, and in 1980 his doctoral thesis. Obtained a post at the USSR Academy of Sciences.
Since 1978, has taught at the Plekhanov Institute of the National Economy, Moscow, being steadily promoted. From Associate Professor, after defending his doctoral dissertation in 1980, he became Professor and then head of the Department of International Economic Relations.
Since Mikhail Gorbachev came to power in the USSR in 1985, Khasbulatov has been actively working to support democratic processes and the ideals of Perestroika.
In early 1990, Ruslan Khasbulatov was elected people's deputy for No. 37 Constituency, Grozny, Checheno-Ingush ASSR.
During the First Congress of People's Deputies of Russia in May–June 1990, Boris Yeltsin was elected chairman of the Supreme Soviet of the RSFSR and proposed Khasbulatov for the post of his first deputy.
In June 1991, after Yeltsin was elected president of the Russian Federation, R.I. Khasbulatov became chairman of the Supreme Soviet of the Russian Federation.

For the first time in their history, the Chechen people had an opportunity to realize their age-old dream of independence without bloodshed. By this vote, Khasbulatov cynically and cold-bloodedly condemned his own people to a terrible war. That resolution was subsequently exploited by Shakhrai, Lobov, Filatov, and later by Avturkhanov, Khadzhiev, and Zavgaev, to block a meeting between Yeltsin and Dudaev. It was absolutely clear that, if that meeting took place, there would be no war. It was Ruslan Khasbulatov who then started insisting that Moscow should send troops into Chechnya, which provided Russia with a formal pretext for unleashing a brutal war, and claiming in the process to be acting within international law.

I took up my ministerial duties on 18 November, and a week later, on 26 November 1994, the first invasion of Chechnya by Russian troops, masquerading as 'opposition forces,' began. Many of our historians, including Dalkhan Khozhaev, have proposed this should be considered the date the First Russo-Chechen War began, and with good reason. That was the day the armies of Russia and Chechnya came face to face in Grozny. That was the day Chechens saw Russian tanks burned out by grenade launchers, observed columns of captured aggressors and their armed henchmen, and had their faith strengthened in themselves and their brave sons and daughters who had taken up arms. It was the day the romantic war cry of 'Liberty or death' became a grim reality for Chechens.

It is a day I will also never forget, because it saw the first entry in the death toll of my friends. Khusein Guzuev's was the first name in that melancholy list. He left three children, two girls and a boy. May Almighty Allah prolong their lives and make them worthy of their talented and courageous father!

There followed a succession of anxious days as Russian planes began bombing Grozny, and the hospitals and cemeteries began to fill with civilian casualties. In every town, district, and village, militia detachments formed as people prepared for a cruel war, although many still harboured the hope that the forces of reason in the world, and in Russia itself, would halt this growing insanity. I often reflect on the words at that time of one of my friends: 'Our fathers fought Russia in the detachments of Khasan Israilov and Mairbek Sheripov. Our grandfathers fought Russia in the years of the Civil War. Before that our forebears fought Russia ceaselessly in the times of Sheikh Mansur and Imam Shamil. For some reason I had imagined our generation would be the only one in all these centuries to be spared a war with Russia, but we have not been able to defy our destiny as Chechens.' It seems to me now that every generation of Chechens is doomed to fight its war with Russia, and that this will continue until the day we gain national independence. Only freedom will halt the endless bloodshed, and that is why 'Liberty or death!' has such a historic resonance for Chechens.

On 11 December, full-scale invasion by Russian troops began, and they no longer bothered trying to conceal their aggression under the fig leaf of an 'opposition.' By this time I had friends I could trust and, with our own financial means, we began acquiring weapons, ammunition and military equipment. We formed a small but close-knit unit in which each person knew his friends would not abandon him in time of trouble. Throughout Chechnya, dozens and hundreds of such detachments formed spontaneously, made up of relatives, neighbours, and friends.

In addition to these preoccupations, I had ministerial duties to perform, although the Ministry building looked more like a military headquarters than a peaceful institution attending to cultural matters. Then, on 21 December if I remember correctly, Djohar convened a meeting of all the government ministers at the Presidential Palace. He informed us of a telegram received from Yeltsin. Previously, Djohar had met Pavel Grachev in the hill village of Sleptsovskaya in Ingushetia, and the Russian minister of defence had publicly promised there would be no war between Russia and Chechnya. Now Djohar read us Yeltsin's telegram. I do not remember it verbatim, but it was along the lines of, 'Citizen Dudaev is to present himself in Vladikavkaz (North Ossetia) at such and such time in order to discuss the disarming of illegal units.' The telegram gave a very limited time for Djohar to appear, and was couched in the terms of a peremptory ultimatum.

Djohar read out the telegram and asked the members of the government for their reactions. Everybody fell over themselves to assure the president that such a trip was out of the question, that it would be a humiliation both for Djohar and the entire republic. He let everyone have their say, but I kept quiet. The matter seemed too weighty and complex for an instant emotional decision. The tone of the telegram was unquestionably arrogant, but it seemed to hold out at least some hope of stopping the bloodshed which had begun and opening negotiations. I said nothing because the atmosphere in the meeting was overheated, and I did not want to put Djohar in an awkward position by advocating something which really would look like a humiliation and loss of face for him.

When the responses came to an end, Djohar said, 'It is easy for you to talk like that because it is not you but I who will answer before the Almighty for the catastrophe this war will bring upon our people. I bear that responsibility before Allah and the people, and I will do everything in my power to stop the war.' He immediately turned to his assistant, Movlen Salamov, and gave his instructions: 'Send Yeltsin a telegram or, if that is not possible, report through ITAR–TASS, that I will go to Vladikavkaz at the time appointed.' After these words the rumble of voices in the hall was stilled and a total silence descended. Djohar added, 'I have heard what you have to say, and my decision is that I will go there to negotiate.' This incident was witnessed by dozens of people, and again shows how hard Djohar tried to prevent war.

Some time later, Ivan Rybkin, ex-chairman of the State Duma of the Russian Federation, told me that, when Yeltsin's entourage drew up this curt telegram, they were confident that Djohar would send them a hostile, negative reply. When they received his agreement to come and negotiate, the Russians immediately withdrew all suggestion of negotiation and intensified their bombing of Grozny. By this time the war was gaining momentum. Russian troops were moving through Chechen territory from three directions at once, making for Grozny, and of course neither the Russian regime nor the Army had the least intention of calling a halt to their military operation. They had simply been looking for another propaganda coup to the effect that they had invited Dudaev to negotiate but he had refused. When their trick failed, the war only intensified and became more savage.

The people Djohar had included in the delegation for negotiations, Amaliev, Abubakarov and a number of oil traders, tried to persuade him that we should not fight under any circumstances, should accept any Russian conditions, and submit to any ultimatums. I remember one of them arguing, 'Our fathers fought Russia for 50 years in the nineteenth century, but it was a futile struggle and we achieved nothing. Now we will only destroy our people without achieving any result, and we still won't be independent.'

Djohar abruptly silenced this panic-mongering talk. 'What do you mean, "a futile struggle?" What do you mean, "no results?" Are you not ashamed to make such assertions? Quite apart from the matter of honour, did not that courageous struggle compel the Russian Empire to pay more attention to the Chechens than to any of the peoples it did subjugate? Did not the Chechens receive the right to resolve disputes in accordance with our own traditions? Were the Chechens not free of the obligation to serve in the Russian Army, where each man suffered for 25 years like a convict sentenced to hard labour? Were Chechens not given the right to bear arms freely, while others were forced to girdle themselves with string? It is thanks to the valour of our ancestors that Chechens have to this day remained Chechens. To this day, even after 70 years under the godless power of the Communists, after the ordeal of the Deportation, we have remained Chechens! Is that not enough for you? Are these not "results?"'

Then Djohar said, 'We have done everything to prevent this war, and now we must do everything we can to rouse our people to repel aggression, to get them to fight. We shall do everything to make that happen!' Declaring that the date of the government's next meeting would be announced later, Djohar drew matters to a close.

After that, I went back up to my office to work. Part of the wing of the building where the library and memorabilia hall were situated was already in ruins after the bombing. I made no attempt to move anything to a place of safety, because Djohar had warned us that removing items from the capital might create panic. In my office the shock wave from bombs had blown the doors off their hinges and fragments of window glass were everywhere. With few exceptions, none of the staff were in the building. I secured my office's entrance doors with wire, and together with my friends left the wrecked Ministry. From there we went straight to enrol in a volunteer unit which was being formed near the Presidential Palace. My military career had begun.

The New Year Assault launched by the Russian Command on 31 December 1994 found me and my comrades in the Presidential Palace. That was also the General Headquarters of the Armed Forces of the Chechen Republic of Ichkeria and the base of its commander, Aslan Maskhadov. From time to time Chechen units, totally outnumbered by the attacking Russian regiments and battalions, called Maskhadov for reinforcements.

I remember Aslan that day, his face haggard, his eyes red from lack of sleep, wearing his military tunic and colonel's hat, monitoring a rapidly changing military situation. He was fully informed of the deployment of our units and the enemy's troops, and tried with the meagre reserves at his disposal to lend at least some measure of support to those who were under particular pressure. It was from that day that I began to feel a deep respect for this mild-mannered and invariably courteous man. When danger threatened from every side, those around him could see the steely courage and indomitable will emerge which are the essential attributes of a real military commander. To the end of my days I will thank the Almighty for making me a contemporary and political companion of such exceptional people as Djohar and Aslan.

In response to one of the requests for reinforcements, Aslan ordered me and my modest unit to deploy to the area of the First Municipal Hospital. There were five of us, including Said-Khusein Tazbaev, my fellow student at the Voronezh Arts Institute, who had been working as a teacher in Gudermes.

The others I will not name in order not to jeopardize their safety, apart from noting that only one of us had ever served as a regular soldier in the Soviet Army. Our weaponry consisted of assault rifles and one Mukha grenade launcher. It took us a long time to reach our destination because Grozny, as 1994 drew to a close, was a vision of hell. There are no words to describe the detail of what was going on during the assault. In any case, the picture could never be complete because there were thousands of skirmishes, isolated battles, and ferocious man-to-man fighting. The roar of planes, the clatter of tank tracks, the endless cannonade, the gunfire merging into a constant rattle, the glare from buildings on fire, smoke spreading over the ruined city, the soot-covered snow, and the corpses littering the streets: that is what I remember of that New Year's Eve in Grozny, like anyone else who took part in those battles, I imagine.

Even against the background of the appalling human tragedy then unfolding, for some reason it is our dogs in Grozny which have particularly stuck in my mind. We met them all the way from the Presidential Palace to our destination. Lost, scared by the thunderous cacophony of war, they came running over to us, whining pitifully, and pressed against our legs. Their eyes begged us for protection. To these terrified creatures, we humans probably seemed superior beings capable of bringing this nightmare to a halt.

In the very centre of the city, on Victory Prospect, stood grandiose residences which for some reason were called 'Stalin' apartment blocks, although everybody knew they had been built by German prisoners of war. Here the shelling was particularly intense and we had to keep our heads down, advancing barely 100 metres in over an hour. From time to time we were forced to shelter in the entrances or cellars of apartment blocks. The people living on this avenue were nearly all Russians, so it was odd to see Russian artillery demolishing their homes with such gusto. Many houses were already ruined and in flames. When we dived for cover into one of the cellars, we found many people sitting motionless in semi-darkness, with only the light from candles and smoky home-made paraffin lamps. There were wounded people, and dead bodies lay by the walls.

In one corner I noticed a man in a fur hat, which he was wearing in the manner of a Russian villager, with one earflap lowered. His face was black with soot and registering profound grief, almost despair. I recognized him as Ruslan Saikhanov, the minister of culture before Abdulla Kindarov. He recognized me too, stood up and came over. Saikhanov had married a Russian, which in Soviet times was common practice among Vainakhs who intended to make a government career. Marrying a Russian was considered a sign an 'ethnic' had renounced their national roots and traditions, adopting instead the nationally indeterminate 'culture' of the Communists. We talked and I asked him, 'Why did you not take your family out to the country?'

'Who could have known it would come to this? War, real war! They've gone mad, bombing the city, killing everyone indiscriminately. What is going on? How did it come to this?' I knew he was addressing these bewildered questions not so much to me as to himself, trying to understand what had suddenly destroyed that whole seemingly unshakable world, and hurled him and thousands of others into the infernal abyss of a barbaric war.

Only people profoundly sure of their principles can face such tragic turmoil with equanimity, seeing them as a spiritual ordeal to be got through. I met many such people, imperturbable in even the most dangerous situations. These were the people who endured, and continue to endure, the incredible burden of this war, a war which can hardly be called merely unequal, so wholly incommensurable in numbers and technological might are the Russian aggressors and the Chechens defending their homeland.

Every Vainakh, no matter how firmly established as a towndweller, is certain to have an ancestral home in a particular village. That is why nearly all Chechens evacuated their families to the countryside in good time and only returned to the city if they intended to defend it against Russian troops. Many Chechens invited Russian neighbours, friends and work colleagues to move with him to their village. Some accepted the invitation and survived, while others, listening to the incessant Russian propaganda claiming that Chechens were taking Russians to the countryside to use them as hostages, chose to remain in Grozny and were killed in their tens of thousands by shells, bombs and bullets.

I can confirm this from my own experience. Along with my family, I evacuated to my home in Urus-Martan five families of Russian officials at the Ministry of Culture. I invited everyone, but the others declined. Those I took away survived, while all those who stayed behind in Grozny, as I learned later, died.

Let me tell you about what had led to my being at the Voronezh Arts Institute in the first place, and how I met Ruslan Saikhanov. It all began when Aindi and I saw Chechen boys of our own age very expertly dancing the *Lezginka* on television. We thought their dancing was brilliant, but what bowled us over was their costumes: the brightly coloured long Circassian coats with decorative cartridge pouches, daggers on jointed silver belts, *bashlyk* hoods which fluttered dashingly as they leapt and span, and shaggy Chechen-style Astrakhan hats.

Aindi and I decided there and then to find out where in Urus-Martan we could learn such fiery dances and be issued such magnificent costumes. We soon tracked down an amateur arts circle and went to enrol. To our delight, we were accepted without ado and immediately became the dance group's most diligent pupils. We never missed a lesson, come rain or snow, although we had six kilometres to walk there and another six kilometres back.

In eighth grade, when Aindi and I were thirteen or fourteen, our dance group was invited to an 'International Dance Festival of the Peoples of the World' in Kishinev in Moldavia. We won first prize and came home feeling like champions. After that Aindi and I had no doubt that our next stop was the Grozny School of Choreography.

When I graduated, I went to work in the theatre, virtually the only place where issues of any social significance could be aired in the Chechen language. After a time, I decided to study at the Voronezh Arts Institute, which had a national cultures studio headed by Aleksey Dundukov.

Our studio's graduation performance was produced by Dundukov in 1981. It was based on a quasi-dissident book by the Georgian writer, Nodar Dumbadze. *White Flags* was to have a considerable, if rather quirky, impact on theatre productions the length and breadth of the USSR. The novel dealt with conditions in Soviet prisons and labour camps and the fact that innocent people could end up in these appalling conditions. It managed to get published, but Dumbadze fell into official disfavour. Our production caused an uproar. 'Vigilant comrades' hastened to alert the appropriate authorities, and thereafter, by a special directive of the USSR Ministry of Education, all theatre institutes in the country were ordered to carry out an advance check on student graduation productions to ensure they were in line with official ideology. Students had previously been able to base their production on any literary work they chose. We contributed to the fact that the totalitarian regime in the USSR became one or two turns of the screw more repressive.

The Artistic Committee of the Checheno-Ingush Theatre decided to include *White Flags* in its repertoire, but after a successful premiere, in which I played the hero, Zaza Nakashidze, Ruslan Saikhanov had the production taken off, remarking that, 'In Russia we have only red flags.' What an irony that the troops who destroyed his home drove into Grozny under red flags. Such were the memories brought back to me by this encounter with him in a Grozny cellar on New Year's Eve, 1994.

We did finally reach the First Municipal Hospital and met up with the resistance unit holding the position there. It was commanded by Khusein Isabaev, with Said-Magomed Chupalaev, who had been a taxi driver, as his second in command. I already knew Said-Magomed. He had often visited us in the theatre in the early days of the revolutionary events, but this was the first time I had met Khusein. His unit proved to be one of those under the command of Shamil Basaev, who had ordered them to occupy this position, and now the five of us were here to provide support. I greeted Said-Magomed and he exclaimed, 'Akhmed, is it really you!' He turned to the fighters and said, 'Lads, we have a minister in our ranks!' I had known a number of others in the unit before the outbreak of war, and was soon acquainted with the rest, checking out who was from where and discovering, as is always the case with Chechens, shared relatives and friends.

We merged with the unit and prepared to storm the hospital, which had been occupied by Russian detachments. An order came from Aslan Maskhadov, however, not to attack or return fire from the Russian soldiers holed up in there. They had taken hostage all the patients, medical staff, and visitors to the hospital, and were threatening a massacre if we attacked or fired at them. This incident features in *Purgatory*, a film by the Russian chauvinist, Alexander Nevzorov. He falsified many aspects of the situation, spicing it up with a few 'Chechen atrocities,' including a ludicrous scene where a Russian soldier is crucified, but did not bother to disguise the fact that the Russians had taken those in the hospital hostage. This is relevant to the question of who was first in the Russo-Chechen Wars to initiate the wretched practice of mass hostage-taking, sometimes in hospitals. There is a sad irony in the fact that the whole world knows all about the seizing of the hospital in Budyonnovsk by a detachment under Shamil Basaev, but very few people know that, a year and a half previously, one of his units was blockading Russian soldiers in a hospital where they had taken the occupants hostage.

Over the following days I noticed the lads were constantly trying to make life easier for me and to shield me from danger. I was touched, but tried not to avail myself of this unconventional ministerial perk, taking my turn at combat duty with the rest of them, participating in night patrols and shifts. This continued until 11 January. The night before, orders from the president had been broadcast on television (which by a miracle was still functioning in a few places) for all government ministers to attend a meeting. For security reasons, the venue had to be enquired after at the Presidential Palace.

On the way there we again encountered numerous stray dogs, but how they had changed over those ten days! They had gorged on human flesh, readily available because the streets and squares were littered with the bodies of Russian soldiers. The dogs had put on weight as a result of their hideous diet and were reluctant to let us pass, snarling and following us with eyes which were no longer asking for protection but had a feral gleam. Maskhadov several times made radio contact with the Russian commander and offered an armistice for the streets to be cleared of these soldiers' bodies which, in full view of everyone, were being gnawed at by dogs and rats. It was only when the sight of these disfigured corpses so horrified new troops being brought in that they started deserting en masse that the Russian commanders were forced to remove them. We let them get on with it.

On arriving at the Presidential Palace, I was told to go to Chernorechiye, and reached the village just in time. Djohar conducted the meeting and, when it was over, turned to me. 'Praise be to Allah, we have plenty of people willing to fight. Everybody should do what he is best at. There has been an anti-war demonstration in Khasavyurt, where there are many refugees from Chechnya. Take Dik-Magomed and see what you can do to help them.'

After that, he took me to one side and added, 'The situation with the refugees is complicated. I want you and Dik-Magomed to find ways of resolving their problems and bringing order to the distribution of humanitarian aid. That is your official task. The unofficial task is to go to Makhachkala, meet Mukhu Aliev, and find out about the Dagestanis' intentions.'

I cannot detail all the matters I was to discuss with Aliev, who at that time was the chairman of the People's Assembly of Dagestan, because he is still alive and known throughout Russia as a former president of the republic.

Aliev agreed to receive me, but immediately stated, 'The people of Dagestan have decided where their future lies, and see it only within the framework of Russia.' I said, 'Perhaps you only think that the peoples of Dagestan (I emphasized the plural) have already decided. Perhaps what you really mean is that the officials of Dagestan have decided. At all events, I am here to discuss other matters. We respect the choice of every people, and even the attitude of individuals, including yourself. We insist, however, that you should respect the choice of the Chechen people. We too have decided, and not in favour of Russia. That does not mean that we are against Russia, it means that we are for ourselves, for our own independence.'

After that I conveyed to him what Djohar had ordered. He promised to talk about it to Magomedali Magomedov, the then leader of Dagestan. Aliev received us hospitably, and we went back to the refugees in Khasavyurt.

Their situation was truly dreadful. I could not imagine myself coping with the task. To see their suffering and be unable to help was very painful. I went back to Djohar and asked him to relieve me of the mission and let me return to my unit, telling him it was not the kind of work I was suited for.

Djohar listened, and entrusted the work wholly to Dik-Magomed. I was pleased and surprised to have persuaded him so easily, but in fact he already had a new assignment in mind for me as foreign minister of the Chechen Republic of Ichkeria. The incumbent, Shamsuddin Yusef, had settled in Turkey and was not doing his job.

When Djohar put the proposal to me, I again tried to dissuade him, pointing out that I had no experience or knowledge of diplomacy. My trip and confidential discussion with Mukha Aliev hardly counted as a fully fledged diplomatic mission, so really I had no relevant experience at all. Djohar replied that he had prepared all the necessary briefing materials and instructions for me, and I could learn on the job. We discussed the matter at length, and Djohar continued to insist until finally I said, 'Djohar, when you told me to take on the duties of minister of culture, I did so. I came home and went to work. But now I really would ask you not to oblige me to leave the republic. I have a family here, and sons, and when at the appointed time the war is over, if we are still alive, I would not want people to say I had run away, had an easy life abroad, and returned only when everything here had settled down again. When my children ask me where I was in the war, I want to be able to reply without avoiding their eyes. I ask you again to let me stay in Chechnya. I will try to be of as much help to you here as I can.'

In March we came together for another meeting, this time in Kurchaloy, and Djohar ordered me to create a Seventh Front from divisions drawn from the Urus-Martan region. I was appointed commander of the front, and am glad to say it was at least an appointment over which Djohar and I were in complete agreement. I was to report to Aslan Maskhadov at General Headquarters, show him Djohar's order, and receive material assistance.

I knew that units from Urus-Martan region were fighting in many parts of Chechnya, but they were very dispersed. Most were in Ruslan Gelaev's division, but he was currently recovering from wounds. I needed to bring these units together, reinforce them by recruiting new fighters, and supply them with arms and equipment. They were to be reorganized and fully integrated into the armed forces of the CRI. Such was Djohar's order.

Accompanied by Said-Khusein Tazbaev, I made my way to Vedeno, found Aslan and gave him Djohar's order. I have to smile when I recall Aslan reading the documents, and then saying he could only let us have a solitary anti-tank mine. That was all he could spare for the newly created front. We lifted the mine. It was heavy. Said-Khusein weighed it in his arms and asked me, 'Are we really going to lug this thing through the Sharoy-Argun Gorge to

Shatoy and on to Martan-Chu?' That was our route to Urus-Martan. We laughed and decided to leave it in Vedeno. A little later Aslan sent us $10,000.

In Vedeno we procured a different kind of help for the front, and very substantial it proved to be. Our celebrated bards, Imam Alimsultanov and Gilani, were there and we were all delighted to see each other. I told them, 'I have been ordered by Djohar to organize a new front. You must come and help us recruit people with your songs.' They agreed enthusiastically, seizing what they saw as an opportunity for using their art to strengthen the Resistance. We agreed that Imam and Gilani would make their own way to Shatoy in a Niva off-roader with all their equipment, and we would rendezvous there.

We met up in Shatoy, hitched the Niva to a tractor so it could cope with the gradients and mud, and after a few adventures along the way made it to Urus-Martan. Later, using my powers as minister of culture, I issued a directive creating the Tolam (Victory) music group, with Imam and Gilani at its heart. We travelled with them through local villages, meeting the people and groups of fighters. Djohar's order to create a new front was already widely known in the region and the republic.

In order to explain why this project, fraught with difficulty, was so important we need to look at its prehistory. After Yeltsin's shelling of the Russian parliament in 1993, Moscow succeeded in inducing Tatarstan which, like Chechnya, had declared itself independent, to sign a federal treaty. In the process, Yeltsin announced his intention of signing a similar treaty with the Chechen Republic, taking due account of the 'special national characteristics' of the Chechen people. This was seen by our own and Russian analysts as indicating that the Kremlin was prepared to compromise in order to restore normal relations between the two countries.

However, Yeltsin's peace initiatives got no further than that. The problem was that by this time Russia's generals had purloined and sold off almost all the military hardware, weapons and equipment of the troops withdrawn from East Germany and the other former satellite states in Europe. Deeply implicated in embezzlement on a vast scale, the generals needed a major war to enable them to write off weapons and military hardware they had in fact already sold. They decided to unleash their aggression on the Chechen Republic, knowing that the Chechens had stood up to Russia for centuries, and today still had the courage to confront a military challenge, even though Russia was now a major world power. That is why Yeltsin's own utterly corrupt entourage, in cahoots with those thieving generals, prevented the president of Russia from seeing the open letter in which Djohar Dudaev expressed readiness to enter into negotiations about a treaty between Chechnya and Russia. I know for a fact that Yeltsin was prevented from seeing it, because, as described below, in May 1996 a Chechen government delegation of which I was a member met Yeltsin in the Kremlin and presented him with a copy of Dudaev's letter. It was obvious from his reaction that he had never seen it before.

Officials in the Russian Presidential Administration had all these years been telling Yeltsin that Dudaev had rejected proposals for negotiations and refused to take any step towards a compromise with Russia's interests. I am sure that a personal meeting between Yeltsin and Dudaev would have prevented a Russo-Chechen War which continues to this day, and which analysts rightly consider the bloodiest military conflict in Europe since the Second World War. Unfortunately, the War Party in Moscow proved too influential.

The first warning sign was the setting up in June 1994 of a Provisional Soviet under Umar Avturkhanov which, with the consent and direct support of Moscow, proclaimed itself the supreme authority in the Chechen Republic. Despite lavish funding from the Russian Treasury, these pro-Russian forces managed to gain a foothold in only two Chechen localities, the Nadterechny and Urus-Martan regions. The Provisional Soviet in Urus-Martan, headed by Yusup Elmurzaev, declared the city completely loyal to the Russian Federal government. Because of this, when the war began, Urus-Martan was one of the safest places in Chechnya, and tens of thousands of refugees streamed there from all parts of the republic, almost quadrupling the city's population of 40,000. Along with ordinary refugees, the republic's Communist Party and economic establishment made its way there and this, indeed, was the sum total of the anti-Dudaev opposition.

When they try to divide our nation into 'good' and 'bad' Chechens and to find supporters among our people, the Russian colonialists invariably fall into their own trap. At the outbreak of the war, Russian propaganda solemnly declared Urus-Martan a 'zone free of Dudaev's fighters.' Despite the long history of Russo-Chechen wars, they still fail to understand the national characteristics of Chechens who, when the latest Russian invasion occurs, immediately create a buffer of people who declare themselves supporters of Russia and mitigate the blows inflicted by the invaders on Chechen fighters and the population in general. During the Caucasian War in the nineteenth century, this buffer consisted of those who were called 'peaceful' Chechens. In the present war, intentionally or not, the function was performed by the anti-Dudaev opposition. It is difficult to tell whether this wartime shock absorber develops consciously or instinctively, but more important is the fact that Urus-Martan became an island of safety in the midst of a savage war, and we took full advantage of that.

Initially I chose Roshni-Chu for my headquarters, and stayed with Dayan Basnukaev. Young people came to join us, and we often travelled through the villages, meeting fighters in the forests. Everything progressed until, by the summer of 1995, the newly formed Front could boast 500 fighters and commanders which, by Chechen standards. was a major fighting force.

In a short period we succeeded in creating a pro-CRI government movement in Urus-Martan. I was born in the city and knew the political landscape, who was in the pro-Russian opposition and who supported us. I feel I have a duty to highlight the special part played by Ruslan Takhaev, who did a tremendously important job in the underground, helping me immensely in contacts with the population. Ruslan was and remains a patriot committed to his Fatherland. At that time the Russian intelligence agencies included him in their list of Chechens to be assassinated.

Needless to say, the Russian Army Command and intelligence agencies knew the situation in the city. They were, however, stymied by their own propaganda. They could not subject Urus-Martan to bombing or shelling because that would have exposed the Kremlin's cornerstone lie that 'only a handful of outlaws in Chechnya supported Dudaev. The destruction of a major Chechen city which had supposedly declared itself an ally of Russia would show up just how few allies Russia really had. We made good use of the situation and Urus-Martan became a safe haven for us. It was our rear. Imam, Gilani, and Birlant Ramzaeva, a true folk singer if ever there was, arranged concerts in squares and the courtyards of houses, where they sang patriotic songs with great professionalism, and there was nothing the city's pro-Russian administration could do to stop it. Music and song have a special place in Chechen culture, at the very core of which are the traditional heroic epic songs, the *illis*. Each of these glorifies the exploits and deeds of a historical hero or military leader and serves the Chechens not only as a kind of history textbook but, no less importantly, as a guide to how to behave.

New times and a new war called for new illis and, in my judgement, Birlant, Imam, and Gilani rose brilliantly to the challenge, raising the patriotic spirit of their packed audiences, and their pride in Chechen fighters who were again confronting the aggressor.

By a special decree of President Dudaev, Ali Yandarov was appointed our official Ichkerian prefect in Urus-Martan. Yusup Elmurzaev knew about this, of course, but made no attempt to interfere. Each got on with his business and left his opponent to get on with his. In turn, Ali Yandarov began appointing the heads of village administrations in the Urus-Martan region. We regularly convened meetings of these village chiefs and gave them specific tasks to create new groups of fighters in their villages, to supply them with ammunition, food, and money.

The money to finance our units came directly from the Russian Treasury, because we left pro-Russian heads of villages in no doubt that they had better share the money they were allocated for the needs of their villages, for salaries and so on, with their Ichkerian counterparts. As the saying goes, 'War is money.' Accordingly, we enabled Russia, which was spending huge sums on its aggression in Chechnya, to pay also our armed forces' expenses for repelling that aggression. If we had been relying solely on financial assistance from outside, our situation would have been dire indeed.

Eventually, we arranged a great meeting in the village of Goyskoye of the commanders of all the existing and new units in the region. A large military force was organized to provide security for the meeting, at which each commander reported how many fighters he had, how well supplied he was with arms and ammunition, and what other problems he needed to resolve. Our front-line forces were impressive: we were ready for major military operations. We had also organized and equipped three large military bases in Martan-Chu, Tangi-Chu, and Roshni-Chu.

In just two months we had created an impressive military and political organization in Urus-Martan region and put in place security measures to safeguard our politicians. These were so effective that on several occasions we conducted meetings and conferences of the Ichkerian government in Urus-Martan itself.

There were no problems about bringing our wounded fighters to the city's hospitals, and we also brought fighters in from other parts of the republic for rest and medical treatment. This meant that men from other regions were glad to join our units. In particular, we had many fighters from the neighbouring Akhchoy-Martan region. Urus-Martan became a powerful base for our armed forces, and remained so until the end of the war. Without exaggeration, we can say that it played an important part in our victory in August 1996 over the occupation forces.

IV

Russia and the Organization for Security and Cooperation in Europe

Zakaev is appointed to negotiate a ceasefire with Russia under the auspices of the Organization for Security and Cooperation in Europe, during which Russia launches a massive military attack. Shamil Basaev's Budyonnovsk Raid attempts to halt the war. Trickery in negotiations by both parties. Attempted assassination of Russia's General Romanov, probably by his own side. Russian massacre of civilians in Samashki. Zakaev organizes disruption of Russian-sponsored 'new elections.'

It was at this time that I first found myself drawn into the negotiating process. In the evening of 23 May 1995, I received an order from the president to come and see him in Shatoy immediately. By three o'clock the next morning I and a detachment of 200 men were in Shatoy. I reported my arrival through an intermediary, and Djohar sent the head of our Security Service for me. I billeted the fighters in various houses, appointed Shamil Isaev commander of the unit in my absence, and went to see Djohar. Our attorney general, Usman Imaev, was also present. We exchanged greetings and Djohar told me, 'Tomorrow, 25 May, you and Usman need to drive towards Dubi-Evl. On the bridge between Dubi-Evl and Dachu-Barzoy, you will find vehicles from the Organization for Security and Cooperation in Europe waiting. You are to travel with OSCE representatives to Grozny and hear proposals from the Russian side.'

In the morning we got into Usman's open UAZ jeep, he took the wheel, and we drove towards Dubi-Evl on the border between the territories controlled by us and the Russians. That morning saw the start of a great deal of activity in the air. Planes hurtled above us at low altitude, their engines roaring. We were not fired on, but could hear bombs exploding in the far distance. 'We had supposedly agreed all military operations would cease during the negotiations,' Usman remarked as another squadron flew over us.

We reached the bridge, where Russian officers and the OSCE representatives were waiting. The white jeeps with blue lettering and the OSCE emblem took up position in front and behind our battered UAZ with its large Ichkerian flag on the bonnet, and we moved off towards Grozny. I will never forget those emotional moments when people standing at bus stops along our way caught sight of the Chechen flag, raised their arms in greeting and shouted, 'Nohchichoe! Allahu Akbar!' to express their solidarity and support. In Grozny itself we were greeted not only by citizens but even by the pro-Russian Chechen police who, entirely openly, stood to attention and saluted the flag of Ichkeria.

We arrived at the OSCE Mission, which was located in a mansion on a quiet little street which was almost undamaged. We went in and were introduced to the negotiators on the Russian side. The delegation was led by the former Communist functionary, Nikolai Semyonov, the one who lost out to Doku Zavgaev in the late 1980s in the Communist Party election. After that he returned to Russia but, when the war began and the Russians captured Grozny, Yeltsin sent him back to Chechnya as 'Head of the Territorial Administration,' as the occupation regime was styled. He was accompanied at these talks by his deputy, Vladimir Zorin, who flew in from Moscow, and Lecha Makhomadov, a pro-Russian Chechen politician.

Our negotiations began with, essentially, just one item on the agenda: how to stop the fighting. While we were discussing that, however, we were contacted by Aslan Maskhadov. He reported that that morning, as we were starting these negotiations under the auspices of OSCE, Russian troops had broken through Vashtaroy to Selmen-Tauzen, and through Makhkety to Vedeno, where Aslan was located. In addition, the Russians were mounting a full-scale assault on the Shatoy region and had occupied Dubi-Evl and Dachu-Barzoy.

Usman Imaev informed the Russian representatives, 'We are walking out because you have violated all the agreements. Not only have you not ceased hostilities during these negotiations as agreed, but you have exploited them to mount surprise attacks on Shatoy and Vedeno. In this situation, the Chechen leaders have decided to discontinue all negotiations and contact with the Russian side.'

We demanded that the OSCE representatives should ensure our safe passage back to territory controlled by the Chechen forces. When we went outside, Chechens, including many women, approached our car. They put in a sack of provisions, footwear, and other things they hoped we would find useful. We were touched by this gesture of support.

When we reached Dachu-Barzoy, all hell had been let loose. There was the ceaseless din of exploding shells and rockets, gunshots merged into an incessant crackling, and the engines of armoured vehicles roaring deafeningly as long columns moved southwards. The Russian commanders at first flatly refused to let us to pass through the front line, and only the insistence of the OSCE representatives obliged them to agree.

Placing ourselves in the hands of the Almighty, we careered south towards Shatoy, squeezing out of our UAZ all the speed of which it was capable. We arrived in one piece, although our vehicle was peppered with bullet holes, and reported to Djohar. He was already aware of what had happened and said, 'I never supposed from the outset that the negotiations would get anywhere, but we had no right to refuse to take part. We cannot pass up any opportunity to stop the war. This was just another dirty trick by the Russians, but it is unlikely to have done them any good.'

When Djohar and I were alone, he told me to send my troops back but stay for a few days myself in Shatoy. Russian troops had launched an offensive in the Urus-Martan region, targeting a strike at our bases but retreating with a bloody nose. The situation was still tense, however, with the enemy likely to resume the offensive at any moment, so my unit should return to base. As for Shatoy, our troops were on their way from Vedeno, where Ruslan Gelaev and his fighters were also deployed. There were adequate forces in Shatoy.

Djohar was occupying a house on the outskirts of Itum-Kale, and the next morning we headed back to Shatoy in two Nivas. I was in the same vehicle as Djohar, and we were already approaching Shatoy when there was a landslide directly in front of us. Our driver managed to brake in time to avoid an accident. To this day I do not know whether the landslide was coincidental or an assassination attempt. We got out of the cars, Djohar examined the rubble, and asked if we had any spades in the vehicles. There were two shovels. Djohar took one and, without more ado, began clearing the road. We asked him to let one of us have it but he just shook his head and carried on shovelling soil into the ravine. At this point, there was a second, even larger landslide. We managed to jump back out of the way, but there was no longer any question of clearing the road manually.

We turned round and went in search of a detour. We had to drive back almost to Itum-Kale, but there turned on to a byroad and drove towards Shatoy through amazingly scenic countryside I had never seen before. On the way, we passed ancient military towers built of white stone on cliffs and promontories, and I was surprised in one tiny village to see byres built of marble. I remember Djohar laughed and said, 'Only Russian kings and princes lived in marble buildings, but the Chechens keep cows in them.' There were now only two families in the village, the rest having left to escape the bombing. Their hospitality was exemplary and they treated us to probably the best lunch I have had in my life.

It was evening before we reached Shatoy, and that same night we left to drive to Usman Imaev's base. Before the war, Djohar had ordered roads to be built in this area. The official in charge of road building was Nuzhden Daaev, who at first worked in our government but, with the arrival of the Russians, moved to the same position in Salambek Khadzhiev's puppet administration. The road building had not been completed by the beginning of the war and, when we got to a bumpy section, Djohar said we should send Daaev orders to finish the work. This off-the-cuff remark surprised me, but I later discovered that such instructions from Djohar were effective irrespective of whether a particular minister was on our side or working for the puppet regime.

At the time of these events, we had only six members of the CRI Council of Ministers still active: Kazbek Makhashev (minister of the interior), Usman Imaev (attorney general), Elza Sheripova (minister of justice), Dalkhan Khozhaev (minister of the Archives Department), Khozh-Akhmed Yarikhanov (minister of education), and myself as minister of culture.

It took us almost the whole day to reach Usman's base. He had five or six fighters there. We loaded arms and equipment into the vehicles and, bringing Usman and his men along with us, headed for Roshni-Chu. When we arrived, Djohar ordered me to assemble a detachment of 50 men. We already had 46 men in Roshni-Chu under the command of Adam, and those accompanying me made the numbers up to precisely 50 fighters. We were issued with new uniforms and Djohar left, telling us to report for duty in Shalazhi. Musa would contact me there and tell me where to take the detachment.

I appointed Khusein Isabaev as my deputy and took the detachment through the foothill forests to Shalazhi. Said-Khusein Tazbaev came with me. At the agreed rendezvous we met Musa, who told me to leave the detachment in the village and go with him to Djohar, who was waiting. Djohar was sitting in a Volga on a country road. I got in and he told me to delegate command of the detachment of fighters to Musa, and myself wait at one of our bases for an important mission in about a week's time. We agreed a password to identify Djohar's intermediary. Musa took the detachment assigned to him to Shalazhi that day, and Said-Khusein Tazbaev and I returned to our base in Roshni-Chu.

Five days after this, the 'Budyonnovsk Raid' occurred. I received written orders from Djohar to go with Usman Imaev for negotiations with the Russians, which were again held under the auspices of the OSCE. I learned that Usman was already on his way to Grozny, but I had no idea how I was supposed to get there, given that there was a cordon of security checkpoints all round the city. I summoned Ali Yandarov, our Urus-Martan prefect, and asked if he could help. He replied laconically, 'I'll get you there, if we survive.' Learning from my experience of the last negotiations, I changed into civilian clothes and we set off in Ali's car. He knew some abandoned byroads, and we were able to drive without incident to the OSCE headquarters. By the gate, I noticed Russian soldiers and some of our fighters escorting Usman, and they told him I had arrived. The OSCE representatives came out and took me into the building.

Talks had effectively started on 13 June, after telephone negotiations between Shamil Basaev and the Russian prime minister, Viktor Chernomyrdin, while the Chechen fighters were still in Budyonnovsk. In these early stages Usman and I were negotiating with the Russians on such technical issues as the route to be taken by the Chechens when they left Budyonnovsk and other detailed arrangements. The teams worked together for one and a half months.[2]

We agreed at the outset to deal separately with political, economic and military issues. Although military matters came last in that list, they were the first to be addressed, as our priority was to halt the military operations and violence rife in the republic. As a means of providing public security, we agreed to establish Community Self-Defence Groups of 25 citizens in every community (of which there were over 420). Moreover, the Russians undertook to arm and equip these units, which totalled more than 10,000

---

[2] The Russian delegation was headed by Vyacheslav Mikhailov, nationalities minister. Their negotiating team consisted of General Anatoly Kulikov, deputy minister of the interior, who was in charge of all Interior Troops and also chief of the Joint Command of Russian Forces in Chechnya; and Vladimir Zorin, head of the Territorial Administration. The Russians' puppet administration in Chechnya was represented by Abdulla Bugaev.
After the first meeting, the Chechen side was joined by Aslan Maskhadov, chief of staff of the CRI Armed Forces; Akhiad Idigov, chairman of the Chechen parliament; and Khozh-Akhmed Yarikhanov, head of the CRI Further Education Department. Finally, as members of our analysis team, we were joined by Dalkhan Khozhaev, minister of the Archive Department, and Said-Khasan Abumuslimov, member of the CRI parliament and historian.

volunteers. Their weapons were to include assault rifles, machine guns, grenade launchers and sniper rifles, plus ammunition.

For us this was a huge success, because at the time we could arm only 2,000-3,000 fighters to face the thousands of Russian Federation soldiers deployed throughout the republic. If the agreement were to be implemented, we would see a more than fourfold increase in our military strength.

All the matters discussed at the negotiations were agreed with Djohar Dudaev. Our activists in Urus-Martan saw to it that, every time our team went to Grozny, it did so as a triumphal procession. Thousands of people lined the streets of the towns and villages through which we passed, and cheered us enthusiastically on our way with banners and Ichkerian flags. It was a nationwide show of support by the people of the republic for their armed forces. As we proceeded, our convoy of two or three cars was joined by columns of hundreds of others, decorated with crests and flags of Ichkeria. With this guard of honour we drove into Grozny, where we were again greeted by residents of the capital, including the pro-Russian administration's police who saluted our flags. This show of support was greatly heartening, and confirmed our belief that the people of Chechnya were fully behind us and appreciated our military achievements.

During this period of general elation, we saw a great influx of volunteers into our units. In accordance with the agreement, we formed them into 'Community Self-Defence Groups' although, needless to say, our hopes that the Russian High Command would arm them were soon dashed. This was, nevertheless, a huge boost to our strength, because we were able subsequently to arm them by various means ourselves.

We agreed to establish Special Observer Commissions with Chechen, Russian and OSCE representatives in every region of the republic. Their task was to monitor compliance with the ceasefire and other agreements, including an agreement to disarm our military units. The creation of Community Self-Defence Groups in towns and villages was to proceed in parallel with disarmament of units of the CRI Armed Forces, and the Russian side was required to buy up the surrendered weapons. Huge amounts of money, we discovered, were forwarded from Moscow for this purpose. The official Russian media presented the whole highly confused process, in which, frankly, both side were doing their best to outwit the other, as 'disarmament of illegal armed groups.'

Meanwhile, after their failure in Budyonnovsk, the minister of the interior, Viktor Yerin, and Sergey Stepashin, director of the KGB, which had been renamed the Federal Counter-Intelligence Service and is now the Federal

Security Bureau, were dismissed. General Kulikov was appointed minister of the interior of the Russian Federation and left for Moscow, his place, also at the negotiating table, being taken by General Anatoly Romanov. The chief of the Joint Command of Russian forces in Chechnya, General Romanov, and the chief of staff of the CRI Armed Forces, Aslan Maskhadov, thus became co-chairmen of these Special Observer Commissions, with OSCE as arbiter. The same structure was mirrored in every region of the republic.

At one meeting of the delegations in Khankala, which I was co-chairing with Romanov's deputy, General Pavel Maslov, the head of the OSCE Mission in Chechnya, Sandor Meszaros, suddenly asked, 'Mr Zakaev, why are you not implementing the agreements we have reached?'

I told him, 'There is no obstacle on the Chechen side to implementing them. I am the minister of culture and want only to get back to a peaceful life. Believe me, nothing will make me happier than to disband my units and return to civilian life, if, of course, we really are terminating this war.'

General Maslov asked, 'Are you talking about disarming the units of the Urus-Martan Front?'

'Absolutely,' I answered. 'I am talking about disarming the units under my command in order to create Community Self-Defence Groups in the communities of the region as officially agreed. My units average 12-15 men from each community in the region. In accordance with our agreement these will need to be doubled to bring the number in each up to 25 men. However, in some units I have volunteers from other parts of the republic who will return to their communities when Community Self-Defence Groups are formed there. I would like to take this opportunity to invite you and the OSCE representatives tomorrow morning to Tangi-Chu to observe the disarmament process for yourselves.' General Maslov promised to come and bring reporters to the event, and the head of the OSCE Mission said he would come as well.

The next morning, at a gathering of the villagers in Tangi-Chu, I lined up 25 of our volunteers, 11 of whom were armed. General Maslov, members of the OSCE Mission, and a whole crowd of journalists arrived in two helicopters. With a flourish, my 11 fighters laid their weapons down on the ground in front of them, and the village elders, adopting various photogenic poses, stood motionless to be photographed. The agreement required the elders to approve volunteers to be included in their Community Self-Defence Groups. The journalists, some of them Western, immediately started filming and taking photographs. To the accompaniment of much clicking and whirring of cameras I stepped forward and invited General Maslov and the OSCE representatives to come closer.

'So, gentlemen, you see before you 25 of our volunteers. The village elders here have approved them as volunteers for their Community Self-Defence Group. Is that in accordance with our agreement?'

'Absolutely,' General Maslov duly confirmed, and the OSCE representatives nodded agreement.

'You will note that the eleven fighters who are members of my units have laid down their arms. There they are, on the ground before you. The other fourteen volunteers have no weapons and you must arm them. You can buy these rifles off the eleven fighters and give them new weapons, or if you prefer, you can leave the weapons where they are and consider that as discharging your obligation to them. Under the terms of our agreement, however, you are required to issue assault rifles, grenade launchers and 1 sniper rifle to the remaining fourteen fighters with, of course, the requisite ammunition. Here is a list of what you are obliged to provide in accordance with the agreement.'

I handed Maslov the list. He took it, went over to the men and started counting the rifles on the ground. These included one machine gun and a grenade launcher. The officers accompanying General Maslov carefully recorded the make and calibre of the surrendered weapons and the journalists busily filmed everything, clearly anticipating the reports they would file on the 'disarming of Chechen illegal armed groups.' I turned to General Maslov.

'Now, Comrade General, I would like to hear from you when and where we will receive the agreed arms for this Community Self-Defence Group.'

The general's face turned purple. His eyes flashed with anger and, unable to control himself even in front of the reporters and members of the OSCE Mission, he yelled, 'This is a complete travesty! I came to witness disarmament and Zakaev is demanding extra arms! I categorically refuse to be a party to this!'

The enemy never had any intention of arming our community volunteers. Nevertheless, the occupying forces did not prevent us from setting up Community Self-Defence Groups, which we ultimately regularized as local commandants' forces for maintaining public order. Djohar Dudaev ordered the appointment of regional commandants throughout the republic, and these in turn appointed military commandants for the towns and villages in their regions. The new groups were incorporated into the CRI Armed Forces and, when armed from our own reserves and resources, increased the strength of Chechnya's army several times over. The Russian High Command, with all its intelligence-gathering and analytical agencies, could

IV: Russia and the Organization for Security and Cooperation in Europe 53

hardly fail to notice that every day the negotiations and the associated ceasefire continued was strengthening the forces of the Chechen Resistance. They decided to sabotage the talks. On the political stage, Salambek Khazhiev and Umar Avturkhanov were stripped of their principal roles in the puppet administration and replaced by Doku Zavgaev, the republic's former Communist Party boss, who was now sent back to Chechnya, the Russian leaders planning to legalize him later through 'elections.'

Negotiations came to an abrupt end on 6 October 1995 with the attempted assassination of General Romanov as he was driving with a security escort over a railway tunnel near Minutka Square in Grozny. It is still unclear who was responsible for this operation. I think it entirely possible that the occupying forces themselves carried it out, because the Russian High Command were making every effort to restart the war. They were well aware that Romanov had publicly promised Aslan Maskhadov, 'While I am in command of Russian forces in Chechnya, I will not permit any resumption of the war.' An alternative theory suggests that Romanov paid for the fact that, under the pseudonym of 'General Antonov,' he had been in charge of the slaughter of civilians in Samashki. The mass-circulation Russian newspaper *Moskovsky Komsomolets* actually carried an article titled 'General Romanov pays for the crimes of General Antonov.'

A massacre in Samashki was perpetrated by Russian troops on 7-8 April 1995. The formal pretext was an ultimatum to surrender to the Russian troops surrounding the village 264 assault rifles, which it was said were known to be in the village. If the villagers failed to comply by 7.00 am on 7 April they would face an all-out assault. Everybody, including the Russian commanders, knew perfectly well that there was nothing like that quantity of weapons in Samashki, from which the Chechen fighters had withdrawn the day before. Nevertheless, without even waiting for their ultimatum to expire, the Russian criminals subjected the village to intensive artillery bombardment the preceding night. Artillery shells blew the village houses to pieces, burying under the rubble men, women, and children alike. When any movement was noticed in the village, where people were desperately trying to escape the shelling, the Russian troops opened fire with assault rifles and machine guns. The bombardment lasted from 10.30 to 1.30 at night, and in the morning the village was subjected for three hours, from 7.00 am, to massive bombing from the air. No journalists, human rights observers, or Red Cross representatives were allowed in and nobody was allowed to leave, not even columns of women and children.

At 6.00 pm on 7 April, the Russian killers mounted a large-scale ground offensive against the defenceless village. Artillery was moved up and bombarded the centre at close range. The left-hand part of Samashki was in flames. Armoured vehicles attacked the area around the mosque and Russian troops occupied the outskirts. At 8.00 pm bombs again rained down. Some of the Chechen fighters who were natives of Samashki made their way back into the village through the surrounding dense undergrowth and put up furious resistance, enabling a small number of villagers to escape. Tanks fired point-blank at people's houses.

The next day, 8 April, the village was subjected to renewed air and artillery attacks. The worst atrocities took place that evening when troops stormed through Samashki. Some 500 villagers were sadistically butchered, the murderers sparing no one. In the school, thirteen boys in grades 1-3, were battered and hanged with wire. A nearby inscription written in the victims' blood read, 'Museum exhibit: the future of Chechnya;' and 'The Russian bear awakens.'

I will not dwell any longer on this appalling topic, because anyone can readily find descriptions of these atrocities, committed in Samashki by the savages of the Russian Army, in the free press, on the Internet, and in reports by Russian and international human rights organizations and independent journalists. The pseudonymous 'General Antonov' was in command of the Samashki slaughter, and I will only add that there is no shortage of reasons to believe that the attempt on his life was carried out by an unknown group in revenge for these monstrous crimes. To the best of my knowledge, the CRI Armed Forces had no plan to eliminate him. In his place, Moscow sent some other commander whose name I no longer remember, and who was replaced shortly afterwards by General Vyacheslav Tikhomirov. The attempt to assassinate Romanov certainly brought our negotiations to a halt.

In November 1995, then, Zavgaev was sent from Moscow to replace Avturkhanov and Khadzhiev. Yeltsin declared him the head of a 'Provisional Transitional Government of Chechnya,' and in December 'elections' were to be held, in order to give at least a semblance of democratic legitimacy to the latest Russian stooge. Needless to say, everybody well understood that these 'elections' were a farce, in the tradition of the pantomimes at which the USSR's former Communist leaders, now transmogrified into 'political leaders of democratic Russia,' were so adept.

Wondering how best to derail these stage-managed 'elections' of Zavgaev, Dalkhan Khozhaev and I drew up a plan of action and showed it to Djohar. He thought it excellent and authorized me to go ahead. It was very simple: on the day of the mock elections, our fighters would occupy the regional centres and block all the country's roads, paralysing any possibility of political activity by the puppet regime. Our plan was based on the confident calculation that, faced with a new and unexpected situation, the Russian Command would need a minimum of three days to crank up its cumbersome war machine before it could respond. That would give us more than enough time to disrupt the farce and return our fighters to base without suffering losses. As for air attack, we were certain that, in the presence of a throng of Russian and foreign journalists, the Russian commanders would be hostages of their own propaganda, not daring to bomb the Chechen 'voters' who, as they had already announced, were 'loyal supporters of the new government,' i.e., Zavgaev.

Prior to 14 December, that is before the officially announced date for the 'elections,' we carried out two experiments, blocking roads in the Urus-Martan and Achkhoy-Martan regions, and taking careful note of the response of the occupying forces. As we had predicted, their reaction was remarkably slow, and both times we had well over three days to withdraw our troops and avoid losses.

On the night of 13 December, I moved the units under my command into Urus-Martan. We immediately blocked all the roads into the city and occupied the main streets. We took control of all the strategic centres, except for buildings occupied by the puppet administration and the pro-Russian police. We did that to avoid smirmishes and clashes. We were determined to prevent the shedding of Chechen blood on either side, whatever people's political persuasion. Additionally, if we had taken over these buildings and disarmed the opposition, the Russian Command might have been tempted to bomb Urus-Martan. Given the crowded state of the city which, in addition to its usual residents, was now affording shelter to tens of thousands of refugees, that could have led to horrendous civilian casualties. Leaving the puppet administration and police more or less alone, we anticipated that, true to type, they would assure their Russian masters they had the situation under control, depriving them of any excuse to subject Urus-Martan to artillery bombardment and bombing. We certainly did not want to expose the city to risk, not least because its 'pro-Russian' status made it such a useful base for us behind enemy lines.

Meanwhile, the city was electrified. Residents gathered in the squares and streets, and here and there impromptu meetings were held at which some of the speakers berated while others extolled us. Many citizens did not disperse even at night, warming themselves at bonfires and discussing the situation. Any 'elections' were the last thing on their minds. We had exceeded our intended stay in the city and it was time to leave. At any moment some provocative incident might be staged and lead to bloodshed. Finally, when we had been there for seven days, a messenger came from Djohar with orders to withdraw. That was timely, because our informants were telling us the puppet administration, under relentless pressure from the Russian Command, was planning to use firearms against us that day.

With Djohar's order to leave in my hands, I decided on a move which might be regarded as foolhardy if I had not carefully thought through the psychology first. That day a meeting was being held in the pro-Russian administration's offices of the opposition commanders to work out the final details of their attack on us that night. We knew all about it from our intelligence sources. In late afternoon, as the early winter twilight was falling, Dalkhan and I, escorted by just two of our lads and armed only with pistols, drove to the administration's building. As we approached this headquarters of the opposition, panic broke out. There were shouts: 'We've been betrayed!,' 'We're surrounded!,' 'It's Zakaev!' The policemen moved to their positions, we heard the clatter of bolts being closed.

Meanwhile, we entered the building and went up to the first floor where the meeting was being held. I greeted the security guards and asked, 'Where are our brothers meeting?' They showed me the room. Looking inside, one of the guards said, 'Zakaev is here.'

Without waiting for an invitation, we went in. Alerted by the shouting and commotion down in the square, but still not aware of what was happening, the police commanders were clustered round a table covered with maps of the city and its surrounding district, on which they were planning their attack on us. They were completely flummoxed. We greeted them, they reciprocated, and I asked where we could sit down for a moment to talk.

They indicated some chairs, we sat down, and one of them said, 'Akhmed, what are you doing here? There is supposed to be a war starting any time now!'

I asked, 'Who with?'

'You.'

'Praise be to Allah,' I replied. 'My only war is with the Russian occupying forces, and I will never be at war with you. We are disputing the ownership of our country with the invaders, but why should we dispute it with you, our brother Chechens?' Our country belongs to all of us. We have no wish to see even a hair fall from anyone's head in this town; we have no such intentions. Even less do we have any intention of opening fire here, killing people. On the contrary, it is to stop the bloodshed in our country that we have prevented these farcical 'elections' of Zavgaev, which were only a stratagem to make the war more brutal and block all the ways of bringing it to a peaceful conclusion. That is why we have not permitted these so-called elections. That was our mission. We are looking only for peace.'

They were very pleased that a situation so close to bloodshed had resolved itself so unexpectedly. Joy lit up their faces and could be heard in their voices. This was the first, unforced meeting outside an official setting of Chechens who found themselves, so to speak, on different sides of the barricades. I was very struck by how easily we could resolve our differences when we did not have the Kremlin puppet-masters behind the backs of one of the parties, manipulating our words and gestures. I will never forget this first successful attempt at internal Chechen dialogue.

The next morning I withdrew all our troops from the city, and as a bonus the local police sold us a large quantity of weapons and made us a present of ammunition, cartridges, and grenades for grenade launchers. We were particularly pleased to receive 7.62mm cartridges, which were always in short supply. The Russian Command provided the pro-Russian police with assault rifles of just this calibre, delivering lavish supplies of ammunition. The main thing, though, was that everyone could see Zavgaev's elections had been high farce, although Russian propaganda shamelessly announced that he had supposedly been supported 'by 90% of Chechen voters.' That lie, however, was so pathetic and obvious that even Kremlin officials were embarrassed to repeat it. Operations to disrupt the Zavgaev 'elections,' which served also to demonstrate the growing power of the CRI Army, were conducted not only by us in Urus-Martan, but in nearly every other region of the republic, with the exception of Nadterechnyi and Shelkovskoy. Naturally, Grozny, packed to overflowing with Russian troops, was also beyond our reach at that time.

V

Occupying Grozny

Salman Raduev's disastrous hostage-taking in Kizlyar backfires, but Russia's subsequent propaganda and military operation in Pervomaiskoye fails spectacularly. Temporary occupation by CRI forces of the Chechen capital of Grozny in a show of strength to discredit Russian claims of victory in the war. Zakaev commands Chechen forces in the battle for Goyskoye. Russia assassinates President Dudaev, temporarily replaced by Zelimkhan Yandarbiev.

Gudermes was the second largest city in the republic, and here CRI divisions fought serious battles with the Russian occupying troops. The fighters attacked Russian checkpoints and troop concentrations and were under the command of Salman Raduev, the CRI prefect of Gudermes region. Raduev was a fairly high-profile figure in the First Russo-Chechen War. I first saw him in March 1995, when Djohar was chairing a meeting in Kurchaloy. At that time, he was still a clean-shaven young man who had been a Komsomol (Young Communist League) official in the recently ended Soviet era. He struck me as very calm, quiet and modest.

Our second meeting was in January 1996, after our operation in Urus-Martan. He contacted me through Urus-Martan activists and we met in a house in the city. Salman wanted a meeting with Djohar. I was in constant contact with the president and agreed to pass on his request, but Djohar's first reaction was, 'There's no hurry.' Salman had to cool his heels for a few more days in Urus-Martan. He met Djohar in one of the foothill villages; I don't remember now whether it was Tangi-Chu or Roshni-Chu. He departed, and on 9 January all the news media were reporting that Chechen militants had seized a hospital in Kizlyar, just over the border in Dagestan. Not only I, but every Chechen fighter I have discussed this episode with, and indeed civilian residents of the republic, reacted very differently to this than they did to Shamil Basaev's raid on Budyonnovsk. The Budyonnovsk Raid was seen by Chechens, and all over the world, as retaliation for the monstrous terror unleashed on our republic's civilian population by the Russian invaders. The sympathies of many people in Russia were openly or tacitly on the side of the Chechen fighters. Even the hostages in the Budyonnovsk hospital were not uniformly hostile to the Chechens, and several women named their newly born baby boys Shamil. A young woman journalist, one of the volunteer hostages who bussed in to Chechnya, married one of the lads in Shamil's detachment.

The seizing of the hospital in Kizlyar, however, was a farce pretending to be a tragedy, although it had more than its share of tragic consequences. Over time, it became clear that not even Budyonnovsk could bring about a stable, long-lasting peace. If Budyonnovsk was not a strategic success, the occupation of the hospital in Kizlyar brought us nothing but discredit. Firstly, the Russian Command, determined to prevent a repetition of Budyonnovsk, did not even consider cessation of the war. On the contrary, they intensified it; secondly, it provided the Kremlin with evidence to support its propaganda campaign in Russia and throughout the world, which sought to represent us as 'terrorists;' thirdly, the attitude of the peoples of Dagestan, who had been expressing overt sympathy for the Chechens' struggle against Russian aggression and had been helping our refugees, cooled markedly after what was seen as an attack on Dagestan. The Kremlin did its utmost to aggravate this rift between our brotherly peoples. Fourthly, and in my opinion most damagingly, the hostage taking at Kizlyar Hospital led many Chechen fighters, especially the younger ones, to regard such methods of 'forcing Russia to make peace' as wholly justifiable, which subsequently led on more than one occasion to ideological and political defeats for us.

My main grounds for believing that actions like Budyonnovsk should not under any circumstances be repeated are moral. I believed, and still believe, that in the Russo-Chechen wars the Chechens, to use religious terminology, always represented good because they were defending their land and liberty. The Russian troops, no less certainly, embodied evil as they attempted to seize our lands and deprive us of our freedom.

Besides moral considerations, I am conscious of purely pragmatic grounds, based on what I have seen of Russian generals over many years of negotiations. I could see they would never allow a repetition of the 'disgrace of Budyonnovsk,' which many pro-Kremlin journalists in Russia likened to the 'disgrace of Port Arthur' during the Russo-Japanese War. In all negotiations there is, of course, a certain amount of disingenuousness arising from a desire to maximize gains for one's own side. Nevertheless, when we were discussing the agreement to disarm our units while simultaneously arming Community Self-Defence Groups, the question arose of which of our troops should be considered 'illegal.' The Russians, of course, wanted the matter decided within the framework of the Russian law 'On Defence,' under which all Chechen troops not subordinate to the security ministries of Russia would be classed as illegal. Under the Chechen law 'On Defence,' no armed group submitting to the authority of the CRI could be considered illegal. After signing these agreements, we and our Russian partners heatedly debated which of the two laws 'On Defence' the agreement should be based on. Our delegation unofficially included Shirvani Basaev, Shamil's younger brother, who attended talks fairly regularly, no doubt in order to keep Shamil informed. Finally, driven to distraction by our endless disputation, General Kulikov jumped up from his place at the table and, turning to Shirvani, yelled, 'Just you try a repeat of Budyonnovsk on me! Tell your brother, just let him try barging his way into any corner of Russia again! Just let him try! Tell him that!'

I mention the incident in order to emphasize the Russian leaders' determination never to be forced again into 'negotiations under duress.' This was borne out by events during the Second Russo-Chechen War. Accordingly, seizing the hospital in Kizlyar in January 1996 was never going to do us any good, either in military, political, or propaganda terms. Russian television, making no attempt to hide its glee, kept up a running commentary from Kizlyar, stressing that 'the Chechen insurgents have again taken hospital staff and patients hostage.' Reaction in Chechnya and internationally was negative in the extreme.

Raduev was initially demanding that, in exchange for the lives of his hostages, Russia should withdraw its troops from the entire North Caucasus. Then he more modestly demanded withdrawal of troops only from Chechnya. In the end, he reduced his demand to just allowing his men to return to Chechnya. He said something along the lines of, 'What has happened has happened. We are prepared to release the hostages in return for safe conduct to Chechnya.'

The operation was initially planned as a military mission to take out the Russian helicopter base in Kizlyar. As the war went on, the Russian air force 'elite' troops degenerated into savages. Operating with impunity because of the lack of Chechen air cover or significant anti-aircraft defences, Russian planes and helicopters felt completely at ease in our skies and embarked on a campaign of bloodthirsty terror against the civilian population, even hunting down lone travellers on the roads, to say nothing of attacking towns and villages. There were numerous instances of Russian pilots firing missiles and dropping bombs on funeral processions. The helicopter regiment in Kizlyar was thus not only a legitimate military target, but a strike against it would serve as retribution and an object lesson for Russia's sadistic aviators. Aslanbek Ismailov, who planned the Budyonnovsk operation, told me that there had been no prior intention to seize the hospital, and that it came about only because wounded Chechen fighters had been taken there in city ambulances.

Encountering resistance from the forces defending the helicopter base, Raduev called for reinforcements, and Chechen fighters, led by Khunkar-Pasha Israpilov and Turpal-Ali Atgireyev, fought their way through to Kizlyar. These fighters too found themselves surrounded by Russian troops and, in order not to dissipate their forces, joined Raduev's unit which had occupied the hospital. By this time, the total number of Chechen fighters had risen to 200. Khunkar-Pasha and Turpal-Ali had completed their combat mission, and seizing the hospital was entirely the brainwave of Raduev.

I was present when he telephoned Djohar from Kizlyar. Like the rest of us, Djohar was dismayed by the news. He silenced Raduev with the words, 'Prepare to die with dignity.' While events in Kizlyar were at their height, we were depressed to see the reputation of Chechen Resistance forces sullied in this manner. The situation was saved, however, by the Russian troops. Contrary to their intentions, but acting wholly in the spirit of Kulikov's hysterical ranting, they radically changed the attitude of people not only in Chechnya but in the world at large. Having supposedly agreed to allow the Chechen fighters to return to Chechnya with a group of hostages, they decided simply to kill everyone, Chechens and hostages, before they reached Chechnya. Near the border between Dagestan and Chechnya, Russian helicopters caught up with the buses moving along the road and fired missiles at them. The Chechens and hostages were unscathed, but one of the missiles hit a police car escorting the column. Our fighters, knowing only too well what would be coming next, turned the buses off the road and drove into Pervomaiskoye, the nearest Dagestani village. On the way, they disarmed and took prisoner 38 Russian riot police at the checkpoint into the village. Giving the villagers an opportunity to leave, the Chechens immediately began preparing defences, digging trenches and passageways. They had sufficient ammunition to last several days of intense fighting.

The village was soon surrounded by many thousands of Russian soldiers, equipped with armoured vehicles, aircraft and artillery, including *Grad* (Hail) and *Uragan* (Hurricane) multiple rocket launchers. The operation was under the command of the newly appointed chief of the Federal Security Bureau, General Barsukov, but Yeltsin stage-managed a very public, televised dressing down of the main Russian marshals and generals for this 'repetition of Budyonnovsk,' and sent the whole lot of them off from Moscow to the scene. As one of the Russian feature writers observed, 'Such an assembly of marshals and generals was last seen only in May 1945 in Berlin.' General Barsukov swore a solemn oath to Yeltsin that he would under no circumstances allow the Chechen fighters to escape from Pervomaiskoye, and immediately upon arrival in Dagestan on 15 January sent in a large force of special operations troops to attack the village. They managed to force their way into the outskirts, but there encountered devastatingly accurate Chechen machine-gun fire, and were also subjected to missile attack from their own helicopters sent to support them. With some 100 fatalities, they hastily retreated. Alexander Litvinenko had been despatched with his entire FSB Special Department to Pervomaiskoye and later told me that, before going in to attack, the troops were boasting they would need no more than half an hour to sort out the Chechens. In fact, after half an hour those of them still alive were fleeing back out of the village.

After the retreat of the special operations forces, the village was subjected to indiscriminate bombardment from Hail and Hurricane rocket launchers which, incidentally, are banned by international conventions as weapons of mass destruction. The Russian High Command dismissed questions from journalists concerned for the lives of the hostages with a claim from General Mikhailov, Chief of the FSB Press Centre, that there were no hostages in the village because 'they were shot yesterday on the orders of Raduev,' and the missile strikes were accordingly 'exclusively on the positions of the terrorists.' This was, of course, a blatant lie.

I later learned many details about the fighting in Pervomaiskoye from Khunkar-Pasha Israpilov and Alexander Litvinenko. Khunkar-Pasha told me what happened on the Chechen side, and Sasha filled in the picture on the Russian side. Defence of the village was under the command of Khunkar-Pasha and Turpal-Ali Atgireyev. Sasha Litvinenko related how, after the failure of one attack, General Barsukov began shrieking hysterically, 'What am I going to tell Yeltsin?' Another of the Russian generals, summoned to report to Minister of the Interior General Kulikov, raised his hand to salute and fell in the mud at the minister's feet, dead drunk. Fierce fighting continued for three days, in the course of which the world's attitude towards the Chechen fighters changed radically. People could not but admire the heroism and stoicism of 200 Chechen fighters successfully resisting attack by thousands of Russian troops.

On the night of 17 January 1996, our fighters launched a surprise attack, broke through a triple encirclement, and fought their way back to Chechnya, without in the process losing a single hostage or prisoner.

Sasha Litvinenko told me that, when Russian soldiers located some distance away from the point of breakthrough heard the Chechens had broken out of the encirclement and left Pervomaiskoye, they were openly jubilant, because they saw each order to storm the village as little better than a death sentence. The Russian marshals and generals once more disgraced themselves in full view of the world and, as an excuse, began telling journalists fairy tales about imaginary 'underground concrete bunkers,' although it was far from clear when the Chechens could have built these. The Russian lies about the supposed shooting of the hostages were shown up when all the hostages returned home safe and sound, and very willingly told reporters how the Chechen fighters had risked their own lives to keep them safe during the breakout.

In February 1996, Djohar ordered me to prepare a meeting of all the commanders of fronts, directions and sectors. We selected the village of Alkhazurovo. Djohar first received Aslan Maskhadov, and they conferred for over an hour. He then invited the rest of us over, and we went to where he was staying.

After the exchange of greetings, Djohar hung a map on the wall and began the meeting. The commanders began complaining about various difficulties. The first was the commander of the Achkhoy-Martan direction, who complained he was short of this and that. Djohar let him finish, then handed him a handkerchief and memorably said, 'Take this handkerchief! Wipe away your tears and snot. I have nothing else to give you.'

He turned to address us all: 'What are you expecting from me? Our country is under occupation. The enemy has taken everything from us, so now we have to take everything we need from the enemy. If you are expecting me to provide you with food supplies or ammunition, do not waste your time. If you have joined up to fight for my sake, I release you from that obligation and you can go home. But if you have gone to war in the name of the Almighty and the freedom of your people, then wherever you look you will see the enemy you have to fight!' Without another word, Djohar rolled up his map and left the house. I went out after him, hoping to persuade him to come back, but the president gave me the names of a number of commanders with whom I was to come and see him. He indicated a time and place and left. Aslan Maskhadov had already gone, having discussed all his concerns with Djohar.

Those who attended this new meeting were Shamil Basaev, Aslanbek Ismailov, Ruslan Gelaev, Abu Movsaev, Dalkhan Khozhaev and myself. We went in to find Djohar talking on the phone. He half-rose to acknowledge us and motioned us to sit down. Ten minutes passed, 20, 30, 40 ... Djohar was still talking on the phone. We waited patiently. Shamil chuckled, leaned over to us and said, 'You know what this is about? Djohar is showing us who is head of the house.'

Djohar finally put the phone down and, as if nothing had happened, we started to discuss our future military plans. This was when we began working on the March operation to recapture Grozny. We agreed a date for the beginning of the operation: the night of 5 March. By this time it was already obvious that the Kremlin was not going to back down from its decision to crush our independence by force. The Russian leaders had imposed their protege Zavgaev on our people and were energetically marketing him as 'the only realistic leader of Chechnya.' Additionally, Russian officials were continuing their political soap opera, scheduling 'parliamentary elections' for the summer. The war was becoming ever more brutal and extensive, as if there was no question of negotiation or a peaceful settlement. Given this situation, we needed to do something spectacular in order to knock the stuffing out of the Russian Command's propaganda campaigns, which were gaining momentum, and its triumphalist hubris, which was growing by the day. In terms of political impact, Grozny seemed the best place for a large-scale military operation. Even with the news blackout which the occupation forces had created around Chechnya, they would be unable to conceal a major operation in Grozny from the Russian and world public, and it would be made clear to everyone that the war was continuing, the Chechen Resistance had not been broken, and that the Russian generals' victory fanfares were entirely spurious.

Djohar again summoned Aslan Maskhadov to discuss the operation. We radically increased our intelligence gathering. Data about the location, size and armaments of Russian military units, the location of checkpoints, routes for advancing, and the best places to mount ambushes were entered on maps. We discussed issues of coordination and numerous other matters, including supplies. Each commander of a front or direction was allocated an area of Grozny for which he was personally responsible and over which he needed to establish control. My own area included Departments 12 and 20 of the city, the towns of Aldy and Chernorechiye as far as Zavodskoy region, including the Zavodskoy district police station, and territory as far as Minutka Square and the checkpoint in Voikova. Overall command of the operation was entrusted to Ruslan Gelaev and the operational headquarters was to be run by Aslanbek Ismailov.

In Grozny I had people I could trust, not least in the pro-Russian police force and civilians working in various institutions of the puppet regime, and they supplied me with reliable intelligence. We also had sabotage groups active in Grozny. As a result, I had a detailed picture of the kind of occupation forces my troops would face and how best to act to minimize losses and maximize results. The overarching objective was to blockade Grozny for three or, depending on the situation, four days; to show our strength, how organized we were, and our determination. The Russian Command would, as usual, need at least three days to formulate an adequate response.

At the agreed time, I entered Grozny with my units through the Chernorechiye forest from the direction of Alkhan-Yurt. We passed the sewage treatment plants in the forest, suppressed enemy resistance, and occupied the area allocated. From Alkhan-Yurt to Chernorechiye I left a 'living chain' of men for bringing in reinforcements if necessary, evacuating the wounded, and passing back captured equipment. I left one detachment in reserve in Goyskoye and another at the road junction by the traffic police post. We were the first to enter the city, and the rest of the forces, following along our corridor, moved deeper into the city, fighting and occupying the areas for which they were responsible. I stopped at Okruzhnaya, beside the new bus station, roughly in the middle of my area of responsibility.

The operation was effective and successful in every respect. The enemy was completely demoralized by our unexpected appearance and the initiative was wholly with us. Russian troops retreated to the city centre, often abandoning equipment and heavy weapons, and our forces suppressed pockets of resistance and followed close on their heels. Some of our troops, forcing their way into enemy-held territory, fought them in the city centre. On the night of 7 March 1996, Djohar arrived in Grozny by way of our corridor. Just as he arrived, I received orders from Gelaev to withdraw from Grozny on 8 March. Our main forces had already been withdrawn. I reported the order to Djohar, and said that Aslanbek Ismailov and I were in agreement that we should not give the enemy the opportunity of celebrating International Women's Day on 8 March; in other words, that we should stay in Grozny for at least one more day and leave the city during the night of the 9 March. Djohar clearly knew nothing about Gelaev's order and did not like it. However, he said that during a war orders should be obeyed and did not countermand it. Djohar spent this last night in Grozny with us. We toured the part of the city controlled by our forces, stopping to talk briefly to the fighters. Djohar had not been in Grozny for over a year, since the end of January 1995, and he was interested in everything there was to see, although, with all the destruction in the city, it was hardly a pleasant excursion.

I was not too worried about the president's security, because Russian troops had retreated from our area of responsibility, and those who remained were holed up behind fortifications and just wanted to be left alone. As for the pro-Russian police, they fled at the first sight of us, except for a squad of riot police in Chernorechiye who instantly came over to our side and helped us. When we were leaving Grozny, I told them it was up to them to decide whether to come with us or stay in the city. There were ten of them: three came with us, while the rest chose to stay, wholly unconcerned that one of them might be an informer and turn them over to the mercies of the Russian intelligence agencies. Later I learned they had had no problems. They carried on working in the riot police until August, before finally joining us.

It struck me long ago, and I still believe today, that our withdrawal from Grozny in March 1996 was a big mistake. When we were finally victorious in August that year, we really only repeated what had already been accomplished in March, when we also had a greater advantage in terms of manpower. In March 1996, we probably had an opportunity to end the war victoriously, and much of our recent history might have turned out very differently. If only ... But, as they say, there is no place in history for the conditional tense, and everything happens at the time ordained.

The March Operation had some very important results. As anticipated, it had a huge international impact and greatly strengthened anti-war sentiment in Russia. The voices of well known political and public figures in Russia became more insistent that the regime should stop playing with puppets and start negotiating with the real authorities in Chechnya, President Dudaev and his government. The stridency of pronouncements by Russian generals and security ministers tailed off markedly.

Quite apart from the political and propaganda success, we captured valuable assets in Grozny: vehicles, especially the UAZ jeeps and trucks we desperately needed, large stocks of uniforms and military equipment, weapons and ammunition. In other words, we did exactly what Djohar had told us to: we took everything we needed from the enemy.

We did not only capture supplies, but also bought what we needed from the enemy, especially ammunition, of which we were in constant need. This trade was not without complications, as the Russian military, while cheerfully selling us arms and ammunition, thought it prudent to put conditions on how they were to be used. If we bought munitions from officers of the interior troops, they insisted they should not be used for shooting at them. Ministry of Defence officials insisted we should not use the ammunition they sold us against them. We had to give our word of honour to both of them, and in order to keep our promise, had to use ammunition purchased from the interior troops only against troops of the Ministry of Defence, and vice versa. The situation was comical, but demonstrated very clearly just how unprincipled and demoralized our enemies were. Russian soldiers and officers at that time, and still today, had just two goals in Chechnya: to survive and, if possible, make some money. To summarize, all our military supplies came from Russia: the money, the weapons, and the ammunition. Money we obtained from the puppet institutions; arms and ammunition we captured in battle or bought from the enemy with the money from the puppet regime. There was no 'stream of Arab dollars' into Chechnya. If we had been relying on outside help, we would not have lasted two months.

At the conclusion of the March Operation, we held a meeting to consider its results: the losses on both sides, the assets captured. We analysed how coordinated our forces and those of the enemy had been, our successes and failures. I was only too aware that the Russian High Command were unlikely to leave our raid on Grozny unpunished, and had every reason to believe their main strike would come in my direction, more precisely, at the village of Goyskoye. Immediately after our withdrawal from Grozny, the enemy began moving troops towards Goyskoye, making little effort to disguise the fact that they had selected it for assault.

Goyskoye extended 2 kilometres from east to west and 500 metres from north to south. It consisted of only 150-200 houses which, by Chechen standards, counts as a fairly small settlement. For all that, Goyskoye was strategically important both for us and the enemy, because it occupied a key position in an unbroken front line stretching as far as the republic's western border with Ingushetia. The front line ran through the three western regions of Chechnya: Sunzha, Achkhoy-Martan and Urus-Martan. All supplies for our troops defending the highland and foothill parts of these regions passed from us along what we called the Military Highway (and the Russians called 'the Wolf Trail'). If you look at the map of Chechnya, the front line ran through the villages of Arshty, Bamut, Staryi Achkhoy, Yandi, Shalazhi, Gekhi-Chu, Roshni-Chu, Tangi-Chu, Martan-Chu, Goyskoye, Saadi-Kotar (Komsomolskoye), Alkhazurovo, and on to Chishki. By capturing Goyskoye, the enemy would be able to cut our communications, and even move round to the rear of our troops, threatening them with encirclement. That would have obliged us to give up defending a front line and re-group for guerrilla warfare.

Russian troops had previously attempted to break through but had always been unsuccessful. Exceptionally fierce battles were fought on the approaches to Bamut, Staryi Achkhoy, and Yandi, but all the villages occupied by troops of our Southwestern Front backed on to the forest-covered Black Mountains, which gave our soldiers a substantial advantage in defending them. Only Goyskoye lay on a plain surrounded by fields, and the lack of natural cover made it, from the enemy's perspective, the most vulnerable sector of the front line. Furthermore, Goyskoye, unlike most other front-line villages where fighting had continued for a long time, had not yet been abandoned by its inhabitants. The Russian troops would be able to use this against us, to blackmail the people of Goyskoye, threatening to raze their village to the ground. Their blackmail often worked. The residents of a besieged village would ask our soldiers to leave and, as we were fighting this war against Russian invaders for the lives and freedom of our people, including these villagers, we had to respect such requests. The Russian Command was adept at exploiting this vulnerability. Quite apart from military considerations, the enemy had propaganda reasons for wanting to strike at Goyskoye. They never wearied of claiming that all the towns and villages in Urus-Martan region were loyal to Moscow and its placemen, but any Russian journalist could refute the claim by publishing a photo or video of the Chechen fighters stationed in Goyskoye and our checkpoint at the entrance to the village.

Accordingly, immediately after our withdrawal from Grozny, the Russians began massing troops and heavy equipment in the hamlet of Chekhkar. Troops and equipment were moved mainly from the eastern regions of the republic, as we knew from intelligence reports and information coming from Chechen groups on the far side of the River Argun. Chekhkar was immediately before Goyskoye, separated only by a strip of farmland.

The enemy began issuing ultimatums. Our troops were to lay down their arms within 24 hours, then 48 hours, The occupying troops threatened that if their ultimatums were not met, they would raze Goyskoye and its neighbouring villages to the ground. Delegations of old men turned up in the villages we controlled, urging the local residents to obey the demands of the Russian military.

We must give credit to the inhabitants of Goyskoye: despite the terrible psychological pressure they were under, they behaved very honourably. There was no panic in the village, though tales of the bloody terror visited by the Russian sadists on the peaceful villagers of Samashki were fresh in everyone's memory. The people of Goyskoye understood that their village was going to bear the brunt of the Russian attack, and that the attack had to be resisted. They lost no time in evacuating their families to safety and removing their property. The number of people in the village decreased dramatically, and those remaining were nearly all men. On 12 March it was decided we should hold a meeting of the remaining villagers to secure their agreement to our fighting a battle there.

I was one of the speakers at that meeting close to the mosque. I explained the situation in the republic and the strategic importance of Goyskoye in resisting Russia's aggression. I passed on to my listeners a request from President Dudaev that they should understand why we were having to expose their homes to the risk of destruction during the fighting. The residents, with few exceptions, agreed that at this crucial moment Goyskoye would not disgrace itself by capitulating and resolved to 'leave the village to our warriors.' This was an expression commonly used in Chechnya in such instances. After meetings of residents, many other Chechen villages in our southwestern territory, such as Bamut, Yandi, and Staryi Achkhoy, were similarly 'left to our warriors.'

From then on we began seriously readying Goyskoye to withstand attack. We dug general-purpose trenches, concealed passages, and bunkers. We moved in people, brought in arms and ammunition, and established a duty roster. There was no need to persuade our soldiers to dig trenches and shelters, because everyone knew that a slipshod attitude towards this, admittedly very heavy, labour was likely to lead to major losses, as we had discovered to our cost on more than one occasion in the early days of the war. With our limited manpower, the loss of even ten fighters was unacceptably high.

We deployed a total of some 300 fighters to defend Goyskoye but, given the necessity of alternating our men in the village, even at the battle's most critical moments there were no more than 180 in action. Overall responsibility for the defence of Goyskoye was entrusted to me. I delegated command of the right flank to my deputy, Khusein Isabaev, and myself took control of the left. This concentration of our units on the flanks was because, as we could see from their positioning, the Russian troops were preparing to strike their main blow not from north to south, at the centre of the village, but from the northeast and northwest, evidently hoping to take Goyskoye in a pincer movement.

Periodic bombardment of the village by artillery and from the air began. The enemy performed some manoeuvres in front of us, armour occasionally approaching our positions. Our troops destroyed it or drove it off by firing grenades and Bassoon wire-guided anti-tank missiles. It was obvious that the enemy's aim was to soften us up with aerial and artillery bombardment before a major assault, while probing for our weaknesses. The shelling and air attacks were timed precisely for the beginning of namaz, or morning prayer, in the hope that at that moment we would leave shelter and fall a prey to their bombs, missiles and shells. The soldiers even joked how considerate it was of the Russians to summon us to prayer with their *adhan*. It did, though, oblige us to get up an hour or an hour and a half earlier than usual to perform our ablutions before the morning bombardments, in order to be ready for namaz.

The enemy shelling of Goyskoye began on 18 March 1996, and on 20 March, after a barrage of artillery bombardment, Russian armour moved on the village, supported by infantry and helicopters. One helicopter was shot down by heavy machine gun fire, but managed to land in a cloud of smoke behind the Russian positions. An anti-tank missile hit and burned out a tank, after which the enemy rolled back. Skirmishes of this kind continued almost daily, but the occupying troops showed no inclination as yet to mount a decisive assault. There was even something of a lull in late March and early April. The intensity of the shelling and air strikes fell away abruptly. We assumed the enemy was preparing something major, and were not mistaken.

Early on the morning of 4 April, Goyskoye was subjected to attack of an intensity I had not witnessed since the infamous New Year Assault on Grozny. It was unimaginable. The village was subjected to bombardment by artillery, including multiple rocket launchers and powerful self-propelled guns. There was continuous mortar fire. Squadrons of planes dropped bombs, including thermobaric 'vacuum bombs.' When the planes had dropped all their bombs and were flying back to base, helicopters flew in and, hovering over the outskirts of the village, began shelling until they had emptied missile bays designed to hold 52 S–8 rockets. The planes returned and resumed bombing. The artillery bombardment continued unabated. For the first time in the war, the enemy used heavy ground-to-ground missiles against us. This hell lasted until 11.00 am, when the occupying forces, under cover of armour, began their ground assault.

I have to say that our soldiers showed supreme courage and heroism in this battle. It was noteworthy that, for the first time, we saw Russian soldiers standing up full height as they advanced, stepping over the bodies of the dead. Unquestionably, they had been pumped full of drugs before the assault to anaesthetize their sense of fear. Despite this, on many stretches of the front our soldiers themselves furiously engaged the enemy in man to man combat. It became evident that the enemy attack was petering out and that the day was ours, but just at this moment I learned that, on the right flank commanded by

Khusein, the enemy had succeeded in breaking through into the village. It transpired that during the night one of the units, on the orders of Ruslan Gelaev and without notifying me or Khusein, had abandoned its post and withdrawn from Goyskoye. It was at this gap in our defences that Russian troops made their breakthrough.

When we heard about it, I and Isa Munaev's group rushed there and came upon Nurdi Bazhaev's detachment. Nurdi told us they had already managed on their own to expel the enemy from the village and were now combing the southeastern outskirts for soldiers in hiding. By evening, the enemy began moving away from our positions in every sector, firing green flares to avoid being fired on by their own side. I inspected our positions. In some places the enemy had forced us back to our third line of defence. On the left flank, where my headquarters were, the enemy had come right up to our trenches. One of their armoured personnel carriers was taken out directly on the roof of our headquarters dugout. It became a landmark, indicating the furthest point to which the enemy had succeeded in advancing. We tallied our losses for the day: 17 dead and 39 wounded.

I would like to mention the heroic death of Visita of Martan-Chu. Seeing the enemy advancing, he ran towards them and took out an armoured personnel carrier with a grenade launcher. Then he climbed on to another APC and threw a hand grenade into the hatch, thus effectively halting single-handed the advance of the enemy deep into the village. He stood up straight and started spraying the Russian mercenaries with assault rifle fire and putting them to flight. Unhappily, Visita himself was mortally wounded in the battle, and late in the afternoon died in the arms of fighters from his own village.

In one of the trenches we came upon a desperately sad sight: seven young fighters had fought to the last bullet, but hand grenades were thrown at them by Russian mercenaries who had reached their trench. Six were killed and one was lying with his throat cut by shrapnel. Fortunately, this young man survived. I later saw him several times and, if I am not mistaken, he is still alive.

That day we also lost Said Zhansaev. He was one of the lads I had rescued in the summer of 1995 after they were surrounded by the Russians in Dagestan. The boys were from Azerbaijan and were coming through the mountains with a consignment of Arrow anti-aircraft missiles. They were spotted by the enemy, but at this precise moment we had an armistice with the Russians in connection with the Budyonnovsk negotiations. When we heard of their plight, on Djohar's orders and accompanied by the OSCE, Khamad Kurbanov and I immediately went to Dagestan and rescued them. They were sixteen or seventeen years old and, surrendering to the enemy one dud missile without a battery as evidence they had been disarmed, we took them back with us to Chechnya. Djohar received them warmly and they asked to join my division. Now two had been killed here in Goyskoye. The loss of these and our other lads grieved me deeply.

That day, as we were able later to ascertain from prisoners, the enemy lost more than 350 men. Our prisoners told us two motorized rifle companies, totalling 240 soldiers, were annihilated almost to the last man and officer. A 'Yermolov' battalion of Cossack volunteers took part in the battle and suffered casualties of over 20 dead and about 150 wounded. The surviving 130 Cossacks deserted. The enemy also suffered heavy losses in terms of hardware: 3 tanks destroyed, 12 APCs and infantry fighting vehicles, two helicopters and one Su–25 aircraft. The plane was shot down by heavy machine gun fire by fighters covering the bridge to the east of the village. Its destruction was witnessed by many residents of Urus-Martan and Goyty who were following the battle from a distance. I was told later that not only the townspeople, but even the pro-Russian officials of Urus-Martan, shouted 'Allahu Akbar' in unison when they saw the enemy plane crash to the ground. Episodes like that show better than any propaganda how united the Chechens are in their hatred of an empire which for centuries has been visiting death and enslavement on them. Assuredly, it is not the lot of every Chechen to be a soldier fighting that empire. There are, alas no few among us who from faint-heartedness or because of some other circumstance go into the service of the invaders, but I have not the slightest doubt that even those Chechens who see fit to call themselves 'Russians' harbour a hatred of that state in their hearts. That is the surest guarantee that sooner or later our Fatherland will be free of the Russian Empire, Insha'Allah!

After we had repulsed the assault, the enemy resorted to its earlier tactic of shelling the village and mounting raids, each time retreating with losses. We held Goyskoye, and prevented an enemy breakthrough of the front. So the days passed until, on 21 April, Dalkhan Khozhaev, my chief of staff, suddenly appeared in Goyskoye together with Ali Arsemikov, our Ichkerian prefect of Urus-Martan. They brought me the terrible news that my younger brother had died. I needed to go to the funeral, and left Dalkhan to deputize while I was away. After giving necessary orders and quickly briefing Dalkhan, I went with a heavy heart back with Ali to Urus-Martan. My brother had suffered from epilepsy since he was little. Of all the members of our family, he was particularly attached to me. He feared for me and was eager to join and protect me, but his illness denied him that. On the day he died, he suffered 12 seizures, his heart failed, and he was gone. Our relatives decided to wait to bury him until the following morning so that I too should be able to bid him farewell. Ali and I arrived in Urus-Martan and found the gate to the courtyard wide open, our custom on days of celebration or mourning. People came to commiserate, and I could hear the wailing of the women. I took my place in the courtyard to accept condolences. When darkness fell and the stream of visitors had ended, I went into the house and sat by my brother's body. Shortly before, I had heard two rockets explode, to judge from the sounds, somewhere to the southwest of Urus-Martan.

As I was sitting beside my brother, the walkie-talkie I always carried with me suddenly buzzed. Someone was trying to contact me through all the noise and interference. I made out the call sign and realized it was someone in the entourage of the president. That evening I had an appointment to meet Djohar and supposed that one of his people was trying to find out where I was and why I had not come to see him. I did not attach too much importance to it. It was only the next morning, as we were getting ready to go to the cemetery, that someone came and told me Djohar had been wounded, and our military prosecutor, Magomed Dzhaniev, who was next to him, had been killed. My informant had no further details. After the funeral, I performed the collective midday namaz with everybody and then went straight from the cemetery to Roshni-Chu. I waited there for someone from the leadership to contact me. Zelimkhan Yandarbiev's nephew came to tell me his uncle was waiting for me in nearby Gekhi-Chu. It was Zelimkhan who told me Djohar was dead.

I could not believe it. It was just too incredible. My head told me one thing, but my heart would not accept the dreadful news. I tried to convince myself there had been some mistake. At the same time, suppressing that hope, I had a growing sense that we had been orphaned in the midst of war, that with the death of Djohar we had lost an immensely important source of strength. With these conflicting emotions of hope and despair, I went with Zelimkhan to the house where Djohar lay. I was conducted to a room in which Alla, his wife, was sitting with a black scarf on her head. Djohar was lying on a carpet spread on the floor. His eyes were wide open and I tried to close them but could not, because the eyelids had been burned away. There were burns on his face. His right arm was damaged above the elbow, but the wound which had caused death was in his back, which had been hit by shrapnel. I spoke to Alla and realized that death must have been instantaneous. He would have been dead even before he fell to the ground. At the time of the missile strike, he was leaning on a vehicle talking by satellite phone to the liberal Russian politician, Konstantin Borovoy.

Djohar's relationship with Borovoy was one of trust, even friendship. I remember once Konstantin Borovoy turned up with Russian soldiers' mothers in Goyskoye where the CRI Military Prosecutor's Office held Russian prisoners of war and, on Djohar's orders, several groups of prisoners and deserters were handed over to him. I knew Djohar kept in contact with a number of Russian politicians, and that his contacts had intensified in late March 1996 after Boris Yeltsin as president of Russia issued a statement that he was prepared to negotiate with him. A mediator was even named: Mentimir Shaimiev, the president of Tatarstan. Shortly afterwards, the Tatar president's aide arrived in Grozny seeking ways to contact Djohar. Yeltsin's peace initiative was very obviously prompted by the forthcoming presidential election in Russia. Recognizing how unpopular the war with Chechnya was, Yeltsin decided to turn public opinion in his favour by presenting himself to the voters as a peacemaker. Neither Djohar nor the rest of us had any great expectation that these peace talks would yield more worthwhile results than the last, but it would have been imprudent for political reasons, and military reasons too, to turn them down. Negotiations would give us some respite from the ceaseless fighting, drastically reduce the influence of the pro-Russian opposition in Chechnya, and bring an influx of volunteers into our units as they always had in the past. When I saw Djohar after Yeltsin's announcements, he told me I would most likely again have to be a member of the Chechen delegation to discuss the location of the talks, the issues to be discussed, and the ground rules. We anticipated there would be three options: Moscow, a foreign country, or Kazan, the capital of Tatarstan.

Apart from Konstantin Borovoy and Mentimir Shaimiev, the Russian prime minister, Viktor Chernomyrdin, maintained contact with Djohar through Ruslan Aushev, the president of Ingushetia. Chernomyrdin sometimes also got in touch through Arkadiy Volsky, chairman of the Union of Russian Industrialists. When we had been negotiating back in 1995, Volsky several times asked Usman Imaev and me to arrange a personal meeting with Djohar to discuss what he described as 'a matter of the utmost importance.' Djohar was very selective about whom he met in his official capacity, and therefore instructed us to find out first what it was that Volsky wanted to discuss. He, however, stubbornly refused to reveal any more, saying only that he had a very important proposal for Djohar from Viktor Chernomyrdin.

Djohar finally agreed to meet Volsky and we were sent to collect him. On the way, he suddenly asked how we thought Djohar would react if he were offered a limitless sum of money and guarantees of safe passage to a country of his choice. We warned him not to make any such proposal, because Djohar would indubitably find it very insulting. Volsky nevertheless decided to go ahead with his mission. Upon hearing the proposal, Djohar frowned but did not vent his anger on the messenger. I well remember his reply to Volsky, who was visibly nervous.

'You are only the intermediary, passing on to me what you have been asked to convey, so I have no grudge against you personally. Please, therefore, try no less punctiliously to convey my answer to Mr Chernomyrdin, and have it brought to the attention of Mr Yeltsin, who is undoubtedly aware of this suggestion. Tell them they have absolutely no understanding of the people against whom they are waging war or of their leaders, or of the nature of what is happening here. Let us suppose for a moment that I were to accept your dishonourable offer. What would it change? Would the Chechens stop fighting? Would they lay down their arms if I were out of the way? Have you learned nothing from the experience of past centuries? There was an instance in history when Imam Shamil went into captivity, adopted Russian citizenship, swore allegiance to the tsar and accepted money from him. Did that stop the Chechens fighting for their freedom? Shamil departed, he was replaced by other leaders, and the struggle continued. Understand one thing: Yeltsin and I did not start this war, we inherited it and there is nothing we can do about that. But he and I can stop it: that is within our power. For that, you need to offer us not money and a cosy life in a foreign land, but long-term peace, freedom and equality.'

Arkadiy Volsky listened attentively to Djohar and said he fully understood what had been said. He promised he would report his words to the Russian prime minister. With that he returned to Grozny. After that meeting Volsky spoke more than once to Djohar on the phone. So Djohar had quite extensive contacts, and the Russian intelligence agencies were, naturally, apprised of that fact as they worked on their plans to assassinate the Chechen president.

Did Djohar know of the latest technical capabilities of the Russian intelligence agencies and the military? Did he knew he was putting his life at risk by talking on a satellite phone? I have read that the system for guiding a missile down on to a telephone signal was a recent development which Djohar might not have known about, but I do not believe that was the case. Djohar was a general in strategic aviation, a man familiar with many of the latest engineering and electronic innovations. He not infrequently demonstrated his knowledgeability of these matters in conversation with us. One conversation in particular comes to mind, when Russian troops had fired rockets at Shalazhi. Fortunately, on this occasion none of the residents were killed, the damage being only to buildings. Djohar was pacing up and down the room, and said, 'I swear, if I did not fear the wrath of the Almighty, I would do something to myself to stop this evil. I know the Russians will never make peace while I am alive. If Allah were to end my life, the lives of many thousands of Chechens would be saved.'

I am not claiming anything is certain, because only the Almighty knows the whole truth of what happened, but I cannot help thinking that Djohar deliberately took unwarranted risks in order to open the way to peace in our land. Having just come from the funeral of my beloved brother, I now sat beside the lifeless body of another man I had revered and loved. I will not speak of the grief weighing heavily on my heart at that moment; sometimes words are powerless to convey our feelings. After some time, Kazbek Makhashev, our minister of the interior, and a representative of the attorney general entered the room. Because of the high status of the deceased, formal investigative procedures were essential. Photographs had to be taken and testimony collected from witnesses. I went out.

The next day, 23 April, our comrades-in-arms began to arrive from the different regions of the republic. Shamil Basaev came, Khozh-Akhmed Yarikhanov, Akhiad Idigov, Dokka Makhaev, Ruslan Gelaev ... Some 20 commanders, members of the government and of parliament assembled. When we got over the initial shock, we began discussing the issue of a successor. In practice, there was little to discuss. In accordance with the law, the president could be succeeded only by the vice-president or the speaker of the parliament, that is, by Zelimkhan Yandarbiev or Akhiad Idigov. Everybody, including Akhiad, agreed that for the duration of the war, until a new presidential election could be held, the acting president should be Zelimkhan. The only objection came from Ruslan Gelaev, who said we should consider Aslan Maskhadov, who for some reason had been unable to come. It was explained to Ruslan that, as chief of the General Staff, Aslan, was ineligible.

From the first reports of Djohar's death, the Russian media began speculating about which of the 'warlords' had enough power to 'head the separatists.' All sorts of names were bandied about, with the clear intention of stirring up jealousies between our comrades-in-arms, but also to insinuate the idea that the Chechens would choose a new leader the way brigands choose a new chief, without any legal considerations, purely on the basis of his power.

Their speculation was wide of the mark: the president's successor was chosen in strict accordance with the letter and spirit of our Constitution.

The second issue we discussed was the funeral arrangements. Mindful of past experience, when the Russian occupiers had desecrated the bodies of our leaders and refused to reveal where they were buried, it was decided that Djohar should be interred in a secret place known only to a few of his immediate family and one member of the government. The head of Hadji-Murad, preserved in alcohol in the Kunstkammer in St Petersburg, or the grave of Sheikh Mansur, whose whereabouts the Russian authorities have still not revealed, were warning enough of the fate which might befall our president's remains if the occupiers should discover where he was buried.

The way the invaders subsequently treated the remains of another of our presidents, Aslan Maskhadov, and the bodies of many of our fallen commanders and ordinary soldiers, confirmed how justified our apprehensions were. Djohar was buried that evening, the location of his grave known only to his nephews, Lecha Dudaev and Musa, one representative of the government, and the Mullah who performed the necessary rites.

The news of Djohar's death spread instantly through the republic and then the world. Many Chechens simply refused to believe it. There were mule-headed individuals who insisted that Djohar had only been wounded and that the news was a rumour deliberately spread by his comrades to put the Russian intelligence agencies off the scent while he was sent abroad for medical treatment. Supposed 'eyewitnesses' popped up who claimed to have been in touch with Djohar after the official announcement of his death. Chechens were understandably reluctant to reconcile themselves to such a loss, and only too eager to believe rumours that he might still be alive.

Finally, on 24 or 25 April, I no longer remember exactly, on behalf of the government, Khozh-Akhmed Yarikhanov, who was living legally in Grozny as Djohar's representative in negotiations, went to the OSCE Mission's headquarters and officially confirmed the president's death at a press conference. I made a statement to the same effect on Ichkerian television. (Later, at my extradition trial in London, this broadcast figured as one of the main crimes I was accused of. The representatives of the Russian Prosecutor's Office tried to present it as a 'threat to commit terrorist attacks against Russia.') After that, in every locality throughout the country, including Grozny, Tezet mourning ceremonies and sacrificial rituals were held. In Urus-Martan it was initially intended to conduct the Tezet at my home, but because we were still in mourning for my younger brother it was decided not to conflate these sad events and the ceremony of condolence was held at the house of our prefect, Ali Arsemikov. The ceremony was attended by thousands of people, including police and officials from the pro-Russian administration. Even Zavgaev felt obliged to express his condolences on nationwide television.

Our opponents too acknowledged that, with the death of Djohar, the Chechen people had lost an outstanding politician and true leader. You might love Djohar or hate him, support or oppose his policies, but everybody recognized the immense authority he had among the people and the Chechen commanders and fighters. The death of our president was truly a national tragedy, but did not break the spirit of resistance, only further strengthening our resolve to continue along his path of independence and the building of a free Chechen state. The person who, in my opinion, succeeded best in conveying these sentiments was a Russian journalist, Natalia Televnaya, who wrote in her article, 'A Land and Its Destiny,' 'All that is said about the "Dudaev regime" falls down in the face of the incontrovertible fact that only the mighty national consciousness of a people, united by a single will and a common destiny, could have withstood the murderous brutality of an aggressor whose reserves of manpower exceed those of Ichkeria by a factor of over 150, and which does not hesitate to commit any crime in its efforts to crush the Chechen people. But while there remains on this Earth a single Chechen, he will know himself, always and everywhere, to be a citizen of Free Ichkeria. That is the great, historic victory of Djohar Dudaev, a victory which has made him the glorious future hero of an epic which will certainly be composed in the Caucasus.'

VI

Yeltsin's Phoney Victory

Russians begin 'Operation Iron Ring' with a massive assault on Goyskoye but Zakaev's troops have withdrawn to the foothills the preceding night. Acting President Yandarbiev ignores security warnings and is almost captured. Yandarbiev and Zakaev fly to Moscow for 'negotiations' with President Yeltsin, a ploy to boost Yeltsin's ratings before the forthcoming election. After signing an agreement on cessation of hostilities, with the Chechen leaders still effectively hostage in Moscow, Yeltsin flies to Grozny Airport to declare the conflict ended.

After Djohar's funeral, I returned to Goyskoye. The village was under enemy bombardment almost round the clock, with only a few hours of relative calm. It was clear that, behind this incessant harassment, the Russian military were preparing another assault on the village. After we officially confirmed that Djohar was dead and named his successor, the Russian 'hawks' seemed to get their second wind. The politicians stopped talking about an armistice, and the military started talking about the imminence of 'Operation Iron Ring.' Specifically, General Vyacheslav Tikhomirov, chief of the Joint Command of Russian Troops in Chechnya, stated publicly that before 9 May, that is, the anniversary of the Soviet victory over Germany, he would 'put an end to the Chechen separatists and outlaws.' During the First War, a number of terms were regularly used in Russian propaganda for designating us. These were: 'outlaws,' 'terrorists,' and 'separatists.' I noticed a pattern: when negotiations of some description were in the offing or in progress, we were referred to as 'separatists;' when negotiations broke down and hostilities were resumed, they called us 'outlaws' and 'terrorists.' As General Tikhomirov used all three terms in his statements, I realized Moscow had not yet finally decided whether to go all out for the forcible suppression of Chechen independence or, after all, to start a dialogue to find a political solution.

In early May, Zelimkhan Yandarbiev through Bakar, his security chief, summoned me to his headquarters. I waited until dark and, accompanied by Dalkhan Khozhaev, Said-Khusein Tazbaev and an escort of several fighters, left Goyskoye, intending to return before morning. On the outskirts of the village of Gekhi-Chu we were met at an agreed spot by Yandarbiev's bodyguards, transferred to another car, and drove to neighbouring Shalazhi, Zelimkhan having evidently moved there shortly before. He was living in the home of the head of the village administration.

Zelimkhan met us in the hallway and conducted us to his room. He knew I had a good, trusting relationship with Djohar and that his death had been a heavy blow for me. Accordingly, very tactfully, as if in general conversation, he said that Djohar's death was an irreparable loss for all of us, but that we must regard it as another trial the Almighty had seen fit to subject us to. We must rise to the challenge and continue on our path as righteously as Djohar. Zelimkhan then asked me about the situation in Goyskoye, the morale of the fighters, and my overall assessment of the situation. He moved quietly on to staffing matters. Zelimkhan was in possession of Djohar's full presidential archive. All the documentation relating to the last few months had been transferred to him as Djohar's successor. From Zelimkhan we learned that he had prepared decrees on new appointments and a reshuffle of the country's leadership. Said-Khasan Abumuslimov was to be appointed vice-president. Zelimkhan appointed me aide to the president on national security. Ruslan Gelaev was reinstated within the system of the CRI Armed Forces.

I need to explain why Gelaev needed to be reinstated as commander of the Southwestern Front. As already mentioned, the strategic importance of Goyskoye was as a village on a continuous front line which the Southwestern Front of the CRI's Armed Forces defended, from Ingushetia in the west to the border of Chechnya's Shatoy region in the east. In effect, this meant that two western regions of Chechnya, Urus-Martan and Achkhoy-Martan, and a substantial part of Shatoy region, were under the control of our armed forces. Retaining them had not only the obvious military value, but a no less important political significance because, in negotiations with Russia and statements addressed to the international community, we could point to the fact that the Chechen conflict was not a mere insurgency but a war between two countries which had a front line. Under international treaties, a military force has the political status accorded to a state only if it is in control of a defined territory with its own operational system of administration.

That is why, quite apart from moral and propaganda considerations, it was very important for us to maintain the front and not allow the Russian occupying forces to compromise its integrity. Djohar did his utmost to ensure that the front-line villages, over which there was continuous fighting, remained under our control. In addition to Goyskoye, whose defence he entrusted to troops of the Southwestern Front's third sector, that is, the Urus-Martan sector under my command, there were also Bamut, Stary Achkhoy and Yandi, which faced daily bombardment and frequent attacks by the invader. Those were the circumstances in which Russian troops succeeded in breaking through the front near Yandi, and later again at Stary Achkhoy. They finally managed to take also Bamut. The commander defending Yandi was Suleyman Aslambekov. Djohar was in Shalazhi when he received news of the fall of Yandi. He took a number of bodyguards with him and Magomed Dzhaniev, the military prosecutor, who had just brought him some report, and immediately headed for Yandi, saying it must be retaken at all costs. It really was important, because we needed the political trump card of controlled territory before the prospective talks between Yeltsin and Dudaev.

When he reached Yandi, Djohar contacted Suleyman Aslambekov to ask where he was. Suleyman reported he was in the southern outskirts, although in fact he had not yet got there. He did not realize Djohar was already there. That is how we came to lose Yandi. Russian troops, outflanking the defenders of Stary Achkhoy and Bamut which were to the west of Yandi, were able to force them to retreat in order to avoid being surrounded. The surrender of Yandi caused a chain reaction of failures which led to the front being broken. Our soldiers retreated south and took up a new line of defence backing on to the foothills and under cover of dense forest. The occupiers decided against further developing their offensive for the time being.

Djohar convened a small meeting to determine how the Russian troops had been able to break through at Yandi. I know that, besides Suleyman Aslambekov, it was attended also by Kazbek Makhashev, the republic's minister of the interior, and it was from him that I later heard the details. While waiting for Djohar to arrive, Kazbek began discussing what had happened with Suleyman. Suleyman told him it was all the fault of Zakaev and Isabaev, because when they began fighting in Goyskoye they set in motion the whole juggernaut of the Russian occupying forces in Chechnya. Kazbek was taken aback, because he knew that surrendering any one of the villages on the front line, including Goyskoye, would have been a strategic disaster. He also knew that the decision to defend Goyskoye was not some whim on our part, but a direct order from the president. He warned Suleyman, 'God forbid you should say that to Djohar! That is no explanation. Why not just tell him exactly what happened?'

Suleyman ignored this advice and repeated his claim when Djohar arrived for the meeting. Djohar stripped Suleyman of his command of the sector and all other military duties, adding cuttingly, 'Do whatever you like with your life, just steer clear of military matters.'

Ruslan Gelaev, the commander of the entire front, was also involved in this conflict. Djohar had summoned me on some matter and, while we were discussing it, the president was informed that Ruslan Gelaev had arrived. Djohar instructed that he be admitted. Ruslan came in, greeted us, and placed on Djohar's desk a request to be allowed to resign. He said this was because of the surrender of Yandi, but that he would nevertheless continue to fight the invader on his own with a group of 100 men. I tried to persuade the two of them not to take any rash decisions, but Djohar took Ruslan's letter and signed it. He said, 'You have made a very wise decision. Do whatever you think is right, just not what you have been doing up till now.'

Ruslan said goodbye and left. I turned to Djohar and begged him to think again. He heard me out, but replied, 'That is my final decision. I know what I am doing.'

Djohar was also drafting a decree releasing Aslan Maskhadov from his position as chief of the General Staff and planning to replace him with Mumadi Saidaev. He announced this in the presence of Kazbek Makhashev, Mumadi, Movlen Salamov and myself. The four of us urged him not to do so, and he agreed to wait for the time being, but added,

'You are not aware of all the circumstances. There is a lot you do not yet know about this issue, but you will.'

Instead of appointing Mumadi chief of the General Staff, he appointed him director of operations. Shortly after, Djohar was assassinated and there the matter rested.

Let me explain briefly what happened to relations between Djohar and Aslan Maskhadov. There was a serious problem, because by this time our so-called 'Islamists,' now more widely known as 'the Green Commissars,' had spun a dense cocoon round Aslan with the intention of manipulating him and turning him against Djohar. Regrettably, they were partly successful. Aslan ignored several meetings to which Djohar summoned him, as nearly all the fighters and commanders knew. There was a sense of a developing split. Moreover, some of our commanders, together with their fighters, ostentatiously sided with Aslan, carrying out only his orders and instructions. These were in eastern Chechnya and included Magomed Khambiev, Apti Batalov, Turpal-Ali Atgireyev, Ruslan Alikhadzhiev, and Islam Khalimov. At the same time, other 'eastern' commanders, like Aslanbek Ismailov ('Little Aslanbek'), Aslanbek Abdulkhadzhiev ('Big Aslanbek'), and many others fully supported Djohar and maintained constitutional propriety.

At the beginning of the war, a delegation had arrived from Iran wanting to meet Djohar. They told him that, for a start, they had brought two million dollars to support the Chechens, and intended to continue to give us financial support, only not publicly, because the Iranian government did not want to sour relations with the Russian government. Djohar replied through an interpreter, 'If you want to help us as your fellow Muslims, do so openly. We want nothing to do with these secret handouts because they will only cause us a lot of trouble later. We cannot accept them.' With that, he sent the Iranians packing.

Djohar was absolutely right, as we saw only too clearly during the Second Russo-Chechen War, because our situation only really worsened when all this money began sloshing around among us. The Chechen Resistance broke into factions as all the top commanders began sending out representatives to raise money, and started enticing fighters into their own camp by promising them better arms and supplies. The money caused a split which is still evident today.

Somewhere along the line, our Green Commissars managed to intercept the Iranians, accepted their money and all their subsequent donations, directing a significant proportion to Aslan as 'aid from our Muslim brothers,' and thus managed to consolidate their hold on the chief of our General Staff. They eventually managed to drive a wedge between Djohar and Aslan. Later, after he became president himself and came face to face with the devious and unscrupulous behaviour of these individuals, Aslan said it was retribution from the Almighty for breaking with Djohar and failing to understand his position.

Such was the situation when Djohar was killed. Aslan Maskhadov continued to hold the post of chief of the CRI General Staff, but Ruslan Gelaev and Suleyman Aslambekov were relieved of their posts and positions. All these documents, including drafts of decrees Djohar had not got round to issuing, were now in the hands of Zelimkhan. It was because he had these that Zelimkhan raised the question of whether to bring Gelaev back to the CRI Armed Forces. After Zelimkhan outlined his intentions, I said I had no comment to make about Gelaev, Aslambekov and Abumuslimov. I was fully in favour, but did have reservations about my own appointment as presidential aide for national security because it was very unclear to me what was to be done about Goyskoye and the fighters currently under my command. Zelimkhan asked who I wanted to replace me in Goyskoye. My deputy, Khusein Isabaev was in Urus-Martan at that moment, recovering from an operation for peritonitis, so I proposed Nurdi Bazhiev.

A brief word about Nurdi. He was a born warrior, able, supremely brave and resolute. Of medium height, stocky and fair-haired, his appearance earned him the call sign 'Silver Fox,' but among themselves the fighters called him 'Nurdi the Bassoon.' He was a highly skilled operator of the Bassoon (AT–4 Spigot) wire-guided anti-tank missile launcher, and also of grenade launchers. He had single-handedly put out of commission more than 50 pieces of Russian armour.

The next question was what would become of the fighters in my sector. At this point, Dalkhan Khozhaev, my sector chief of staff, spoke up. He had probably already given some thought to the matter, because his proposal was succinct and detailed. He suggested Zelimkhan should form a presidential special operations team on the basis of Sector 3 of the Southwestern Front. Dalkhan added that, as chief of staff of the sector, he knew the mood of the fighters and there was a risk that many of the volunteers might disperse if there was a sudden change of leadership. Accordingly, it would be better first to form a presidential special operations team and, some time later, let it pass under the command of another person. Zelimkhan liked the idea, and that night drew up and signed all the requisite decrees and instructions. The troops of Sector 3 were redesignated a presidential special operations brigade, I was appointed presidential aide for national security and simultaneously commander of the new brigade. I could make the necessary appointments and transfers within the brigade on my own authority.

We also discussed the situation in Goyskoye and the overall position in the Southwestern Front's zone of responsibility. I told Zelimkhan I thought it made no sense to try to hold on to Goyskoye, because now the enemy had captured Bamut, Stary Achkhoy, and Yandi, the settlement had lost its earlier strategic importance. The new front line had moved south, right to the foothills, so that it would make better sense to withdraw our forces from Goyskoye, where they might find themselves encircled, and deploy them to consolidate the new front line. Zelimkhan agreed, and it was decided that, at the first sign of a new assault, we would withdraw from the village, but remain there for the time being in order to inhibit, as best we could, the Russian troops' scope for manoeuvre in Urus-Martan region. We went back that night, I gathered the commanders, and briefed them on the new presidential decrees. As agreed with Zelimkhan, I made no mention of the order to abandon the village before the next assault, or of our plans to form a special operations brigade. Dalkhan and I announced only Zelimkhan's decree concerning my appointment as presidential aide for national security and the transfer of command for the defence of Goyskoye to Nurdi Bazhiev.

A few days later we received intelligence that the Russian troops were preparing a massive assault the following day. I assembled the commanders and informed them of the order of our president and commander-in-chief that the defenders of Goyskoye should withdraw from the village no later than three o'clock the following morning. Before that time, all our units withdrew from Goyskoye in a quiet, orderly fashion. The last to leave were Dalkhan and I. As we were on our way, some groups separated from us. The Samashki fighters departed. Balavdi Beloev headed off through Saadi-Kotar towards Barzoy.

By dawn we were in the foothills in dense forest. We decided to set up a temporary camp there as our military bases were higher in the mountains, and during the day there were Russian reconnaissance aircraft flying which might find us on the march and call in aerial or ground fire. I had just over 100 fighters left with me in our makeshift camp. Hidden beneath the dense forest canopy, we sat to await further developments and were not disappointed. Precisely at the time for morning namaz, the invaders subjected abandoned Goyskoye to a great barrage of bombardment from the ground and from the air. There was relentless shelling by artillery, including blanket bombing from multiple rocket launchers and mortars; wave after wave of bombers targeted Goyskoye; helicopters buzzed round the village perimeter firing missiles, and again all hell was let loose until 12 noon. After that, the armoured columns and infantry moved in and, naturally, in an abandoned village, met no resistance. Nevertheless, as we learned later, Russian generals were that evening telling television reporters fairy stories about 'fierce fighting' for Goyskoye, the 'hundreds of Chechen outlaws' they had killed, and so forth. The BMP–3 Infantry Fighting Vehicle we had captured was there with its broken down engine. We had stripped it of its armaments, but this hapless vehicle had a moment of, probably worldwide, fame as the Russian generals pointed towards it and assured journalists the Chechen outlaws were equipped with the very latest armoured vehicles, 'more advanced even than those at the disposal of the Russian Army.'

In reality, this had been a humiliation for the invader. To have put so much effort into preparing the assault, to have unleashed so much firepower on this small village, to have sent in such numbers of armoured vehicles and infantry, and not to have a single murdered Chechen fighter to show for their pains! It was as if in a boxing match a heavyweight boxer was geared up to deliver a devastating punch and put all his strength into it, only to find himself punching empty air. Listening in our temporary camp to the hours of artillery bombardment and the exploding bombs and missiles, we concluded that Russia's infamous Operation Iron Ring was under way.

That same day, the invaders began advancing through Shatoy, Barzoy, and Surat into the mountains and were effectively to our rear. For the first time in the war they advanced south of the villages in the foothills and established a line where the forest of the Black Mountains began. They supposed their advances were a great military success, although our units had suffered no losses and retained full combat and manoeuvring capability. While still there, we heard that the enemy was planning security sweeps in the villages of the Urus-Martan region. I was also informed that there would be a sweep, beginning at dawn the following day, in Roshni-Chu where Zelimkhan Yandarbiev was currently located. I lost no time in getting to the village that night and stationing fighters at intervals of 50-100 metres to provide a corridor for the safe removal of the president. When I reached Roshni-Chu, I sent someone to fetch Zelimkhan's nephew, who was the head of his security detail. When Bakar came, I passed on my information and advised that Zelimkhan must leave Roshni-Chu tonight. He could sit out the operation in my temporary camp. I told Bakar of the corridor I had established to ensure safe passage. He promised to report all this to Zelimkhan and left. We saw Ruslan Gelaev arrive in the village. Bakar returned a couple of hours later and told me, 'Zelimkhan is not in Roshni-Chu. You need not worry about him. He has moved to another place.'

I said, 'Look, Bakar, what happened to Djohar is still fresh in our memory. If Zelimkhan has not in fact gone away, it could be disastrous. Do not forget that you bear personal responsibility for his safety.'

Bakar replied that he understood, and could vouch for the fact that Zelimkhan was no longer in Roshni-Chu. Having received that assurance, I led my fighters back to our camp.

Zelimkhan was extremely casual about his own safety. When Dalkhan and I were with him the night he was writing the decrees mentioned above, I noticed on the table a case with a telephone exactly like the one Djohar had been using at the time of his death. I said in surprise,

'Zelimkhan, are you really using this telephone? You surely know what happened to Djohar when he used one, and it is barely two weeks since he died.'

Zelimkhan gestured airily and said,

'I do not use it. It is just lying there.'

As it transpired, he did make use of it on one occasion, and when he decided to make a call with it a second time, it was only by the grace of the

Almighty that nobody was killed. The house in Shalazhi where he was staying was promptly subjected to missile bombardment and demolished. Fortunately neither Zelimkhan himself, his guards, nor the houseowners were injured.

That night before the security sweep, Zelimkhan, despite Bakar's assurances, disdained security measures and remained in Roshni-Chu. At dawn the Russians surrounded the village and began checking the houses. Zelimkhan and his two guards took the bags containing the CRI presidential documents and archives and hid in the attic of the house where he was staying. The owner told me later that, at the beginning of their operation, the Russians contacted Zelimkhan by his radio call sign and invited him to surrender. Eventually, an officer entered the yard of the house with some soldiers. Zelimkhan's Niva was parked under a tarpaulin in the yard. The officer asked the owner, who was working in the yard, 'Is President Yandarbiev staying here?'

'Well, yes, actually,' the man said unflustered. 'He is hiding in my attic.' The officer responded with a grin, appreciating the joke, and gave orders to the soldiers to thoroughly search all the buildings, the orchard, cellars and attics. Hearing the order, Zelimkhan and his bodyguards readied their weapons for a fight, determined to sell their lives dearly. The occupying troops searched everywhere, but did not bother going up to the attic. That is the only reason Zelimkhan and his guards escaped death, because needless to say they would never have allowed themselves to be taken alive.

When the sweep was over, the owner fetched civilian clothes for Zelimkhan and his guards and drove them through the Russian checkpoint at Gekhi to Dokka Makhaev. Dokka contacted Shamil Basaev, who came to Gekhi with a group of fighters and removed Zelimkhan to Makhkety. All this we found out later, but in the meantime returned to base.

One night I noticed lights glowing in the vicinity of our camp. These were pieces of phosphorescent, rotten wood and, as I looked at them, I hit on the idea that we could use them as lighting. The problem was that, at night under the dense forest canopy, it was pitch dark in the camp. We could not light fires, because that would have given away our position to the Russian troops only a few hundred metres away. Moving about the camp at night was a big problem. In the morning, I sent fighters out to collect a lot of these rotten boughs and told them to place them at the side of our paths and the entrances to our bunkers. When night came, sure enough, the tracks and turnings of our camp glimmered helpfully and we were able to find our way. These phosphorescent lamps were invisible from the air and from the plain, and we now had 'neon' street lighting. My men were very taken with the innovation.

Meanwhile, having heard that there had indeed been a security sweep in Roshni-Chu, I did my best to discover where Zelimkhan was. We had had a convention since the beginning of the war that the president's safety was primarily the concern of the commander in whose area he was at the time. I had a purely practical need to know whether Zelimkhan was in the Urus-Martan region or had moved to a different sector. Zelimkhan, like Djohar before him, typically, stayed in one of three villages while in the Urus-Martan region: Gekhi-Chu, Roshni-Chu, and Shalazhi. My informants told me he was in none of them. I made enquiries and was eventually told by Djohar's former chief bodyguard, Abu Arsanukaev, that the best person to ask was Dokka Makhaev. Dokka told me Zelimkhan had been ferried across the River Argun and was now the responsibility of the Southeastern Front. Meanwhile, on our Southwestern Front, Operation Iron Ring, much hyped by the Russian Command, was gaining momentum. Extra military units and armour were constantly being sent from eastern Chechnya in our direction. General Vladimir Shamanov appeared regularly on television threatening to crush us with a 'single mighty iron fist.'

During one of these worrying nights, I had a dream. There was a station, trains hurtling through it, and Djohar standing on the platform. I am not superstitious, but this dream somehow confirmed a growing anxiety that we had stayed too long in this temporary camp, and that I should not delay a moment longer before pulling my fighters back to somewhere safer. We received new intelligence about impending security sweeps in Urus-Martan and after that in Gekhi. We had seven passenger vehicles and a few trucks between a hundred of us. Also one cannon, removed from the celebrated infantry fighting vehicle. We had additionally several heavy machine guns, and I ordered Khusein Isabaev who, barely back on his feet after surgery, had re-joined us, to take care of our 'artillery piece' and the machine guns. He drained oil from the truck engines, greased our cannon and machine guns to protect them from rust, and buried them in a safe place. We decided to abandon the trucks.

Down below, there was a strip of unoccupied land 300-400 metres wide between two Russian units. This narrow corridor was the route we would need to negotiate in complete silence. Fortunately, the night was exceptionally dark and we moved stealthily down to the plain, pushing the cars with their engines switched off. We made it to Tangi-Chu without incident, rested a little, and were fed by people loyal to us. Then, before dawn, we continued on our way. Fortunately, the enemy, having concentrated all their forces in the foothills, had dismantled their checkpoint between Tangi-Chu and Urus-

Martan, so not only did we not need to destroy that obstacle, we were actually able to start the car engines. By 4.00 am or so we were in Urus-Martan. I sent the main contingent of fighters on to Gekhi, where they were to be under the command of Dokka Makhaev, and myself stayed behind with several comrades in Urus-Martan, yielding to the entreaties of Ichkerian television to give an interview on current developments in the region and throughout the republic. At 5.00 in the morning, I and my companions went on to Gekhi to rejoin our fighters.

The house-by-house searches began in Urus-Martan at 8.00 or 9.00 am. We knew it would be the turn of Gekhi the following day, so we assembled all the fighters from Gekhi, Valerik and Katar-Yurt and took a long, circuitous route through Kulary to Yermolovka, where the searches were already over. Around 300 fighters arrived in Yermolovka, with all our weaponry and vehicles. We had managed also to evacuate our television equipment from Urus-Martan. After spending 24 hours in Yermolovka, with our men and vehicles distributed round people's homes, we heard that the searches in Gekhi were over and the cordon had been lifted. Dokka Makhaev and the fighters from Gekhi returned to their village.

At this time I received orders from Zelimkhan to attend a meeting in Makhkety. I decided to take Dalkhan Khozhaev and Said-Khusein Tazbaev, together with a number of fighters as bodyguards. We planned to drive along the Rostov-Baku Highway to Novye Atagi, from there to Dubi-Evl, then follow the course of the River Vashtar as far as Selmen-Tauzen, and proceed to Makhkety. We first sent a local resident ahead in a car to check the road. He reported back that the coast was clear, except for Chechen police at the traffic police station by the turning for Grozny. We decided the Chechen policemen would cause no problems and set off in two jeeps. We were in Chechen military uniform and armed. At the traffic police station, we stopped and greeted the men. They returned our greeting and saluted us as soldiers. The same day we reached Makhkety, exactly as planned. The meeting was already in progress and discussing forthcoming Russo-Chechen talks in Moscow.

After the death of Djohar, we had severed all contact with the outside world, not only with Russia but also with the representatives of OSCE because, although OSCE did condemn the murder of the president of Chechnya, we felt it had done so less than vehemently. Our adversary found this situation very unnerving. For all their propaganda, the Russian Command were perfectly aware that our forces were far from defeated. Our entire military and political infrastructure was intact, and they surmised we must be preparing some large-scale retaliation, as we always had before. It was true that the invader had for the first time in the entire war managed to reach the foothills, and in one or two places even to advance into the mountains. Our forces had, however, been moved out of danger in good time, and the Russian assaults had done no real damage. Having reached the foothills, the Russian troops just camped there without advancing further, which made no military sense.

For all these reasons, the Russian representatives made strenuous efforts to establish contact with the Chechen side through the mediators from the OSCE Mission in Grozny. When we arrived in Makhkety, Zelimkhan was just talking about this situation. He had been approached by the OSCE representatives on behalf of the Russians with an offer to attend peace talks in Moscow with President Yeltsin. It was an important meeting, attended by all the military and political leaders of the CRI: Aslan Maskhadov, Akhmad-haddzhi Kadyrov, Said-Khasan Abumuslimov, Kazbek Makhashev, Shamil Basaev, newly appointed as vice-president, and Khozh-Akhmed Yarikhanov, who had left Grozny and cut off all diplomatic contact on Zelimkhan's orders. Zelimkhan informed us that contact had been resumed on the initiative of the Russian side. Prime Minister Viktor Chernomyrdin had sent an intermediary, Khusein Beybulatov, to ask him to agree to attend the meeting with Yeltsin which should have taken place with Djohar. In Russia's bureaucracy, many political and diplomatic initiatives continue through inertia unless definite instructions are received from the top to terminate them. That is what had happened here. Despite the murder of Djohar and our firm announcement that we were terminating all contact with the Russian side, the mechanism preparing these negotiations had carried on functioning, and the arrival of Chernomyrdin's representative was one of the major stages in the preparations. Perhaps, too, they had decided in Moscow that the new CRI leaders, lacking Djohar's high profile on the international stage, might prove more conciliatory. Most probable, however, is that Yeltsin and his administration were just continuing their election charade, of which one of the most vote-catching components was holding peace talks with the 'Chechen separatists.'

We discussed the proposal, and opinions were divided. Some were in favour of negotiations, while others were categorically opposed, saying we could not trust the Russians an inch and that they were capable of absolutely every kind of deceit and maltreatment of our delegation. I remember Aslan Maskhadov and Shamil Basaev were the most outspoken in their opposition to any visit to Moscow by Zelimkhan and other Ichkerian leaders. Many of those present supported them. When Zelimkhan asked my opinion, I was in a quandary. The fact that he had announced his proposed negotiating team before the discussion, and that it included me, meant that now, although personally inclined to agree with Aslan and Shamil, openly supporting them might seem to stem from excessive caution and concern for my own safety. So I said that I saw positive and negative aspects to the proposal. On the positive side, irrespective of any results, was the fact that negotiations would tell the outside world that, despite Djohar's death, the political and military foundations of our state were intact. The main negative aspect I saw as the universally recognized dishonesty of the Russian leadership, which could easily arrange a plane crash or use a slow-acting poison on us.

Shamil jocularly remarked, 'A plane crash would be okay, but if you came back poisoned it would be a real drag. We'd have to spend forever looking after you, trying to find medicine, shuttling doctors all over the place ...' It was black humour, but it lightened the atmosphere.

The discussion came to an end: people's opinions and positions were clear, and we all waited to hear what Zelimkhan would decide. He said he would accept the offer, and on that the meeting ended. We returned to our region the same day. I divided the brigade between four towns: one to Goyty, one to Novye Atagi, one to Alkhan-Yurt, and the remainder to Yermolovka. Dalkhan Khozhaev was left in command of the brigade and Said-Khusein Tazbaev and I, together with some bodyguards, returned to Makhkety. From then until our departure to Moscow, I stayed there, involved in preparing for the negotiations.

We tried to anticipate all the scenarios the Russian side might devise. The Kremlin had been determined to see this meeting go ahead, and we knew they would be trying to extract maximum political and propaganda advantage from it to ensure victory for Yeltsin in the looming presidential election. We were prepared for any twist events might take and had countermeasures ready for every conceivable outcome of our trip, even the most radical. We prepared very flexibly and thoroughly.

After we had finally decided to go to Moscow and the date was already set, we heard that the Russian intelligence agencies in Nalchik had arrested Alla Dudaeva and Musa Idigov, one of Djohar's nephews and former bodyguard, who was accompanying her. Musa Idigov was one of the two close relatives of Djohar who knew where he was buried. That same evening, on Zelimkhan's orders, an emergency meeting attended by almost all the members of our delegation was held in Makhkety. There were two items on the agenda. First, the urgent need to move Djohar's body, now that one of the people who knew where he was buried was in the hands of the Russian intelligence agencies. Needless to say, the Russians would be primarily interested in confirming that Djohar was dead and, if that were the case, where he was buried. The second item was whether, in the light of Alla Dudaeva's arrest, we should go to Moscow at all. We debated this at great length, going over all the arguments. In the end, we decided we should still go, but make the first item in the negotiations a demand for the immediate release of Alla and Musa.

So it was that, at 6.00 am on 27 May 1996, an OSCE car arrived in Makhkety bearing Tim Guldimann, the Mission chief. Escorted by him, we drove towards Shali, then on to Novye Atagi, and there changed vehicles. Zelimkhan, Said-Khasan Abumuslimov, Khusein Bekbulatov, and I got into an imposing Chaika limousine with Ismail of Novye Atagi, an exceptionally brave man devoted to our cause, at the wheel. We asked Zelimkhan where he got the Chaika, and learned that this extremely expensive limousine had been sent from Moscow by our fellow Chechen businessmen. They had bought it for 200,000 US dollars specially for Djohar Dudaev when there was speculation in the Russian media about negotiations between him and Yeltsin. In the Soviet era it had belonged to a member of the CPSU Central Committee, USSR Foreign Minister Andrey Gromyko if remember aright. It had been fully fitted out for official occasions, and the state flag of Ichkeria flew over the bonnet.

Despite the early hour, in every village through which we passed there were thousands of people waving Chechen flags. They gave our motorcade a great welcome, wishing us good speed and that we should return with peace. I say again that such demonstrations of mass support from the population gave us confidence in the rightness of the cause we were fighting for, and faith that our efforts were truly in the interests and in accordance with the aspirations of our people. This, in turn, placed a great burden of responsibility on us to pay attention to everything that was going on in and around the republic. There was a clear sense of history being made. This was the first meeting at such a high level in the centuries of conflict between Russia and Chechnya. I was aware that, whatever its outcome, it would open a new chapter in relations between us.

On our progress from Makhkety to Ingushetia we drove past several Russian checkpoints. Nobody tried to stop our motorcade because the Russian military had been advised that we were coming through. Tim Guldimann told us our safe passage had been guaranteed by the Russian president personally. At the checkpoints, not only were we not obstructed, but neither were the many hundreds of vehicles of our spontaneous escort, decorated with flags and portraits of Djohar and Zelimkhan.

We were all excited, but at the same time anxious. We talked about everything except the reason we were making this journey. In spite of all our preparatory planning and analysis, we knew we could not possibly anticipate all the manoeuvres the Russian leadership might try on. Everyone was attempting to play down the excitement, so we talked in a relaxed manner and shared our impressions of the journey. At the border with Ingushetia we were met, on the orders of President Ruslan Aushev, by a local riot police unit which accompanied us then all the way to the airport at Sleptsovskaya. I emphasize that, just as in Chechnya, the people of Ingushetia gave our motorcade a warm welcome, clearly demonstrating their support. We were met at the airport by President Aushev and members of the Ingush government.

Before boarding the plane, we had to decide how many people would fly to Moscow. Our delegation was accompanied by 50 fighters from the Presidential Lifeguards. It was decided that we would take 30, the same as the number of Russian troops from the Presidential Security Service whom Yeltsin had sent for our protection on the plane. The TU–154 on which we were to fly, one of Yeltsin's aircraft, was spacious and fitting everyone in was no problem. Ruslan Aushev promised to find space in the barracks of the local riot police for the rest of our soldiers and the volunteer guards who had come to Ingushetia on their own initiative. There were a lot of them. Khusein Isabaev and Alu Gaisumov had come with me, and they decided that they too would await my return. Khusein told me everything was in order at our bases, where Dalkhan Khozhaev and Aslanbek Lesov were in command.

We boarded the plane, landing at Vnukovo Airport where we were met by the representatives of the Kremlin directly responsible for receiving us. We agreed with them that our delegation would be guarded by eight armed fighters. The remaining 22 would wait for us in the plane which, immediately after landing, was towed away to a quiet, deserted stand in a remote corner of the airport. We were assured that the plane had plenty of food and everything else needed, and that our fighters would want for nothing. Our lads promptly hung an Ichkerian flag at the entrance. Even before we left the airport, the Russian military moved in armoured vehicles and surrounded the aircraft with what appeared to be special operations forces, which I imagine were the FSB's Alpha unit. The Russians were evidently blissfully unaware that, if they got up to any dirty tricks, we had take the precaution of deploying several groups of our fighters in Moscow. This was our insurance policy against a worst case scenario: if, for example, the Russians arrested our delegation. If events had developed along those lines, each group had a well thought through action plan of appropriate countermeasures.

We were whisked from Vnukovo Airport to the Kremlin in the record time of just 17 minutes, the route evidently having been cleared of traffic and cordoned off. We drove into the Kremlin, got out and passed through metal detectors. These were not specially in our honour but a routine part of Kremlin security. We ascended to one of the halls on either the first or second floor and were met by Sergey Stepashin. By that time he was no longer director of the Federal Security Bureau and had been appointed head of administration in Chernomyrdin's government. Not long ago somebody asked me who in the Russian government was overseeing the 'Chechen problem' in the 1990s. At different times the names of Oleg Lobov or Doku Zavgaev were mentioned, but confidential information from people closely involved with the regime at the time suggests that, until 1999, the person principally responsible was Stepashin.

We went up some stairs and were asked to wait five minutes or so. Our delegation consisted of Chechen Acting President Zelimkhan Yandarbiev, Said-Khasan Abumuslimov, Khozh-Akhmed Yarikhanov, Movlen Sala-mov, Movladi Udugov, Khusein Bekbulatov, and myself. We had made a point of also including 'S. Basaev' in the list of delegation members. This was Shirvani, the brother of Shamil, and we deliberately gave only his initial. We heard later that, while we were waiting, the names of our delegation were taken for Yeltsin to look through and that, when he came to the name of Basaev, he sat bolt upright in his chair and yelled, 'What? Shamil Basaev is in the Kremlin?' It was hurriedly explained to him that this was not Shamil Basaev but his brother. That was one of our little surprises for Yeltsin, and we had no doubt the Russians would have a few of their own in store for us. As indeed they had.

While we were waiting, Movlen Salamov began anxiously enquiring where we could perform namaz. After he had asked three or four times, Khozh-Akhmed, whom I never remember missing a time for prayer no matter how difficult the circumstances, said, 'Would you believe it! Movlen, who never performs namaz, has suddenly been overwhelmed by piety in the Kremlin.' We laughed, and somebody explained to Movlen that when travelling it is permissible to perform a shortened version of the midday namaz at the same time as afternoon prayers.

We were finally invited through to Yeltsin. The Russian president was ensconced in the chairman's seat at the end of the table, and to his right were Lobov, Zavgaev, Chernomyrdin, Stepashin, Mikhailov and Kulikov. We went in, greeted him, and Yeltsin gestured to us to sit on his left, facing his ministers. Many people will have seen this boorish incident on television, but I shall describe it in my own words, not least because some interesting details were missing from the television report.

Yeltsin, with his characteristic bear-like growl, turned to face us and said, 'That's it. The fighting is over. Sit down.'

Needless to say, none of us did. This was one of the scenarios we had thought through in advance, and we had agreed that if the Russians' puppet, Zavgaev, was present at the meeting, with Yeltsin trying to pose as the arbitrator in a 'dialogue between Chechens,' as if we and their collaborators were on an equal footing, we would refuse to enter negotiations, no matter what the consequences might be for us personally.

Zelimkhan moved towards Yeltsin who, when we had come in, had not had the common courtesy even to half rise from his chair. His security chief, General Korzhakov, immediately popped up from nowhere to 'cover' his boss. Zelimkhan said, 'Boris Nikolaevich, this is not what we agreed. We were told we would meet you privately to discuss matters relating to the Russo-Chechen conflict.'

Yeltsin said, 'No! There never was any such agreement. I have no intention of discussing anything with you in private. You are not my equals. Sit down! That's enough. You have done fighting. Let me hear no more about it.'

Zelimkhan declared that in that case we were here to no purpose. We would leave Moscow and they could discuss whatever they liked with each other. He then asked loudly, 'Where is Guldimann?'

Tim Guldimann appeared, and told Yeltsin, 'Boris Nikolaevich, you are mistaken. We had a firm prior agreement that the format of the meeting would be direct negotiation between you and the Chechen side. The presence of Zavgaev at the negotiations was not discussed and was not part of the agreement. As the official facilitator of your meeting, I am categorically opposed to your terminating this carefully arranged dialogue with the Chechen Resistance.'

Having listened to Guldimann's statement, Yeltsin looked him up and down, and growled, 'And who the hell might this be?' Lobov explained that Tim Guldimann was the Mission head in Chechnya of the Organisation for Security and Cooperation in Europe.

Yeltsin slapped his hand down on the table and said in a threatening voice, 'No one will leave this room. Lock the doors.' At this, Zelimkhan said to Guldimann, 'Your Mission is responsible for our safety. You guaranteed our unimpeded return to Chechnya.'

Tim Guldimann again addressed Yeltsin. 'I shall be obliged to report to the OSCE that the Russian side has violated all the protocols of this meeting previously agreed by your own and the Chechen representatives, as well as with the OSCE. I confirm that the OSCE is wholly responsible for the Chechen delegation, and we shall now leave this room.'

Yeltsin's face went crimson as Guldimann was speaking. He glared at him ferociously and then at those seated to his right. 'Get up!' he barked. You should have seen how nimbly those gentlemen, who a moment before had been sitting there looking gravely statesmanlike, leapt to their feet when yelled at, and left the table, almost knocking the chairs over in their haste. Yeltsin rose abruptly from his seat, proceeded to the side from which he had just so impressively dismissed the Russian delegation, sat himself down in the middle, put his clasped hands on the table and said to us, 'Now will you sit down?'

Zelimkhan said, 'Now we will.'

Tim Guldimann, without a moment's hesitation, by-passed Korzhakov and took Yeltsin's place, demonstrating that it was he who was chairing the meeting and would be refereeing the proceedings. None of these details found their way into the report on the TV news programme *Zerkalo* (*The Mirror*).

It was interesting to watch the reactions of those present, my opposite numbers in past negotiations, – Kulikov, Mikhailov and the rest of them. Even before we sat down, there was a brief verbal exchange between Zelimkhan and Zavgaev, Zavgaev remarking, 'All this' (meaning the war) 'started because of you.' Zelimkhan retorted, 'No, it all started because of you, and will continue for as long as you continue meddling in our affairs.'

While this verbal skirmishing was going on, Kulikov, who was wandering about near the table, leaned towards Mikhailov and said, 'I told you their place was not in the Kremlin but in Lefortovo with the FSB, or at best in high security at Matrosskaya Tishina.'

Yeltsin, meanwhile, was already seated at the table. Zelimkhan was the first on our side to sit down, after which the rest of us followed. The talks began, and immediately, as we had agreed among ourselves, Zelimkhan passed Yeltsin the open letter Djohar Dudaev had written before the war began. It showed how hard he had been trying to avoid a military confrontation with Russia and the extent to which he was prepared to compromise in order to do so. Yeltsin read it carefully and said, 'No, I have not read this letter before and did not know it existed, most unfortunately.'

Before proceeding to discuss the major issues, Zelimkhan said, 'Boris Nikolaevich, we wish to inform you that Djohar Dudaev's widow, Alla, has been arrested at Nalchik Airport and is presently being held by the Russian intelligence agencies. We demand that she and the person accompanying her should be released immediately.'

Yeltsin replied that he had not heard about the incident, and asked Chernomyrdin what had happened. Chernomyrdin replied, 'Yes, we have information that Citizen Anna Fyodorovna Kulikova has been detained in Nalchik for using forged documents.'

To this Zelimkhan responded, 'That is just a pretext for arresting her. You and we know perfectly well who she is, and we would like you, Boris Nikolaevich, to give us your word that she will be released without delay.'

Yeltsin promised that would be done, and instructed Chernomyrdin, 'Find out at once where she is and make the necessary arrangements. She is to be released before the Chechen delegation leave Moscow.' Chernomyrdin wrote this in his notebook and instructed Kulikov to deal with the matter.

With that resolved, we moved on to the major issues, each of which led to heated discussion. In the end, Yeltsin said, 'You will know I have announced that a presidential election will be held in Russia on 16 June, and I am stating to you as a fact that all military action on the territory of Chechnya will cease. You for your part must undertake that you will observe the truce. We need finally to resolve this problem of the relations between us, and will do everything possible to find a political formula satisfactory to both sides to end the conflict. Today we shall not discuss the status of Chechnya, whether it is an integral part of Russia or an independent state. Today we shall talk only about how to cease hostilities.'

Our delegation accepted this proposal, and it was agreed that the next stage in the negotiations would be to discuss political issues, including the status of Chechnya; in effect, to continue the work of the earlier negotiations in Grozny. For the present, both parties agreed to limit negotiation to a cessation of hostilities from 1 June of the current year, and the signing of an official document to that effect.

During its drafting, we insisted that Chechnya should be referred to as 'the Chechen Republic of Ichkeria.' With that agreed, it was decided to take a break. When the two delegations were apart, Yeltsin, as Stepashin and Mikhailov told us later in Nazran, gave them his assessment of the Chechen delegation: A prickly lot, he said. 'I like them.'

To this Mikhailov responded, 'Boris Nikolaevich, now you know what we were up against in the negotiations in Chechnya; see how they stick to their guns even here in the Kremlin.'

Yeltsin replied, 'Fine, but we still need to bring this to an end.'

After the break, the second round of negotiation began. Yeltsin returned to the hall, and I remarked to Khozh-Akhmed, 'I don't see this man ever leaving the Kremlin of his own free will.'

That was clear from Yeltsin's body language: he was not just the president of Russia, he owned the place. He was the Tsar. Despite the fact that Yeltsin was highly unpopular with the Russian public, he had tremendous authority. You could see that in the way he behaved, and in how Russian politicians and ministers reacted to that behaviour.

By the time he returned, the text of the treaty was all but ready for signing. Mikhailov, who was sitting one along from Yeltsin, with Chernomyrdin between them, decided to have his say. He leaned towards Yeltsin and said, 'Boris Nikolaevich, if you sign this document with the formulation 'the Chechen Republic of Ichkeria' we will appear to be recognizing the independence of Chechnya.'

Yeltsin banged Mikhailov on the head and said, 'Shut up! I know what I'm doing.' Then he turned to us and added, as if to gauge our reaction, 'We shall change the title in our Constitution as well.'

In the Russian Constitution the official title of Chechnya was given as 'the Chechen Republic.' In an instant, Yeltsin had resolved an issue over which the Chechen and Russian delegations had been deadlocked during a month and a half of negotiation in Grozny. That was typical of his approach to complex political problems: he took an axe to them. He, and all those around him, were fully aware that such matters were decided by him alone. Yeltsin made no bones about it.

We signed an agreement on the cessation of hostilities and, at Yeltsin's insistence, the Russian signatory was Chernomyrdin. Yeltsin asked Zelimkhan for one further concession in return for officially naming Chechnya in the document as 'the Chechen Republic of Ichkeria;' he asked him to sign with only his name and surname, without designating himself as president of the CRI. That request was one surprise we had not foreseen. The talks might have stalled again, because we were ready to refuse to sign the document, but Yeltsin cajoled Zelimkhan: 'Zelimkhan, the whole world knows you are the president of the CRI, just as the whole world knows that Chernomyrdin is the prime minister of Russia. There will be many more signatures of all sorts of people on this document. Even Doku Zavgaev may sign somewhere on the back to indicate he has no objection to what we have agreed between us. Don't let us lose this truce over a few empty formalities.'

Frankly, I knew from past experience exactly how much ceasefires with the Russians were worth and had no illusions about the document's significance. I was well aware that the truce would hold until the Russian presidential election was over, and that then the war would resume. The real value for us of these negotiations lay in the very fact of their being conducted at summit level. That not only legitimized us in the eyes of the world as an equal party in the Russo-Chechen conflict but, more importantly, demonstrated our status as the only political force capable of representing Chechnya. For Yeltsin, of course, it was no more than a public relations stunt in his campaign for the presidency, enabling him to fly to Chechnya and declare that the war was over. Both sides had achieved their main aim in the negotiations, so I had no objection to Zelimkhan signing in the style Yeltsin proposed. For us, this had been a major political success.

The question now arose of when we would depart. Yeltsin turned to our delegation and said, 'I think you should, and hope you will, stay tonight in Moscow. We would value the opportunity to extend our hospitality to you.'

We had foreseen this, anticipating that we would not be allowed to return the same day to Chechnya. Zelimkhan accordingly protested mildly, 'Boris Nikolaevich, thank you, but it is probably better if we leave today and return on the same plane to Chechnya.'

Yeltsin was insistent: 'No, Zelimkhan, you cannot fly straight back home just like that. You have come to Moscow and it is our duty to treat you hospitably. Chernomyrdin has already prepared somewhere for you to relax until tomorrow morning.'

This Chernomyrdin immediately confirmed. 'Yes, Boris Nikolaevich, everything is ready. They will be taken straightaway to a country residence at Barvikha. The place has been prepared for the president and his entourage.'

It was clear enough that we would not be flying home that evening. Zelimkhan then proposed that we should stay at a hotel, but Yeltsin declined that suggestion too, assuring us they really wanted to give us a hearty welcome and be good hosts. We had no option but to agree to stay at the house in Barvikha.

As promised, we were driven straight from the Kremlin out into the countryside. As we travelled along, I said to the president, 'Zelimkhan, it is 100 per cent certain that, either tonight or tomorrow morning, Yeltsin will fly to Grozny while we are still here.'

Zelimkhan disagreed. 'Impossible. That would be such a blatant display of cowardice and weakness that I really cannot see Yeltsin opting for it.'

I said, 'Let us wait and see.' Zelimkhan and I even bet on it.

We finally arrived at the residence. If I am not mistaken, it was the villa of Nikolai Podgorny, a former member of the Communist Party's Politburo and chairman of the USSR Supreme Soviet. The accommodation was very spacious, comfortable, and in a scenic location. We prayed, and then the table was laid for dinner. Naturally, there was no vodka, and we were specifically informed that all the meat was halal. We sat down at the table, but no one was in any hurry to touch the food, mindful that Byzantine ways still prevaled in Moscow and that we might well be poisoned. These concerns were compounded by the absence of Tim Guldimann, the sole guarantor of our safety in this hostile city. We all looked round and enquired where he was. Guldimann finally joined us at the table and we had dinner.

The first news bulletins the next morning informed us that Yeltsin was in Chechnya. He gave a speech at Grozny Airport in front of some Russian military unit, thanked the officers and men for their 'courage and valour,' announced that he had decided to run for a second term as president, and declared that the war in Chechnya was over. All this was broadcast from very early morning by the Russian media, but was immediately followed by news analysis and comment. Many Russian and foreign analysts pointed out that Yeltsin had only dared go to Chechnya while effectively holding our delegation hostage. There was much debate over whether this should be seen as a sign of strength or weakness on his part, whether it was a diplomatic triumph or a disgrace. Our people in Chechnya were not slow to add fuel to the fire. Shamil Basaev swiftly issued a statement that Yeltsin had left Chechnya unscathed only because the president of Chechnya was being held hostage in Moscow.

Yeltsin, it transpired, had flown to Chechnya with Zavgaev in tow. That day or the next, the pro-Russian television service in Chechnya was claiming that it was only in response to persistent requests from Zavgaev that Yeltsin had felt obliged to meet up with us in some obscure location in Moscow, that Yeltsin did not regard us as genuine political opponents, and had only deigned to treat us more or less graciously as a favour to Zavgaev. All the main news media in the republic were under Zavgaev's control and we had no access to them. We had no video footage of the meeting in the Kremlin for screening on our own Ichkerian television, but then the *Zerkalo* news programme, presented by Nikolai Svanidze, came partly to the rescue. By the end of the week, after Zavgaev's vainglorious claims, Svanidze's broadcast showed millions of viewers Yeltsin having to move from his seat to sit opposite Zelimkhan Yandarbiev. It showed us succeeding in having Zavgaev removed from the negotiating table, and the Russian side being obliged to alter the entire format of the negotiations at our insistence. While we were in Moscow, media representatives were not permitted to meet us for press conferences or interviews. However, there was no blocking of the phone lines, and we took full advantage of that, calling a number of Moscow-based journalists we knew from Chechnya and telling them how the negotiations had gone and what had been agreed.

From the villa in Barvikha we were taken straight to Vnukovo, where our plane was waiting. As we approached, the Russians stood down the security cordon around the aircraft. Our troops were in place and waiting for us. We flew back to Sleptsovskaya and were again warmly welcomed by Ruslan Aushev, the president of Ingushetia, and members of his government. We spent that night in Ingushetia, accommodated in several different houses, and each of us met a lot of people who wanted to talk to us, to share our impressions of the trip to Moscow, and just to express their support. We could feel how happy the Ingush were at our political and diplomatic success, and how sincerely they empathized with their Chechen brothers.

The next day we returned to Chechnya. I was with Zelimkhan, still in that imposing Chaika. At every town and village we were met by thousands of people eager to see us. Zelimkhan spoke at these impromptu rallies, and that was how our trip to Moscow concluded. We got back safely to Makhkety and, as time passed, concluded that we had not been poisoned.

These negotiations had a huge impact, both in Chechnya, in Russia, and in the global media. Attitudes towards us changed radically. We knew we already enjoyed the sympathy and support of the Chechen population in general, but even officials of the pro-Russian administration could not conceal their consternation at Zavgaev's behaviour at the meeting in Moscow, or their contempt for his blatant lying about it as exposed by the *Zerkalo* programme.

I should mention that the main thrust of that programme was directed not at Zavgaev but at the hysterical attacks on Yeltsin from Zhirinovsky and Bryntsialov, his opponents in the presidential election. The latter excelled himself, declaring with great pathos that he had wept only twice in his life: the first time with grief when his mother died, and the second with shame when the president of Russia received in the Kremlin 'those Chechen bandits under the leadership of Yandarbiev.' Of course, others in Russia shared his sentiments, but the sympathies of an absolute majority of the Russian public were on the side of the Chechens. This was not least because, during the war, the Russian media had truthfully revealed the atrocities perpetrated in our land by the Russian Army. At the same time, the Russian public could see for themselves how rare that sort of thing was on the Chechen side.

    The Russian media had given extensive coverage to the activities of the Association of Soldiers' Mothers, following the story of Russian women who travelled to Chechnya in the hope of gaining the freedom of sons who had been taken prisoner. Everyone had seen the sympathy and compassion with which Chechens treated these selfless women, giving them food and shelter and helping them contact the Chechen commanders. From the beginning of the war we freed more than 1,000 Russian prisoners of war after intercession by the mothers, in return for an oath from the soldiers not to take up arms against the Chechen people again. With such a background, no amount of ranting from the likes of Zhirinovsky, Bryntsialov, Prokhanov or Nevzorov could take away the honour and respect the Chechen Resistance had gained in the minds of the Russian public.

VII

Reoccupying Grozny

Yeltsin plans to go ahead with his 'new elections' in Chechnya to legitimate a Russian puppet. Immediately the Russian presidential elections are over, war is resumed and it is claimed the Ichkerian government has been defeated. The Chechens reoccupy Grozny to discredit the Russian claims. Under American pressure, the Russian military are prevented from razing the city by, possibly nuclear, missile attack. General Alexander Lebed is sent to negotiate and a ceasefire agreed. Most Russian troops withdraw from Chechnya.

From early June 1996, as a continuation of the Moscow meeting, we began negotiating in Nazran with a Russian delegation headed by Stepashin and Mikhailov.

Among the participants were four deputy prime ministers of the Zavgaev administration. These were Khasan Musalatov, Vakha Sagaev, Batruddi Dzhamalkhanov, and Alani Osmaev. The Zavgaev government announced that on 16 June, the same day as the presidential election in Russia, parliamentary elections would be held in Chechnya. We talked with Zavgaev's four representatives informally and asked them not to go through with this electoral pantomime in order not to disrupt all prospect of a peaceful political settlement of the Russo-Chechen conflict, which would be the inevitable result if Zavgaev and his supporters did not abandon their plan. We told them not to hinder our efforts to reach agreement on all issues with the Russians, and that after that we would conduct a free general election in the republic. If they went ahead with the 'elections' planned for 16 June, we would consider ourselves freed from all our commitments and take commensurate countermeasures, which could mean only one thing: the resumption of full-scale hostilities.

All four of them assured us they would pass on our conditions to Zavgaev and, if he did not accept them, they would resign, with appropriate public statements. After this conversation, we signed a further agreement with the Russian side, building on the previous Moscow ceasefire agreement and, for the first time, agreed that the document should contain the 'canonical' designation of our country found in the Russian Constitution as 'the Chechen Republic,' rather than the 'rebel' designation, 'the Chechen Republic of Ichkeria.' The Russian representatives saw this as a great victory and thought they had put one over on us but, like the Zavgaevites, were unaware that Zelimkhan Yandarbiev had issued a special decree shortly before, permitting the designation in official documents of our country both as 'the Chechen Republic of Ichkeria,' and 'the Chechen Republic of NohchiCho.' At the foot of the document, the Zavgaevites were designated as representatives of the Russian Federation, and we were designated as representatives of the Chechen Republic. When Lobov read the document, he asked Zavgaev in perplexity, 'Great, but where are you if the separatists are the representatives of the Chechen Republic?'

The Zavgaevites were hung out to dry but, joking apart, by obsessing over formulations, we sometimes did more harm to ourselves than the Russian representatives did. Whenever we showed flexibility over these matters, we invariably came out on top.

Despite our warnings, Zavgaev went ahead with his sham 'elections.' The only Zavgaevite deputy prime minister who did resign was Khasan Musalatov. He contacted Aslan Maskhadov and said, 'I kept my word, and cannot answer for the other three.'

So ended this phase of our negotiations. The Russian authorities, as we had always anticipated, had not the slightest intention of honouring the agreements signed. The second round of the presidential election in Russia ended on 3 July, and on 11 July the invaders mounted an air raid on Makhkety, targeting precisely the houses we had stayed in while preparing for the Moscow negotiations. In the raid, 28 civilians were killed. That same day, Russian troops stormed the village of Gekhi.

As it happened, Dalkhan Khozhaev, Khusein Isabaev and I had left Makhkety early in the morning for Alkhan-Yurt, where our brigade headquarters was located. At ten or eleven o'clock in the morning, however, there was a Russian air raid on that village too. When we got there we heard about the assault on Gekhi and that Dokki Makhaev's brother, Alkha, had been killed in battle. I suspect that the ongoing negotiations with Russian representatives had lulled our fighters into a false sense of security and they had relaxed the measures essential to prevent a surprise attack by the invaders.

After the bombing of Makhkety and the attack on Gekhi, we decided again to terminate all contact with the Russians. It was obvious that, after a brief period of calm, the war was being resumed with no reduction in its scale and ferocity. At this point almost all our forces were based in villages around Grozny. It was now that we began to prepare Operation Jihad for the liberation of Grozny.

On 20 July 1996, Alu Gaisumov and I went to my home. My parents were grief-stricken by the death of my younger brother, and no less distressed by the death of Djohar. My mother often wept over that and said it had left all Chechnya's warriors orphaned. My father and mother knew Djohar well, because he never missed an opportunity, after the meetings we often held at my home in Urus-Martan, to spend an hour or two in their company over a cup of tea, chatting with them about this and that. No matter what rumours our enemies spread about Djohar, for my parents he remained a Chechen *K"onakh*, a knight of honour and true national leader. They loved and respected him deeply. We spent two hours with my parents, and my younger sister videoed our family evening together. It is the only recording made of my father during his life.

I had to be in Makhkety the following morning for a meeting, and before leaving I wanted to see Dalkhan, who was in Alkhan-Yurt. Alu and I went to see him. I told him about the next morning's meeting with Zelimkhan and collected from him reports for the past week from the commanders of the various units of the Presidential Special Operations Brigade. These provided all the essential information on how many men we had, the amount and type of weapons and related ammunition, reports on armed clashes and the losses on each side. This information was updated weekly by all the commanders of fronts, sectors and individual brigades, and was forwarded to the commander-in-chief, Zelimkhan Yandarbiev, and chief of staff, Aslan Maskhadov, so the Chechen leader always knew our real strength and capabilities. That was very important in the planning of joint army or regional combat operations. Our army was composed entirely of volunteers, which meant the soldiers could go home at any time on leave or even permanently, or move to another unit if they met up with friends or relatives. That was why we really needed constantly to update information on the status of every unit.

Armed with Dalkhan's reports, Alu and I travelled to Novye Atagi, and from there by a familiar route following the course of the River Vashtar to Selmen-Tauzen and on to Makhkety. At this hour of the night the coast was clear. We were well aware of the locations of the Russians' permanent checkpoints in our republic and how to get round them. As regards mobile checkpoints, they usually set these up after 8 am, so we always moved at night or in the early morning. The occupation troops were duped by their own propaganda. They kept telling themselves and the Russian public that the war in Chechnya was over and, as one Russian political analyst quite rightly commented, 'the difference between the Chechen Resistance and the Russian Army was that the Russian soldiers felt they were doing a job, while the Chechens were fighting a war.' War has its own rules. There is no time off in war, no weekend, no slavish adherence to procedure and tidy timetables.

By 5.00 am we were at Dubi-Evl, and went on from there to Makhkety, where we found Said-Khusein Tazabaev in the house of our friends. He had been wounded a month earlier while travelling on a commission for me. The occupiers knew many of the routes we used, including the one along the Vashtar, and sometimes mines were laid there by traitors collaborating with them. They were few in the First War, but they did exist. One of these mines was tripped by the car in which Said-Khusein was travelling. We had left him in Makhkety to be treated, and our friends there brought a good doctor to see him. He met us now, fit and ready for combat. Said-Khusein told us the commanders from nearly every part of Chechnya had assembled in Makhkety.

This truly was to prove a historic meeting, and the decisions taken decided the outcome of the war, although, of course, there was no knowing that at the time. We discussed the actions we could take if Russia went ahead with its planned elections to a sham 'Chechen parliament.' It was the first of a series of meetings which led to the August 1996 operation to liberate Grozny.

As we anticipated, in tandem with the presidential election in Russia, whose first round was held on 16 June 1996, Zavgaev and his administration staged their own charade of elections to a so-called 'parliament of the Chechen Republic,' reporting to their masters in Moscow that 'in accordance with the Constitution of the Russian Federation, all governmental institutions in the republic are fully functioning and constitutional order has been restored.' No less ceremoniously, they went on to announce that in Chechnya 'the war is over, with only 40 outlaws at loose in the mountains, but these brigands are incapable of significantly influencing the situation in Chechnya and cannot turn back the wheel of history.' Such was the rhetoric and bombast of Mr Zavgaev.

In Russia, the first round of the presidential election was declared to have been successfully completed, and a second round was scheduled for 3 July. After this, Aslan Maskhadov convened a new meeting in Dubi-Evl to discuss the major military operation we were planning. If the first meeting had been attended not only by high-ranking commanders, but also mid-level commanders, participation in the second was restricted to commanders of fronts and directions. It was at this second meeting that we began elaborating a specific plan of action, calculating our forces and resources, assigning responsibilities for the forthcoming operation, and considering organizational aspects.

After all present had spoken and agreed on the need for Operation Jihad, Ruslan Gelaev stood up and, to everyone's surprise, stated that, in his opinion, the operation would not be successful and seemed little better than a gamble. Bearing responsibility before the Almighty for the soldiers under his command on the Southwestern Front, he was not prepared to take part in it. At just this time, active combat operations were under way in Shatoy region in the direction of Barzoy, under the command of Balavdi Beloev. The occupation troops had attempted to seize Barzoy with one mechanized infantry regiment. The village was protected by Balavdi's fighters, who not only fought off all attacks but mounted a spirited counter-attack and surrounded the regiment. Our latest reports were that Balavdi was negotiating with the encircled troops, offering to spare their lives if they laid down their weapons and surrendered. Ruslan Gelaev had come to our meeting directly from the vicinity of Barzoy. He stated his intention of forming all the forces of the front into a single fist and moving them up to Barzoy. He proposed an alternative plan to our meeting's participants: to focus all our efforts on the Shatoy region and move forward from there, liberating one village after another, to Grozny, eventually driving the enemy out of the republic.

This, of course, was Gelaev's personal view, and we could see he believed he was right. Nevertheless, all the other participants, including Vakha Arsanov, Shamil Basaev, Aslanbek Ismailov, Nurdi Bazhiev and the others, including me, were unequivocally in favour of the Grozny operation. We agreed that Gelaev would apply his forces to fighting in the Shatoy region, and all other forces would participate in the operation to liberate Grozny. There was no question of its being cancelled. Gelaev left the meeting for Shatoy, and we got down to discussing organizational matters. Shamil Basaev was given overall responsibility for the operation, and Aslanbek Ismailov was appointed chief of staff for planning it. From that moment preparing the operation was our first priority.

At the same meeting it was agreed that, in order to minimize possible casualties among the civilian population, we should give the residents of Grozny advance warning of their city's impending liberation. A communiqué was drafted and approved. Needless to say, it did not give the exact date of the operation, but warned that it was imminent. Residents of Grozny were requested to leave the capital before fighting began and to take shelter for the time being with their families in the villages and regional centres of the republic. A second communiqué was addressed to officers in the pro-Russian Chechen police. They were asked to resign in good time from their positions and join the Chechen troops, or to disperse to their homes. If the Chechen policemen were unwilling to do so, they were advised that our fighters would not use arms against them unless they opened fire first. It was the Russian occupying troops, not they, who were our target as an army.

Around 20 July, our activists began distributing leaflets with these requests around the city. Rumours immediately began circulating throughout the republic about the operation we were planning, and the rumours were even more effective than the leaflets. From a variety sources, we received intelligence that the Russian troops, the Russian Legation in Chechnya under Lobov, Zavgaev's administration, and indeed virtually everybody else in Chechnya, were aware of the proposed action.

The communiqué produced exactly the psychological impact on the enemy we had been hoping for. The invaders and their adherents were expecting us to attack Grozny at any time, and we kept them on the hook for over two weeks. Without waiting for us to attack, they instigated their own counter-propaganda, assuring people on the local television that the Chechen Resistance lacked the forces for any halfways serious local military operation, let alone for capturing Grozny. General Tikhomirov, head of the Russian military presence in Chechnya, departed for Moscow. It was unclear whether he was going on vacation or leaving for good. He was replaced by General Pulikovsky as acting commander. General Tikhomirov was known as a hawk and had publicly stated that in the course of his period in command 'an end will be put to the Chechen outlaws.' His departure indicated to us that the invader and Zavgaevites really did believe there would be no attack on Grozny. By the time we approved the final date for the operation, the night of 5 August, the enemy had already tired of waiting and was caught off guard. I was commanding the Presidential Special Operations Brigade and was to take control of the same area as during the March operation. Naturally, before the operation started we thoroughly reconnoitred the part of town where we were to operate. We knew the deployment of the Russian units, approximately how numerous they were, their military procedures, transportation routes and weaponry: all the things you need to know about an enemy before you strike. All the other commanders studied the districts where they were to operate with the same degree of meticulousness. We had had plenty of time to do this.

On 3 August, I met Aslan Maskhadov and his deputy, Islam Khalimov. Aslan asked me, 'What do you think, should we perhaps cancel this operation? Maybe Gelaev is right after all? If the operation fails, people may become disillusioned with us and we might lose the last forces we have.'

I responded that our task, as I saw it, was to do what needed to be done, and what would be would be. Everything is subject to the will of Allah.

'My view is that we have no option. This is our only opportunity to turn the tide. Even if we all die, the operation will have been a victory. Even if we have not prevailed over the enemy, we will not have submitted. We will have passed on the baton to future generations, for those who continue the struggle.'

Aslan said that was his opinion too, and that he had just wanted to make sure our views coincided.

The decision was taken and Aslan asked me to pass on written orders to the commanders on my direction who were involved in the operation. Islam Khalimov handed them to me. From the commanders' reports which Aslan had received, we should be able to count on over 1,300 fighters. With those numbers, we decided to liberate our capital in an operation which, as it transpired, proved crucial to the outcome of the war. We talked through all the details. Precisely at midnight on 5 August, all the commanders were to report to headquarters that they were ready. The codeword was 'Subhan'Allah' ('Glory be to Allah!'). The next stage, as we were approaching Grozny, was to be notified using the code word 'Alkhamdulillah' ('Praise be to God!'). And at 5:30 am we were to indicate combat readiness with the words, 'Allahu Akbar' ('God is Great!').

The units directly under my command were in a number of villages in the vicinity of Grozny. At the time appointed, we advanced towards the city along the previously designated routes. Khusein Isabaev, my deputy in the brigade, entered Grozny from the direction of District 12. The soldiers under his command had been billeted in Goyty and Novye Atagi. I entered Grozny with the rest of the brigade, who had been in Alkhan-Yurt, Yermolovka, and Kulary, by way of Chernorechiye, following the same route as during the March operation. At 5.30 am, all the brigade's units were in place, ready to start fighting. Bislan, the head of our reconnaissance unit operating in Chernorechiye, informed me that at precisely 6.00 am each morning two armoured personnel carriers with soldiers left the compound and drove to fetch water from the spring between Chernorechiye and Okruzhnaya. We should wait for these APCs to emerge before opening fire. Listening in on my walkie-talkie to commanders' reports, I knew that only Vakha Arsanov's units had managed to reach their positions by 5:30. They were operating in Staropromyslovsky region. Vakha's soldiers had already engaged the enemy. In our part of the city, however, and in the centre all was silence. It was clear that many of our forces had not entered the city limits on time. I contacted Khusein and then went to visit his fighters, to decide on the spot where they should take up and reinforce positions. When I drove into Aldy, I could see that Khusein had lost no time in setting his people to work digging trenches. The task of consolidating our positions was in full swing. The troops commanded by Shamil Basaev, Aslanbek Ismailov and other units advancing on Grozny from the east, from the direction of Shali, Makhkety, and Vedeno, were to enter Grozny from Aldy along a corridor held by us. Khusein reported that these units had not yet appeared.

Taking in the situation, I decided we could well afford to wait for those two APCs to leave their compound. According to Bislan, they usually had 30 soldiers perched on the armour or inside. Although the enemy must surely have known from radio reports that fighting had broken out in Staropromyslovsky, as if they had not a care in the world the APCs drove out of the gates of their compound at their usual hour and headed at speed for the spring. I do not know whether the soldiers in the command post had decided that clashes on the far side of town were no concern of theirs, or whether they were blindly following orders, but before I relate what happened to them, let me say a few words about the Russian command post in Chernorechiye.

During our March operation, the Russian command post had been to the left of the entrance to the village, in an infant school. After that fighting, however, the occupation troops had moved it to the right-hand side, into one of the abandoned boarding houses on the shore of the Grozny reservoir, popularly known as 'the Sea of Grozny.' This had doubtless been done to prevent the post being surrounded again, as had happened in March. Now it was protected from the rear by an expanse of water, which made defending it much easier. The building itself was protected on three sides by trenches and barriers of concrete blocks and barbed wire. It had been turned into a fortress and driving the enemy out would have been nearly impossible, but luckily that was not our aim. We needed only to seal these fortified sites, keeping the soldiers holed up inside by small arms fire. We could not resist the temptation, however, to get our hands on those two APCs, so I gave the order to hold fire until they left the compound.

Battle commenced just as I was returning to Chernorechiye from my inspection of Khusein Isabaev's positions in Aldy, and everything happened before my eyes. Khanpash ambushed and began shelling the armoured vehicles. One was was put out of action immediately, the surviving soldiers lying on the ground and shooting back. I and Alu, my driver and bodyguard, found ourselves to the rear of them. Alu jumped out of our vehicle, fired a grenade launcher at the enemy, and then opened fire with a machine gun. The other APC raced across the dyke of the reservoir before suddenly swerving and taking to the water. It was evidently amphibious and the soldiers were hoping to get back to the command post that way. Our soldiers fired several grenades and the armoured vehicle sank. Later that day we managed to pull it out and recovered worthwhile arms and ammunition. Our boys joked afterwards that it was the first time in Chechen history we had had simultaneously to fight a land and 'sea' battle.

The battle was no sooner over than Khusein radioed to say that the columns of soldiers led by Shamil Basaev and Aslanbek Ismailov had appeared in Aldy. Alu and I turned and went back there. It was an impressive sight, the first time I had seen so many Chechen fighters in one place. Our men were marching, weighed down with arms and ammunition, with the barrels of grenade launchers rising up above their shoulders. Heavily laden trucks and jeeps were driving slowly along. In one of them sat Shamil Basaev, Abu Movsaev, and the Little and Big Aslanbeks. We stood and talked for five minutes and I learned where Shamil was going to locate his headquarters. They could delay no longer, because it was already light and they had yet to take up their positions in the city centre and dig in.

As soon as the column of fighters began entering Aldy, the local elders assembled to ask Khusein to withdraw to save the village from being attacked, but seeing the scale of the forces advancing on Grozny, they silently turned and went home, recognizing that major events were in train and their petitioning would be futile.

And indeed large-scale fighting was already taking place in Grozny. The troops commanded by Ruslan Alikhadzhiev, Islam Khalimov, and Magomed Khatuev had begun the assault on Zavgaev's 'Government House' and other 'government' buildings in the very heart of Grozny. Some overzealous officials of the Zavgaev administration had come to work early and found themselves in an unenviable predicament. Others fortunate enough to be late for work that day turned round and hastily left the city. As we know from radio intercepts, there was complete panic, even hysteria, among Russian units in the city. For example, we heard radio communications between the Russian No. 6 checkpoint and Grozny Commandant's Office (call signs 'Radius' and '800'), in which the office responded to desperate requests for help, 'Unable to assist.' This was followed by some suggestions: 'Now under cover of darkness, kidnap a couple of Chechen families. Announce you have hostages. Using them as a shield, remain in your building. Establish a defensive perimeter. I recommend this last option.' There was, however, no hostage-taking. The checkpoint responded, 'This lot...' (referring to the Chechen fighters surrounding the checkpoint), '... the ones in this area don't give a stuff about Chechens or non-Chechens. It is us they are after. They are not going to fall for that... we will find... solution... thanks for all the help.'

In Chernorechiye, after the destruction of the two APCs, the fighting subsided, but the following day we had a very unpleasant surprise. The occupiers we had blockaded in the command post did not immediately resign themselves to the situation and attempted to regain the initiative. Before the start of the August operation, there had been a change of personnel in the Chernorechiye command post. Russian Ministry of the Interior Troops were replaced by a large Special Operations Unit transferred from Vladikavkaz. This may have been prompted by the leaflets we had distributed in Grozny. Whatever the cause, we found ourselves confronting a strong, audacious and well-trained enemy.

From our signals intelligence we gathered that the occupiers trapped in the command post were preparing a group to break out of the boarding house and seize a two-storey building on the main road through the village. After the March operation, when we destroyed the old command post, the occupiers had established a temporary post in this two-storey building, later moving on to the boarding house. Our information now was that they intended to seize the abandoned building and gain a vantage point from which to cut off our movement along the village's main thoroughfare and to be able to fire on the surrounding territory. Their plan was also to move a large group of troops into the city from the vicinity of Achkhoy-Martan, where they were occupying land known locally as the Field of Kulikovo. The enemy was evidently unaware that I had taken the precaution of blocking the Rostov-Baku Highway with two detachments, one of which had taken up a position where the Chernorechiye Forest began, while the other was at the fork in the highway which led to Grozny.

Despite this, occupying that two-storey building would give the enemy a major tactical advantage in the area for which my brigade was responsible. The house was in a district under the control of Ramzan Tsakaev's unit, and I warned him of the information we had, so that he could prepare a fitting welcome for the enemy's assault group. Unfortunately, Ramzan did not given this information the priority it deserved, and during the night the Russian Special Forces occupied the building unopposed. At the morning General Staff meeting (and we held daily morning and evening Staff meetings), Ramzan, looking rather shamefaced, admitted the enemy's assault team was now in the previous command post, adding defensively that he had 'never expected such daring from Russians.' It really had been audacious, and created a major headache for us. They had jeopardized our control of the village and were now to our rear. It was a classic illustration of the consequences of underestimating an enemy.

At that meeting we decided to expel the enemy from the building at whatever cost. To check the situation, I took a few fighters and went there with Ramzan. We reached it within ten minutes. The Special Operations troops were firing from the windows in all directions and it was plain that, under cover of all this shooting, they were consolidating their position in the building and intended to stay there for an extended period. Two five-storey blocks were end on to the two-storey house. I asked Ramzan whether the residents had left and he said there was almost no one living there, other than people sheltering in the cellars. The buildings had been occupied by his fighters to curtail any further movement by the enemy, but I pointed out that it was unlikely they would try to move deeper into the village. It was much more important for them to control the main road through the village. If we did not get them out of the building then, under cover of fire from their group, the enemy might try to occupy more houses along the road. Ramzan agreed, and added that that would enable them to control the main road from the edge of the forest to the dam itself, which was our link with Khusein Isabaev's division in Aldy.

Under fire from the Russians, we skipped into one of the five-storey blocks and considered how best to storm the occupied building. Our plan was that six machine-gunners, three from each of the five-storey buildings, would open incessant fire on the windows of the old command post. Two grenade launchers would be fired at the main entrance of the building to unblock it. Under cover of machine-gun fire, eight fighters would immediately storm it and occupy the ground floor, clearing it of the enemy with hand grenades. Simultaneously, the stairs leading to the first floor would be controlled by gunfire. The Russian troops on the first floor would then be invited to lay down their arms and surrender. The whole operation was to take no more than three minutes.

I am glad to say it went exactly as planned. Our assault group suffered no casualties, dead or wounded. Securing the ground floor, our fighters blocked the stairs. The enemy lost ten or so soldiers, and seven chose to surrender. The remainder holed up on the first floor and rejected our offer to lay down their arms.

I gave orders not to storm the first floor in order to avoid needless losses, and had to be very insistent about this because Musa Khaddzhimuradov, exhilarated by the recent fighting, kept demanding that I should allow them to storm the first floor too. He had just turned 17 and was the youngest fighter in our brigade. I did my utmost to shield him from harm but had little success, because in every battle Musa would pile into the thick of the fighting. He was fearless and would happily take on a much stronger opponent without giving a thought to the possible consequences.

I was introduced to him long before the August operation by Alu Gaisumov, a neighbour of Musa's in Chernorechiye. He was actively involved in the March Operation, both in preparing and fighting in it. During that operation too Chernorechiye was part of my zone of responsibility, and Musa with his detailed knowledge of his native village and its surroundings gave us much valuable assistance with intelligence. When he became a fully fledged member of the brigade, he gave up smoking, learned to perform namaz and, with his selfless bravery and openness became everyone's favourite. Needless to say, he was the first to volunteer to attack the building occupied by the Russian special troops, and I had to restrain him from attacking the first floor on his own. It was obvious that the enemy's plan to dominate the road had failed, and no less obvious that the remnants of the group, ensconced on the first floor, would either surrender within a day or two or try to break out at night and get back across the road to their colleagues in the boarding house. I told Ramzan to get his men to keep the first-floor windows in their sights, but we have to give the Russian troops their due: under a hail of bullets from our fighters, they began jumping down from the first-floor windows and, firing back, fought their way across the road to their own side. In the process, several of them were killed and they had to leave behind all their ammunition. We also got our hands on the latest model of an infantry gun and a large fixed radio station. From the radio it was clear that the troops had been planning to hold the building for a long time. In order not to tempt fate again, I ordered our fighters to occupy all buildings along the road in groups of two or three and so the episode was brought to a conclusion. We exchanged six prisoners for hostages held by the invader in Municipal Hospital No. 9. As regards the seventh prisoner, he decided to remain in Ramzan Tsakaev's division to teach our men how to operate the captured gun. When the war was over, he went home to Vladikavkaz but, we later heard, a few days after his return was found murdered.

As well as Chernorechiye, my area of responsibility included Voykova, which also had a Russian command post, beside a bridge across the Sunzha. On this direction Arbi Baraev's unit was active, as was a jamaat attached to my brigade for the duration of the operation. These two detachments occupied a chemical factory, and shelled the command post, pinning down the Russian soldiers manning it. Isa Munaev, who was to proceed through the Zavodskoy region to Okruzhnaya, reported that he had occupied the Zavodskoy police headquarters, where no resistance had been offered. Across the street was another Russian command post which Isa's fighters had blockaded. They were firing at it at close range. Fighting was intense throughout the city.

We had no doctors or nurses in our ranks, so we needed to identify a hospital to which, if necessary, we could bring our own and any civilian wounded. I drove out to Okruzhnaya to the Ministry of Railways' hospital and met the duty doctor and nurses. The medical director of the hospital was not there, and I told them that if they wished to leave the city we would ensure their safe passage, but would be very grateful if they did their professional duty by staying to help the wounded. The doctor asked for five minutes to consult his colleagues and enable each doctor and nurse to make their own decision. A few minutes later he returned to say they would all stay in the hospital and carry out their duties. I noted down their names, and later all these men and women were honoured with state awards. We now had a hospital where wounded fighters and Grozny residents could receive medical care.

When I emerged, I heard the sound of fierce fighting coming from the Okruzhnaya bus station. Two APCs with soldiers riding outside on the armour had been sent from Khankala to Chernorechiye to relieve the command post we had blockaded. Finding that they could not get through, the invader's troops had decided to break through past the chemical factory to the Voykova command post. They had evidently been in radio contact with the soldiers pinned down there and had been told they would be able to break through to them. They were sadly mistaken. Our fighters almost immediately put both APCs out of action with grenade launchers, and fierce hand-to-hand fighting followed, using not only firearms but also knives and daggers. It was soon over. By the time I arrived on the scene the several dozen Russian soldiers and officers had been killed. One burnt-out APC had stopped right next to the steps at the entrance to the chemical factory and the second was smouldering a short distance away. One Chechen lad died in the melee, a civilian. Seeing the fighting, he piled in on the side of our soldiers. His shirt was ripped off, leaving him in his vest like many of the Russian soldiers. In the confusion one of our fighters accidentally shot him. We had later to negotiate with his relatives, who were intent on finding out whose unit had been involved in the battle at the bus station and who exactly had fired the shot. After establishing all the details, they were planning to declare a blood feud against our fighter. We managed to nip this conflict in the bud, explaining to the dead boy's relatives that it had been a tragic accident and that their young man's death had not resulted from malice. They were honourable people, accepted our explanation, and renounced their right to vengeance.

At about noon, Khusein Isabaev radioed to say that helicopters had appeared over his territory. By then I was back in Chernorechiye, accompanied by Alu, Adam, and my namesake, Akhmed. We took a shortcut across the dam to Aldy and drove from there to District 12. By the time we arrived, our fighters had already shot down three helicopters, and in the course of the fighting we shot down two more. This was a huge success, because we had no heavy or specialized weapons to use against air targets. The helicopters were shot down mainly by machine-gun fire. The downed aircraft were immediately stripped of their S–8 cluster rockets, which the pilots had not had time to fire. We took this valuable booty back to our positions, and sent some to the city centre for the fighters assaulting the complex of 'government' buildings as well as the KGB/FSK/FSB building and central command post. Our soldiers learned to fire these missiles using pipes of the requisite diameter, or even just off sheets of slate, which the enemy found very disconcerting. They knew we had no heavy weaponry, were not expecting to be subjected to missile bombardment, immediately discontinued active operations and went purely on the defensive.

That first day of the operation, the fighting continued unabated throughout the city until nightfall. On the second day, we unexpectedly discovered that our strength had increased many times over, because spontaneous military units converged on Grozny from all directions. These were not part of our army or under CRI control. We called them 'Redskins.' These people chose their opponents, fought for as long as they felt like it, and might then just go back home. It was the purest guerrilla warfare. In addition to the Redskins, other units began arriving in Grozny which, for one reason or another, had not been included in the operation but were nevertheless under the command of the CRI Armed Forces.

On the second day, an infamous ultimatum was issued by General Pulikovsky, giving the Chechen units 48 hours to withdraw from Grozny and threatening otherwise to transform the city into 'a volcano crater' using massive air and artillery power. Statements were also made by Stepashin and

Mikhailov, who it transpired, were currently in Chechnya. They threatened Zelimkhan Yandarbiev and Aslan Maskhadov that the whole negotiation process would be called off and all prospects of a political settlement of the conflict torpedoed if Chechen forces were not immediately withdrawn from Grozny. Zavgaev, cowering in the main Russian military base at Khankala, claimed on television that he and the Russian troops had the situation in Chechnya 'completely under control,' although at that very moment the building of his 'government' was ablaze and his officials had either fled or were hiding in the cellars.

On the third day of the operation our ranks began to thin again. Heeding General Pulikovsky's ultimatum, the Redskins began pulling out. This exodus caused panic among the residents of Grozny, who misunderstood the situation and thought it was our forces being withdrawn. Columns of many thousands of residents also began leaving Grozny, mainly through Chernorechiye towards the south and through Staraya Sunzha to the north, by way of Microregion 6.

I remember that when I returned to Chernorechiye that day I encountered a vast column of cars with refugees clogged in a hopeless traffic jam. Driving forward, I found that Musa Dadaev from Zakan-Yurt and several fighters from the Presidential Guard had set up an impromptu roadblock to check the refugees' ID. I asked him what they were doing and he said they were pulling collaborators out of the column. I ordered them to clear the road immediately and let everyone pass without hindrance. They were greatly puzzled by this, as they genuinely thought they were engaged in important and valuable work for the state. At that moment, however, mortar strikes were taking place all over the city, and if a shell landed in the midst of this crowd of refugees there could be terrible casualties. Musa called off his fighters, and the traffic jam cleared within 20 minutes.

Many people came to ask us if we were going to leave the city after a few days of fighting, like during the March Operation. We told them very unambiguously that we would not be leaving Grozny. 'Either the occupying forces will leave or we will die here.' People did not doubt our resolve to fight to the last, and hastily evacuated children, women and the elderly. Adult men stayed behind to secure their homes and property. By the end of Day Three of the operation, almost all the Redskin units had left, along with most of the civilian population.

Meanwhile, General Lebed flew to Chechnya and stated that he did not know anyone with the authority to order turning Grozny into a volcano crater. We learned that the United States had reacted very sharply to General

Pulikovsky's ultimatum, stating that it was out of the question to subject a city in which there were still tens of thousands of civilians to massive bombing and shelling. I believe General Lebed's disowning of Pulikovsky's ultimatum came precisely because Moscow had taken note of the position of the United States. General Lebed went on to declare that it was time to stop talking about volcanoes and get on with ending the war. It became known that he had met Aslan Maskhadov in Novye Atagi and they had agreed a ceasefire, to start from 20.00 hours on 11 August.

A number of criminal groups took advantage of our operation in Grozny to help themselves to other people's property. In that respect, we found General Pulikovsky's ultimatum very useful, because it caused all these gangs to flee. When the city was clear of them, we ordered our units not to allow any of these freelance squads back in, from the date the armistice agreement came into effect. An exception was made for Redskins who were willing to be incorporated into our official military institutions and observe strict military discipline. This was implemented, with the result that my brigade was augmented with a number of new units and strengthened considerably. I know the same thing occurred on other directions. Lists of fighters were drawn up, duty details assigned to the various areas, and patrols were formed with orders to strictly prevent any form of looting. After the ceasefire, the city was wholly under the control of our forces. Russian troops were still pinned down all over Grozny.

On the afternoon of 10 August, I heard that the 'Werewolf' Special Operations Group of the Angara Interior Troops Regiment had surrounded and stormed Municipal Hospital No. 9 and taken hostage the entire medical staff, patients and visitors to the hospital. Here is how the incident was described by Russian human rights activist, Alexander Cherkasov:

> The medical staff had a firm agreement with the belligerent parties that neither side would enter the territory or interfere with the functioning of the hospital. The Chechen commander stationed next to the hospital gave this undertaking and they did not intrude. Russian soldiers, however, entered the hospital and demanded that insurgents should be surrendered to them. They put the young nurses against a wall, alleging that shots had been fired at their group from the hospital. Using the medical staff as human shields, the group searched the hospital, the attic, the basement, but found no one. When the Russian special troops went out into the courtyard, a shot rang out and the commander of the group was seriously wounded in the hip. The doctors and a nurse took the wounded man into

the hospital and attended to his wound. The soldiers contacted their headquarters by radio and were informed, 'We are unable to assist. Hold out to the last man.' The special troops then took up defensive positions in the hospital building, establishing firing points on each of the floors, closing and booby-trapping the doors, and declaring, 'Nobody leaves.'

There were some 90 medical staff in the hospital, around 300 sick or wounded patients, and about 100 relatives looking after them, including some 20 children. The commander of the group gave the Chechens an ultimatum: 'If you allow us to leave without firing a single shot, we will do so.' The Chechens agreed to give them that opportunity, but the soldiers dragged matters out until evening, when they said they had received orders not to leave, and if the Chechens opened fire or attempted to storm the building, they would kill hostages by throwing grenades into the basement where the patients were located. The Russian Army terrorists regularly contacted their headquarters by radio and were ordered not to leave the hospital, to which Russian soldiers were being drawn up in small groups from buildings in the surrounding area. The Russian terrorists' commanders refused to release even women, children and patients able to walk, asserting to the doctors that this could be decided only by the commander of the regiment. The deputy medical director was permitted to walk to the driving school to talk to him. The commander agreed only to allow 50 women and children to leave the hospital.

On 12 August, Russian soldiers tried to break through from the territory of the driving school towards the hospital but were repulsed by Chechen forces. The soldiers who had seized the hospital then resumed negotiations on the conditions for their release. The commander of the Chechen detachment met one of the commanders of the soldiers entrenched in the hospital. Several nurses and doctors were used as a human shield for the latter. The Russian agreed to withdraw his men, but demanded security guarantees. The deputy medical director repeated his earlier proposal that the hostages should voluntarily provide the soldiers with a human shield and accompany them all the way to their destination. At 15.00 or 16.00 hours on 12 August, agreement was reached, and both parties promised in future neither to occupy nor to shell the hospital. The Russian terrorists left the building, surrounding themselves with a human shield of 100 volunteer hostages, and when they reached the main force in the driving school the hostages were released. When the members of the human shield returned to the hospital and the medical staff were preparing patients for evacuation to the premises of the International Red Cross, mortars were fired at the hospital and one nurse was killed. Two other nurses, two doctors and one female patient were wounded.

I would only add that, as mentioned, we too were involved in freeing hostages taken by the Russian Special Operations troops. We exchanged six of the prisoners of war captured in the old Chernorechiye command post for hostages.

As agreed, on 11 August the two sides ceased fire, and from that day serious Russo-Chechen negotiations began. This time I was not involved, and we only received orders, on the basis of which we could deduce what had been agreed.

Finally, in Atagi an armistice agreement was signed which included the establishment of joint command posts and disengagement of the two sides. This last point meant that the Russian troops we had holed up were able to withdraw to their two main military bases in Chechnya, in Khankala and at Sheikh Mansur Airport, which the enemy called 'North' Airport. Prior to the signing of these agreements, Russian troops had made repeated attempts to break through into the city to relieve the units we had surrounded. There were also attempts by besieged Russian troops to fight their way out of the city, but these were all thwarted by our fighters. Mindful of these enemy actions, we kept some of our divisions outside the city in positions where they could control the main highways into Grozny.

The two units of my brigade posted on our southern direction to cover the Rostov-Baku Highway and the fork to Grozny frustrated an attempt by a major force of Russian troops to break in from the south to Chernorechiye to rescue the troops pinned down there. The enemy, after losing several armoured vehicles, thought better of repeating the attempt and dug in under cover of the forest near the fork. As for the troops besieged in the Chernorechiye boarding house, after the failure of their foray into the old command post they became quiescent. There were similar situations in many other areas in August 1996 as Aslan Maskhadov and General Lebed signed their Accord in Khasavyurt for a ceasefire and disengagement.

Russian ultra-nationalists later accused Lebed of having 'handed the city over to the Chechen rebels,' claiming that the Russian troops had had the men and capacity to turn the tide in their favour. To these charges, Lebed rightly responded that he had, on the contrary, saved Russia from the public humiliation of the spectacle of columns of thousands of Russian prisoners of war passing in a 'parade of dishonour' through the streets of Grozny in full view of the world, as during the Second World War columns of German prisoners of war had been paraded through the streets of Moscow.

That really was the way everything was going, because the Russian troops in Grozny were completely demoralized. It was only a matter of a few days before they would have surrendered. After the armistice agreements were signed, Ruslan Gelaev's units entered the city, and that too made a great impression, graphically demonstrating to everyone that the CRI Armed Forces had not only the units directly involved in the operation to liberate Grozny, but also powerful reserves. It had an important psychological effect on both the Chechen population, for whom it was further proof that we had no intention of withdrawing from Grozny, and on the Russian forces, increasing their demoralization. General Lebed, by signing the Atagi Agreements, did indeed save his country's army from ignominy, because Russian troops, although they left Grozny under a white flag and escorted by our fighters, left bearing their arms. For me it was, nevertheless, a magnificent and unforgettable sight. In the four centuries of Russo-Chechen military conflict, this was the first time such vast numbers of Russian troops bearing white flags had filed past Chechen fighters.

Everyone was elated. As people heard of the agreement to establish joint command posts and disengage troops, they began returning to Grozny. It was a feeling we may never experience again, that intense, heady savour of victory, that gradual release of the soul from the inhuman stress associated with the war, even though at that moment we were by no means certain that it was all over. Like many of our compatriots, I had prayed to Almighty Allah to grant us the victory, and He had answered our prayers. No matter how the destiny of the national liberation struggle of the Chechen people might develop in the years to come, we had known the taste of victory, hard won, gained at the cost of many sacrifices which could never fully be recompensed, but nonetheless joyous and longed for. Many probably remember the extraordinary changes this sense of victory effected in people. No one was any longer feuding with anyone else, people forgave old grudges, and the unity of our people in its striving to build its own, independent state was suddenly a reality.

VIII

After the Khasavyurt Accord

Zakaev leads the Chechen team negotiating with Lebed, who had been instrumental in saving Yeltsin during the August 1991 coup attempt. Lebed's career. He is seen as a likely successor to Yeltsin and a supporter of a peaceful solution to the Chechen problem. The Ichkerian government is effectively in control of the country. Lebed and the Chechen chief of the General Staff, Aslan Maskhadov, develop friendly relations and are seen as presidents-in-waiting. A smear campaign in 1996 claims Lebed was planning a coup d'etat with Chechen support. Yeltsin dismisses him from all posts. It is the first step in a long-term plan by the Russian intelligence agencies to take over the Russian state.

When our troops were withdrawn from Grozny, I met Zelimkhan Yandarbiev in Novye Atagi. The headquarters of the president of the CRI was at that time located in a private house. After retiring as commander of the Presidential Special Operations Brigade, I continued to perform my duties as minister of culture and presidential aide on national security. There were many matters I needed to discuss with Zelimkhan in connection with the new political situation, particularly because we were facing numerous institutional changes. Under our agreements with the Russians, a coalition government was being formed. Aslan Maskhadov, chief of the General Staff of the CRI Armed Forces and head of the government delegation for negotiating with Russia, had been appointed chairman of the Cabinet of Ministers of the CRI. At our meeting, Zelimkhan informed me he had signed a decree establishing the composition of the new government delegation, and that I had been appointed to lead it.

A round of talks was shortly to be held, and our delegation needed to agree with the Russian side a draft joint declaration by CRI President Zelimkhan Yandarbiev and Russian Prime Minister Viktor Chernomyrdin on the need to establish a joint commission. This was being set up on the basis of the accords signed by the parties on 31 August 1996 in Khasavyurt.

Zelimkhan told me the Russian delegation, headed by General Lebed, would arrive in Chechnya within the next few days, so I needed to convene our own delegation as a matter of urgency. Its composition was little changed, except for the absence of Aslan Maskhadov and Said-Khasan Abumuslimov, who had been appointed CRI vice-president. Their new status meant it was no longer appropriate for them to be ranking members of the negotiating team. In spite of that, we discussed all the issues with them and all decisions were collegiate.

Tim Guldimann remained in charge of the OSCE Mission in the republic, and knew of the changes in our negotiating team. As leader of the Chechen delegation I was now in regular contact with him, and we met often to discuss current issues. He told me the Russian side, including General Lebed, was reluctant to continue working with him. This was the situation in the second half of September 1996 at the first meeting between Alexander Lebed and myself as leaders of the two delegations. It took place in Novye Atagi, in the home of Rizwan Lorsanov.

Before this meeting, I had seen Lebed only on television. He had been prominent since the period of Perestroika. I knew a lot about him, but set about learning more after he appeared as the main protagonist on the Russian political scene for settling the 'Chechen problem.' I found it interesting to spend time in his company, and the better I got to know Lebed, the more I felt it was entirely predictable that he should be the individual to turn up in Chechnya with authority to resolve the conflict. As we later discovered, he had had extensive experience of carrying out what he himself described as 'certain missions' in conflict hot spots. During and after Perestroika, his involvement in these missions was much less as a peacemaker than as a punitive strongman. To understand his behaviour in Chechnya at this dramatic turning point, we need to understand the man. Dr Elisabeth Heresh wrote about him in detail in her book.

In Russia, desperately starved of heroes, General Lebed's popularity grew by leaps and bounds. Commander of the 14th Army in Transnistria, a big, broad-shouldered man with blue eyes and a powerful, metallic voice, Alexander Lebed was a very colourful personality. He was one of those officers whose mere physical appearance make a great impression on Russians. The Russian people were seeking an alternative to both the discredited grey, faceless Party functionaries of the Communist era and the 'democratic' leaders, who differed from them only in their more blatant rhetoric.[3]

Alexander Lebed had been a participant in the Afghan War. Describing his experiences there, he remarked to me that waging war is a very dirty job. He said his service in Afghanistan radically altered his attitude towards the Communist regime and the entire Soviet state system. He called that war a senseless political gamble which was the beginning of the end for the Soviet Union.

In late July 1982, Lebed was wounded and returned from Afghanistan. The same year he began studying at the Military Academy, graduating in 1985. His career continued to advance and soon he was put in command of a division which, on 21 December 1988, was sent to Baku, the capital of Azerbaijan.

On 20 February 1988, the Council of People's Deputies of the Nagorno-Karabakh Autonomous region, which is part of Azerbaijan but populated mainly by Armenians, passed a resolution to secede from Azerbaijan. The Karabakh crisis began and continues to this day.

In April 1989, Alexander Lebed was sent in to Tbilisi, the capital of Georgia, where local intellectuals demonstrated in support of calls by the Confederation of Caucasian Peoples for the republic to secede from the USSR. On 9 April there were mass student demonstrations in Tbilisi in favour of Georgian political independence, and it was to crush these that he was sent there at the head of a regiment of his parachute division. The protesters greeted the appearance of the soldiers with shouts of 'Pigs' and 'Invaders.' The soldiers opened fire and rushed in to disperse the protestors, wielding entrenching tools. Sixteen of the protestors were killed, and four subsequently died from their wounds. Colonel Lebed claimed he had not given any order to fire, and said that if his soldiers had been shooting, it was only in self-defence.

Alexander Lebed was also involved in bloody events in January 1990 in Baku. After each deadly confrontation in the Baltic states, Baku, and Tbilisi, Mikhail Gorbachev tried to evade responsibility by issuing exactly the same statement: 'I am deeply shocked by what has happened, as I was not informed in advance.' He appointed a commission to investigate each incident and find the culprit. Lebed told me it became obvious to him that he might be used as a sacrificial pawn in the Kremlin's chess games.

---

[3] E. Kheresh, *General Lebed,'* Rostov on Don: Feniks, 1998. Elisabeth Heresch, *Alexander Lebed: Krieg oder Friede*, Munich: Langen Müller, 1997. I am indebted in these pages to Dr Heresch for the thoroughness of her fact-finding.

Elizabeth Heresch writes that on 17 August 1991 General Lebed received orders from the commander of airborne forces, Lieutenant General Pavel Grachev, to bring the Tula airborne division to full combat readiness 'for the southern option.' The southern option was code for sending troops to the Caucasus. The order stated that General Lebed should await further instructions on where exactly his division was to be deployed. On 19 August he received new orders from the Airborne Troops headquarters to proceed to the Supreme Soviet building, better known as the White House.

Lebed carried out these orders to the letter. Later, General Alexander Korzhakov, Chief of Personal Security of the Russian President, came to tell him Yeltsin wanted to talk to him. Shortly after, Lebed found himself in Yeltsin's office and heard from him what was going on. Yeltsin said that, on the night of 18 August, a 'State Emergency Committee' had been formed in the Kremlin which included USSR Vice-President Gennadiy Yanaev, USSR Prime Minister Valentin Pavlov, USSR Minister of Defence Dmitry Yazov, KGB Chairman Vladimir Kryuchkov, USSR Minister of the Interior Boris Pugo and a number of others. Lebed was told that Yeltsin had created a staff headquarters to oppose the coup and was in constant telephone contact with the heads of foreign states. After giving this briefing, Yeltsin asked Lebed straight out if he was prepared to join him in defending the White House and Russian democracy, or at least to give an assurance that his soldiers would not fire on the defenders of the White House.

In reply, Lebed confidently stated that his soldiers would shoot only under orders, and that he would not give them any such order. He added that he trained his soldiers to shoot at enemies, and that he did not regard the defenders of the White House as enemies. His men were not mercenaries, they were soldiers, sons of the people. He was prepared to defend the White House, but in order to move soldiers and hardware up to the building through the crowds, the protesters would need to have it explained to them that the soldiers were no threat to them. After that, Yeltsin went out to Lebed's troops and said, 'Soldiers! I believe that at this tragic hour in Russia's destiny you will take the right decision. The honour of the Russian Army must not be stained by the blood of our citizens.' I need specifically to emphasize that Lebed said his troops would not fire at their own people, and that Yeltsin said the honour of the Russian Army must not be stained by the blood of 'our citizens,' so that my readers may better understand the actions of those same soldiers in Georgia, Azerbaijan, the Baltic states, and subsequently in Chechnya. We need to be in no doubt as to who, for Lebed as for Yeltsin, was 'us' and who was 'them' in the USSR, which at that time still existed, and later in the 'territories of the former USSR.'

Lebed was well aware that siding with the people might lead him to outright disobedience of the orders of his superiors, if they were to issue instructions to storm the White House. Fortunately, however, as he put it, he received no orders from his superiors at that time. It remains an open question, of course, how he would have acted if he had.

Elizabeth Heresch writes that, that same day, Lebed was summoned by the USSR minister of defence, Dmitry Yazov. Lebed reported on the situation to Yazov, and concluded by commenting that any precipitate action by troops could lead to numerous casualties and unforeseeable consequences. Yazov listened, and then instructed Lebed to prepare a plan for taking the White House. Lebed produced the plan within ten minutes but, in response to a direct order to storm the White House, again expressed concern that such an action would lead to numerous civilian casualties. Despite this protracted toying with his superiors, Lebed did carry out one order: he gave the White House security teams an ultimatum to disarm immediately, threatening otherwise to launch an attack within the next few hours. The assault did not take place because the commander of the Alpha Special Forces unit refused to take part in it.

By the evening of 21 August it was clear that the coup had failed. Two days later, Gorbachev, 'the Captive of Phoros,' arrived back in Moscow. Events then developed rapidly. On 8 December 1991 Russia, Ukraine and Belarus jointly formed the Commonwealth of Independent States (the CIS). On 21 December they were joined by eight former Soviet republics, although Georgia, Lithuania, Latvia, and Estonia refused to join. The Chechen Republic declared its willingness to join the CIS, but Moscow categorically rejected the proposal.

On 25 December 1991, all institutions of the USSR ceased to function and Russia, as the successor state to the USSR, became a member of the United Nations Security Council. It vetoed the issue of recognition of the Chechen Republic when other union republics became members of the United Nations. For Lebed, as someone who had grown up inside the imperial system, the collapse of the USSR was a defeat and he made no bones about it. He recalled it ruefully, and told me in conversation that if the Soviet Union had not collapsed there would have been no Russo-Chechen War.

In June 1992, Yeltsin appointed Lebed commander of the 14th Army stationed in Tiraspol, the capital of Transnistria. During Perestroika, Moldova, like all the other union republics of the USSR, declared itself a sovereign state and stated that its top political priority was reunification with Romania. Transnistria too declared itself independent and announced that it was seceding from Moldova. The Moldovan government demanded withdrawal of the 14th Army from its territory, citing Paragraph 15 of the 1992 Helsinki Declaration under which interstate relations should exclude such Cold War practices as stationing foreign troops on the territory of independent states. Chisinau drew an analogy with the Baltic Republics from which, on the basis of this paragraph, Russian troops had been withdrawn. The government of Transnistria countered this with a statement that it saw the presence of the 14th Army on its territory as a guarantee of stability and security.

On 19 June 1992 the Moldovan government appealed to the UN for help, and Moldovan troops launched a military operation in Transnistria which was the beginning of a civil war. On 21 June Moscow ordered the 14th Army to intervene, and on 23 June Lebed was sent to Transnistria to resolve the conflict. He effectively terminated the Moldovan Army offensive with artillery strikes against their units, which were preparing to storm Tiraspol and retake Transnistria. On 9 July, the Moldovan president, Mircea Snegur, and the Russian president, Boris Yeltsin, signed an agreement for the peaceful settlement of the Transnistrian conflict which, amongst other things, provided for withdrawal of the 14th Army. In September of that year, Yeltsin promoted Lebed to the rank of lieutenant general in recognition of his services to Russia.

Referring to the Agreement, the Moldovan government called for the withdrawal of the 14th Army to be speeded up, and the Russian government confirmed that, in accordance with the Agreement, Russian troops would be withdrawn from Transnistria. General Lebed was strongly opposed to this, taking the view that withdrawing the 14th Army would adversely affect stability in the region.

Meanwhile, the political environment was changing. The outbreak of war in Chechnya, the conflict with Moldova over Transnistria, and with Georgia over the situation in Abkhazia and South Ossetia were jeopardizing Russia's move to join the Council of Europe. Moscow was obliged to declare a number of peace initiatives, hence the Russo-Moldovan Agreement on withdrawal of Russian troops from Transnistria. Lebed returned to Moscow and addressed the State Duma, stating that after withdrawal of the 14th Army Moldova would 'look like Chechnya,' where a bloody war was being waged. Following his speech, the Duma voted against ratifying the withdrawal agreement, and declared Transnistria a region of geostrategic importance to Russia. The deputies later advised Yeltsin to recognize the independence of Transnistria, establish diplomatic relations, and incorporate it in the CIS.

Pavel Grachev issued an order to restructure the 14th Army in accordance with the withdrawal agreement, which Lebed resisted. Grachev offered Lebed several other posts, but he refused them and, on 30 May 1995, tendered his resignation. The final decision rested with Yeltsin, who vacillated. Yeltsin's political nous told him that Lebed's resignation could further boost the general's popularity, and that in the next year's presidential election he could be serious competition. Only on 14 June did the Yeltsin administration report that General Lebed had tendered his resignation as commander of the 14th Army, and that Yeltsin had accepted it.

After resigning, Lebed began to concentrate on politics. On 11 January 1996, he officially announced his candidacy for the Russian presidency. He was quick off the mark in recognizing that Chechnya could be advantageous to his election campaign. In his speeches he focused on two major themes: strict discipline must be reimposed on the country, and the war in Chechnya must be brought to an end. He met with businessman Boris Berezovsky, who was working at Yeltsin's campaign headquarters and offered his support. This was seen as a move to draw votes away from Gennadiy Zyuganov and the Communists, which would help Yeltsin to be re-elected.

The Russian presidential election was held on 16 June 1996 with an almost 70% voter turnout. Yeltsin gained 35%, Zyuganov 32% and Lebed 14.5% of the vote. The second round of voting was scheduled for 3 July, and on 17 June Yeltsin signed two decrees. In one he appointed Lebed secretary of the Russian Security Council, and in the other appointed him presidential aide for national security. On 10 August, after the start of Operation Jihad in Grozny, Yeltsin appointed Lebed his representative in the Chechen Republic, and from then on Lebed dedicated himself to resolving the Russo-Chechen conflict.

Our work with Lebed was just beginning. Working with him was much less onerous than with his predecessor, Vyacheslav Mikhailov. Lebed did not have a history of crimes committed in Chechnya. He spoke openly about them, and criticized the Russian government for ever allowing the war to begin. During our first meeting, we agreed the main points of a joint statement. We also agreed that there would be a meeting between Prime Minister Viktor Chernomyrdin and President Zelimkhan Yandarbiev on 3 October 1996 in the Hall of International Negotiations at the White House in Moscow. It was plain that the highest level of the Russian government had decided to continue the peace process from where it had left off.

I never forgot what was said immediately after the signing of the Khasavyurt Accord by Vladimir Lukin, at that time chairman of the Russian Duma's Foreign Relations Committee. He was a member of the Russian delegation at the talks, and when Said-Khasan Abumuslimov, the CRI vice-president, approached him to express his pleasure at the signing of the agreement, Lukin said literally, 'Don't worry. In five or seven years' time Russia will be strong again, and will then remember who was a friend and who was the enemy.'

One day, during an informal meeting with Lebed, I asked him how he felt about Lukin's remark. We were having dinner at the time in the home of Rizwan Lorsanov in Atagi. Lebed answered frankly, 'Unfortunately, colleague, not only Lukin and Yavlinsky are thinking this way, but also very many leaders of parties, independent politicians, businessmen, government officials, and, needless to say, the military. In other words, everyone who has any connection with government. That is why everybody in Russia considers me a traitor.'

Anatoly Kulikov, the Russian minister of the interior, had indeed publicly accused Lebed of treason. All Russia's politicians and officials considered the Khasavyurt Accord a 'betrayal of Russia.' Even certain Russian oligarchs who had made their billions during the military operations in Chechnya were baffled as to why Lebed had stopped the war. They publicly expressed their indignation that he had allowed 'humiliation of the Russian Army' and accepted an agreement so 'shameful for Russia.'

As an example, Alexander Lebed told me of a discussion he had had during one of his meetings with Boris Berezovsky. Berezovsky had enquired what his thoughts were about Chechnya and what he was planning to do about the problem. Recognizing Chechen independence, Berezovsky believed, would lead to the disintegration of Russia, which he considered unacceptable. Lebed replied that by 2001 he would have eaten Chechnya for breakfast and resolved all the problems associated with it.

I understood why Lebed was being so open with me. He was trying to get me and the rest of the Chechen team to put our trust in him and his policies. He really needed our support to achieve his goal, which was to become president of Russia. Yeltsin was seriously ill, and the recent election race seemed finally to have undermined his health. When somebody asked him about the state of Yeltsin's health, Lebed replied that Yeltsin today was like Brezhnev in the 1980s. Asked by Germany's *Der Spiegel* whether he saw himself becoming president in the 2000 election, Lebed replied, 'Perhaps much sooner.'

How did the Chechens give support to Lebed? The Chechen leaders first tried to avoid public displays of euphoria over our victory in the war, in order not to stir up needless hatred of Lebed on the part of Russian ultra-nationalists. At Lebed's request, we refrained from organizing a military parade on 6 September 1996 to mark the fifth anniversary of Chechen Independence. On that day, we confined ourselves to commemoration of those who had lost their lives. President Yandarbiev appealed to the Chechen population for universal mutual forgiveness and reconciliation. A decree was signed and published extending an amnesty to all who had collaborated with the occupation regime but were not personally guilty of bloodshed. Aslan Maskhadov and General Lebed received an invitation from Ernst Muehlemann, chairman of the Commission on Chechnya, to speak at the opening of the autumn session of the Parliamentary Assembly of the Council of Europe about the peace process in Chechnya. The Russian government protested about this, fearing that it could lead to recognition of the Chechen Republic. Maskhadov and Lebed accepted the invitation, but at Lebed's request, Maskhadov then declined to go to Strasbourg, in order not to give opponents of the peace process in Chechnya additional grounds for attacking Lebed.

I am sure Lebed knew we received intelligence about everything happening in Moscow in government circles, including information about secret meetings in the security agencies. I was perfectly aware that, after the defeat of Russian troops on 6 August and before signing the Khasavyurt Accord, Lebed as secretary of the Russian Security Council, had tasked the military leaders with compiling a plan and submitting a proposal to create a legion 50,000 strong. At a meeting with the military he said, 'If the Chechen Army is associated with wolves, Russia needs to prepare 50,000 wolfhounds to deal with these wolves.' The legion was to be established at breakneck speed, with one week for the decision to be taken, one week to form it, and one month for combat training. There was no response from the Ministry of Defence or the Ministry of the Interior, and only after Lebed put them under intense pressure did he receive a reply signed by the chief of the General Staff, General Kolesnikov, and chief of staff of the Interior Troops, Lieutenant General Maslov, to the effect that the earliest the brigades could be operational was late 1999.

Being familiar with the hierarchy in the Russian security agencies, I knew for certain that the ultimatum from Acting Commander of the Joint Group of Forces in Chechnya General Pulikovsky, in which he threatened to turn Grozny into the crater of a volcano, which was released to the media on

9 August 1996, must have been agreed with Lebed. It was Lebed testing the response to an escalation of violence in Chechnya not only of Russian society, but primarily of the West. It all demonstrated that these peace initiatives from the Russian side were being forced out of them and were purely temporary. For that reason, I did my utmost to speed up the peace process. We needed to move on from the format of joint commissions and joint command posts to contractual agreements between the two governments and their agencies. During our meetings, I pressed on Lebed the need to dismantle the joint command posts.

That concept had been relevant and effective while our troops were being disengaged, but by now it was obvious that continuing with them was becoming risky. There had been clashes between Chechen fighters and Russian soldiers. Lebed's idea of using only military units which had not participated in hostilities in Chechnya was feasible only for the Russian side. The Chechen Armed Forces simply did not have anybody in them who had not participated in the war, or suffered at the hands of the Russian Army. The wounds inflicted were too fresh, and it was impossible to compel Chechen fighters to feel friendly towards Russian soldiers. They did not accept all the rules and regulations which Russian soldiers lived by. In Russia, soldiers were drafted into the army, but in Chechnya the fighters were volunteers who came to the defence of their Fatherland. There was a huge gulf between them.

I was frequently in the Central Command offices where Aslanbek Ismailov was the CRI's joint commandant with General Ovchinnikov. As soon as I entered the checkpoint, I could see the relationship between the Russian soldiers and Chechen fighters who had to work together. The Chechens made no attempt to hide their sense of superiority, or their contempt for the Russian soldiers who were obsequious towards their superiors in a way that was totally alien to our fighters. There was a broadcast on Russian television which graphically illustrated everything I was telling Lebed about the joint command posts. The reporter interviewed a Russian soldier who complained, To the Chechens we are occupying troops who have been defeated. They look down on us. They regard us as less than human, as fascists who destroyed their towns and villages and murdered their relatives. I really do not know what we are supposed to be doing here. What sort of friendship can there be? What sort of working together? They treat us like stray dogs. They do not even call us by our own names. 'Hey, Fido, over here!'

Another incident occurred while I was visiting Aslanbek Ismailov. According to the rota, the CRI commandant was on duty that day. (Under the agreement, the Chechen and Russian commandants were on duty on alternate days.) The headquarters was located in the city centre, at the Dynamo football stadium. I was in the staff room when a report was radioed in to Aslanbek from Khankala:

'Comrade General, in the vicinity of Duba-Yurt unidentified armed men are obstructing a column of Interior Troops.'

'Well, what is a column of Interior Troops doing in the vicinity of Duba-Yurt?' Aslanbek enquired.

'It is a planned move in preparation for troop withdrawal in accordance with the agreements with the Chechen side,' came the reply.

'Why have I not been informed of this movement?' Aslanbek demanded, raising his voice. 'Why has it not been agreed with us? Are you deliberately trying to provoke a conflict? Haven't you had enough fighting?'

'No way, Sir, Comrade General!' the officer in Khankala squealed.

'No way, Sir, you haven't had enough fighting or no way, Sir, you are not trying to provoke a conflict?'

'No way, Sir, we are not trying to provoke a conflict, Comrade General. We have not had any problems up till now. This unit is being temporarily deployed to Khankala.'

'Put me through to the commander of the unit,' Aslanbek ordered.

'I am unable to do so, Comrade General. It is not technically possible,' the officer responded.

'Then inform them all from me, Russians and Chechens alike, that if they do not immediately disengage, or if they start firing at each other, I'll send in an air squadron and bomb the lot of them to kingdom come!'

After this threat, Aslanbek hung up, turned to me and said, 'You know, Akhmed, throughout this war I longed to see how they would have behaved if we had had aircraft.'

At this moment, General Ovchinnikov suddenly appeared from the off-duty room. In great agitation, hastily putting on his spectacles, he asked, 'What aircraft? Where do you have air units?'

When Ovchinnikov noticed me, he became even more agitated, but greeted me correctly. He was a typical hereditary Russian officer, a neat, buttoned-up staff officer.

'It is not a matter of where I have them,' Aslanbek retorted. 'I am talking about the aircraft you and I have at our joint disposal, colleague. Or is the Russian Air Force no longer under our joint command?'

'Ah, I see,' Ovchinnikov said with obvious relief. 'I misunderstood.'

'I know,' Aslanbek retorted. 'You thought I was talking about Dudaev's Air Force.'

Then he added, 'If we had had time to create anti-aircraft defences, to train a few squadrons, the war might never have happened.'

General Ovchinnikov reflected for a moment, before agreeing.

Even at this level, between two joint commandants, there was a lack of mutual trust. We can readily imagine the situation between the private soldiers of the two armies. Citing these and other grounds, I did my best to persuade Alexander Lebed of the need to disband the joint command posts as soon as possible.

I knew the general met Aslan Maskhadov informally, and that they talked through all issues together. They developed a very close, trusting relationship, both personal and working. Aslan treated Lebed as a future president of Russia. In exactly the same way, Lebed treated Aslan as a future president of Chechnya. Each was in no doubt that, once he was president, he would be able to persuade his partner to come to the compromise political solution which they desired. Maskhadov hoped that when Lebed became president of Russia he would recognize Chechnya's independence, while Lebed hoped to persuade Maskhadov that Chechnya would be much better off staying under the umbrella of Russia, perhaps with some special status.

I was working flat out, reporting regularly to Zelimkhan Yandarbiev on how preparations for his meeting with Chernomyrdin were proceeding. At meetings of the State Defence Committee we discussed issues around forming a coalition government. Some of Zavgaev's ministers agreed to join it, although Zavgaev himself called the Khasavyurt Accord an 'ambitiously conceived deception' and refused to take any part in forming the coalition government it called for. The principle of how the Cabinet was to be set up was a formality. Our first priority was getting the law enforcement agencies staffed. Kazbek Makhashev, CRI minister of the interior, was confirmed in that post in the new government. At one of our meetings, he reported that staffing the Ministry of the Interior was 90% complete and that the Chechen militia were ready to assume their responsibilities by replacing the existing joint command posts. At the same meeting, Aslan Maskhadov, who combined his functions as prime minister with his responsibilities as chief of the General Staff, reported that more than 80,000 soldiers and commanders were now registered with the General Staff. These data related to the end of October 1996. In early August of that year, when we entered Grozny, we had had only 1,300 soldiers, so in less than two months the strength of our armed forces had increased more than sixtyfold! This was gratifying. Even after a 20-month war which had cost more than 100,000 lives, our nation was capable of mobilizing so many people. Admittedly, later, as we sought to settle the country down to life in peacetime, this presented a huge problem. At the same meeting, the issue was raised of Akhmad-haddzhi Kadyrov, mufti of the republic, and of the CRI deputy foreign minister, Yaragi Abdullaev. Mumadi Saidaev, head of operations of the General Staff, presented information to the effect that in the Soviet period both had had KGB connections. Yaragi Abdullaev was absent from the meeting, so discussion was confined to Akhmad-haddzhi Kadyrov who, according to the Operational Department, was associated with the KGB while studying at the Bukhara madrassa. Kadyrov openly admitted that it was impossible to study religion at the time without filling in a form agreeing to collaborate with the KGB. He also said that in the last 8-9 years nobody from the KGB had been in contact with him, and that he now had no ties with that institution or its shortlived successor, the Federal Counter-Intelligence Service. He added that he was prepared to swear to the truth of his words on the Qur'an. The foreign minister, Ruslan Chimaev, said they would consider the issue of Yaragi Abdullaev at the Foreign Ministry, and Mumadi Saidaev would be invited to participate.

I have to admit I was very surprised to learn that Yaragi Abdullaev had any sort of contact with the KGB. On reflection, though, I could see that, studying at the Foreign Languages Faculty of the Checheno-Ingush State University, and then defending a postgraduate thesis, Yaragi was bound to be taken in hand by the KGB. People who could speak foreign languages at a professional level no doubt did pose a potential risk for a Communist system which had fenced itself off from the rest of the world behind its infamous Iron Curtain, as they had access to far more accurate information than ordinary Soviet citizens. As for Kadyrov, Zelimkhan Yandarbiev said there was no need for him to swear on the Qur'an because he believed him already. The other participants agreed and, I have to admit, they really did believe him.

After the meeting, Zelimkhan asked a number of us to stay behind: Aslan Maskhadov, Said-Khasan Abumuslimov, Akhmad-haddzhi Kadyrov, Kazbek Makhashev, Khozh-Akhmed Yarikhanov, who had just been appointed chairman of the YuNKO Oil Company, and myself. He wanted to discuss the forthcoming visit to Moscow. The document to be signed by Yandarbiev and Chernomyrdin, Zakaev and Lebed had a very long title: 'A statement of the necessity of a Joint Commission in accordance with the principles for determining the basis of relations between the Russian Federation and the Chechen Republic signed on 31 August 1996 in Khasavyurt.' By this time, the document had been finally agreed with the Russian delegation and President Yandarbiev. Zelimkhan said he would like to discuss with us the composition of the delegation we would send to

Moscow. He added that Shamil Basaev had asked him to include two or three people involved in the Budyonnovsk Raid.

This, of course, was a very sensitive issue. The room fell silent, no one wanting to speak first. Aslan broke the silence, saying this was provocative, and at best irresponsible and completely pointless. He added that he was not prepared even to raise the issue with Lebed. Aslan continued that it was far more important now for us to resolve the issue of compensation for the damage caused in the republic and other pressing social problems. He was acutely aware that the burden of responsibility for dealing with social problems lay with him as chairman of the Cabinet of Ministers. Zelimkhan responded that he understood these concerns but, at the same time, also understood Shamil Basaev's wish to rehabilitate the young men who had risked their lives with him to put an end to the war. Many of these young people should be brought in to assist in building the Chechen state. He instanced Aslanbek Ismailov, commandant of the republic; Abu Movsaev, minister of public safety; and several others who had participated in the Budyonnovsk Raid and now held important positions in the government. He added that the sooner the Russians got used to this situation, the better for everyone.

Aslan was unmoved. 'You know the reaction of the Russian ultra-nationalists to the Khasavyurt Accord and what major problems Lebed has with them. We should not aggravate what is already a difficult situation for him.'

All present remained silent. It was one of those occasions when both sides are right. I asked Zelimkhan why he wanted us to agree this issue with the Russian side at all, and suggested, 'If we tell them we want to include participants of the Budyonnovsk Raid in our delegation it will cause a heated debate and we will never reach agreement. If we just quietly include them in the list, nobody will even question it. Providing, of course, that the list does not include Shamil Basaev himself.'

After a brief discussion, everyone agreed with that proposal.

Zelimkhan then turned to me and said he wished to congratulate me on my promotion to the military rank of colonel and the award of the Order of Pride of the Nation. He explained that he had found Djohar Dudaev's last decree in his archive, signed on 12 April 1996, conferring on me the rank of colonel and the Order of K"oman Siy for the defence of Goyskoye. He added that he would make me a gift of the original decree signed by Djohar, and keep only a copy in the archive. It was a gift I appreciated enormously. Everyone congratulated me wholeheartedly.

On this we parted. I went on to Grozny where I had an appointment with cultural workers that afternoon. In addition to political activities, I had also my duties as minister of culture to perform. In this I was greatly helped my first deputy, Makkal Sabdullaev, a poet, playwright, true Chechen, and patriot. Makkal agreed to work with me when the war was at its height. As deputy minister, he met with artistic companies and carried on political work with them. People's Artist of the CRI Birlant Ramzaeva sang many patriotic songs with lyrics by Sabdullaev, and these were very popular. Songs with his lyrics were performed also by Raisa Kakhermanova and the Zhovkhar folk music group. Our artists travelled to highland villages and performed for Chechen fighters. Their work, nominated by Makkal Sabdullaev on behalf of the Ministry of Culture, was recognized by the CRI government. By decree of President Yandarbiev many artists were awarded the title of Distinguished Artist and People's Artist of the Chechen Republic. There were others, however, who accepted similar titles from the Russian government. Thus, Dikalo Muzykaev became a Distinguished Artist of the Russian Federation, while Musa Dudaev and Dagun Omaev accepted the title of People's Artist of the Russian Federation. A number of other actors and performers accepted Russian awards. Accordingly, that afternoon of 30 September 1996, I was meeting all the artistic collectives and workers of regional departments of culture.

The meeting was held at the Manual Sports Stadium, and a very considerable number of people attended. First Makkal Sabdullaev briefed them on plans to reorganize our ministry and the organizations under its control. During the war all these institutions had worked as an integral part of the Russian Ministry of Culture, and that needed to change. It was proposed to release from their duties, while a process of re-attestation was carried out, everybody in our ministry who was in charge of state cultural institutions. An attestation commission was being set up. I trusted Makkal Sabdullaev implicitly, and appointed him to head it, satisfied that he would approach the task in a highly responsible manner. During the war, I repeatedly heard people in the arts say that they and their groups should stay outside of politics, because their mission was to preserve and revive our national culture. Taking advantage of the fact that nearly everybody active in Chechen culture was present at the meeting, I told them what I thought of the way they had acted over the past year or two. I said,

> My friends and colleagues, what many of you were engaged in during the war was no revival of culture, but aiding and abetting the occupying army in our country to destroy our national culture and our nation itself.

It was you they paraded for the whole world to see, as if in your person the Chechen people was grateful to these butchers whom you called 'liberators.' Is that what you call 'keeping art out of politics?' You were not only embroiled in politics, you were the principal political weapon in the hands of the executioners of the Chechen people. I am telling you this to disabuse you of any notion you may have that you were not complicit in the tragedy of our nation. I am telling you this so that you can truly reconsider your position. Needless to say, nobody is going to persecute you. President Zelimkhan Yandarbiev has signed a decree of amnesty for all who collaborated with the occupying forces, but you well know the history of what happened in the past in even the most democratic countries in similar circumstances. You must surely know the attitude of the nations of Europe after the Second World War to those in their midst who had shamed themselves by collaborating with an occupying regime. Nevertheless, I fully support President Yandarbiev's policy. We are a small nation which has suffered huge losses and must value the life of every individual. But we must also learn from the past in order not to make mistakes in the future.

The Chechen delegation, headed by Zelimkhan Yandarbiev, travelled on the morning of 2 October 1996 to Sleptsovskaya Airport in Ingushetia, where we were met by President Ruslan Aushev. We flew on his plane to Moscow, as provided for in the minutes of the meeting between President Yandarbiev and Russian Prime Minister Chernomyrdin. At Vnukovo Airport we were officially met by Alexander Lebed, Sergey Stepashin, and Vyacheslav Mikhailov. From the airport, our motorcade proceeded with a security service escort to Smolensk Square and the Red October Hotel which, since the days of the Soviet Union, had been used for receiving VIPs. Aslanbek Ismailov was in my car and was one of the participants in the Budyonnovsk Raid we had included in our delegation.

The next morning, Lebed came to the hotel to accompany us to the White House to meet Chernomyrdin. Aslanbek and I were again in the same car and, as we drove along, I remembered the first time I had been in the White House, in the days when it housed not the government but the Supreme Soviet of Russia.

It was 2 October 1993, exactly three years previously and just one day before the White House was shelled by tanks, watched live on television by the rest of the world. Sheykhi Khazuev and I were in Moscow and went, purely out of curiosity, to stand in the square in front of the Supreme Soviet. Then, just as a lark, we decided to see if we could get inside.

Several thousand supporters of Alexander Rutskoy and Ruslan Khasbulatov were in the square and around the White House. We made for the main entrance, stepping between the tents which were temporarily home to a wide variety of people, from down-and-outs to worthy professors and academicians. It was an overcast autumn day. People lit campfires and, to judge from their expressions and the snatches of conversation we overheard, were in no mood to compromise. The air was heavy with Russian revolutionary ardour and the spirit of rebellion. Before we could reach the main entrance, we had to negotiate a number of checkpoints manned by armed guards, a mixture of civilians and soldiers. Sheykhi had the ID of his elder brother, a former deputy of the Supreme Soviet of the Checheno-Ingush Autonomous Republic. He presented this document to anyone who wanted to check us and said we were 'a delegation from the Chechen Republic.' We were allowed through without hindrance, and at the entrance to the building the security service officials treated us with marked cordiality and conducted us to the office of Isa Alleroev, a deputy from Chechnya. We found Abdulla Bugaev in Isa's office. We greeted them, asked how things were going, and how Ruslan Khasbulatov was feeling. Sheykhi and I identified ourselves as representatives of the Chechen diaspora in Moscow and asked whether they needed any help from us. Isa thanked us but said they did not need anything; they had the situation under control. After this exchange of courtesies, Sheykhi and I left the office. None of the hundreds of worried-looking people scurrying down the corridors of the White House took the slightest notice of us, and we were free to go anywhere in the building. Sheykhi and I came upon a hall where the Supreme Soviet was in session. Occupying his chair in the praesidium was Chairman Khasbulatov, looking very tired, indeed exhausted.

Sheykhi and I were present in the chamber when Khasbulatov, on behalf of the people's deputies, proclaimed Rutskoy president of Russia. Khasbulatov invited Rutskoy to take the oath of office on the White House balcony, in front of the people gathered there to defend the Supreme Soviet. Sheykhi suggested we should find a convenient spot from which to observe this historic moment. When we came down into the hall we ran into Sazhi Umalatova, our countrywoman, who at that moment was general secretary of the Communist Party of the Soviet Union. After the collapse of the USSR, when Mikhail Gorbachev abdicated as president of the USSR and general secretary of the CPSU Central Committee, disgruntled Communists at the

USSR Congress of People's Deputies decided to elect a new general secretary, and the mantle descended on Sazhi Umalatova.

While, playing on our rights as fellow countrymen, we were chatting to Sazhi, Aman Tuleyev came up. He was chairman of the Legislative Assembly of Kemerovo province, where he later became governor. Sazhi introduced us to Tuleyev as her fellow countrymen who had come to Moscow to support Rutskoy and Khasbulatov. Tuleyev enquired about the situation in Chechnya and Sheykhi, looking suitably important, said that the situation was complex, but under control. If the conversation had gone on much longer, he might have had to explain who or what exactly he had under control in Chechnya, but we were rescued by the general secretary of the CPSU, who exclaimed that Rutskoy was going out to the balcony. She invited us to join her, and Sazhi and I hastened out there, to her subjects.

Emerging on to the balcony, her hand upraised in the manner of a Brezhnev, Sazhi greeted the toiling masses gathered below in the square, the crowd responding with a tumultuous ovation and cries of greeting. Actually, it was not entirely clear whom they were greeting, because the newly appointed president of Russia appeared on the balcony at the same time. He was surrounded by guards wearing flack jackets, as indeed he was himself, and even had an army helmet to foil any attempt at assassination by snipers for Yeltsin. Alas, it became obvious that it was Rutskoy who was in the limelight, eclipsing all the other exalted personages, and it later emerged that there had indeed been snipers lurking in the buildings round the White House.

Rutskoy repeated the words of the presidential oath, something along the lines of a vow at this crucial moment in the destiny of Russia to serve the nation and its people with might and main. The whole event struck me as worthy only of a rustic amateur dramatics society. There was, nevertheless, something sinister in the crowd below, redolent of imminent bloodshed. As I looked around, I noticed a complete absence of television or newspaper cameras. At the end of the inauguration ceremony, Sheykhi and I decided our mission in support of our fellow countrymen in the White House had been accomplished and left the building the way we had entered, telling the guards we would be sure to return.

Along with the rest of the world, we watched the subsequent events on television: the tanks firing point-blank at the seat of government; Ruslan Aushev and the Kalmyk leader, Kirsan Ilyumzhinov, entering the building for talks with the rebels; and then Khasbulatov, Rutskoy and General Makashov getting on the bus which would take them to Lefortovo Prison. Alexander Litvinenko later told me that, in the following days, more than a thousand and a half people were killed in Moscow. For days in a row, dead bodies were being collected across the capital in trucks covered with black tarpaulins.

I told Aslanbek as we drove along that, after Yeltsin had so flamboyantly bombarded the White House and killed so many people in the very centre of Moscow, I no longer doubted there would be war unless the Chechen government compromised with the Kremlin. On this October morning in 1996, I was now again on my way to the White House. We were there by eleven o'clock and met at the entrance by Sergey Stepashin. Accompanied by Lebed and Stepashin, we took the lift to the sixth floor to Chernomyrdin's reception room and office. The reception room was sumptuously decorated and fitted out with comfortable furniture. There were fresh flowers everywhere, and exotic fish swimming in aquariums. All this luxury would have given the impression of a strong, wealthy and prospering country to anyone who had never been a hundred kilometres beyond the Garden Ring Road. The members of our delegation seated themselves, or walked around the reception room admiring the decor.

Stepashin invited us to make ourselves at home and disappeared behind the massive doors leading to the next room. Keeping us waiting in this manner was not in accordance with the protocol for the meeting which I had agreed and signed with Lebed. I could see there was a hitch, and mentioned this to Zelimkhan. At that moment Lebed came back, obviously very agitated about something. He apologized to Zelimkhan and said Chernomyrdin's previous appointment had overrun by ten minutes. I took him aside and said,

'Is there a problem because we changed the composition of our delegation at the last moment?'

Lebed replied,

'No, it's just the usual Russian shambles.'

I said,

'Don't let it worry you, Alexander Ivanovich, we Chechens know we were out of luck with who colonized us.'

He laughed out loud just as Stepashin came back to invite us through to Chernomyrdin. On the way in, Stepashin asked what was so funny, and Lebed said he would tell Chernomyrdin.

We followed Zelimkhan into the enormous hall for formal meetings. Viktor Chernomyrdin came to meet Zelimkhan, and shook hands with the rest of us. As he shook hands with me, he looked very closely at my Order of the Pride of the Nation. So closely, indeed, that everybody noticed and Lebed felt obliged to explain that this was the highest award of the Chechen Republic. Chernomyrdin was followed by their invariable negotiator, Vyacheslav

Mikhailov, and several other high-ranking officials. We took our seats round the table, Zelimkhan sitting in the middle opposite Chernomyrdin and I sitting opposite Lebed. We were all officially introduced, Zelimkhan presenting the Chechen representatives and Chernomyrdin the Russian. The document to be signed had already been agreed, and accordingly, after official statements, the four of us, Yandarbiev and Chernomyrdin, Zakaev and Lebed, signed the act establishing a joint commission without further discussion. After the signing, Lebed passed on to Chernomyrdin my remark about our colonialists. Chernomyrdin responded,

'He might be right.'

After a pause, he added, to general laughter,

'Or perhaps Russia was out of luck with who we colonized.'

Overall, to use the journalistic cliche traditional in such situations, the meeting was held in a warm and friendly atmosphere. From the White House we were taken to the airport, with Lebed and Stepashin accompanying us. This was our last meeting with Lebed while he was secretary of the Russian Security Council. From 7-9 October he was in Brussels, meeting the secretary-general of NATO. Lebed urged the alliance to engage more actively in dialogue with Russia. 'The members of NATO are euphoric,' Reuters news agency reported. 'NATO sees Lebed as a leader capable of action.'

Meanwhile, however, a vicious circle was closing round him. President Yeltsin's Administration, led by Anatoly Chubais, began accusing Lebed of having started his election campaign for the presidency. Chubais's office suddenly announced they had foiled a coup Lebed was plotting. After our return from Moscow, Dmitry Rogozin, the leader of a movement called 'The International Congress of Russian Communes,' had arrived in Chechnya and met Isa Umarov and Movladi Udugov. They duly arranged meetings for him with a number Chechen commanders or, as they were increasingly being called, 'emirs of jamaats.' As later became known, during these meetings Rogozin declared that the unleashing of the Russo-Chechen War was 'all the fault of the Jews surrounding Yeltsin,' and that government of the country could only be put back in the hands of Russians by a military coup, which Lebed had decided to lead. Lebed would need the support of Chechen fighters. Isa Umarov promised to raise '1,500 mujahideen' to support Lebed. A videotape made by Udugov of Rogozin's meetings with the 'emirs' and of Isa Umarov's promises duly landed on the desk of Russia's minister of the interior, Anatoly Kulikov, whom Lebed had urged Yeltsin to fire for his involvement in the war in Chechnya.

VIII: After the Khasavyurt Accord

Chernomyrdin called an emergency meeting of the Russian government on 16 October 1996 to investigate 'the Lebed affair.' Following this, Kulikov held a press conference at which he announced, 'Prime Minister Chernomyrdin has received documents about a coup being plotted by Secretary of the Security Council Lebed.' Kulikov also declared he had irrefutable evidence that Lebed had been promised the support of 1,500 Chechen fighters to enable him to seize power in Russia. Kulikov further made reference to an article in a foreign newspaper which called Lebed 'the next Russian president.' The following day, 17 October, President Yeltsin appeared on television to read a decree dismissing Alexander Lebed from the post of secretary of the Security Council and presidential adviser on national security.

Unlike Kulikov and his numerous overt and covert enemies, Alexander Lebed was not a member of the Russian state security apparatus. Yeltsin was periodically being admitted to hospital with serious health complaints and might not survive until the next presidential election. In order to make sure General Lebed did not attain the highest office in Russia, he was removed by means of dirty tricks concocted by Russian and Chechen agents of the Lubyanka. I talked a lot to Lebed, and knew he was confident of winning the election. Lebed was no pacifist, but he was someone who could be called an honest opponent. He knew how to keep his word, and the duplicity and deceitfulness, so typical of Russian politicians, were alien to him. It was precisely this fair dealing that caused General Lebed to be inimical to those already planning to deliver Russia into the hands of the intelligence agencies. That is why Lebed, who had put a stop to the war in Chechnya, was dismissed from all his positions in the government, while the careers of Generals Kulikov and Kvashnin soared. Kvashnin became chief of the General Staff, and Kulikov remained minister of the interior and was also appointed deputy prime minister of the Russian Federation.

IX

Divide and Rule

The Russian intelligence agencies step up their activities in post-First War Chechnya, exacerbating divisions among the Chechen leaders. They arrange covert funding for rival presidential candidates. The intention of fielding a unity candidate of the Resistance in the Chechen presidential election collapses. When Aslan Maskhadov is elected, Acting President Yandarbiev hastily enacts a succession of Islamist reforms before Maskhadov's inauguration. A wave of kidnappings of pro-Chechen westerners and journalists working in Chechnya, coordinated by the Russian intelligence agencies, follows, inspiring copycat kidnappings by Chechen criminals organized and armed by Moscow, and eventually corrupting senior office-holders in the CRI government. A crime wave ensues.

It gives me no pleasure to recall how, after establishing the Joint Commission and returning from Moscow, I found palace intrigues in full swing in Chechnya too. One day when I was at work in the Ministry of Culture, 'little' Aslanbek Ismailov, 'big' Aslanbek Abukhadzhiev, and Abu Movsaev, head of the CRI Department of State Security, came to see me. This was no surprise. We often met and, after the March Operation, had developed a relationship of trust and friendship. The matter they wanted to discuss was, however, a surprise. After the exchange of greetings and the traditional mutual enquiries after family, Aslanbek Ismailov said, 'We have decided you need to be made the Chechen Reagan.'

At first I did not know what they were talking about, but then they explained they wanted to nominate me as a presidential candidate. The analogy with Reagan was a reference only to our shared acting background. I gathered from my friends that they were confident of success. I objected strongly, pointing out not only that I was not Reagan, but that Chechnya was not America. I tried to persuade them that the last thing we should do was pursue a path that could split both our own ranks and Chechen society. I said I believed Zelimkhan's decision a few months ago to nominate Aslan

Maskhadov for president was a good, wise decision and that we should do nothing to cause dissension.

Aslanbek Ismailov listened to what I had to say, before commenting, 'You must have been very tied up in your work, Akhmed, if you do not know that Zelimkhan long ago backtracked on that agreement and is planning to stand for president himself!' 'Even if this is so,' I said, 'which I find hard to believe, we should not go down that path.'

At that point I was sure we would reach agreement, as we always had before when disagreeing about particular issues. As far as the presidential election was concerned, we agreed it was vitally important to find the right, consensus-based solution. My visitors, however, were strongly opposed both to Aslan Maskhadov and Zelimkhan Yandarbiev.

Against Zelimkhan, they argued that he had facilitated a split in Chechen society. They said that ordinary people blamed Zelimkhan for turning Chechen against Chechen before the war. My friends believed that Zelimkhan's crude outbursts against the opposition had done much to undermine support for Djohar and his government, and that all the feuding had been exploited by Russia as an excuse for instigating a full-scale war against us. I totally disagreed, because it seemed to me that all that had gone wrong in Chechnya before the war was part of an ingenious and meticulously planned operation by the Russian intelligence agencies. It was carried out in a highly professional manner, using the latest developments in ethnology and information technology, and with lavish financial backing. The operation drew on a huge legacy of experience of the USSR, which had been remarkably successful in this area throughout its existence.

The gangs headed by Gantemirov, Labazanov, Avturkhanov, Suleymenov, Kelimatov and others were euphemistically referred to in the Russian media and in comments by Russian politicians and heads of the intelligence agencies as 'the political opposition to the Dudaev regime.' However, throughout the republic and in Grozny itself, overtly criminal gangs were operating which had all the latest weaponry and even armoured vehicles. For example, Ruslan Labazanov was a career criminal. His gang could appear and mount a roadblock wherever they pleased. If any passer-by dared to say anything, they were ostentatiously murdered. There was a great increase in random killings. The bodies of Chechens, Russians, or Cossacks would be discovered, murdered for no reason and without even a pretence of robbery. The aim was simply to terrorize Chechen society, and discredit the Chechen state in the eyes of international public opinion by showing it to be incapable of maintaining law and order. These murders were committed by a group headed by Adam Deniev, later revealed as a ranking KGB lieutenant colonel. As soon as Russian troops invaded Chechnya, Ruslan Labazanov, to say nothing of other gangster leaders, appeared wearing the epaulettes of a lieutenant colonel of the recently renamed Federal Counter-Intelligence Service, which left no possibility of doubt as to who was ordering him to rob and murder.

In this era of rampant gangsterism, the remnants of the old Soviet police force in Chechnya were demoralized. Some became traitors to the Chechen government. On one of the occasions when, in later years, I met Khasbulatov, he told me he saw Dudaev's authority as stemming from the fact that Djohar was the first and only Chechen general in the history of the USSR. Khasbulatov thought he could undermine Djohar's prestige by persuading Yeltsin to promote Aslakhanov and Ibrakhimov, a couple of colonels in the police force, to the rank of general. Needless to say, Djohar's authority did not suffer from this manoeuvre, but these two souped-up generals between them completely demoralized the Chechen police. Our recently formed security agencies lacked the experience to counter the devious methods of the Russian intelligence agencies. The impression successfully created was of an ineffectual Chechen government, causing widespread anxiety in Chechnya about the future.

These gangs appeared to be separate, but all deferred to the same master in Moscow, on whose orders they would meet together, as happened on 26 November 1994 and after the outbreak of war. Contrary to my friends' opinion, neither plain speaking nor tactful politeness from anyone in the Chechen government, including Zelimkhan, would have had the least impact on these gangs or their leaders, who had been unleashed by the Kremlin and were directly controlled by Russia's intelligence agencies. The majority of the Chechen population supported their elected president, and Zelimkhan Yandarbiev took most of the stick at that time.

Zelimkhan was uncompromising towards anyone disloyal to the ideal of independence, both as vice-president and as someone who had been at the forefront of the national liberation movement from the outset. He felt an obligation towards Djohar, whom he had persuaded to resign from his post as commander of a strategic aviation division in Estonia to lead the struggle of the Chechen people for freedom and independence. Zelimkhan had soberly assessed the situation at that time, and recognized that the people would not follow him or his associates in the Vainakh Democratic Party, or other leaders of unregistered public associations such as Lecha Saligov, Said-Khasan Abumuslimov, Yusuf Soslambekov, or Movladi Udugov. A leader at such a turning point of history, if he is to lead his people in a resolute but mortally dangerous struggle, must be possessed not only of the personal courage and dedication which Zelimkhan unquestionably had, but also of the kind of personal charisma possessed by Djohar. Zelimkhan knew that.

Zelimkhan had sound political instincts, and I took it as further confirmation of this when, a few months previously during negotiations in Ingushetia, Said-Khasan Abumuslimov had told me Zelimkhan was proposing that we should field Aslan Maskhadov as the sole Resistance candidate in the forthcoming presidential election. He was himself indubitably an able politician and ideologist, but not a leader who could stand at the head of the united people of Chechnya. I believed at the time he was fully aware of that. The fact that, with Djohar's death, he had become acting president, was a transitional situation, and recognized as such by Chechen society, his associates, and Zelimkhan himself. The news that he had changed his mind and decided to run for president came as a complete surprise to me.

This meant that the forces of the Chechen Resistance might split into factions. This meant that yesterday's comrades might find themselves on opposite sides of the barricades, and that could destroy all our achievements in consolidating independence. Indeed, it could lead to civil war. We were fully mindful of what happened in Afghanistan at the end of a ten-year occupation of that country by Soviet troops. Russian troops, whenever they withdrew from anywhere, left behind a legacy of bloodshed. If we failed to remain united, we might prove no exception. I said all these things to my friends, who had been tested in battle and whom I respected and trusted wholeheartedly. If anyone else had been arguing over this with me, I would have suspected they were in the pay of the Russians, but I trusted these three as I trusted myself. They tried to argue that, if elected president, Aslan Maskhadov would in any case split the Resistance because he had favourites among the commanders and was hostile to others. They had little doubt 'which side of the Argun' he would favour.

The Chechen Republic is divided geographically into eastern and western territories by the River Argun, which originates in the mountains and flows down the Argun Gorge into the River Terek. Maskhadov's ancestral village was Alleroy, in the east of the republic. During the war, Maskhadov invariably stayed on the far side of the Argun. My three friends, being from Shali, were also from that side, and would accordingly have been well aware of the situation there during the war. They failed, nevertheless, to persuade me we should support the emerging split, while I failed to persuade them we should rally round Aslan in the election. It was the first time in the past year that we parted without reaching consensus. As they were about to leave, Abu said, 'I have to tell you, Akhmed, since you will not agree to be our candidate we will nominate our Baldy.'

Baldy was their nickname for Shamil Basaev, but here they faced a problem, in that Shamil was not yet 35 years old, and our Constitution required any candidate for the presidency to be at least 35. If Shamil Basaev was to be nominated the Constitution would have to be changed. That reassured me, and I thought that in any case Shamil would not agree to stand. He would assess his chances and not want to lose. I thought too that Shamil was very pragmatic, with the ability to think like a statesman. If he became president, Chechnya would be diplomatically isolated and Russia would never accept the election result. I decided my friends would be unable to talk him round, and there would be plenty of opportunities for us to continue the discussion.

After we parted I met Dalkhan Khozhaev and we discussed this disturbing development. We decided to go and talk to Zelimkhan and find out exactly what his intentions were. We needed in any case to have a detailed discussion of the fact that Alexander Lebed had been dismissed. He was the person responsible on the Russian side for implementing the Joint Commission agreement and his removal was not only a political defeat for him, but a victory for the forces in Russia advocating a military solution to the Russo-Chechen conflict. We had no idea who Yeltsin might now appoint to take responsibility for the peace process in Chechnya, or how relations between Russia and the Chechen Republic of Ichkeria might develop. We had even been liaising with Lebed over the presidential election in Chechnya, although the OSCE Mission in Chechnya was taking care of the organizational and financial aspects. The problem was that the Mission's mandate required agreement in principle with Russia. Given the current uncertainty, it seemed an act of criminal irresponsibility for us to start wrangling about power among ourselves. Dalkhan and I saw eye to eye on these issues, and needed to talk them through with Zelimkhan Yandarbiev.

Using the internal government communication system, we learned that Zelimkhan was staying at Rizwan Lorsanov's house in Atagi. The normal telephone system had been wrecked during the war and mobile telephones did not work in the republic either, so we had to get by with an internal radio-based system set up by our communications specialists.

When we reached Atagi and turned on to the street where Rizwan lived, we noticed cars parked along its entire length. I was surprised to recognize people I had not seen since the USSR collapsed: officials from the

Council of Ministers of the Checheno-Ingush ASSR, old friends who had worked before the war in Djohar Dudaev's government, people who had worked during the war in the pro-Russian administrations of Khadzhiev and Zavgaev. Now they were all lining up to be received by Acting President Yandarbiev, whom not so long ago they had been roundly cursing. It confirmed once more, if confirmation were needed, that nothing was sacred for these people. They were devoid of honour or self-respect. Their god was their boss and their religion was money. They could corrupt anyone the least bit susceptible to their wiles. They were not coming to Zelimkhan empty-handed, and the fixer behind these meetings was a relative of Zelimkhan's, the unsinkable Idris Khamzatov.

Khamzatov had his own philosophy, and held that it was fine to take money off the likes of these unscrupulous officials. You would be punishing them after a fashion, while yourself remaining a good Muslim. As I watched them coming to 'pay their respects' to Zelimkhan, I began to see what had changed his mind. Khamzatov and his ilk had boxed him in. Hovering around him 24 hours a day, they had not only set up a profitable business but had managed to persuade him he was the only person capable of leading Chechens to a radiant future. They assured him that the people adored him, and would be dismayed if at such a crucial moment in our history he were to abdicate responsibility in favour of someone else, even someone as respected as Aslan Maskhadov. Their flattery proved effective.

Dalkhan and I had to wait over two hours before being received, but that gave us an opportunity to talk at length to Vice-President Said-Khasan Abumuslimov. He confirmed that Zelimkhan had decided to run for president. I asked whether this had been discussed with Aslan Maskhadov. Not yet, I was told, but Zelimkhan and Aslan were to meet the next day. I told Said-Khasan I knew for a fact that, almost from the moment he had told us Zelimkhan would nominate Maskhadov as our sole candidate for the presidency, Aslan had been preparing his election campaign energetically. He had assembled a team and had the support of many commanders of fronts, sectors and directions, such as Vakha Arsanov, commander of the Northern Front, Ruslan Alikhadzhiev, Turpal-Ali Atgireyev, Khunkar Israpilov, Magomed Khambiev, Apti Batalov, Dokka Umarov, Khamzat and Idris Labazanov, Islam Khalimov, all the jamaats, all the Chechen clergy, including Mufti Akhmad-haddzhi Kadyrov, and all the pro-Russian opposition in Chechnya. He even had the support of Russia. Given this situation, if Zelimkhan did not publicly repudiate his intention, he would lose the election and in the process split us into two camps, making us far more vulnerable to provocations from our enemies.

Dalkhan added that we might miss a historic opportunity to build a fully fledged, independent Chechen state, and that we must anticipate many problems with Russia in the future. Russia had not in the end recognized us, and our 'deferred status' might well turn into a deferred war. It was far more important to maintain unity among the Resistance forces and consolidate Chechen society than fret over who held the nominal title of president. All of us, including Aslan Maskhadov, were on the same side. We had nothing to hold against him because, throughout the ordeal of the war, he had shown steadfast commitment to the ideal of independence and to the Chechen people. Said-Khasan, as usual, agreed with all our arguments and gave us to understand he was on our side, but no less emphatically gave us to understand that, as a friend and comrade-in-arms of Zelimkhan, and as his vice-president, he would support him. He remained true to type and sat resolutely on the fence.

I told Said-Khasan I had no doubt Aslan Maskhadov would hold to his intention of standing, and that indeed those who had rallied round him would not allow him to do otherwise. Zelimkhan and he, Said-Khasan, would be wholly responsible for the consequences if, with their experience and understanding of politics, they went ahead and created a crisis. While the war was in progress, they had told Aslan they would nominate him as president, but now it was over and the elections were to be held, they wanted him to wait. He could only assume they did not trust him, or thought him too inexperienced to be president. None of us had any reason not to trust Aslan and, given his ambitious nature, which we were all familiar with, he was bound to feel insulted.

Our impassioned discussion was interrupted by Zelimkhan's assistant, Sultan Takalashev, who invited us to come to see the acting president. We walked across the courtyard to another house. Rizwan's home was built to a typical Chechen design, with a courtyard containing two houses, one larger and one smaller. We needed to cross from the smaller house to the larger. The courtyard was crowded with visitors and armed guards. Everybody in the yard, whether we knew them or not, came to greet us and wish us good luck. This was a time when we were very popular and respected in Chechnya. For them we were still the heroes who had defeated Russia and won our independence. Knowing the differences emerging between us, I found this thoroughly depressing. At the same time, that respect obliged me and everyone else who was aware of the likely consequences of a split to try to head off a conflict.

With these thoughts on our minds, we went into a large hall to Zelimkhan. He was standing in front of a mirror, trying on a Circassian coat, the national costume of Chechnya. We greeted him and Zelimkhan reciprocated. He was in good spirits and asked us if it suited him. Then he removed it, laid it on a table, and took a mantle like a wide cloak more usually worn by Muslim clergy. He put that on and again asked how he looked in it. Dalkhan and I watched this performance in silence and Zelimkhan, as we said nothing, had to comment on the cowl himself. 'I feel more free in this robe,' he remarked, turning in front of the mirror.

His statement was portentous. Zelimkhan was at a crossroads and had not yet decided which direction he thought we should take: whether towards building a Chechen nation state, or frittering away all we had achieved in favour of the disputations of religious demagogues. Neither we nor Zelimkhan had any profound knowledge of Islam, and his preference for the Islamic vestment with the words that there was 'more freedom' in it, proved fateful.

The Chechen national costume, severe, without needless adornment, girdled by an embossed silver belt with a dagger, draws the wearer up to full height and makes him focus. One can hardly imagine a Chechen in national dress lounging about casually or behaving heedlessly, and it is inconceivable that a Chechen in national dress could fail to comply with our *'edal* traditions, our *ghillakh* norms of behaviour, or wide-ranging *siy* code of honour. For a Chechen observant of our national standards of conduct, the way he should behave in any particular situation in life is prescribed and fixed for all time: how to greet his elders or juniors, a woman or a man, the words in which he should express grief at a funeral or joy at a wedding; how to work in time of peace and how to behave in time of war. There is no room for argument or debate when every detail of conduct in any situation which may arise is regulated by tradition, etiquette, and a code of honour. The outward expression, the visible sign that a Chechen is prepared to adhere strictly to the standards embodied in our customs is the Circassian coat, our national costume.

In a mullah's robe a person does indeed feel more free than in the austere vestment of a warrior. He can sprawl on a soft divan, indulge in casual gestures or thoughtless utterances. He can call religious truths into question by the hour, quoting theologians, but theological disputations rarely bring people to a universally agreed resolution, as witness the myriad sects and trends within the single religion of Islam. And do we not find at the founding of these sects and trends their very own theologian, most often clad in a robe analogous to the one whose voluminous folds so appealed to Zelimkhan?

Zelimkhan, alas, subsequently chose the path which allowed 'more freedom.' Any problem on which Chechen tradition gave unambiguous moral or legal guidance could be swamped by verbiage disguised as religious rhetoric. The traditional Chechen ethic was born of religion. It is my profound belief that Islam, being divine revelation, cannot contradict the nobility and human dignity in relations between people which are crystallized in our traditions. That is why for me, as unquestionably for the vast majority of my fellow countrymen, my national identity, my 'Chechenness,' never came into conflict with my Islamic identity, the religion I profess. At that point we did not yet know that we were, however, moving towards discord between nationality and religion, although we had a sense of foreboding.

Dalkhan and I wanted to talk to Zelimkhan about the issue which had brought us to him, but he would not listen. He said only, 'I respect your opinion, as you are well aware. The decision about putting forward a single candidate from the Resistance forces must, however, be taken at a meeting of the State Defence Committee, which as of now remains our principal political authority.'

Although the war was considered to have ceased upon the signing of the Khasavyurt Accord, no presidential decree had yet been issued officially rescinding the declaration of martial law, which meant that the State Defence Committee was still Chechnya's supreme governing institution, even though we already had a functioning Cabinet of Ministers headed by Aslan Maskhadov. A number of parliamentary deputies led by Akhiad Idigov had also come together to administer the country. I believed Zelimkhan was intending to introduce a number of his own supporters into the State Defence Committee in order to have the issue of nominating a single candidate for the presidency decided in his own favour. I no longer doubted that his political judgement was faltering. I told him it would be a major mistake on his part if he tried to go back on the earlier agreement in respect of Maskhadov, as Said-Khasan Abumuslimov had mentioned. I said I believed he should remain above this situation, and get the State Defence Committee to confirm the previous decision to nominate Aslan as the sole candidate from the Resistance.

I tried to get him to see that Aslan would in any case be nominated, and would agree to stand in view of the trust placed in him by his comrades-in-arms. He would see it as his duty to them and to the people of Chechnya, and a responsibility he must assume for their future. This was so obvious that it seemed difficult for anyone not to understand events would develop this way. Zelimkhan, however, exploded and in a raised voice started claiming he had never given any such undertaking about Aslan's candidacy, and that Said-Khasan had simply misunderstood him. Said-Khasan, stammering slightly as he tended to when agitated, said, 'What am I supposed to have misunderstood? What did you mean, if not that Aslan should be nominated for president, when you told me that in the elections, when they were held and if we lived to see the day, we should support Maskhadov and follow his lead? You said yourself that the entire Chechen people, including the pro-Russian opposition, would support him!'

Zelimkhan replied, 'I meant that Aslan would be suitable if we had to discuss a candidate for the presidency with the Zavgaevites. As acting president, I bear responsibility before the Almighty for everything that happens or may happen, which is why there is no way I can today just renounce my role as leader, the first person in authority.'

It was obvious that Zelimkhan had made an irrevocable decision and no longer considered us, his former comrades-in-arms, to have a voice in the matter. He was consulting quite different people. I recalled that a few days before, on his return from Moscow, he had called a meeting of the State Defence Committee to discuss one single issue: adopting in Chechnya the Sudanese penal code advocated by Shamsuddin Batukaev. On the one hand we clearly needed a criminal code of our own. We were still operating the criminal codes of the USSR and the RSFSR, to the extent that they did not conflict with Chechnya's sovereignty. I did not see this as particularly terrible and thought we could make do with them until we had devised our own penal code, as other countries in the Commonwealth of Independent States were doing. In our case, however, someone was leaning very strongly on Zelimkhan, urging him to embark on populist actions in terms of religion.

There had been a sharp exchange at that meeting between Akhmat-haddzhi Kadyrov and Zelimkhan. Kadyrov said he knew where this wind was blowing from. It was Wahhabi ideology and he knew who was behind it. If Zelimkhan continued heeding Bagauddin of Dagestan, it could lead to the shedding of blood in Chechnya over religious differences. This was effectively the beginning of a differentiation in our midst between 'traditional' and 'pure' Islam. That meeting had ended with a resolution that, after certain modifications, the Sudanese penal code would be adopted. It was decided to set up a commission to draft a new penal code for the CRI. The commission included Minister of the Interior Kazbek Makhashev, Minister of Justice Elza

Sheripova, the mufti of the republic, Akhmat-haddzhi Kadyrov, and Shamsuddin Batukaev as a scholarly *alim*.

I could not see any need at that time to be in such a hurry to decide these religious matters, in which Zelimkhan and we, his comrades-in-arms, were far from expert. Zelimkhan responded that what he most feared was his answerability to God. This was a line of argument it was difficult to counter. When he came out with it at the precise moment he had run out of other arguments, it struck me Zelimkhan liked the idea of appeals to heaven as a means of terminating debate.

We moved on to discuss the situation in Russia and the fact that Yeltsin, having sacked Alexander Lebed, had yet to appoint anyone to replace him. Zelimkhan said we would continue the peace process, which was irreversible, that we had made a point of not commenting on the abrupt dismissal of Lebed as the central figure in the peace negotiations to demonstrate that we regarded it as a domestic issue of Russia. One thing we were agreed on was that Yeltsin had made a political decision to end the war, and that it made no difference to us which individual we continued to pursue the peace negotiations with. We also concluded that our agreement with Russia to hold presidential and parliamentary elections in Chechnya on the basis of the 1992 Constitution of the Chechen Republic of Ichkeria was an extremely important political step forward for us. That was true, although the achievement was tarnished by our emerging disagreements. We said goodbye to Zelimkhan. As we left, Dalkhan said he would go to see his mother and might stay with her overnight. She lived in Atagi. I went back to the city with Alu Gaisumov and the others accompanying me. I saw only too clearly that a new phase in relationships within the Resistance was beginnng.

A short time later, Aslanbek Ismailov, Aslanbek Abukhadzhiev, Abu Movsaev and some of their supporters met Akhiad Idigov, the speaker of parliament, and insisted he should call a meeting of deputies to change the article in the Constitution which delimited the age of presidential candidates. I later heard Aslanbek Ismailov claim they had paid Akhiad 20,000 dollars 'in support of parliament.' Akhiad persuaded the deputies who were in the republic at the time of the need to change the Constitution and they duly did so. Shamil Basaev then officially announced he would run for president, and from then on all the internal dissension we had managed to keep private became common knowledge throughout the republic. For the couple of months until the elections were over, nearly everyone in the republic tried to persuade the candidates to unite and put forward one agreed candidate.

X

Excluding the European Union

Ivan Rybkin, a moderate, replaces Lebed and negotiations resume. The Russians are determined to exclude the Organization for Security and Cooperation in Europe from mediation between Russia and Chechnya.

On 21 October 1996 the Russian media reported that Ivan Rybkin had been appointed secretary of the Russian Security Council. The appointment of the ex-chairman of the Russian State Duma signalled that President Yeltsin and Russia's top leaders were staying with their current policy on Chechnya. Rybkin was a professor with a degree in technology and a doctorate in political science, and seemed clearly not to be a hawk. He had previously sent an appeal to the Constitutional Court of the Russian Federation challenging the constitutionality of Boris Yeltsin's decrees of 23 and 25 August 1991 dissolving the Communist Party after the coup attempt. In September of that year, he wrote to Yeltsin asking him to suspend the decrees pending a ruling by the court.

At that time, Rybkin was seen as a social democrat hostile to both the extreme left- and extreme right-wing parties and associations. He evidently believed Russia's many problems could be solved only in a society at peace with itself and pursuing national reconciliation. Ivan Rybkin was in favour of sensible state regulation of the economy, and believed the former Soviet republics needed to be reintegrated on a new federal or confederal basis. He saw the Commonwealth of Independent States as a step in the direction of such reintegration, with priority given to human rights over the rights of the various nations and states. Aslan Maskhadov announced Rybkin's appointment as secretary of the Russian Security Council and presidential envoy to Chechnya at a meeting of the Cabinet of Ministers. After the business of the meeting was over, Aslan asked Khozh-Akhmed Yarikhanov, Movladi Udugov, Kazbek Makhashev and me to come to his office. There he told us he had had a meeting with Ruslan Aushev, and that Russian officials wanted to propose to us, through the president of Ingushetia, that we should meet informally in Aushev's country residence, without participation of members of the OSCE Mission in Chechnya.

When Aslan invited our comments, I reminded him that the Russian representatives while Alexander Lebed was in charge had been keen to minimize the role of the OSCE mission in our relations with them. Despite all the fits and starts, Russia's negotiators had a consistent position in respect of the Chechen problem. They wanted our dialogue, our process of negotiation, free of intermediaries or international institutions. The fact that the OSCE Mission had from the outset been an active mediator in negotiations clearly vexed Moscow. When the Russian leaders decided to engage in direct political dialogue, the OSCE Mission was an obstruction because it could, when necessary, ensure the implementation of bilateral agreements. That, of course, was the last thing Russia wanted. I told Aslan the Kremlin was doing everything in its power to isolate us from the international community and, in particular, to keep us away from the institutions of Europe. I reminded him and my colleagues of his decision not to go to Strasbourg for the opening of the autumn session of PACE, to which, together with Lebed, he had been invited to talk about the peace process in Chechnya.

Maskhadov did not like that, and said he did not think it had been a mistake. He would do the same today. He added that resolving our republic's social problems, which was what the Chechen people expected of him, was far more important than any politicking. Strasbourg would not pay any pensions or benefits to Chechens, and we could look only to Russia for solutions to our economic problems.

'I know,' Aslan continued, 'why I was put in charge of resolving the republic's social welfare problems. The intention was that I should break my back on them, fail, and lose face.'

We could see that Aslan was referring to Zelimkhan, who had appointed him chairman of the Cabinet of Ministers, responsible for the most intractable economic and social problems of a republic devastated by war. 'But,' he added, 'I intend to disappoint my so-called friends!'

Aslan said this so vehemently that continuing the discussion might have reduced our conversation to personalities. Out of respect for his age and merits, I refrained from pursuing the topic. I said I stood by my opinion and deeply believed that working together with international institutions was not politicking but vital if we were to succeed in establishing an independent state.

As often before, Khozh-Akhmed Yarikhanov defused the situation by ticking me off for straying from the subject. We were not discussing a trip to New York to meet the UN secretary-general but to Ingushetia to meet

Ruslan Aushev and our Russian colleagues. We all agreed that the meeting could do no harm and might, indeed, prove useful. In drawing our own meeting to a close, Aslan said in a conciliatory tone that he shared my concern about the OSCE, adding that he had no doubt at all that the organization would continue to be present in Chechnya at least until the presidential election. He also said he would agree the matter of our trip to Ingushetia with Zelimkhan Yandarbiev.

After the meeting, Movladi Udugov said he would like to come back with me to my office at the Ministry of Culture. When we got there he said he had come to snoop around and ask if I could lend him an office as he currently had nowhere to work. His problem was that, under Zavgaev, the Ministry of Information and the Press had been located at 'Government House,' which was burned down during the fighting in August. Nearly all our ministries were in the same predicament. Even Aslan Maskhadov's government was tucked away in the managerial offices of the Terek Furniture Factory. The presidential residence was being readied in the vicinity of Terek, in a building on Karpinsky Kurgan, but the building work was still in progress. Zelimkhan Yandarbiev's entire administrative apparatus was housed in Atagi in the home of a local businessman, and Zelimkhan conducted official meetings and received visitors also in Atagi, at Rizwan Lorsanov's house. In this respect I had been relatively lucky. The Zavgaev government's Ministry of Culture even before the August Operation had been housed in the premises of the Armed Forces Cadets Association at the Manual Sports Stadium. This building had been almost unscathed during the fighting and my ministry 'inherited' it when the Ichkerian government institutions relocated to Grozny.

I promised Movladi I would try to free up a room for his office. He thanked me and said one room would be quite sufficient and he would only stay until a suitable alternative building could be found for his ministry. Then Movladi moved on to what I took to be the main issue he wanted to discuss. He said he was going to run for president and asked me to stand as his vice-president. He went on to say that the Islamic Renaissance, all the jamaats and Islamic regiments commanded by Islam Khalimov, Isa Umarov and Supian Abdullaev had decided to support the election of Aslan Maskhadov, but they had reliable information that Zelimkhan would try to talk Shamil Basaev and Aslan out of running for office. Zelimkhan's plan was to make use of authoritative elders who had lost several sons in the war, people like Lecha Makhaev of Gekhi, three of whose sons had been killed. It was thought that at the meeting Shamil might agree to stand down on condition that Aslan did the same. In such a situation, Aslan would have little option, unless he wanted to be stigmatized as a person who, in pursuit of power, had chosen to ignore the request of worthy and respected members of society. That could lose him a vast number of votes among those who supported Chechen independence. Even if he went on to win, he would no longer be the universally recognized leader of the nation.

Accordingly, Aslan's campaign headquarters had decided to take the heat off him by having several more candidates nominated for the presidency, so preventing Zelimkhan's supporters from being able to accuse him of being the person mainly responsible for sowing dissension in the ranks of the Resistance. He, Movladi, was one such candidate. If I would join him, he thought we would be a strong team and might even gain something out of it politically. I categorically rejected the suggestion, to which Movladi responded, with a sigh, that it was a pity we were not yet ready for serious political competition. I asked Movladi if Zelimkhan knew yet that he had gone over to Aslan's camp. He said no, not yet, and I said, 'Movladi, what you are doing is not serious political competition but a serious political mistake. If we continue down this road, ultimately the only people to benefit from our intrigues will be the people occupying the Kremlin.'

Movladi said, 'Well, Akhmed, what else can we do in the present situation? We have no voice, all we can do is take one side or the other. Perhaps in the end everything will turn out better than we think. In any case, if we go into the elections with just one candidate, people will complain it was uncontested and undemocratic.'

This was clearly disingenuous, because Movladi knew very well that the election would be contested and that at least ten candidates for the presidency would be registered. I told him as much, and said I felt strongly that we must prevent Zelimkhan and Aslan from causing a split and compel them to take the right decision. If all the members of the State Defence Committee took a common position on the matter, they would have to reconsider. For my own part, I said, it mattered little whether Zelimkhan or Aslan became president. What mattered most was to maintain unity in our ranks. Movladi nodded, as if taking in my arguments, but then said, 'You are right, of course. The only trouble is that there are now three contenders: Zelimkhan, Aslan and Shamil.'

It seemed clear that at this early stage Shamil and his supporters could still be persuaded not to contest the election. Zelimkhan and Aslan were the main contenders, and this was already having a negative effect on the relationship between the Resistance fighters and other supporters of independence. At this time, events were being held throughout the republic which were attended by large numbers of people. Rituals with sacrifices and distribution of the meat to the needy were being performed in memory of those who had died in the Jihad, and traditional steles (*'hollam'*) were being erected on their graves. Like other ministers and commanders, I often took part in these commemorations and it was impossible not to notice how concerned people were about the way things were going in the republic. The main questions they asked were about the elections. How would they affect our future relations with Russia? Which of the candidates had a serious prospect of winning, and would they serve the people well? Would the nomination of several candidates cause division and destroy our unity?

There were also many questions asked about Djohar Dudaev. Rumours were being persistently spread to the effect that he was still alive and had gone abroad for a time, either to be treated for his injuries or to persuade the international community to recognize our independence. It was asserted that, during his absence, Djohar had appointed Zelimkhan to act for him 'because he had most trust in Zelimkhan,' and that when Djohar returned Zelimkhan would cede the presidency to him. Every time I took part in events of this kind, I had to refute these rumours. I told the people that, unhappily, Djohar really had been killed, that he had been buried in secret, but in the near future the situation would change and make it possible for the location of his grave to be made known to everyone.

However, even in the face of reasoned argument and the testimony of eyewitnesses, people continued to believe he was alive. It was an irrational belief, but caused by the fact that everyone in Chechnya, other than those opposed to our independence, revered Djohar so much that they were unwilling to believe he was dead. When I told people about his death, they accepted what I said and agreed he had died. I was told, however, that after I left, the general consensus was that I had to say Djohar was dead because I had sworn on the Qur'an to keep the secret of his disappearance, and so could not tell them the truth.

It did not take long to find out that these rumours were being deliberately spread and encouraged by a number of well known individuals, like Salman Raduev who had recently returned to Chechnya after medical treatment in Turkey. On one occasion I saw Raduev on television being asked at a rally why Zakaev was so insistently claiming Djohar was dead. To this he replied, 'I do not know why Zakaev should be saying that, but I can swear on the Qur'an that I have come to this rally after parting with Djohar, who is alive and well.' There was a roar from the crowd and shouts of 'Allahu Akbar!,' 'May Allah bless you, Salman, for bearing such good news!'

The first thing I did the next morning was go to see Raduev in his office at Sheikh Mansur Square in the centre of Grozny. He seemed to have more bodyguards posted there than Acting President Yandarbiev. One of the guards told me to wait while he reported my arrival to Salman, apologetically adding that such were their instructions. I assured him there was no need to apologize; he should just do his job. A couple of minutes later out jumped Raduev, all agile dynamism, to say my arrival was an honour and a delightful surprise. He took me to his office, which had a portrait of Djohar Dudaev hanging on the wall.

He noticed the interest I was taking in his office, and said Zelimkhan had arranged it through the district prefecture for his organization, The Veterans of the Battle of Pervomaiskoye. After the customary mutual enquiries after friends and relatives, I told Salman I had seen his speech on television at the rally the previous day. I asked him, 'Salman, how can you lie to people like that? And more importantly, why are you doing it? This is just what our enemy needs: implying to Chechens that Djohar, as they claim, unleashed a war, then abandoned the republic and fled abroad to live the high life. Do you really not know these are exactly the rumours they are energetically promoting?'

Salman registered great amazement, and asked me to clarify exactly which Djohar I was talking about. 'What do you mean, which Djohar?' I exclaimed. 'I am talking about Djohar Dudaev, our first president, may the Almighty accept his jihad!' Salman said, 'Amen. May the Almighty accept his jihad.' Then he added, 'Akhmed, is it not written in the Qur'an that a person who has given his life in jihad cannot be considered dead? He is more alive than the living! That is why, when people come to mention the death of Djohar, I say to one and all that it is not true, that Djohar is alive! That, after all, is what it says in the Qur'an, and which of us can take exception to what it says in the Qur'an? And as for the fact that I arrived at that rally having just parted with Djohar, it is absolutely true. I was referring to my two-year-old son who, in honour of Dudaev, I have named Djohar!'

After these explanations I was left speechless. I knew, of course, that Raduev was an opportunist to the marrow of his bones, but had never imagined him capable of such casuistry and outright deception. Later, I discovered that all Raduev's nonsense was part of Zelimkhan Yandarbiev's election strategy. I talked to Zelimkhan himself about this. I asked him why, as acting president, he did not release an official statement about Djohar's death and put an end to all these rumours that he was still alive and would return any time now. The rumours really were discreditable to Djohar's memory, when it was our duty to uphold his reputation and protect it from gossip and slander. Zelimkhan's response was that he would not issue any such statement or tell anyone that Djohar was dead because 'people would be very upset.' The real reason for his failure to terminate the rumours became clear, however, when his headquarters published a campaign poster depicting Djohar Dudaev and Zelimkhan Yandarbiev side by side, with the slogan, 'Together to the end!'

Yandarbiev was no doubt entirely justified in aspiring to formal leadership, but at that moment it was beyond his reach. I proposed to him an ideal course of action to put an end to all our dissension and make us a united team again. It was a course everyone would have accepted. I advised Zelimkhan that, as Djohar Dudaev's closest comrade-in-arms and the man who had brought the war to a triumphant conclusion, as someone who had been directly involved in every political move to establish a sovereign Chechen state, he should rise above the contention and nominate Aslan Maskhadov as his successor. This was, of course, the approach to transference of power subsequently used, although in a thoroughly perverted form, by Yeltsin and Putin. In our circumstances, the effect would have been very different. It would have enjoyed the support of our people and of the Chechen Resistance fighters. Russia and the international community would have accepted it. Aslan Maskhadov would have felt obligated to Yandarbiev as the patriarch of Chechen politics who had entrusted him with guiding the republic forward. Zelimkhan would in any case still have been a universally acknowledged, authoritative unofficial leader, immune to criticism no matter what shortcomings or blunders might be made by his successor.

You cannot argue with history, of course, and things happened the way they did. Zelimkhan did not accept my arguments and went on to lose the election, convincingly beaten in the polls by both Aslan Maskhadov and Shamil Basaev. Maskhadov felt he had scored a victory in this political skirmish over Zelimkhan and the various other candidates. He was to show gratitude only to those who had worked for him during the campaign, and those staffing his campaign headquarters were by no means all patriots or supporters of Chechen independence. Carrying out the instructions of their handlers in the Russian intelligence agencies, they worked on aggravating our internal strife. It was only much later that I learned why we had found it impossible back then to agree the nomination of a single candidate: the Russian intelligence agencies made use of all their agents in Chechnya and deployed all their financial and other resources to make sure that did not happen.

Almost from the beginning of the negotiation process, in other words, from 1995, they were infiltrating their agents into Aslan Maskhadov's entourage. A week after negotiations began, Lom-Ali Alsultanov resurfaced, having a few months previously decamped to Moscow with our government's money. He returned the money, not to Djohar Dudaev whom he had constantly called his 'idol' before the war, but to Aslan Maskhadov, a member of his own Teip. Shortly afterwards, Maskhadov's team was further augmented by the arrival of Alkhazur Abdulkadyrov Abdulkhadzhiev, chief financial officer of the Terek Bank, through which the pro-Russian governments of Salambek Khadzhiev and Doku Zavgaev had conducted their business. These people began gradually to influence the situation, and there is no doubt today that they were working for the Russian intelligence agencies.

Another example. The major sponsor and activist in Shamil Basaev's campaign headquarters was Ruslan Atlangeriev, a Lubyanka agent since the days of the KGB. Not everybody in Zelimkhan Yandarbiev's election headquarters was beyond reproach either. Khamzat Idrisov was blatantly selling positions in the coalition government to former ministers of the pro-Russian government of Zavgaev. In short, the Russian intelligence agencies threw all their resources into ensuring that Aslan Maskhadov gained the presidency, but in such a way that, after the election, the three major candidates should be at each other's throats. They made sure that Maskhadov's rivals, two highly influential figures in the republic, after losing the election became radically opposed to him, with all the risk of future armed confrontation which that entailed.

In Russia, the calculation was that this would make it easier to put pressure on Aslan, who was a man of impeccable honesty and courage but completely out of his depth in politics. Unfortunately, after he won the election, opposition to him and his policies automatically turned into opposition to the independent Chechen state. It was predictable, and exactly what Moscow wanted. What made it all the worse was that the leaders of this anti-state opposition were not the corrupt officials of earlier pro-Russian governments or the out-and-out gangsters fed by the Lubyanka, but men who had fought and shed blood for our independence. The situation was aggravated by the fact that, after their electoral debacle, Shamil Basaev and Zelimkhan Yandarbiev harboured resentment not only against Maskhadov but against the entire Chechen people who, they felt, had slighted them. Their subsequent behaviour can only be called harmful to the Chechen people and their state. I am reminded of a joke from the Soviet period. Little Vladimir Ulianov (Lenin) asks his mother what his brother Alexander was hanged for.

'For the people of Russia!' says his mother. 'Never mind, Mum,' he replies, 'when I grow up I'll sort out the people of Russia!' Shamil and Zelimkhan, having lost the election, were similarly determined to sort out the people of Chechnya.

After that meeting and exchange with Raduev, I went on to my office in a fairly wretched mood. The waiting room was crowded and, as usual, many of the people there had little connection with cultural matters or the work of artistic companies, which is what I was supposed to be concerned with. People came with a great variety of problems, ranging from pensions and welfare payments to seeking help to find people who were missing. That day, Kazbek Makhashev came to see me on behalf of Aslan Maskhadov, and told me that that night, when the working day was over, we were to drive to Ingushetia at the invitation of President Aushev. I needed to be at the government complex by 6.00 pm to set off with Aslan and the others who had been invited. I asked Kazbek what the purpose of the trip was, and whether it was related to the informal meeting with Russian officials we had discussed at the previous day's Cabinet meeting. Kazbek said it was entirely separate, a personal invitation, passed through him, from Aushev. I knew Kazbek was a close friend of Ruslan's, and he explained that the president of Ingushetia just wanted to invite us over to meet up in an informal, brotherly, Vainakh way for a pleasant evening. Besides Aslan, Kazbek, and myself, Ruslan had invited Khozh-Akhmed Yarikhanov and Movladi Udugov.

At the agreed time, we gathered by the government building and, shortly afterwards, a motorcade of seven or eight vehicles was heading for Ingushetia. It took us about an hour on the Rostov-Baku Highway to reach the border, where we were met by Mukharbek Didigov, the Ingush prime minister. Didigov got into Maskhadov's car and we continued, escorted now by the Ingush riot police. It was striking how Ingushetia had changed in the last two years, with excellent roads, luxurious two and three-storey houses, and even whole villages built to European standards. Magas, the new capital of the republic, was being constructed at speed. I consider that Ruslan Aushev's presidency was the high point for Ingushetia. He skilfully exploited the situation between Chechnya and Russia to the advantage of his republic. He told me later that, when addressing urgent financial or staffing issues in Ingushetia, he would say openly to Viktor Chernomyrdin, 'If you do not want another Chechnya in the North Caucasus, you need to help us resolve these issues.' The approach worked not only for Ruslan but also for nearly all the other leaders of republics in the region, as I discovered when I later chatted to them. President Kirsan Ilyumzhinov of the Republic of Kalmykia, President

Kokov of Kabardino-Balkaria, and Magomedali Magomedov, chairman of the State Council of Dagestan, told me themselves.

At that time all of them became little autocrats in their own domains and were left to do as they pleased. Corruption, nepotism, and the clan system of power were in full bloom. In my opinion, only two leaders used this decentralization to the benefit of their republics: Ruslan Aushev in Ingushetia and Kirsan Ilyumzhinov, the president of Kalmykia. I am not, of course, going to pretend they were sinless, but it seems undeniable that they did much to benefit their republics. I say that confidently, because I spent time in all the neighbouring republics and saw for myself the most dramatic change precisely in Ingushetia and Kalmykia.

Our procession turned into the courtyard of an enormous palace built in English Victorian style. It was given a modern look by red bricks with a very smooth surface and faceted edges, which were popularly known as 'Italian.' In the early 1990s a factory was built in the Stavropol region to produce bricks using Italian technology. They looked very good, almost toy-like, and were, of course, far more expensive than those produced by factories using Soviet technology, including ours in Grozny. Almost any more or less wealthy Chechen or Ingush who was having a house built privately specified 'Italian' bricks.

We were met at the entrance by Ruslan Aushev, who shook hands and embraced each of us according to Vainakh custom as he welcomed us into his residence. Ruslan personally showed us over the house where we were to spend the rest of the evening and night, all the floors, the halls and rooms. It had everything: a place for official receptions, a billiards room, a cinema and concert hall, a sauna and swimming pool, bedrooms, a kitchen, dining rooms for everyday and for official occasions, quarters for the security staff, including a room with CCTV surveillance screens and another for relaxation. Ruslan also showed us a special room which, at Moscow's request, had been prepared for the meeting which never took place between Djohar Dudaev and Viktor Chernomyrdin.

That was very typical of the Russians, making simultaneous provision for several options when trying to resolve political problems. By this time I knew for a fact that the assassination of Djohar had been specifically authorized by the Kremlin, that same Kremlin which had instructed Ruslan Aushev to prepare a special hall for Djohar's meeting with the Russian prime minister. Chernomyrdin himself kept an eye on its construction, regularly phoning from Moscow to ask Ruslan how it was coming along. The Russian leaders were undecided which option to adopt, so they prepared for both. This confirmed our view that Russian politicians never put all their eggs in one basket. They kept their options open.

Ruslan laid on a welcome truly fit for brothers. Until then I had no idea that Vainakh cuisine could be so varied and include so many courses, supposing the Georgians to be unbeatable in this respect. That evening, however, the Ingush succeeded. The biggest surprise for us, however, was the Vainakh *Sink"eram* Ruslan had organized for us. The word means literally 'entertainment of the soul,' and is usually translated into European languages simply as 'a party.' That, however, does not do it justice.

When the meal was over, Ingush girls wearing national costume entered the hall. One playing an accordion led the way. She struck up a foot-tapping *Lezginka*, and a drummer immediately appeared to provide a frenzied accompaniment to the music. Ruslan, as the host, was the first on the dance floor, inviting one of the girls to join him. He was an amazing dancer. We have a saying that a man's character becomes evident when he dances. Adroit dance steps, accompanied by the clapping of all present and pistol shots provided by the Ingush president's bodyguards and the lads accompanying us, were followed by smooth alternating steps as Ruslan allowed the girl to demonstrate how poised she was even with numerous eyes fixed on her, and her ability to gracefully follow her dance partner's lead.

Vainakh dance is a science. Every movement and gesture is symbolizing something, although today few people other than specialists in folk dance know what. After Aushev, Aslan Maskhadov came out into the circle. I was pleasantly surprised to discover how well he could dance. Growing up from a young age outside the republic, first at a military academy and later as a serving officer, Aslan had nevertheless mastered the intricacies of our national dancing, and that too said a lot about his character. Almost everyone present danced, and I too had to go into the circle.

When the first part ended, the accordionist started playing a lyrical melody and the girls sang a folk song. These are the main, alternating components of a Vainakh entertainment. The difference between Chechen and Ingush partying is that Chechen young divorced women and girls of marriageable age have the right to sit in front of the men, at a distance of 4-5 metres. Very young girls stand behind them. At Ingush parties all the women and girls are standing in front of the men, who are seated. At a Chechen *Sink"eram* the boys and girls communicate through a chaperone, usually the lady of the house where the evening is being held. A distinctive feature at Ingush parties is that there is no intermediary. They communicate directly and all they are saying can be heard by everyone present. Vainakh parties are held either after a wedding, as a continuation of it, or as a separate event in honour of distinguished guests from another village, town or region.

Not only young bachelors attend these parties, but married men too make the acquaintance of young women, express their admiration of them, and invite them to accept their hand and heart. If the proposal comes from a guest, the girl accepts it, even if her fiance is present (the one whom, according to Vainakh custom, she meets beside the spring). Everyone understands that the girl, in accepting the guest's offer, is expressing her respect, but at the end of the evening her consent does not oblige the girl or the guest in any way, and does not detract from her relationship with her real fiance. This is a game, a battle of wits and knowledge of etiquette, and everyone plays by the rules.

The rules of the game for the Ingush are, if I may put it this way, rather more demanding. For example, after listening to a proposal from the guest at a party, the Ingush girl replies that she consents to share his joys and sorrows, and that if he will marry her she is prepared to accompany him to the ends of the earth and live with him for the rest of her days. The man should reply that he is ready to marry her and live with her for the rest of his days. This is also only a game, and at the end of the evening, these mutual non-binding promises remain only as memories of time agreeably spent.

When we reached this stage in the evening, Aslan began looking around in some desperation and motioned for me to come and sit beside him. Our colleagues immediately guessed he was in need of a consultation on these nuances of Ingush hospitality. I explained them to him, what he should say to the girl and how, how she would reply, and reassured him that, despite all the mutual vows of fidelity, he would not have to return home from this party with a second wife.

I knew the ins and outs of Ingush party etiquette from my student years. I had studied at the Theatre Institute alongside Ingush boys and girls, so I was familiar with their customs. We remained on good, friendly terms after graduation, often visiting each other and, of course, throwing parties.

When the present party drew to a close, the girls were taken back to their homes. This is another Vainakh rule: the host who organizes a party is obliged to ensure the girls are returned to their homes safe and sound. Ruslan then invited us to his cinema. He had a large collection of videos of Ingush and Chechen concerts, and was a big fan of Chechen singers and performers. During the viewing, someone commented on how similar the Chechen and Ingush music was. I remarked that Chechen and Ingush music was not just similar but, to all intents and purposes, identical. I said, 'There are no separate Chechen and Ingush dances or music: there is only Vainakh dance and

Vainakh music, because there is only one, indivisible Vainakh people. The names "Ingush" and "Chechen" have been bestowed on us by other nations, and it is these names which divide the Vainakh people.'

'It is not an ethnographical issue; it is politics, and blatantly imperialist politics at that. The unity of the Vainakhs is absolutely clear if we research Chechen-Ingush folklore, music, dance, and art. Or look at our tower architecture. Chechens see these cultural elements as specifically Chechen, and Ingush see them as Ingush. This is one instance where both sides are completely right: this is all our common heritage, the heritage of the Vainakh people. To emphasize this, we should call all the manifestations of our culture and traditions not Chechen or Ingush but Vainakh.'

I found I had delivered a whole impromptu speech, but Ruslan very much liked my ideas and proposed that we should call all our two republics' cultural institutions not Chechen or Ingush but Vainakh. I said we could and should do that in Chechnya after the election of the president and parliament, but I had serious doubts as to whether Moscow would allow them to do it in Ingushetia. The Russian Empire had kept us divided for centuries and was unlikely to agree readily to our reunification. Ruslan countered by saying they had much more freedom than people in Chechnya supposed, and that he could easily decide such matters by presidential decree.

While we were on the subject, I told Ruslan that, as he knew, all our cultural centres were in ruins and we would see it as a truly brotherly gift if the Ingush Republic could assume responsibility for restoring, if not the whole of the theatre and concert complex in Grozny, then at least the small concert hall. This was something that could be done quite quickly and at fairly modest expense. Ruslan immediately called his aide and asked him to make a note of the matter. He invited me to send someone to discuss the details of the projects with one of the deputy chairmen of the Ingush government. He said he would ask his government to decide what could be done. Everybody who heard our discussion started cheerfully goading me on: 'Go for it, Zakaev!' 'Get in there, Minister of Culture!'

Aslan supported me, however, and said I had set a good example for other Chechen ministers to follow. They should take every opportunity to get our ruined republic back on its feet. 'We need to be thinking about this not only when we are sitting in our offices, but even when we are out visiting, as Zakaev has.'

Ruslan Aushev and I became good friends. Later that night, when our colleagues had dispersed, some to play billiards, others to enjoy the sauna or take a dip in the pool, Ruslan invited me and Kazbek Makhashev to come to visit his father. It was late, about one o'clock in the morning, but Ruslan said his father would be waiting up for us. We went home with him and did meet his parents, who were delightful people. Kazbek and I remained on good terms with them, and would go to see them at the end of Ramadan and on other holidays, or just drop in on them when the occasion presented itself.

We returned to Chechnya the following day and I immediately called a meeting with Gapur Aliev, the director of the Chechen Drama Theatre, and his first deputy, Makkal Sabdullaev, to tell them what had been agreed with President Aushev for getting the small concert hall restored. They were genuinely pleased. I gave them names of people in the Ingush government they should meet to talk through the practicalities of the project. I put Gapur in charge, with Makkal as supervisor. The changing circumstances meant that I was becoming increasingly involved in politics rather than culture.

XI

Enter Berezovsky

In October 1996, Boris Berezovsky is appointed deputy to Security Council Secretary Rybkin, an apparently positive step. Zakaev negotiates removal of the last two remaining Russian brigades in Chechnya. An Intergovernmental Agreement is signed with the Russians.

On 29 October 1996, ITAR–TASS news agency reported that, by presidential decree, Boris Berezovsky and Leonid Mayorov had been appointed deputies of the Security Council secretary, Ivan Rybkin. Vladimir Denisov and Sergey Kharlamov, former members of Alexander Lebed's team, were dismissed. Fifty-year old Boris Berezovsky was a corresponding member of the Russian Academy of Sciences and a doctor of economics. For several years he was at the helm of the LogoVaz corporation, was one of the heads of Russian Public Television (ORT), and an active member of Yeltsin's re-election team. His appointment saw the beginning of a process whereby oligarchs began openly coming to power in Russia, deciding not only economic but also political matters. This was the main difference between the Russian economy and the market economies of the West. In the West, Big Business serves the state, financing political parties and movements and supporting them in elections. Here, as in so many other matters, Russia chose to follow its own notorious 'special path.' Russian oligarchs, the representatives of Big Business, decided the government should serve their interests and, by bribing officials, began elevating their own placemen to the political Olympus. The press office of Acting President Zelimkhan Yandarbiev issued a statement that the Chechen leader saw the appointment of Berezovsky as a positive step and hoped he might play an important role in the economic and social recovery of the republic.

On 1 November 1996, at the invitation of the Russians, communicated through Ruslan Aushev, a Chechen delegation travelled to Ingushetia, arriving at the president's country residence at seven o'clock in the evening. The Chechen representatives were Aslan Maskhadov, Khozh-

Akhmed Yarikhanov, Movladi Udugov, and myself. The Russians who attended the meeting were Ivan Rybkin, Boris Berezovsky, Nationalities Minister Vyacheslav Mikhailov, and Sergey Stepashin, formerly director of the Federal Counter-Intelligence Service but dismissed by Yeltsin after Shamil Basaev's raid on Budyonnovsk. He now headed the Administrative Department of the Russian government.

I believe that Stepashin, despite his move, was still the main curator of the 'Chechen direction' in Russian policy-making. Stepashin was still in charge of the Russian network of intelligence agents in Chechnya and, in this capacity, was to take Movladi Udugov under his wing. Whenever there was a break in the negotiations, Stepashin and Udugov would move away from everybody else and start whispering together.

During our summer negotiations, there had been an incident involving Udugov. After he and Stepashin had very obviously taken themselves off to some private corner, Aslan Maskhadov angrily reprimanded him, mentioning the case of Usman Imaev. During negotiations in the summer and autumn of 1995, we had been discussing with the Russian delegation a form of words in the document we were preparing to sign. The Russian side had proposed including a clause in the agreement stating that all military units not recognized under the Russian law 'On Defence' should be disarmed. We were insisting that after reference to the law there should be no mention either of the Russian Federation or of the Chechen Republic. This was very important for us, as it would allow us to decide for ourselves which armed groups were 'legal' or 'illegal.' When this had already been agreed with the Russian delegation, Imaev suddenly joined the Russian officials in trying to persuade us to go back and accept the earlier, Russian wording. Aslan Maskhadov had called him a traitor. In the present instance, the implication behind his remark to Udugov was entirely unambiguous.

This time too, in the Ingush president's country residence, immediately after the formal introductions, Stepashin closeted himself with Udugov, and this time also with Berezovsky. Now, however, there was no reaction from Aslan, as Movladi was one of his entourage, his loyalty vouched for by Islam Khalimov and Isa Umarov, people close to Maskhadov and occupying prominent positions in his election campaign team.

Although Udugov and I were officially meeting Boris Berezovsky only the next day, 2 November, with statements for the press, we discussed all the issues informally that evening. Berezovsky immediately took the initiative, addressing himself first to the members of the Russian delegation:

You know, my friends, the methods you have used in working with our Chechen partners in the past are wholly inappropriate today. At that time a war was being waged. That was before it was decided we should settle all our problems by political and economic means. You tried to trick, to outwit an opponent, to play for time. Now, though, when the war is finally over, thanks to the joint efforts of Maskhadov and Lebed, and also the political will shown by Russia's president, Boris Yeltsin, we need to address problems of an entirely different nature, and the old methods are no longer valid. We have the duty and responsibility on behalf of our peoples to maintain and protect this fragile peace. That, my friends, is not going to be easy. It will be no simple matter after all that has happened and, as we know, there is no shortage of opponents of the peace process on both sides. In order to achieve positive outcomes in our work together, the first requirement is openness, the second is trust, and the third is implementation of the agreements we reach.

To start with, my Chechen friends, for us you are a part of Russia, but for you Russia is an occupying force, an aggressor, and you are an independent sovereign state. Those are completely different positions, different approaches. They say politics is the art of the possible. Friends, colleagues, let us do the impossible by finding an acceptable formula for cooperation, for working together while maintaining and respecting the political positions of the parties. I have every confidence that, observing the three requirements I have mentioned, this is something we can achieve.

Thanks to that approach, we were able to reach agreement on establishing a legal framework for resolving the whole range of problems, political, economic, and social. Almost from the first days of our talks we reached consensus on the necessity of signing a peace treaty. It was agreed this should be signed after the elections in Chechnya. At that moment in time, there was no framework regulating relations between Russia and Chechnya other than the Khasavyurt Accord, which was only a declaration of intent to establish relations between Chechnya and Russia in accordance with the generally recognized principles and standards of international law.

At the initial stage of our negotiations, with the appearance of new political figures on the Russian side, we reached many positive agreements. Both parties, for example, renounced the use of political formulations which were obviously unacceptable to the other side. We agreed to refrain from any more petty political dirty tricks, like the one we were subjected to in the Kremlin during the negotiations earlier in the year, on 27 May 1996. On that occasion, at the conclusion of the negotiations, Vyacheslav Mikhailov emerged exultantly to announce to the press, as if it were a huge victory for the Russian side, that our delegation had signed a ceasefire agreement under a letterhead with the Russian state insignia, thus, according to him, indicating that we recognized Chechnya was part of Russia.

Of course, this really was a serious blunder on the part of Said-Khasan Abumuslimov and Movladi Udugov, who were seated on either side of Zelimkhan during the signing. If, in the heat of the moment, Zelimkhan failed to spot this trick, it was the bounden duty of those two to vet the document carefully before he signed. I am sure the Russians never expected to get away with this, but felt obliged to try to trick us into signing beneath the Russian crest. Mikhailov and his colleagues in the negotiations shared their delight at such petty diplomatic point-scoring, knowing perfectly well that in any case the Russian side had not the slightest intention of honouring any of the points we managed to agree. Alexander Lebed's team, and after them Rybkin's team, refrained from such small-minded mischief making.

A meeting was held at three o'clock in the afternoon on 3 November at Government House in Grozny between Aslan Maskhadov and Boris Berezovsky. Berezovsky said afterwards that his visit was to prepare for a meeting between Aslan Maskhadov and Viktor Chernomyrdin. Aslan for his part confirmed that he welcomed the proposal for a meeting with the Russian prime minister, and wished primarily to discuss economic issues with him. Political issues, he suggested, would best be left for five years, when it would be easier to consider them with a cool head.

Such were the external political processes affecting the republic at that time, but internal political developments were no less important for us. Maskhadov, actively preparing for the day when he would become president, told me while we were still in Ingushetia that it was time for me to make my mind up. My preferred solution of political unity was not going to happen, and I needed therefore to move to a more realistic position. In other words, in a thinly disguised way, Aslan was inviting me to join his team. He immediately went on to discuss organizational detail, telling me that Turpal-Ali Atgireyev would be coordinating his campaign and that Vakha Arsanov had agreed to stand for election as his vice-president. I asked Aslan whether his only criterion in choosing his vice-president had been the degree of his hostility towards their political opponents. Like many other people in the republic, I knew Vakha Arsanov was on terrible terms with Zelimkhan

Yandarbiev and Shamil Basaev. Aslan just laughed, and said his criterion for choosing Arsanov was geographical, because people who knew about these things had told him Vakha, representing the highlands of Chechnya, and he, representing the lowlands, would make a good team.

I knew both Aslan and Vakha well, and had not the slightest doubt that, with their very different characters, their alliance would be short-lived, no matter how they might presently be swearing oaths of friendship and loyalty to each other. I thought better than to upset Aslan with these misgivings, however, and said only that if, at the forthcoming meeting of the Cabinet, we failed to agree on a single candidate, I would indeed make my mind up. It would not, however, be the decision our three prospective candidates were expecting, that I would side with one of them against the other two.

An extended meeting of the Cabinet of Ministers was scheduled for 15 November, to which the elders were invited, together with all the commanders of fronts and directions and the heads of regional administrations. The only item on the agenda was the advisability of nominating a single presidential candidate from the Resistance. The meeting was opened by Dayan of Roshni-Chu, who spoke on behalf of all the elders. He began with a call to pray a *Dua* invocation for all those who had died in the war, that the Almighty should have mercy upon them and accept their jihad; that He should have mercy also upon us who were still among the living. Dayan reminded us of our responsibilities at this crucial moment, because, having given us a military victory over our enemies, the Almighty was continuing to test us. Dayan went on:

> At this time, the whole world is full of admiration for you, your courage and the fortitude you have shown in deadly combat with an enemy which outnumbered you a hundredfold and whose armaments exceeded yours a thousandfold. It is for these qualities of yours that the Almighty granted us victory over our age-old enemy, and hope for the future of our people and our descendants. Along with the victory, the Almighty gave us an opportunity of realizing our ancient dream of creating a free nation on this land, every inch of which is soaked with the blood of our ancestors. I want to say this to you: if you have the wisdom and, most importantly, the patience to bring to its culmination what our ancestors and you, our sons, fought for, then your descendants will remember you with pride and gratitude. But if, at this moment so fateful for the future of our people, you succumb to the intrigues of Iblis and allow yourselves to be

divided, thereby enabling our enemies to destroy the fruits of our victory, our descendants will think ill of you.

We talk of victory, but in reality all we have achieved is unity, and we have gained faith in the favour and protection of the Almighty, and in our own strength. For that unity and faith the whole Chechen people has paid a great price. Our greatest problems, however, are yet to come, because our enemies are not reconciled to their defeat, and this is most certainly not the time for us to fall out between ourselves.

All our candidates are very fine people. Before coming here today, the Council of Elders debated all these issues at great length, and we decided not to give our support to any one of you, because by so doing we would unjustly wrong the other two. We came to the conclusion that it would be best if our candidates decide this matter among themselves. If the Almighty gives a man courage, He also gives him Iman, faith, and wisdom, in order that he should be of use to his family, relatives and his whole people.

To conclude, I want to tell you about something that occurred in the last century here in Chechnya. In those days, Duda, a man greatly respected among the people, died leaving seven worthy sons. The question arose of which should represent the family in place of their departed father. People began suggesting first one and then another of the brothers. Then a wise man came, gathered them together, and said, 'Your father Duda was a very worthy and respected man and you, his sons, are worthy of your father. But if all seven of you want to be Duda, none of you will be. People will first divide you and then defame you as sons unworthy of their father. So this very day, decide among yourselves who is to take your father's place in society, and announce it to the people yourselves.'

I mention this case because it is very similar to our situation today. If Djohar, our first president, were alive today, we would not be here discussing who should be the leader of our nation. But the Almighty has taken him to Himself, and you, the close comrades-in-arms of Djohar, must decide among yourselves whom you will propose to the people in place of Djohar. If you deliberately decide not do that, you will eventually cover yourselves in disgrace and we will all be the losers. That is all I wanted to say to you today.

While Dayan was speaking there was dead silence in the hall. Everybody present was listening intently. I too was listening to his every word, filled with joy that we still had such wise and worthy elders. It seemed to me at that moment that after his speech nobody could possibly argue against what he had said. It was an enormously important moment when Zelimkhan could have announced that Aslan Maskhadov was to succeed him, to become a truly national leader, to break the necks of our adversaries and put an end to the incipient strife. But that was not to be.

Zelimkhan was not present at the meeting because two days previously he had been in an accident and broken his arm. He was being represented by his vice-president, Said-Khasan Abumuslimov. Said-Khasan got to his feet and addressed those present. 'As you know,' he said, 'Zelimkhan has had an accident and therefore cannot be here, but he has asked me to convey to you his view on the matter under discussion.'

Said-Khasan reminded not only me but also many of our fellow fighters who knew him well of Mullah Nesart, a figure in Chechen folklore, particularly as he is depicted in a story in which Mullah Nesart is acting as a Qadi, a Sharia judge, in the countryside. Two villagers come to ask him to resolve their dispute. The chicken of one of them strayed into the garden of the other and began pecking at some recent planting. The owner of the garden threw a stone and killed it. The owner of the chicken came to demand compensation, they began arguing, and decided to refer the matter to the Qadi. After listening to the owner of the garden, who stressed the fact that the chicken had damaged his crops, Mullah Nesart stated that his claim against the owner of the chicken was well founded. Then the owner of the chicken spoke. Mullah Nesart heard him out and then stated that his claim against the owner of the garden was well founded. The villagers looked at each other in perplexity and went home. Then Mullah Nesart's shrewish wife jumped out of the kitchen where she had been eavesdropping and laid into him. 'What sort of a Qadi are you if you decide both sides in a dispute are right! One or other of them always has to be in the wrong, you dolt!' Mullah Nesart listened patiently to his wife's outburst, and said meekly, 'Yes, wife, you too are right.'

Such an inadequate response on Said-Khasan's part could be seen as comical, but only in the short term. It was later only too evident what major misfortunes it caused for the whole of Chechnya. Said-Khasan began by saying that Zelimkhan Yandarbiev had been there at the very beginnings of the Chechen national liberation movement as the leader of the Vainakh Democratic Party. Zelimkhan had been largely instrumental in persuading Djohar Dudaev to return home and head the republic. After Djohar's death, Zelimkhan as vice-president had succeeded him, become the leader of the Resistance, and won the war.

At these words someone shouted from the floor of the hall, 'It was not Zelimkhan won the war but the worthy sons of the Chechen people!' Said-Khasan corrected himself and said that was what he had meant. The main argument he was able to advance to explain why exactly Zelimkhan should be the sole candidate was that he was already president, and his colleagues should not challenge his position, the more so since he had given all of them positions in the government.

To this Vakha Arsanov retorted, 'Why? Did he inherit the position from his seven ancestors? Do you think the Chechen people elected him vice-president? He was not even elected a deputy from his own region, as we all know. It was Djohar appointed him vice-president by decree, and under our Constitution he remains president only until the next election, which is now. I am certain the people will not elect him president in this election, so if Zelimkhan is the single candidate from the Resistance forces we will all lose. I, and the men of the Northern Front which I command, support Aslan Maskhadov for president.'

Said-Khasan asked Vakha not to interrupt him, reminding him he would have time later to express his views. One of the elders who was conducting our meeting called it to order and urged that the speakers should not be interrupted.

Everything that happened in the hall bore the stamp of the 130 years that Chechens had spent under Russian domination. That is a long time, of course, although not long enough to erase from the Chechens' collective memory their past, their code of conduct, their traditions for resolving disputes and reaching decisions. The folk memory and our history testify to the fact that the Chechens have lived in this land since time immemorial, independent of any outsider and in territory which attracted the attention and interest of many powers and empires, not all of which survived to the present day. Contact with Russia has brought us many misfortunes but, paradoxically, it is in peacetime that all the bad influences that contact has brought to bear on the Chechen mentality come to the fore. Not one of our meetings during the war, no matter how fraught the issues we were discussing, was marred by people taking liberties or making disrespectful remarks. One of the major differences between Chechens and Russians has always been that Russians could afford to insult and swear at each other, and then make peace over a bottle of vodka and forget all about it. Chechens, however, say that the wound inflicted by a weapon will heal, while the wound inflicted by an insult never does. That is why Chechens have always been reserved and respectful in all they say. What was taking place that day saddened me greatly, and persuaded me there was little likelihood we would be able to agree on a single candidate.

Next, Aslanbek Ismailov took the floor. He was managing Shamil Basaev's campaign, and said that he and his colleagues had decided to nominate Shamil only after they heard that the Resistance forces would not be fielding a unity candidate. He announced that they had petitioned the chairman of the parliament to amend the present Constitution by lowering the minimum age for presidential candidates from 35 to 30. Parliament had agreed to this. Aslanbek continued,

'None of those who took part in the Budyonnovsk Raid trust Aslan Maskhadov. If he is elected president, he may agree to a demand from Russia for them to be handed over, as stipulated in the agreement of 30 May 1995. Maskhadov is the person on the Chechen side who guarantees implementation of that agreement.'

Of course, Aslanbek did not believe that himself. He was well aware no one would ever hand them over. He continued, 'If Aslan is elected president, he will cause a split among those who fought in the war because he has his own favourites and people he has taken a dislike to. He started all that while Djohar was still alive, gathering his own supporters and using them to oppose Djohar's policies. The reason the Russians killed Djohar was because they were sure he would be succeeded by Aslan as head of our forces, and with him they would find it easier to come to a compromise. We all know, though, that the only compromise acceptable to the Russians is one which diminishes our independence and sovereignty. That is why I and everybody on my side consider it very important that Shamil becomes president. Then we can be sure there will be no compromise with the Russians at the expense of Chechen independence. I urge everyone to vote for Shamil. That is all I wanted to tell you, my brothers and respected elders.'

When Aslanbek sat down, Vakha Arsanov stood up. Neither Aslan Maskhadov nor Shamil Basaev were present at the meeting. When they heard that Zelimkhan would not be there, they decided to send their vice-presidents. Vakha Arsanov greeted everyone, making a point of demonstrating his respect for the elders. He apologized on behalf of Maskhadov for the fact that he was not able to take part in the meeting, and continued, 'I will be brief. You are all aware that I have agreed to stand with Aslan in the elections as vice-president. I want to reply to Aslanbek's complaints and doubts about Aslan. All of us present here today know Aslan well, and none of us have any reason to doubt him. None of the Chechens who survived the war did as much for our victory as Aslan, and no one is more worthy of our trust than he. I will go further than that: I trust Aslan more than my own brothers and I am ready to die for him. At the same time, I want to assure you that, if Aslan were to agree to betray our independence,' – here Vakha put his hand on his Stechkin pistol and paused for a moment, before continuing theatrically – 'I will shoot him personally. I permit and encourage you to do the same to me if I should compromise our principles and betray our country.'

This was all very much in Vakha's style. It was exactly what I had foreseen when I heard that Aslan had invited Vakha to run as his vice-president. I knew he was not someone who would agree to play second fiddle for long, and today, seizing his opportunity, he was doing a very good job of demonstrating that he would be the unofficial leader in their duo. In this, however, Vakha was much mistaken, because there were things he did not know about Aslan's personality. At first sight, Aslan gave the impression of being a mild, amiable person. Behind that mask, however, was a strong-willed man, stubborn and ruthless towards his enemies. I had witnessed highly charged exchanges between Aslan and Djohar. I had been in close proximity to Aslan on many occasions and in very varied situations. I had not the slightest doubt that those who imagined they would be able to manipulate him were mistaken. It was easy to deceive him, because he was ridiculously trusting, but later, after being betrayed many times by people he had trusted, he swung to the opposite extreme and became hyper-suspicious.

After Vakha Arsanov, Vakha Ibrakhimov asked to speak. He had been Djohar Dudaev's aide, and was next to him on the dark day when our first president was murdered. Vakha was one of the few who survived the blast, but was seriously injured. For Vakha Ibrakhimov, this meeting was not just a pre-election game. He was totally convinced that only Shamil Basaev should be president now the war was over, and that only Shamil was capable of keeping the situation under control. Even before Djohar was assassinated, we often met and discussed a variety of matters. Vakha was a selflessly dedicated patriot, a competent politician, and an exceptionally decent human being. His speech took the form of a series of rhetorical questions addressed to the previous speaker.

'What more did Aslan do than Shamil to preserve our independence? Shamil and his comrades-in-arms did much more than Aslan and his supporters. Shamil and his comrades faced almost certain death and, thanks to their daring incursion into Russia, the Almighty turned the tide in favour of the Chechens. For some reason, everyone attributes the success of the August Operation in Grozny solely to Aslan Maskhadov, but did Aslan prepare the operation single-handed? No. And was it not Shamil Basaev who personally directed the operation and was wounded in the fighting? Why is no one here talking about that? I see no reason why Shamil should have less right to be our leader than Zelimkhan or Aslan. Shamil is already our national leader in fact if not officially. Who in our republic, from a two-year-old toddler to the oldest of our seniors, does not know of Shamil Basaev? How many Chechen men and women have named their newborn sons in honour of Shamil? The entire Chechen people have recognized him as their leader. If we, who fought alongside him, just temper our ambitions a little and recognize his leadership in this election, we will all reap the benefit. That is why I, like Aslanbek, urge you to support Shamil Basaev.'

Thus this meeting, which was supposed to be selecting a single candidate from those who had fought in the war in support of Chechen independence, turned into a hustings conducted by representatives of the three main candidates. There were many television cameras in the hall, from our state television, cable TV channels, and local television studios. Our disagreements and disunity were about to be displayed to the entire Chechen population, and not only to them.

I now faced a personal problem. Each of the three candidates thought I should side with them and work in their campaign against the other two. I enjoyed good, even friendly, relations with all of them By entering the campaign headquarters of one, I would automatically become the adversary of the other two. I, Dalkhan Khozhaev, Khusein Isabaev and Makkal Sabdullaev therefore decided that, if we could not secure the nomination of a single candidate, we would put me myself forward as a candidate. We thus escaped the dilemma of campaigning for any one of the main candidates and upsetting the others. Additionally, we would gain a platform for political statements which might help to mitigate the strife, which was bound to worsen after the elections; to be more precise, after Aslan Maskhadov was elected president, as I had not the slightest doubt he would be. The majority of Chechens were simply programmed to vote for him. Needless to say, the pro-Russian opposition, switched over by Moscow to support Maskhadov, was a far from negligible force in getting him elected. If Maskhadov had been put forward as the sole candidate from the Resistance forces and supporters of independence, the pro-Russians would certainly have been against him. As the line-up stood, however, Maskhadov was the only alternative to Zelimkhan Yandarbiev, and as such was 'fated' to win. For the pro-Russian opposition and those in Moscow who controlled them, Maskhadov's victory over Yandarbiev and Basaev would seem a victory over the supporters of independence, by whom they had been defeated in outright military confrontation.

Before the meeting closed, I decided to take the floor and express my opinion of the way the situation had developed. It was useless to hope the representatives of the three major candidates might yet be persuaded to come to an agreement. No one could have put the arguments in favour of unity more compellingly than Dayan of Roshni-Chu already had, so I confined myself to commenting on the speeches we had heard.

I started by saying that, until today, I had hoped we could agree on the subject under discussion, but the presentations on behalf of Zelimkhan, Shamil, and Aslan showed that each of them, and their supporters, were convinced of their own rightness.

'The fact of the matter is,' I said, 'that the only right decision is one adopted with the agreement of all concerned. In this case, none of the three parties is willing to listen to the views of those who disagree with them. I would like to point out to you just how shaky, if we look at the three viewpoints one by one, your certainty is that you alone are right.'

'Our esteemed Said-Khasan, in trying to persuade us that the position taken by Zelimkhan and his supporters is best, gave as his main argument that we must nominate Zelimkhan as our sole candidate in order to spite the Russians. I would argue that, if we were to adopt Zelimkhan as our sole candidate, we would spite only the Chechen people. If we want to spite the Russians, we would do far better to nominate Shamil Basaev.' This produced a lot of laughter in the hall. I continued, 'Now I would like to question my friend Aslanbek's argument that electing Shamil Basaev would save us from any risk of a compromise which would undermine our independence. I would add that, if Shamil Basaev became president, Russia would make sure we became so isolated from the rest of the world that no one would be interested in seeking compromises from us, whether to undermine or to consolidate our independence. Nobody would discuss anything with us. The world will not tolerate a second Yasser Arafat.'

'Now, as regards Vakha Arsanov's claim that nobody has done more for our independence than Aslan Maskhadov. Yes, that is entirely true. It was only after Aslan became chief of staff of our army that the first blood was shed between Chechens. Someone had to take that decision. At a time when Moscow was arming Chechens in order to change our system of government by their hand, Aslan, along with other brave sons of our people, crushed this Russian provocation. He did something which few other Chechens could have brought themselves to do and took responsibility for spilling Chechen blood to defend our independence. But I want to warn all of you present here today, and Vakha Arsanov personally, that if Aslan Maskhadov is elected president without any resolution of our present differences, then the opposition you will face will come not from pro-Russian Chechens, but from those with whom for the past two years you have fought shoulder-to-shoulder against the Russian invaders. And that adversary will not run away as the pro-Russian Chechens did. The result will be a civil war.'

'So what do you suggest?' voices were heard calling in the hall.

'If, when they meet tomorrow, Zelimkhan, Aslan, and Shamil fail to agree to put forward a single candidate, I suggest we propose another candidate, but on the condition that all of us, except those three, unite around that other candidate, including those working in the campaign headquarters of Zelimkhan, Aslan, and Shamil, which will merge into a single headquarters. Of course, I realize this is an ideal. It is unfortunately unrealizable. Apparently, the Almighty is sending us a further ordeal, and we can only pray to Him that it will not prove to be a punishment. I have mentioned this ideal solution only because you asked what we should do. There is always an answer and a solution, but unfortunately we do not always find the right answer or choose the best solution.'

Needless to say, the next day Zelimkhan, Aslan, and Shamil were unable to agree on a single candidate. That is how I became the sixth candidate of the Resistance forces for the presidency. With the passage of time, I realized it was the biggest mistake of my life.

XII

Subverting Independence

The NKVD/KGB/FSB network in Chechnya. Russia's history of genocide in Chechnya. Extent of the destruction in the two recent wars. Russian airbrushing out of history of the role of Chechens in the defence of the Fortress of Brest in 1941. Negotiating with Berezovsky. Russian attempts to undermine Chechen insistence on independence. Outflanking General Kulikov over the continued presence of Russian troops in Chechnya.

    Despite our differences over the forthcoming elections, the government continued to work in a climate of optimism and an expectation of something good, like the entire Chechen nation. There was heated discussion everywhere about the elections and nobody was indifferent. Overall, the atmosphere in the republic was one of elation and victorious euphoria. There was a bitter irony in the fact that a people who, on the eve of the war, had numbered just over a million, and who during the war had seen more than 100,000 men, women and children killed in bombing, artillery bombardment, and torture on an industrial scale in concentration camps, a people who had lost their entire industrial and social infrastructure and were living literally among the ashes of their civilization, this people was being bombarded with propaganda to the effect that in the war just past it had vanquished a nuclear power.

    If for some reason your neighbour bursts into your home, destroys your house, kills some of your family and cripples others, robs you of your property and then, some time later, departs, it is unlikely that you will feel you have been victorious. Of course, if you are a believer, you will thank God that at least not everyone in your family has been butchered, but you are hardly likely to be in a triumphant mood. Likewise, the Chechens in the aftermath of the war had little reason to feel they had come out the winners or as God's chosen people. The Russian intelligence agencies were well prepared, and those Chechens who could see the absurdity of how the situation was developing found themselves unable to resist, as they should have, a full-scale covert campaign designed to encourage the delusion that 'victory' over Russia meant we had not been victims of aggression with a right to demand compensation from the aggressor.

I discussed this a lot with Dalkhan Khozhaev. We could see that our old men were particularly assiduous in trying to induce a mood of triumphalism in Chechen fighters, constantly building them up and all but elevating them to the rank of saints. It was obvious to me that many were continuing to spread propaganda on orders from their handlers in the Russian intelligence agencies. I remember back in 1995 Sergey Stepashin stated that more than a billion and a half rubles had been spent on their network of agents in Chechnya.

It was, of course, impossible to eradicate this network completely. The foundation had been laid back in the 1930s when the NKVD exterminated almost all the Chechen intellectuals and clergy. The network was propagated down the generations. The young would be shown documents indicating that their fathers or grandfathers had been recruited, and then further shown the secret denunciations which led to the imprisonment or execution of their neighbours, fellow villagers, or colleagues at work. After that, the descendants of informers would be invited to collaborate with the KGB if they did not want the information passed to the children and grandchildren of those who had been murdered as a result of those denunciations. In order to avoid the inevitable blood vengeance, they would agree to collaborate. I know this method is used by the Russian intelligence agencies in Chechnya to this day. These same aged Russian agents were used to worsen the split emerging among the leaders of the Resistance. They visited each presidential candidate and tried to convince him that he and only he was worthy to lead the nation. They also worked on rank-and-file Resistance fighters, insinuating that our top commanders' glory had been stolen from them, that they had reaped the power and money and unfairly forgotten about their soldiers.

Meanwhile, negotiations with the Russians continued. We had several meetings with them to discuss three issues: first, the withdrawal of Russian troops (the 101st Brigade of Interior Troops of the Russian Federation and the 205th Brigade of the Ministry of Defence) to beyond the boundaries of the Chechen Republic; second, assistance from the Russian side in locating Chechens who had disappeared during punitive search operations conducted by the Russian Army and intelligence agencies throughout the republic (of whom, according to our information, there were more than 1,500 and who, we discovered, were being held in prisons under false names and without the right of correspondence); third, the signing of an interim Russo-Chechen Intergovernmental Agreement.

The agreement which was to be signed by the Russian prime minister, Viktor Chernomyrdin, and Aslan Maskhadov as chairman of the coalition government of Chechnya, was to be a temporary measure. The two sides agreed that, until the agreement was signed, the laws of the Russian Federation and the Chechen Republic would be applied to enable unhindered movement of citizens, officials and freight; for this it was essential to restore the functioning of the civil airport in Grozny by 1 December 1996, as well as rail and road communications.

Next we needed to sign an arrangement for customs clearance of goods and freight leaving or entering the Chechen Republic. We needed also to conclude an agreement on the extraction, processing and transportation of oil, oil-based products and gas on the territory of the republic. The Chechen side was to assume responsibility for the security of pipelines, extraction and processing sites of oil and gas. After that, a high priority was to resolve social and humanitarian issues, which required measures to restore essential infrastructure in the towns and villages of the republic, to ensure the payment of pensions and wages, and provide for payment of compensation to those who had been affected by the fighting. For the Chechen side, the matters presented in the agreement as compensation were an attempt to disguise the reparations being paid by Russia, enabling Moscow to save face. Even so, Russia attempted to use it for propaganda purposes. Responding to criticism from Russian ultra-nationalists that Yeltsin had recognized the independence of Chechnya de facto and de jure, Kremlin ideologues pointed to the money from the Russian budget sent to Chechnya to address social issues as showing that the republic was being treated exactly like any other constituent part of the Russian Federation. The Chechen government decided not to take issue publicly with this. Instead it was decided to issue a government directive indicating that all funding being received from Moscow was regarded by the Chechen side as reparations, that is, compensation for damage caused to the Chechen Republic by Russian aggression. By presidential decree, Zelimkhan established a commission to quantify the material damage resulting from the war waged by Russia. The commission had already completed its work and estimated the damage caused by military operations at US$ 170 billion. This meant we could receive funding from Moscow for the next ten or fifteen years without any danger of compromising our principles or infringing our sovereignty. All that was required was for us to adopt appropriate regulations for domestic use, and this could continue until diplomatic relations were established with Russia.

The next round of negotiations with Ivan Rybkin to finalize the text of the Intergovernmental Agreement was scheduled to take place in Moscow. I flew there as leader of the Chechen delegation. All the issues relating to the agreements were already practically agreed, but the question of the two Russian brigades which, we knew, Moscow was intending to station permanently in Chechnya, remained unresolved. This had proved a stumbling block in our negotiations, and was the main issue I had to discuss with Rybkin.

I arrived in Moscow on 16 November 1996 on the same plane as Ruslan Aushev, who was flying in to a meeting of the Federation Council. With me were Alu Gaisumov, Said-Khusein Tazbaev, and Yaragi Abdullaev, CRI deputy foreign minister. At Vnukovo Airport, Deputy Security Council Secretary Leonid Mayorov was waiting for us at the bottom of the steps.

Mayorov impressed me as a very decent man. In informal conversation he was vehement in his criticism of the military campaign in Chechnya. We developed a good, trusting relationship. Before we got in the cars, Leonid told me Ivan Rybkin was waiting for me at the Security Council. He asked me to accompany him straight back there, adding that his staff would take those accompanying me to our hotel. I agreed, only saying that Alu Gaisumov would come with me.

We got in the car with Mayorov and were soon at No. 11, New Arbat where the offices of the Russian National Security Council were located. Ivan Rybkin met us at the entrance and led us inside, where we found Sergey Stepashin and Vyacheslav Mikhailov waiting. Although our Russian negotiating partners were planning an informal meeting, that was not how it felt as we found ourselves in the office of the Security Council secretary, which was more like a vast hall than a place where someone actually worked. Only the huge desk with a plethora of telephones and a globe indicated that this was in fact an office rather than a hall for ceremonial receptions. On the wall hung an enormous map of the Russian Federation. To the right of the desk were a leather sofa with two armchairs and a coffee table with newspapers on it. To the left was a long table with chairs for meetings. On the wall opposite the desk were huge bookcases, but instead of books they held files of different colours, evidently full of documents. The whole environment was redolent of the USSR.

After the official handshakes, we did not sit down and I strolled over to the bookcases to look at some documents. My attention was caught by files on a middle shelf, one of which had inscribed on its spine, 'A vengeful Chechen fords the river, sharpening his blade.'

I took it these were documents relating to Chechnya. Rybkin noticed the shelf I had paused at. He was visibly embarrassed, and explained apologetically that this was a poem by Lermontov which a joker on the team of his predecessor had inappropriately left behind. I replied that the joker would have gained a better understanding of why Lermontov's Chechen was sharpening his blade if he had read Tolstoy.

The attitude towards the Caucasian War and the Chechen question is ambiguous in Russian classical literature, and the same ambiguity is still evident among Russian writers and journalists today. Lermontov in his famous *Ismail Bey*, wrote of the Chechens:

> *Wild clans in gorges over which the raptor soars,*
> *Their god is freedom and their law is wars;*
> *They grow up swiftly in the midst of plunder,*
> *Acts of great cruelty, deeds that fill with wonder;*
> *There mothers' lullabies bid them take care,*
> *And in the night they sense the Russian bear;*
> *To kill a foe's not crime but execution;*
> *Their friendship's sure but surer retribution.*
> *The good get goodness, blood begets more blood,*
> *And hate and love are boundless as the flood.*

Despite the obvious sheen of Romanticism, these verses, on closer inspection, are hardly flattering for the Chechens, because the adulation of freedom in combination with wildness and wars as the only law leads merely to anarchy and gangsterism. I do not suppose this is the idea Lermontov, who by his own admission was in love with the Caucasus, was intending to express, but it is clearly imprinted on these lines of his poetry. The truth, however, is that it was only invasion by a foreign army, the army in which Lermontov was an officer, which forced the Chechens to take up arms, forced them to 'sharpen their blades' and be drawn into a war which, as even official Russian history admits, lasted no less than 60 years. Lermontov himself was one of hundreds of thousands of Russians who donned military uniform and whose aggression made war an inevitability and a way of life for the Chechens for many, many decades.

Or take Leo Tolstoy's novella, *Hadji Murat*. Unlike the Romantic Lermontov, Tolstoy was not only a great writer but also a thinker and world-renowned humanist. Here is what he wrote about the Chechens:

> *Nobody spoke of hatred for the Russians: the feeling experienced by all the Chechens, from the youngest to the oldest, was stronger than hate. It was not hatred, for they did not regard those Russian dogs as human beings, but it was such revulsion, disgust and perplexity at the senseless cruelty of these creatures, that the desire to exterminate them – like the desire to exterminate rats, poisonous spiders, or wolves – was as natural an instinct as that of self-preservation.*[4]

Following on from a description of the destruction of a Chechen village perpetrated by bloodthirsty Russian soldiers, these intensely emotional words seem fully justified. But put yourself in the shoes of the Russian man-in-the-street and let us try to imagine what thoughts he will have after reading these lines. We do not have to rely on guesswork, because these thoughts were expressed by a Russian officer who participated in the Chechen War and gave an interview on television: 'After what we have been guilty of in Chechnya, we have no option but to completely destroy this people because they will never forgive us or our descendants.' And indeed, Tolstoy's words about a feeling 'stronger than hate' harboured by Chechens towards Russians, can only convince the latter that there can be no question of any sort of peaceful coexistence between the two peoples. Whether he intended it or not, that is the premise underlying Tolstoy's words. By the end of the Caucasian War in the nineteenth century, even the most 'lenient' Russian statistics admit that more than half the total Chechen population had been killed.

Today's Russian human rights activists and democrats consider themselves the spiritual heirs of the Decembrist revolutionaries who, in 1825, proposed a broad programme of liberal reforms against the absolutism of Russia's monarchy. It is, however, instructive to see just what proposals the Decembrists put forward in respect of the highlanders of the Caucasus, including, of course, the Chechens. Let us look inside the proposal for a new democratic constitution for Russia ('Russia's Truth'), compiled by one of the leaders and main ideologists of the Decembrist movement, Pavel Pestel. For all the liberalism of his views, for all the progressive ideas in his draft

---

[4] Leo Tolstoy, *Hadji Murad, Great Short Works of Leo Tolstoy*, Tr. Louise and Aylmer Maude, New York: Perennial Classics, 2004, p. 629.

constitution which proposes the abolition of serfdom and equal rights for all Russia's citizens, Pestel's commitment to democracy miraculously evaporates when he comes to the problems of the Caucasus. In the second chapter of his constitution, 'On the Tribes Inhabiting Russia,' Pestel proposes:

> Taking into consideration the fact that all attempts have demonstrated indisputably the impossibility of inclining these peoples to tranquility by gentle and amiable means, the Provisional Supreme Board determines:
> 1) to resolutely conquer all those peoples living, and all those lands lying, to the north of the border between Russia and Persia, and equally also Turkey ...
> 2) to divide all these Caucasian peoples into two categories: the peaceful and the turbulent. The first to be left in their habitations and afforded Russian governance and system; and the second to be forcibly resettled into the interior of Russia, fragmenting them in small numbers and distributing them through all the bailiwicks of Russia; and
> 3) to institute in the Caucasian territories Russian settlements and to these Russians reallocate the lands confiscated from their previous turbulent inhabitants that by this means all trace shall be expunged from the Caucasus of its former inhabitants and this region converted into a tranquil and well ordered province of Russia.

Thus, it transpires that the instigator of the project to deport the Chechens and other peoples and to resettle the lands thus 'vacated' with Russian colonists was not the blood-stained dictator Joseph Stalin but the liberal democrat, Pavel Pestel. How interesting too that Tsar Nicholas I, who hanged Pavel Pestel as one of the five ringleaders of the uprising, repeated almost word for word the formulation of the executed democrat in his infamous rescript to his viceroy in the Caucasus, General Paskevich:

> Having thus accomplished one glorious affair (the war with Turkey, *AZ*), you are now charged with another, in my eyes equally glorious and in respect of direct utility much more important: the pacification for all time of the highland peoples or extermination of the recalcitrant.

In Russia, tsars, general secretaries, and presidents came and went, the political system changed; autocracy was replaced by Bolshevism, which in turn was replaced by democracy, but Russia's basic attitude towards the Chechens – 'Subjugate or Exterminate!' – has never changed. The protracted

Caucasian War of the eighteenth and nineteenth centuries brought about the deaths of more than half the Chechen population. The Communists' hatred of the rebellious Chechens cost our people, according to various estimates, the death of as many as 70 per cent from purges, starvation, and the cold when they were transported in unheated cattle trucks in the severe frost of February 1944. The current wars, even according to official statistics, have resulted in the physical destruction of 250,000 Chechens, including 40,000 children under 12 years of age. More than 300,000 Chechens, in order to save their families from destruction, have dispersed around the globe. 'Subjugate or Exterminate!' No single generation of Chechens since the end of the eighteenth century has been left unscathed by this relentless Russian policy.

Meanwhile, Rybkin continued, 'Unfortunately, those who today determine our Russian policy think in the old categories; I would even say, they think in ancient stereotypes.'

'As it happens, one of Russia's principal ideologists is with us today,' I reminded Rybkin, turning to Nationalities Minister Vyacheslav Mikhailov. 'What does the Nationalities Ministry say about all this?'

Mikhailov, who at that moment was standing next to Stepashin, nervously puffed at his invariable cigarette before retorting, 'I am not an ideologist but a simple official and executive.'

As the deputy of Nationalities Minister Nikolai Yegorov, Mikhailov was one of those behind the attack on Grozny on 26 November 1994. In Mozdok, Mikhailov personally met all the leaders of the pro-Russian opposition and gave them detailed instructions to overthrow the legitimate authorities in Chechnya. Akhmed Kelimatov, a zealous collaborator, writes about this in his book *Chechnya in the Clutches of the Devil*.[5]

Rybkin invited us to sit down and, as if oblivious to my spat with Mikhailov, continued, 'I know for a fact that during the Second World War more than 150 Chechens and Ingush were deservedly nominated for the title of Hero of the Soviet Union, and that more than 300 Vainakhs took part in the legendary defence of the Brest Fortress. Directly as a result of Stalin's decision to deport the Chechens and Ingush, only a few received these awards, and even then they were recorded as Dagestanis or members of some other nationality. The second fact, their involvement in the defence of the Brest Fortress, was simply hushed up.'

---

[5] Akhmed Kelimatov, *Chechnya: v kogtiakh d'iavola ili na puti k samounichtozheniiu*, Moscow: Ekoprint, 2003.

XII: Subverting Independence

On a personal note, I should say that the Chechens were well aware of both these facts. In my family, for example, we knew that Moka Khasanov, my father's brother, died defending the Brest Fortress. In the 1980s I went to Byelorussia and visited it, where I saw the marble memorial slabs which list no names. Needless to say, I found no mention at all of my uncle. Usman Balgaev from Elistanzhi was with me, and we were speaking Chechen as we walked down the Memorial Avenue to the defenders of the fortress. There were very few people there, but suddenly an elderly gentleman spoke to us. Hearing our unfamiliar speech, he asked where we came from. Usman and I were obviously not foreigners, but at the same time we were not speaking Russian, and it was evidently this that caught his attention. We told him we had come from Chechnya and the old man was delighted. He was a war veteran and had Chechen friends who had fought alongside him during the Second World War. He spoke very highly of our countrymen. He remembered their names: Khasan, Arzu, Turko, Aziz. He told us that in the summer of 1944 his regiment was lined up and the names of the Chechens and Ingush were called out. When the Vainakhs stepped forward, they were ordered to surrender their weapons on the grounds that the High Command had decided they were to be dismissed from the Army because the Supreme Soviet of the USSR had resolved to deport all Chechens and Ingush to Central Asia and Siberia as punishment for their 'collaboration with the German fascist invaders.' They would be given travel documents by the staff headquarters to enable them to join their families and relatives. On arrival at their destination they would be required to register as persons subject to 'special resettlement.'

The old man told me that he and the others in his regiment felt the tremendous injustice of the decision. A turning point had been reached on all fronts. Everywhere the Germans were in retreat. Nobody now doubted that the Soviet side would be victorious, and just at this moment the order was received to remove the Chechens and Ingush from the front line, deprive them of all ranks and military awards, and exile them to Central Asia. However, despite feeling that tremendous injustice, none of them, the old soldier told us, dared publicly oppose the decision because they did not have the whole story at that time. Stalin was their infallible god whose decisions were wise and unchallengeable. The old man told us that, under those anonymous slabs, lay buried the Chechens and Ingush who died defending the Brest Fortress.

I told this story to my Russian colleagues at the meeting. They all listened carefully but, when I finished, Sergey Stepashin tried to change the subject. 'Yes,' he said, 'of course all manner of things have happened in our history, many trees have been felled, and not only then but now too.' He moved on: 'What is the current situation in Chechnya?'

Stepashin went on to say he had read in the papers that I had been nominated as a candidate for the presidency of the republic. He wondered what my relations with Aslan Maskhadov were like. Did I have points of disagreement with him? I replied that we had no disagreements but that elections were a democratic procedure. Those who had put me forward as a candidate had availed themselves of their constitutional rights and everything was entirely in the spirit of our free Chechen society and in accordance with our laws.

The attitude towards us of Russian officials and the tone in which they communicated with us had changed by this time. Nevertheless, they remained true to their immutable imperial policy of 'divide and rule.' Stepashin went on to say that fighting an election was an arduous task and would require a certain amount of funding. He was certain that Chernomyrdin's government, of which he was a representative, would be willing to find means to support my campaign and that, if I were elected president, Moscow would be only too pleased. I knew they were having exactly the same conversation with all the other major candidates. They knew that divisions were appearing between the leaders of the Chechen Resistance and were eager to extend and deepen them. I thanked Stepashin for his offer but said that the people who nominated me and the 10,000 people who had submitted their signatures in support of me to the Central Electoral Commission in accordance with Chechnya's legislation would doubtless be able to fund my election campaign.

'If Moscow really wants to help with our elections,' I said, 'we need to resolve the issue of withdrawal of Russian troops from the republic, namely the two brigades of the Interior and Ministry of Defence Troops.' I turned to Rybkin. 'Actually, my purpose in coming to Moscow was to discuss this issue, Ivan Petrovich. We really do need to deal with it if we are to keep the peace and conduct the elections in Chechnya. If we cannot agree on this issue, it will rule out the signing of an Intergovernmental Agreement and, of course, it will be impossible to hold elections.'

I did my best to persuade them that having these brigades in Chechnya was completely pointless, and that the continued presence of Russian troops in Chechnya was an irritant which complicated and could jeopardize the entire peace process. There would be people who would commit provocative acts and, after all that Russian troops had been guilty of in Chechnya, no one could guarantee their safety.

Rybkin answered that he fully understood the difficulty of the situation and had discussed the issue with Yeltsin, but had so far failed to convince the president of the expediency of pulling the brigades out of Chechnya because those in charge of the security ministries, especially General Kulikov, were categorically opposed to the idea. Then Rybkin made a proposal: 'Could you meet Kulikov to discuss this issue? I think that would be very helpful.' Although I was not scheduled to meet Kulikov, I accepted Rybkin's offer, noting only that I would have to get the agreement of our Chechen leaders.

At this point, Boris Berezovsky came into the office. He shook hands individually with all present in an uninhibited and confident manner. His behaviour made it clear that he considered himself to be in charge, although he was studiously polite to Rybkin and demonstrated that he understood and respected his formal subordination. Berezovsky sat himself down on Rybkin's right and apologized politely for having interrupted our conversation. He asked me about the situation in Chechnya and the preparations for the elections. Rybkin said we were just discussing the highly sensitive issue of the two brigades stationed in Chechnya. Then, emphasizing that these were formal discussions, Rybkin said, 'Akhmed Zakaev, as secretary of the Chechen Security Council, says that if we do not come to a decision over these two brigades the meeting between the two prime ministers may be in jeopardy.' He added, 'Personally, I think that it would be better not to link the two matters.'

Berezovsky said, 'Thank God, we have no incurable patients and also no issues which cannot be resolved. If our Chechen friends consider these two brigades the main issue then we should decide the matter at a federal level. We have been discussing this issue with our colleagues from Chechnya from the very beginning, and it was one of the most important items at our negotiations in Nazran. I find their arguments compelling. If they are capable of controlling the situation in Chechnya themselves, we should welcome that. I entirely agree that the presence of these two brigades in Chechnya can only lead to armed clashes and provocations. Particularly in the light of our sad experience of recent attempts to create joint command posts.'

To this, Rybkin responded that he too accepted our arguments, but that he was also well aware of the position of generals with very weighty epaulettes. I understood that he was talking about Kulikov, the minister of the interior, and Kvashnin, chief of the General Defence Staff.

'No matter who holds what position,' I said to Rybkin, 'the final decision rests with the supreme commander-in-chief, the Russian president,

Boris Yeltsin. As I understand it, Yeltsin has entrusted the conducting of negotiations to you, and you, Ivan Petrovich, are the plenipotentiary representative of the president of Russia. It is for you to try to persuade him of the expediency of withdrawing these two brigades. Perhaps we could do that together? If you organize a meeting with Yeltsin, I am prepared to make it a joint effort.' Rybkin said the president was still in hospital and it was not currently possible to arrange such a meeting, but he could organize a meeting with Kulikov if I agreed.

When we rose to leave, Alu told me that our men were settled into their hotel. I asked him to let them know we were running a bit behind schedule and that they should not be concerned. We went out into the yard. There were several Mercedes with government number plates and a jeep with a flashing light and bodyguards round it. This was evidently Berezovsky's personal security. Ivan Rybkin offered me a seat in his car. We got in the back and Alu sat next to the driver. As we moved off, Rybkin asked who Alu was: his name, what position he held, and so on. I replied that Alu was a security officer of our government, that he had fought by my side throughout the war. I said he was a very reliable and experienced person, and last but not least he was my friend. I understood what was behind Ivan Petrovich's interest, and added that we could safely speak about any topic in his presence. Rybkin laughed and said, 'You understand everything! That makes it much easier to talk to you.'

Then he became much more serious and added, 'I simply do not know who brought relations between us to this state or why, and what need we had of bombs when we could have talked to each other.' I thought it only tactful not to remind Ivan Petrovich that he had been chairman of the State Duma when Russia's rulers took the decision to bomb Grozny. By this time we had intelligence of the fact that the resolution of the Russian Security Council to launch a military operation in order, as they put it, to 'restore constitutional order' in Chechnya, was signed by Rybkin as speaker of the Duma, by Shumeyko, the chairman of the Federation Council, and by the heads of all the constituent entities comprising the Russian Federation with the exception of President Ruslan Aushev of Ingushetia and Kirsan Ilyumzhinov, the president of Kalmykia.

The real architect of the war, however, its chief ideologist who persuaded Yeltsin to start it, was Sergey Shakhrai. Contrary to a widely held belief, Russia's minister of defence, Pavel Grachev, was not the main instigator of the war. As later became known, Grachev was the last to sign the document. He tried to persuade them all that we should reach agreement with

Djohar Dudaev. He said he had met him, that Djohar was prepared to negotiate, and that it should be entirely possible to reach a compromise. It was only after Sergey Stepashin, the director of the Federal Counter-Intelligence Service, and Sergey Shakhrai openly accused him of cowardice that Grachev added his signature to the document authorizing war.

Rybkin meanwhile came round to his real reason for inviting me to ride with him. He said frankly that Moscow was very keen that Maskhadov should win, and through secret channels had put a great deal of effort into persuading the pro-Russian Chechens, and in particular Zavgaev and other Chechens in his government, to hold back their activists from placing obstacles in Maskhadov's way. Yeltsin had already signed a decree dissolving Zavgaev's government. Ivan Rybkin went on to ask me how else they could help Aslan Maskhadov to win the election. I told him I had perfectly good, friendly relations with all three of the major candidates – Basaev, Yandarbiev and Maskhadov – and that there was no doubt in my mind that Aslan Maskhadov would win.

'If you really do want Maskhadov to win,' I warned him, 'stop supporting him in your media, because that is entirely counterproductive. Every time one of your politicians comes out in support of him on Russian television, it costs Maskhadov potential votes. You still do not understand the mentality of the Chechens, even after we have stood up to Russia for several centuries. If people in Moscow speak out in favour of Maskhadov, Chechens will suspect a trap. For its own reasons, Moscow did not want Dudaev to be president because he was a protagonist of independence. Accordingly, if you support Maskhadov, Chechens will see that as indicating that you have already reached agreement with him to give up independence.'

I went on to assure Rybkin, 'If you are hoping that once Maskhadov is president he will do a deal on independence, you are very much mistaken. At one time, before the war, Djohar Dudaev could have agreed to very major concessions, but today neither Maskhadov nor anyone else in our team could give an inch on the ideal of national independence. If you want Maskhadov because he is not an 'extremist' or a 'radical' but a sober and intelligent politician who enjoys the support of the Chechen people, and if that makes him more acceptable to you than Yandarbiev or Basaev, then fine. So be it. Chechens are not all that bothered with whom exactly you conclude a durable peace as an equal partner. But now, Ivan, after this atrocious war, you ought not to be wondering who you might find it easiest to incline to treachery, but how to restore our relationship with each other, which could perfectly well be a mutually beneficial alliance.'

For a while Rybkin looked thoughtfully out the car window. It was noticeable that my ability to read another person's thoughts had not gone down well. It was equally noticeable that what I had to say was not what he was hoping to hear. He responded non-committally, changed the subject, and before long we arrived at our destination.

When we got out of the cars, Berezovsky suggested Rybkin should go to the White Hall. The villa which housed Berezovsky's club or, as it was known officially, Hospitality Mansion, was on Novokuznetskaya Street. Berezovsky briefly recounted its history to me. Before the revolution it had belonged to a merchant. Berezovsky mentioned his name, but I no longer recollect it. In the Soviet period it accommodated the Political Education Centre. A few years previously, LogoVaz, one of Berezovsky's companies, took a 49-year lease and restored it. The 49-year lease was widely used at the beginning of Perestroika, during the transition to a market economy. As the law stood at the time, premises considered to be of major architectural importance could not be taken into private ownership, so wealthy businessmen and companies negotiated with the officials in charge of particular sites, more precisely, bribed them and, for a nominal payment, rented the building for 49 years.

Accompanied by Boris Berezovsky, effectively the owner, Alu and I had a tour of the rooms, each of which was decorated in an appropriate colour. The LogoVaz Board of Directors met in the Green Room, the Red Room was a restaurant, and through the Rose Guest Room with its piano you proceeded to a bar with a plasma TV on the wall. The Rose Room also had a door on the left which led to a small antechamber with a sofa and several armchairs. This in turn led to the White Hall, where we were to dine. The whole house was fitted out with luxurious Italian furniture. The White Hall was decorated in a distinctively European style and was markedly different from Rybkin's office which we had just left. To encapsulate the difference, if Berezovsky's mansion was the face of emergent Russian capitalism, the way Rybkin's office was furnished was emblematic of the Soviet system which, with all its ponderous pomposity, had been consigned to oblivion.

While we were being shown over the house, the rest of our companions had already taken their places at the dinner table. Ivan Rybkin invited me to sit next to him. The table was covered with a variety of cold dishes, bottles of vodka, brandy, and different wines. The waiter offered us a menu from which to choose among the entrees. Spotting my tacit concern about the meat dishes, Boris Abramovich jocularly reassured me: 'Akhmed, I can promise you that in this house nobody is going to sell you a pig in a poke.

Everything is kosher.' Turning to the others, he added, 'I know many Chechens and have found myself in a variety of situations with them. One thing I have noticed is that, despite their being Muslims, they drink wine and vodka and keep mistresses, sometimes several. Pork, however, they do not eat.' He asked me, 'What is this, Akhmed, a separate, Chechen school of Islam?' 'Of course not,' I replied. 'It is simply the result of 130 years of Russian domination of Chechnya.' Then I added, 'What you have noticed are the results of Chechnya's 130-year history as a part of Russia. I can tell you a joke on this topic. A Russian decided to tease a Tartar for having bow legs. 'Ravil,' he asked, 'why are all Tatar men bandy legged?' 'That I would not know,' the Tatar rejoined, 'but our elders say it is because for 300 years they have been sitting on the Russians' necks.'

The others also had jokes to tell, and then we gradually moved on to more serious issues. The talk came back to the two Russian brigades in Chechnya. Rybkin said he had already given his staff instructions to organize my meeting tomorrow with General Kulikov. I contacted Zelimkhan Yandarbiev by phone and reported that I had a meeting pencilled in the next day with the head of the Russian Ministry of the Interior. Zelimkhan replied that I was welcome to meet anyone at all, just so long as I got the message across to our Russian partners that, without resolving this issue, we could not continue to negotiate.

Later, Alu came in to say he had been contacted by Said-Khusein, who had asked him to tell me that there were ministers of the Zavgaev government in the rooms next to ours in the Rossiya Hotel. They were friends and fellow villagers of Yaragi Abdullaev. They had laid a table and were awaiting my return so they could talk to me. Needless to say, this was no part of our programme or plans and sounded extremely suspicious. I asked Rybkin, because of what had happened, to arrange for us to be moved from the Rossiya to some other hotel. Berezovsky stepped in, said he would organize the move immediately, and asked how many of us there were. He summoned one of his officials and told him to sort the matter out. Twenty minutes later, Boris told me he had booked four rooms on behalf of the Russian Security Council in my name at the President Hotel. Alu took over the further arrangements.

Shortly afterwards, Rybkin and I finished discussing the plan for the next day, and then Alu and I, escorted by Leonid Mayorov, went to the President Hotel. The first thing I did was ask Yaragi how his fellow villagers, ministers of Zavgaev, had come to be occupying rooms next to ours at the Rossiya. He explained that the day before we left for the negotiations, he had been phoned by Vakha, a fellow villager, who suggested meeting up when we were in Moscow. Yaragi said it had not seemed important, and that was why he had not told me about it. When we arrived in Moscow, Yaragi continued, they had asked where we were staying and he told them. He said they wanted to meet me to talk about the situation in Chechnya, about the forthcoming elections, and wanted to offer us material assistance, that is, to finance my election campaign.

Said-Khusein and Alu made no secret of the fact that they did not believe Yaragi, but at the same time showed no sign of disrespect because he was regarded as a member of our team. I too could see that Yaragi was being disingenuous in claiming not to have considered the matter worth mentioning, but did not make an issue of it. I just gave him a strict warning against displaying any more unwelcome initiative.

In the morning Alu and I went down to find Leonid Mayorov already waiting for us in the lobby. We drove to the Ministry of the Interior to meet Anatoly Kulikov, who oversaw the entire security apparatus of the Russian Federation. We did not have far to travel: the Ministry of the Interior building was at the intersection of the Garden Ring Road and Lenin Prospekt. It was a white high-rise building of concrete and glass and we were met at the entrance by a police officer who conducted us to the lift. Kulikov met us in the waiting room and took me into his office. Alu and Mayorov remained behind.

Kulikov's office was very large and, apart from the official furnishings and state emblems, there were a good few of the minister's personal belongings, portraits, and various diplomas on the walls. I did not spend too much time examining the decor, however. If with Ivan Rybkin I had been able from the outset to establish a good relationship of trust, the same could not be said of Kulikov. Although he was studiously polite, there was something blase about him. He had a rather lordly air and was completely different from the person I first saw on a video taken four years previously, in 1992, when an agreement was being signed on the withdrawal of Russian troops from Chechnya and the allocation of military equipment, half of which was transferred to the Chechen side. In four years, Anatoly Kulikov, who had ignominiously lost the war in Chechnya, had somehow contrived to rise from the rank of colonel to that of general. He was now trying rather too hard to present himself as a great statesman with a fund of practical experience behind him. In other words, he was doing his best to measure up to his exalted rank. At the time we are speaking of, this individual really did play a significant role in Russia when decisions of major importance for the state were being taken. His hand was greatly strengthened after he got the better of General Lebed.

Kulikov invited me over to a round table to the right of the long committee table. It was covered with cold dishes, including ham, and a whole battery of bottles of vodka and cognac. The contrast with Berezovsky's hospitality the evening before was striking. Kulikov was evidently not averse to trying, in Berezovsky's words, to sell me a pig in a poke. He asked what I would like to drink, knowing full well that I would refuse alcohol. He had no intention of drinking himself. It was evidently a tactic intended to emphasize the informality of our meeting. I thanked him for his hospitality and said I had already breakfasted at the hotel, but would not say no to a cup of tea. Within a few minutes, tea was brought and we got down to our discussion. Like everybody else we met in Moscow, Kulikov began by asking about the situation in Chechnya, except that he made it clear that actually he already knew everything there was to know, because each morning he was brought a summary covering the whole of Russia.

'Chechnya, of course, figures prominently,' he said, adding, 'However, bare statistics are one thing, and it is quite another to have the opportunity of hearing from someone directly involved in all these processes. When Ivan Rybkin invited me to meet you, I readily agreed.'

Kulikov too was mainly interested in hearing how preparations for the elections were going and how Maskhadov was feeling. How were we coping with the problems, particularly the social problems, which Chechnya was facing? I replied, 'We face many problems but we are not complaining. We are doing our best to solve them, although that is far from easy. The social problems are particularly intractable and can only be dealt with through joint action. A draft Intergovernmental Agreement has been prepared, due to be signed by Chernomyrdin and Maskhadov on 23 November. As things stand, however, the Agreement may not be signed without a final decision about the two Russian brigades stationed in Chechnya. The conducting of the elections is also in the balance. As you know, it is due to take place in early 1997, which means that all Russian troops need to be withdrawn from Chechnya before the end of this year. That leaves very little time, and it seems to me, Anatoly Alekseyevich, that you, as deputy prime minister of the Russian government with overall responsibility for security matters, should actively involve yourself in our negotiations and bring forward the signing of a decree by the president of Russia on withdrawing these brigades.'

When I said this, Kulikov leapt out of his chair and started pacing nervously around the room. 'Never! I will never agree to that!' he shouted. 'We have agreed from the outset that these two brigades are to remain in Chechnya. We have invested a huge amount of money in capital construction of barracks and headquarters buildings, and are we now supposed to hand that all over to Basaev and Gelaev?'

'Forgive me, Anatoly Alekseyevich,' I interrupted. 'When and with whom did you agree this? It has never been discussed with us. The individuals with whom you agreed it, Zavgaev's government, were dismissed yesterday by a decree of the Russian president. You need to consider the situation as it stands today. If we really want to bring this war to an end, those two brigades have to be withdrawn. As a representative of the legitimate Chechen government I must officially inform you that we cannot guarantee their safety. We have warned about this from the outset of our negotiations with the Russian side and our negotiating partners are aware of the issue. All of them are civilians, but you are an army man and know better than anyone what has gone on during the recent war. More than 100,000 of our civilians have been killed. They have surviving relatives in Chechnya. That is not less than 100,000 armed people for whom we currently have no useful work in a republic devastated by war.'

'Exactly,' Kulikov exclaimed. 'I shall have once again to send in the Army and there will be a lot more casualties.' 'Wait a moment, Anatoly Alekseyevich,' I said. 'Have we not just ended the war? Are you wanting to keep these brigades in Chechnya in order to provoke a new influx of troops, a new war?'

'That is not what I said,' Kulikov back-pedalled. 'I will be straight with you, Akhmed. I am categorically opposed to this and that is what I will tell the president. If he nevertheless decides on that course of action, I shall resign.'

'Fine, Anatoly Alekseyevich, one confidence deserves another. Let me be honest with you too. For as long as there remains even one pair of Russian army boots on the territory of Chechnya, there will be no elections and the war will continue. I have said that to your colleagues on the Security Council, and I am telling you now.'

With these words, I rose from the table and my breakfast with Kulikov ended before it had begun. He saw me to the waiting room, where Alu and Leonid Mayorov were waiting. We shook hands with Kulikov and, escorted by the same police officer, went down to our car. We drove back to the President Hotel where, at two o'clock, we had an official meeting with the Russian delegation, headed by Ivan Rybkin. Before the meeting, I told him about my dialogue with Kulikov. Rybkin was already more or less aware of how it had gone, as Kulikov had phoned him and said much the same to him as he had to me. Boris Berezovsky promised Rybkin to arrange a meeting for him with Yumashev, the husband of Tatiana Diachenko, to secure a meeting with President Yeltsin. Such was the reality in Russia: the chairman of the National Security Council had to go through the president's son-in-law in order to see him. Actually, little has changed in Russia since then: all important decisions are taken by a tight circle of individuals, and the institutions of the state only then give them a semblance of political legitimacy.

For an hour we conferred officially, discussing the protocol of the forthcoming meeting between Aslan Maskhadov and Viktor Chernomyrdin. Then the press were invited in and official statements were made. It was announced that a further round of negotiations in Moscow for a peaceful settlement of the Russo-Chechen conflict had been concluded.

The next day, 19 November 1996, I flew back with Aushev to Ingushetia and went on to Chechnya. Aslan Maskhadov, Kazbek Makhashev, Khozh-Akhmed Yarikhanov, Islam Khalimov and I met at Zelimkhan Yandarbiev's. Said-Khasan Abumuslimov was also present. I reported back on the results of my trip and told them that Rybkin and Berezovsky had assured me they would persuade Yeltsin to sign a decree on withdrawal of the Russian brigades. Maskhadov and Yandarbiev showed little interest in this, and I had the impression their thoughts were elsewhere.

A distinct chill could be felt in relations between them. Aslan tried not to show it, but Zelimkhan made no secret of his emotions. This time he did not ask any questions about the negotiations over the Intergovernmental Agreement. He had changed so much he seemed a completely different person. They say the Almighty tests men in three ways: with hardship, wealth, and power. Zelimkhan passed the first test, but not the second or third. His craving for power proved so strong that he accused us of being unfair to him, and even today could not keep quiet. He quietly shifted the focus of the meeting to the elections, reproaching Aslan with having all along been interested only in power. Aslan said that was not true: he had returned to the republic in order to serve his people and, if he had been a careerist then, like many other Chechens, he would have stayed in Russia. Aslan went on to say that Zelimkhan had only offered him the position of prime minister in the belief that he would be unable to cope and be discredited as a politician.

After Aslan's retort, Zelimkhan leapt to his feet, picked up a copy of the Qur'an and threw it on the table in front of him. 'Swear on the Qur'an that was so! Can you swear that these were my exact intentions?'

Aslan reproached Zelimkhan, 'This book, incidentally, is not just a collection of poetry. What way is that to treat the Holy Qur'an? Pull yourself together. Behave rationally!'

So saying, Aslan got to his feet, bade us farewell with a smile, and left, followed by Islam Khalimov. Kazbek Makhashev then tried to steer the discussion in a different direction, reporting to Zelimkhan on how law enforcement in the country was being restored and how long he would need to complete the task. Despite the formal dissolution of the joint command posts, established at General Lebed's insistence and designed to provide a law enforcement system, they were still staffed by ex-fighters. Kazbek, as CRI minister of the interior, had been charged with turning them into regular police departments. That evening proved to be the wrong time for discussing the matter, and soon Kazbek, Khozh-Akhmed and I left too.

The next day, 22 November, I again flew, with Maskhadov's agreement, to Moscow to find out on the ground how things stood with Yeltsin's hoped-for decree on withdrawing Russian troops from Chechnya. Upon arrival, I had a meeting with Ivan Rybkin and he informed me that, as promised, Berezovsky had arranged for him to meet Yeltsin that night. The draft decree was ready for signature. Rybkin said he was confident Yeltsin would sign it. He asked me to inform Aslan and the other members of the Chechen delegation that everything was going to plan and that, in accordance with our protocol, a plane would be sent to Ingushetia to bring them to Moscow.

Alu and I were again staying at the President Hotel, and at 4.00 am I was phoned by Colonel General Leonid Mayorov with the good news that Boris Yeltsin had just signed Decree No. 1590 on withdrawal from the territory of the Chechen Republic of the 101st Brigade of Interior Troops of the Russian Federation and the 205th Brigade of the Ministry of Defence. This was very welcome news! Mayorov added that I should be ready to leave by 9.00 am. He would come with Rybkin to pick me up, as we would be flying to Ingushetia together.

Everything went as agreed, and on the way to the airport Rybkin explained why he thought it was advisable for us both to fly to Ingushetia today and accompany Aslan Maskhadov and the other members of the Chechen delegation back to Moscow to sign the Intergovernmental Agreement. He said the Russian 'hawks' were furious about Yeltsin's decree and might go to any lengths to disrupt the scheduled meeting between Maskhadov and Chernomyrdin. That was why he had decided to bring the Chechen delegation to Moscow personally, on his own plane. Ivan Petrovich saw this as the the only way to forestall possible attempts to sabotage the meeting. In the hierarchy of Russian power, the secretary of the Security Council had only the president and the prime minister above him, so his presence was a very worthwhile guarantee against unpleasant surprises. The morning news broadcasts reported that the Russian and Chechen delegations were meeting today in Ingushetia. Our Russian negotiating partners had so far kept secret the imminent meeting of Maskhadov and Chernomyrdin. This in itself shows how powerful and influential those opposed to a peaceful settlement of the Russo-Chechen conflict were in Russia.

After my talk with Rybkin, I contacted Maskhadov and told him about these changes of plan. While we were flying to Ingushetia, Ivan and Boris Berezovsky gave me a detailed account of Yeltsin's signing of the decree. The Russian Security Council had sent General Kulikov off on an urgent trip to Poland, to ensure that while they were discussing the issue with Yeltsin the militant general should be as far away as possible. My informants told me that Yeltsin was extremely reluctant to sign. He invited them to imagine the fuss the Communists would make in the Duma and what the consequences might be. To get him to sign they had had to provide a lot of arguments in favour, in particular that it was the main condition of the Chechens for continuing the peace process, that without it the elections in Chechnya might be cancelled, and that Maskhadov could not guarantee the security of Russian soldiers in Chechnya. The Chechens would blame Russia for torpedoing the peace process initiated by General Lebed by removing him from power. Finally, allowing the peace negotiations to fail just because of these two brigades would lead to immediate resumption of all-out war, which Russia could afford neither in economic nor political terms, because a new war in Chechnya would turn the whole world against them.

After listening to all the arguments, Yeltsin finally said,

'Very well. I am signing this decree, and on your heads be it. For all the political consequences of this decree I will hold you personally responsible. We really cannot allow a resumption of the war.'

That was how the ill-starred Decree No. 1590 came to be signed. Deeply engrossed in our conversation, we found we had already arrived in Ingushetia. We were met at the airport by Ruslan Aushev, who took us straight to his country residence. Shortly afterwards, Aslan Maskhadov, Movladi Udugov, Khozh-Akhmed Yarikhanov and Tim Guldimann all arrived. As a hospitable host, the president of Ingushetia invited us to lunch where, in an informal setting, we discussed some of the finer points of the imminent meeting and made a few changes to the official procedure. Specifically, it was agreed that the meeting would be held not at the White House but in a country residence near the hamlet of Razdory. A few hours later, we all flew to Moscow on the aircraft of the secretary of the Russian National Security Council. By 7.00 pm we were at Chernomyrdin's residence and the official negotiations between the Russian Federation and the Chechen Republic of Ichkeria concluded with the signing of an Intergovernmental Agreement.

The Agreement had a great impact, not only in Russia but throughout the world, because it had been mediated by the OSCE. In Europe and Chechnya the event was, of course, welcomed. The late night news of all three Russian state television channels showed the meeting and commented on points in the Agreement.

Vyacheslav Mikhailov stated that the working text of the final draft of the provisional Intergovernmental Agreement had been printed in only two copies, one of which was with the Russian and the other with the Chechen side. On 24 November a press conference was held in Moscow at the Arbat Hotel where our delegation was staying, at which Aslan Maskhadov described the signing as 'an important step towards a peaceful settlement' of the conflict.

'This document,' he said, 'provides a basis for resolving the practical economic and social issues between the parties.'

Regarding the Russian presidential decree on the withdrawal of troops, Maskhadov said Russia had made an important contribution towards ensuring that the elections to be held in Chechnya on 27 January 1997 were fully democratic. He gave an assurance that the Chechen side for its part would do everything in its power to ensure that no armed individuals were anywhere near polling stations on election day.

That same day, Gennadiy Zyuganov, the leader of the Russian Communist Party and the People's Patriotic Union of Russia, gave a briefing at which he said he had sent a demand to the State Duma on behalf of three groups of deputies, the Communist Party fraction, the People's Power group, and the Agrarians, to convene an emergency session of the parliament to discuss the president's decree and the Intergovernmental Agreement. 'This agreement,' Zyuganov said, 'does not reflect the realities, and has been signed without consulting the National Security Council.'

Zyuganov stressed that the Praesidium of the People's Patriotic Union of Russia was astonished that both documents, the decree and the agreement, had been signed without consultation with the Ministries of Defence and of the Interior. The Union intended to request the boards of both ministries to examine these documents and decide how they assessed them. It also intended to ask the Ministry of Justice to scrutinize their legality.

Our delegation, headed by Aslan Maskhadov as chairman of the coalition government, returned to Chechnya. The first stage of a peaceful settlement of the Russo-Chechen conflict had been completed successfully, but in the republic both officials and ordinary citizens were preoccupied with the elections and did not see this success as being of great importance. Needless to say, in Aslan Maskhadov's campaign headquarters it was presented as a personal political and diplomatic triumph for their candidate.

Looking back only a few years later on the events described in this chapter, comparing the withdrawal of those two brigades with the pre-war situation in 1992 when Russia had also agreed to withdraw its troops from Chechnya, I saw we had committed a huge blunder on both occasions. I will not touch on the earlier events, but if we had agreed to keep those two brigades in Chechnya on a contractual basis for 5, 10 or 15 years, that would have been tantamount to recognition of our independence by Russia, as Russia retained military bases on a contractual basis only with sovereign republics. Looking back at my meetings with Russia's leading politicians, I am certain that at that time Moscow would have agreed to sign such a treaty, with the involvement of and guaranteed by the OSCE by analogy with Ukraine and other former Soviet republics in the Caucasus and Central Asia. Unlike them, we had a real opportunity to negotiate this on more favourable terms. If those two brigades had remained in Chechnya, they would have served as a guarantee that Russia would not undertake any new aggression against us. In political terms, it could only have strengthened our sovereignty and been a first step towards establishing diplomatic relations between our countries. History, however, cannot be wound back, and the only point in my writing this is to warn those who come after us not to repeat the mistakes we made in the heat of the moment and the euphoria of victory. At the time, however, I thought Yeltsin's decree on withdrawing the last Russian troops from Chechnya was a great diplomatic victory for us, and was happy to have played a not insignificant part in it.

XIII

A Chechen Crime Wave Made in Russia

Heads of other Caucasian republics prepare to establish relations with the CRI. Russian intelligence agencies engineer the murder of six members of the International Red Cross working in Chechnya, leading to the immediate withdrawal of humanitarian support from the outside world. Yandarbiev, still acting president, is aware of the plot but does nothing to stop it. When Russia sees Chechnya will not renounce independence, it resorts increasingly to dirty tricks. Journalists employed by Berezovsky are supposedly kidnapped, inaugurating a crime wave the CRI government cannot contain. Its international reputation is seriously harmed. Failure to nominate a unity Resistance candidate for the CRI's second presidential election. Zakaev's manifesto for a Chechen democracy.

Our perception of the political situation at that time was that we were making good progress towards recognition of our independence, despite furious resistance from Russian ultra-nationalists and the security forces. Very soon, however, we realized that we were not prepared for the new challenges thrown down by the Russian intelligence agencies. They struck their first blow against us in December 1996, shortly after our meeting with a negotiating committee of the heads of the North Caucasian republics. The meeting was held in Chechnya under the chairmanship of Ivan Rybkin, secretary of the Russian National Security Council. He was joined by President Valeriy Kokov of Kabardino-Balkaria, President Ruslan Aushev of Ingushetia, President Magomedali Magomedov of Dagestan, and President Kirsan Ilyumzhinov of Kalmykia. Also present were Governor Nikonov of Russia's Stavropol Territory and Rafael Khakimov, aide to the president of Tatarstan.

Before the meeting the guests were driven round Grozny. More precisely, they were driven through the charred ruins, left after the war, of a city which was once the largest industrial centre in the North Caucasus and renowned for its beauty. After discussion of the main issue of the meeting, our guests, still very much under the impression of the apocalyptic sights of the ruined city, began as one to assure us they would provide every assistance in the task of reconstruction.

President Kokov of Kabardino-Balkaria spoke on behalf of all the guests. He thanked us for our honest, open and, as he put it, rational policy. He admitted that, preparing to come to Chechnya at the suggestion of Ivan Rybkin, he had been concerned that there would be reproaches from our side that our neighbours had not shown the solidarity customary in the Caucasus in our struggle against Russia.

'We could not do that,' Kokov said, 'because we are Russia and our peoples, as you rightly pointed out, have made their choice. Nevertheless, for our part, and here I am talking about the peoples of Kabardino-Balkaria, we also respect the choice of the Chechen people. I am confident that all those in Moscow have had a change of heart on this issue, especially after the Chechen people defended their choice in a war. The proof of this, in my opinion, is to be seen in recent events, namely the Intergovernmental Agreement signed by the prime ministers of Russia and the Chechen Republic of Ichkeria, and the Presidential Decree on complete withdrawal of Russian troops from Chechnya.'

Listening to his and other speeches, I followed my habit of keeping an eye on our old acquaintances, Stepashin and Mikhailov. They were at first exchanging glances full of disquiet, and then began literally to glare at Rybkin, clearly trying to get him to change the subject. However, Rybkin pretended not to notice their signals and made no attempt to interfere with the discussion, scribbling some notes on papers lying in front of him. After Kokov, Kirsan Ilyumzhinov spoke.

'The people of Kalmykia,' he said, 'in just the same way as the Chechens, Ingush, Balkars and Karachais, were deported from their homeland and for many years considered untrustworthy in the USSR. Today, that situation has changed and the attitude towards us in Russia has changed. Now the people of Kalmykia, and I, as president of Kalmykia, decide our own priorities. For me it is abundantly clear that Chechnya is an independent state, and that in Kalmykia I should receive any official representative of Chechnya as the representative of an independent state. If anybody does not like that, I see it as their problem.'

After this, Rybkin entered the conversation. 'Who might not like it, Kirsan?' he asked. 'Moscow? We have long been receiving our Chechen colleagues in precisely that manner. What does that tell us? What do the speeches we have heard from Valeriy Kokov and Kirsan Ilyumzhinov tell us?

They tell us that, within the framework of the Russian Federation, it is possible to enjoy a very great deal of freedom.'

At this point, Aslan Maskhadov addressed Rybkin. 'Ivan Petrovich,' he said. 'The Khasavyurt Accord exists and we have already signed the Intergovernmental Agreement. Let us not discuss the issue of the political status of Chechnya today. The systematic steps we are taking give us a real chance of establishing normal mutual relations.'

At this, Vyacheslav Mikhailov could contain himself no longer. 'Quite right, Aslan Alievich!' he exclaimed. 'We do not need to confront these issues until 2000. There is no shortage of problems needing to be resolved today.'

Aslan then invited our guests to dine in one of the buildings in Grozny which housed his election campaign headquarters. Towards evening, the Ikarus bus on which our guests had arrived, departed for Ingushetia.

The very next day, on 18 December 1996, at one of the regular meetings of our Cabinet of Ministers, Kazbek Makhashev and Director of the Department of State Security Abu Movsaev reported on the murder of six members of the International Red Cross who were working at a hospital in Novye Atagi, established and maintained by that organization. The temporary hospital complex was situated in the lowlands of Chechnya between the foothill villages of Chiri-Yurt and Novye Atagi. That location had been chosen to be accessible to people from several highland and lowland regions, and was probably the only place in the entire republic where they could obtain fully qualified medical assistance. I had been there only a few days before the atrocity with my thirteen-year-old son, who had a leg problem. While the doctors were examining him, I was shown round the hospital by several of the staff. The women told me how their work was organized. All the staff were Chechens, with the exception of five women and one man who worked for the Red Cross. They were paid regularly and were very satisfied with their jobs. I talked to some of the patients who were being treated there, and they too were immensely grateful to both the staff and the organizers of the hospital. Although the doctors were specialists in the treatment of bullet and shrapnel wounds, and there were many with such wounds in Chechnya, they also helped people with a variety of other health problems.

This murderous attack on the Red Cross mission in Novye Atagi was not just the vile, cold-blooded killing of members of the world's most humane profession, but a tragedy on an international scale. At the same time, blasphemous as it seems to put it this way, for certain forces and a particular faction, the mass murder was a very professionally executed black operation which had an enormous impact. After these killings, all the international humanitarian organizations, whose assistance our mangled and impoverished country so desperately needed, terminated their activities within a matter of days and left the republic. Despite their limited experience, the Chechen security forces managed to solve the crime in a very short time. They established who commissioned it, who organized it, and who carried it out. They were unable, however, to catch the criminals, because they fled to Russia. The request from the CRI state prosecutor to the Russian law enforcement agencies for the suspects to be extradited was simply ignored, even though they were provided with all the evidence of the case. The main suspect was Adam Deniev, who by this time was making no secret of the fact that he was a colonel of the Russian Federal Security Bureau. The surmise of Andrey Babitsky, a Radio Liberty reporter abducted in Chechnya in December 1999, that Deniev's gang were responsible for kidnapping him, makes it clear enough what this Russian officer specialized in.

A number of details came to light subsequently. In 2002, Zelimkhan Yandarbiev told me when we met in a hotel in Istanbul that one of the emirs of the Urus-Martan Jamaat came to see him and told him he had been asked by Isa Umarov to murder the members of the Red Cross on the grounds, Umarov alleged, that they were 'working against Chechens and Muslims,' that they 'represent Jew-Freemasons,' and that 'after being treated by them young Chechen men lose their ability to father children.' That emir, after consulting senior emirs in Urus-Martan, refused to carry out Umarov's proposal. The murderous attack happened a week after Umarov's conversation with the emir.

The savage crime committed in Novye Atagi was a landmark. It was the beginning of a campaign of subversion against the Chechen State, the first, immensely damaging act aimed at discrediting the leaders of Chechnya, a campaign to create an image of Chechens as barbarians incapable of forming a state on their own.

We did not at first realize a new war was being waged against us: a vile and loathesome war conducted by the Russian intelligence agencies and their complicit or unwitting natural agents. We found ourselves faced with a growing crime wave, but at the time were busy with other matters and failed to give it the priority it deserved. We carried on working as normal in circumstances which were far from normal.

Meanwhile, during the night of 30 December 1996, all Russian troops left the territory of the Chechen Republic. In accordance with the law governing a presidential election, all candidates other than the incumbent stepped down from their government positions. Aslan Maskhadov resigned as chairman of the Cabinet of Ministers and Zelimkhan Yandarbiev replaced him with Ruslan Gelaev. Movladi Udugov and I resigned our ministerial posts and were replaced by our deputies.

At the height of the canvassing, campaign offices were set up in all regions by the three main candidates: Yandarbiev, Maskhadov and Basaev.

My own reasons for standing in the election I have given above. For Movladi Udugov this was an opportunity to make his mark politically as the leader of a new ideology totally alien to Chechens. Aslan Maskhadov took almost no part in the canvassing and issued no policy statements. Zelimkhan Yandarbiev, however, publicly criticized us all, complaining that we, his former comrades-in-arms to whom he had entrusted government positions, were now disputing his right to the presidency. He claimed that all of us, with the exception of himself, were to blame for the split between those who supported independence and the Resistance fighters. He virtually accused Maskhadov of being obedient to the will of Russia, asserting that if he became president he would betray the ideal of independence. Basaev also criticized Maskhadov, recognizing him as his main competitor. He accused him of having supposedly agreed during negotiations after the Budyonnovsk Raid to hand over Basaev and all the other participants to the Russians. He harangued Aslan on television, demanding he should reveal the source of the funds for a car he had given Shamil on his birthday. These were underhand tactics and Shamil gained no votes by resorting to them. Almost all Chechens regarded him as a national hero, and saw these sordid utterances as a sign of weakness and totally unworthy of him.

Shamil and I also had our own little verbal spat. I had a meeting with voters in the village of Znamenskoye. One of the people present said, 'Akhmed, Shamil Basaev was here yesterday. We asked him why he was criticizing all his rivals except you. We asked him what he thought would happen if you were elected president. Shamil said that if you were elected president there would be holidays and weddings in Chechnya every day. I would like to ask you what you think would happen if Shamil Basaev were elected president.' I supposed Shamil had been referring to my acting career and post as minister of culture, and told the questioner that if Shamil were elected president we would have funerals and mourning every day and international isolation, and they should decide for themselves which they preferred.

That meeting was shown on television, and immediately afterwards my friend Aslanbek Ismailov commented that only three people considered

Basaev a terrorist: Yeltsin, Maskhadov and Zakaev. He went on to say that Maskhadov and I had agreed with the Russians to hand over Basaev and the others involved in the Budyonnovsk Raid after the elections. I met up later with Basaev at his campaign headquarters and we got our relations back to normal. I heard afterwards that he forbade his supporters to criticize me because he knew my response would do nothing for his prospects of winning. He and his representatives later offered me the post of prime minister after he was elected, as they were sure he would be, but on condition that I withdrew my candidacy and endorsed him. I declined the offer, explaining that for me it was a matter of principle not to take sides in the election race between the three main candidates.

Shamil had a good chance of winning, but let himself down by intemperate criticism of Maskhadov, and was further damaged by the fact that Aslan never reacted to it. Of course, the hostility of the pro-Russian opposition played its part in ensuring he did not win. As for Zelimkhan, he never had any prospect of victory, although he counted as one of the main contenders. His entourage helped delude him into believing he was in with a chance, not least because he could abuse his position in the government to further his campaign, making use of so-called 'administrative resources.' Early on in the elections observers in Urus-Martan found 100,000 forged voting slips filled out in favour of Zelimkhan and prevented them reaching the ballot boxes.

In my campaign speeches, I urged people not to vote for any of the three of them. I and my supporters decided our campaign strategy and tactics, which were to talk to the voters about our programme in order to avoid discussing the other candidates' personalities. Our strategy was to gain the ear of the main candidate, Maskhadov. Aslan had said that if he won he would conflate the programmes of all the other candidates and make them the foundation of his own policy.

Our programme differed fundamentally from those of the others. We proposed that the newly elected parliament and president should schedule new parliamentary and presidential elections, to be held within two years on the basis of new legislation. We believed two years were needed to enact appropriate legislation and make the necessary changes and additions to the existing Constitution.

While we were preoccupied with the elections and considering the best arrangements for our state, the Russian security services were not sitting on their hands. In early January, two weeks before the presidential election, they delivered a second blow. Two journalists from the Russian ORT television channel were abducted. Russia's formal agreement to the holding of elections in Chechnya on the basis of our 1992 Constitution, which explicitly declared Chechnya to be an independent state, and involvement of the international community in the form of the OSCE in the elections, marked the end in legal terms of six years of political and military confrontation between Russia and Chechnya. The legitimacy of the Chechen government and of the Constitution of the Chechen Republic of Ichkeria as the fundamental law of a sovereign state was being recognized not only by Russia but by all the countries of the European Community. There were, however, forces in Russia which shunned the light, and from the end of August 1996 they and those Russian leaders whose position we had come to know during the negotiations and called 'the War Party,' embarked on a series of black operations aimed at disrupting our elections or, at the very least, discrediting them. One of the most effective ways was to kidnap journalists.

I would like in this chapter to consider the important matter of the attitude of Russian journalists to the war. That is essential for my readers to appreciate how absurd it is to suggest involvement of the Chechen government in any of these abductions which, in political and propaganda terms, would have been suicidal. Who can doubt that the outcome of modern warfare depends now as never before on the 'news music,' that is, which side the sympathies of reporters and news presenters are on, and the direction in which they are going to move public opinion? Needless to say, confronting the monster of an over-militarized imperial Russia, we had a vital interest in retaining the sympathy of the public in Russia and worldwide. For that sympathy we were wholly dependent on journalists. During the First War, the sympathies and support of the overwhelming majority of Russian journalists were on the side of the Chechens.

I see a number of reasons for this. First and foremost, all of us, Russians and Chechens alike, hatched out of the same Soviet egg. To a large extent we had a shared outlook, part of which enjoined us to support small, weak nationalities trying to wrest their independence in an unequal struggle from much larger powers. From the late 1950s, Soviet propaganda depicted the struggle of the 'oppressed peoples of Asia, Africa and Latin America against colonial empires' in glowing terms Needless to say, this propaganda did not proceed from any philanthropic respect for freedom. It was being put out by Communists who had established a bloody tyranny in their own country and created, not just an empire, but one based on slavery. The USSR's 'freedom-loving' propaganda was dictated by the simple logic of its Cold War with the Western world, but by no means everyone in the Soviet Union was aware of its seamy side. The population took the propaganda at its face value and were sincerely moved by it. People of my generation and older still remember the way Soviet television and radio told us day and night about the wars of national liberation in progress all over the planet. The tone was rapturous when the struggle scored a victory, tragic when the freedom fighters suffered a reverse. At school, we read in our history books about the exploits of Tadeusz Kościuszko, Simón Bolívar, Patrice Lumumba, and many other leaders who led their peoples in the struggle against a motley collection of empires. All that lodged, not only in our memories, but deep down in our subconscious. When Russian troops invaded Chechnya in December 1994, the situation was precisely what we had been accustomed to condemn in earlier years as a crying injustice. A huge colonial power had unleashed an unjustifiable war of aggression against a small people one million strong, who were defending their national independence. Naturally, the sympathies of very many Russian journalists and prominent public figures were on the side of the Chechens.

I do not have much time for Boris Yeltsin and will never remotely be an admirer. He unleashed two wars against the Chechen Republic, bringing down a terrible catastrophe both on Chechnya and on Russia. This individual, whom blind chance elevated to the pinnacle of power in a vast country, had on his conscience both the slaughter of hundreds of thousands of Chechens and the hobbling of democracy in Russia itself. Those two Russo-Chechen Wars served Putin's KGB junta as an excuse for reviving an authoritarian regime in Russia. Despite this, we should recognize that in the Yeltsin years one of the institutions most essential to democracy functioned in Russia with little constraint – free media. The Russian intelligence agencies even at this time were murdering journalists who, like Dmitry Kholodov, dug too deep, but the press and television remained free. This allowed dozens of Russian reporters, at the risk of their lives, to cover the course of the war objectively and make an appreciable contribution to the struggle of the Chechen people for their freedom.

The Chechen armed forces and intelligence services placed no obstacles in the way of journalists, if for no other reason than because we more than anyone had an interest in ensuring that the international community learned as fully as possible the truth of the tragedy which befell the Chechen people when Russian troops invaded their republic. The Russian generals for their part fell into the habit of ascribing all their failures and defeats to media bias, and at the first opportunity called the journalists harshly to account. First in the woeful list of murdered journalists was an American, Cynthia Elbaum, who at the very beginning of the war, on 22 December 1994, died from the shrapnel of a bomb dropped by a Russian plane. There followed the deaths of dozens of Western, Russian, and our own Chechen journalists, many of them shot in cold blood by the Russian Army in full view of numerous witnesses. Those journalists whose bodies the Russian Army managed to hide were declared 'missing without trace.' In this manner, in the First War 20 journalists were killed, 9 'disappeared,' and 36 were wounded. These cases are well known to human rights organizations, which recorded all their names and the circumstances of their deaths, so I will not repeat the information here.

The first kidnapping of Russian journalists in Chechnya, on 19 January 1997, still remains a mystery. The Russian media reported that an ORT television crew, Roman Perevezentsev and Vyacheslav Tibelius, were abducted that day by 'unidentified individuals' near the Chechen village of Samashki on the border with Ingushetia. I call it a mystery, because witnesses of the abduction confirm that both journalists in fact safely crossed the Chechen border into Ingushetia. I do not want to engage in groundless speculation, but the circumstances in which, a month later, the two journalists were 'freed' suggest the whole thing was staged. The Russian intelligence agencies announced to the media that Perevezentsev and Tibelius had been freed on 18 February 1997 as the result of a 'special operation.' If it is possible to cast doubt on whether the two journalists in fact had any difficulty in leaving Chechnya, we can say with complete certainty that no 'special operation' was undertaken by Russian security forces in Chechnya at the time of their release. Neither could there have been, because our armed forces and police were stationed throughout the republic, even in small villages. Additionally, the official version was flatly contradicted by equally official information to the effect that US$ 3 million had been paid to Chechens for their release. I believe that what really occurred was a covert operation by the Russian secret police whose purpose was to broadcast to all the criminal elements in Chechnya that an easy way of making money was to kidnap Russian and Western journalists, specialists contracted to work in Chechnya, and just wealthy citizens.

At this time the entire world was expressing admiration for the heroism of the Chechen people, and for the Chechen government this created a very favourable psychological and emotional climate in our dealings with foreign countries. The purpose of these abductions was to change that climate so that the international community would instead view Chechens with horror and revulsion, to change our image to one of cruel, primitive natives and criminals pursuing not lofty ideals of freedom but bloody ill-gotten gains. It had the added bonus that, by frightening off journalists with the threat of abduction, Chechnya could become a no-go area for news gathering, after which Kremlin propaganda, exploiting the powerful machinery of disinformation it inherited from the USSR, could spread around the globe whatever murky lies about the state of affairs in Chechnya it chose to, without fear of refutation by honest journalists. Unfortunately, this black operation by the Lubyanka and its local political and criminal agents met with considerable success.

We received more reliable information about subsequent abductions. Chechnya is a small country, and the names of kidnappers, where their victims were held, and much else did not long remain a secret. We knew that a vast number of kidnappings in Russia itself were wrongly and cynically attributed to Chechens. A criminal gang or the Russian intelligence agencies would abduct a businessman or a member of his family in Moscow or another city. He would be driven around in the boot of a car for a long time to make it seem he had been taken a long way. He was then hidden in a basement and his relatives would be phoned by someone claiming to be a Chechen commander or 'warlord' whose name was well known in Russia, or his associate, and a ransom demanded. Payment of the ransom in exchange for the victim was made as close to Chechnya as possible, usually in Ingushetia or Dagestan. As a result, one more sensational kidnapping was attributed to Chechens, to which they often had not even an indirect link. Thousands of such kidnappings occurred throughout Russia, but where no Chechen involvement was claimed, they were listed only in the statistical reports of the Ministry of the Interior. Any abduction in which Chechens genuinely or fraudulently figured received detailed coverage in the media. In this way, the Russian agitprop machine succeeded in associating the concepts of kidnapping and Chechen gangsters in the public mind.

I write this not with any ambition to whitewash Chechnya's criminals, but simply as a statement of fact. Engrossed in our political disputes because of the elections and our rival programmes as to how Chechnya should be governed, we did not initially appreciate just how serious these crimes really were, considering them just something our law enforcement agencies would have to deal with. After the elections, when we had split into rival political groups and jamaats, we found ourselves incapable of dealing effectively with a crime wave initiated and orchestrated by the Russian intelligence agencies. Of course, that is no excuse.

I had no campaign headquarters anywhere other than Grozny, on Friendship Square on the ground floor of a five-storey apartment block. It was a one-bedroom apartment I had bought before the war and refitted as a shop.

The block had not been damaged too badly, and I decided it would do. I and my colleagues were there almost every evening to work on our programme. We were not numerous. My chief of staff was Said-Magomed Khachukaev, who was my deputy at the Ministry of Culture. Dalkhan Khozhaev and Makkal Sabdullaev stood in for me and generally came to the headquarters at the end of their working day. My staff included Said-Magomed Khasiev, an anthropologist and expert on folklore; Dalkhan Khozhaev, minister of the Archives Department; Khasan Bakaev, historian; Gapur Aliev, director of the Chechen Drama Theatre; and Ruslan Khachukaev, deputy director of the Russian Drama Theatre. The theatres were not functioning because those in Grozny had been destroyed, but their companies survived as legally recognized entities.

Said-Magomed Khachukaev was a very good manager, and within a few days had organized all the office equipment essential for a campaign headquarters: a photocopier and audio and video recorders. The office prepared leaflets with our campaign slogans, made video clips, and produced audio recordings of my speeches and announcements.

Before compiling our programme, we analysed the situation. Why, for example, was it being said even before the war that the Chechen government's authority extended no further than the ground floor of the Presidential Palace? I have to admit there was a grain of truth in this. We tried to figure out why this was by analysing the nature and structure of the Chechen state. For Chechens, with their mentality and long-standing tradition of democracy, authoritarianism in all its forms and manifestations was intolerable, whether in the shape of a kingdom, a sultanate, a khanate, an imamate, or whatever. Power in Chechnya could be neither inherited nor conferred for life, neither could it be absolute. In Chechnya, power presupposes authority derived from voting. In the past this took the form of a meeting of Teip representatives, and in the present of the secret ballot. Any attempt to sidestep this millennial custom was doomed to failure. For proof, we can look not only to the recent past, but back over the entire known history of the Chechen people.

Before the Chechens came into contact with the southward expanding Russian Empire, the characteristic features of our land's internal social arrangements were stability and harmony. Social and economic rules and principles were strictly defined and clearly formulated. Contrary to the nonsense written by Communist historians indoctrinated by Moscow's ideology, there never was a 'class struggle' in Chechnya or an 'anti-feudal movement,' because there were no feudal lords or peasants dependent on them. That did not require proof, it was simply there in Chechens' memory, as was another fact: that Chechnya had never been a part of Russia, let alone a voluntary part. At the time it came into contact with Chechnya, Russia was an absolute monarchy, a barbaric form of power in which the tsar could treat his subjects like animals. He could sell them, give them away as presents, or massacre entire townships. In Chechnya, on the contrary, human rights were virtually absolute: nobody could kill with impunity, strike or verbally abuse another person, or cause even the slightest damage to their property. Children and the elderly enjoyed a privileged position. As regards the status of women, even women in Europe at that time could only dream of having their rights protected to the same extent as those of Chechen women. For example, the life of a woman was equal in vendetta terms to the lives of two men. To insult her by touch, word or even a look was severely and invariably punished. The Georgian writer, Alexander Kazbegi, wrote that Chechen women were the most free in the Caucasus, because their honour and dignity were protected by law.

In Russia at this time, drunken debauchery was rife and landowners were still availing themselves of the notorious *jus primae noctis*. According to Abdurakhman Avtorkhanov, 'their coming into contact with the Russians gave Chechens not one single day of festive celebration, and only too many days of mourning.' What suffered from contact with Russia, if not most disastrously then certainly most extensively, was the traditional nature and principles of Chechen governance. Throughout their occupation of the country, the Russian colonialists systematically imposed an administrative system alien to Chechens, the main difference being appointment from above, rather than election from below. Village elders, clerks and even the mullahs were appointed by the occupying power. The one indispensable qualification for candidates was subservience to their superiors and willingness to betray their own people, to inform on them, to give and take bribes. This corrosive system of Russian power functioned in Chechnya for over a century, until 1991, irrespective of whether a tsar or the Communists ruled in Russia.

It was precisely because the institutions of our new state did not accord with age-old Chechen traditions of public order that the people could not call it '*Vaineh 'edal*' ('Vainakh power,' 'Vainakh custom'). This was why the new state was unable to wield the necessary authority. In the past, the Chechens had evolved a very advanced form of democracy and social justice, embodied in the institutions of state power. These were such well known communal institutions as the *Mekhk-Khel* and the *Mekhk-Da*. If we translate these terms from Chechen, the former can be rendered as 'parliament,' 'council,' 'shura;' and the latter as 'president,' 'imam,' and so on. The problem is that they carry nuances of meaning unique to the Chechen mentality. These institutions of authority derive from the customs and traditions of the Chechen people, and if we depart from those we lose our identity and condemn ourselves to the kind of difficulties we experienced during the 1990s.

The Mekhk-Khel had legislative and deliberative functions. At its sessions, decisions of national importance were taken which were mandatory for all citizens. Anyone who flouted the regulations of the Mekhk-Khel could no longer be considered a Chechen and was doomed to leave the country or die. The rigour and severity of Chechen laws is illustrated by the saying, 'A man who rises up against the village becomes an outcast; a village which rises up against the country becomes a pile of ashes.' As a result of our discussions, we concluded that by adopting the name 'Mekhk-Khel' for their legislative body, our parliamentarians would defuse the situation. In the first place, the status of the people's chosen representative would he clearly identified. He would no longer be associated with the windbags of the past, with dissolute high-livers, self-important lords or congressmen. Voters would know that for such an important forum as the Mekhk-Khel they must choose to represent them only the very best man in their neighbourhood, unblemished in every respect: intelligent, just, God-fearing, courageous, enterprising, authoritative, and conscientious in fulfilling his promises. The laws and regulations passed would be readily observed, as they would have the support of a millennium of experience and tradition. There would be strengthening of the sense of national identity. Finally, returning to the traditions of our history might put an end to speculation about whether our state should be secular or religious.

As regards the head of state, among the many merits of the title Mekhk-Da, two should be particularly noted. In the first place, formally adopting this new designation of the post of president would further differentiate us from Russia and highlight the uniqueness of the Chechen nation which, should the Almighty so will it, would ultimately be recognized by the international community as a fully fledged sovereign nation under international law. In the second place, the title Mekhk-Da, testifying to the fact that the person elected president was the most worthy person, would enhance the authority of the executive branch, by analogy with the name of the Mekhk-Khel. The orders, decrees, and instructions of the Mekhk-Da would be binding not only because they were in accordance with the Constitution, but also because now they involved the morality and honour of the citizen. Willingness to carry out the instructions of a popularly elected leader is one of the fundamental criteria of Chechenness – 'Nohchalla.'

Mekhk-Khel and Mekhk-Da are institutions of supreme state power, defined in a democracy as government by the people, or power delegated by the people. The supreme authority in Chechen society should grow organically out of the system of local government, represented by the institutions of the Yurt-Khel and the Yurt-Da, both of which would, of course, be elected. The primary source of authority in Chechnya would be the personality of the citizen. The lowest unit of community and state institutions for Chechens is the *Kup* (the local community). This is generally analogous to a ward or district constituency for electing councillors to municipal authorities in European countries. The Kup is a uniquely Chechen institution, and has always played an important role in the life of every citizen, and hence of society as a whole. It has existed in Chechen society since ancient times and is a territorial unit of people living in close proximity, perhaps on the same street or in parallel streets, who regularly communicate and participate in each others' daily life. Kups form naturally, and vary in size and number of residents. From our observations, the range was 400-600 people.

The forming of local government institutions from Kup representatives would signify a rebirth and legal recognition of the traditional Chechen model of local self-government. Not a single person would be overlooked or outside the influence of the authority. In a town or village, representatives of the Kups would form a *Yurt-Khel*, a Council of People's Deputies authorized to decide matters relating to the life of the local community. The Council would elect its chairman, the Yurt-Da, to head the local administration. Thus the Yurt-Da, an extremely important figure in the whole power structure, would have to pass through two filters relating to reliability and competence. First, he would have to satisfy his Kup before being eligible to become a deputy on the local Council of People's Deputies and, secondly, he would have to be chosen by the deputies of the local councils in a multi-candidate election, a substantial barrier and test. After being elected, the Yurt-Da, in addition to being answerable to his Kup and the members of the Council of People's Deputies, would now also be answerable to all the residents of a particular town or village, who could exert pressure on him through their deputies. Given a population in the Chechen Republic of one million citizens, about 2,000 local councillors needed to be elected, each with real power and authority in his Kup and town or village.

The institution of the Kup is optimal for governing Chechen society. During the past 150 years, it has been under constant threat, including even the execution of leaders of Kups. Imam Shamil and his successors, the Russian colonialists, were equally zealous in their efforts to abolish the uniqueness of Chechens by eradicating their national traditions, and specifically their national institutions of self-government.

In order to avoid the coming to power of unqualified, irresponsible people, the entire pyramid of state power in the Chechen Republic needed to be built on the foundation of primary Councils of People's Deputies. The Mekhk-Khel, the parliament, should be formed of delegates from the local councils, the Yurt-Khel, with multi-candidate elections. At the same time, an elected deputy (*Vekal*) of the Mekhk-Khel would remain a member of his local Council. The head of state, the president (Mekhk-Da) would be chosen from among the deputies of the Mekhk-Khel, also in a multi-candidate election and would head the Mekhk-Khel. The Cabinet of Ministers, headed by a prime minister, would also be formed from deputies of the Mekhk-Khel on the recommendation of the Mekhk-Da.

I also proposed introducing a further institution of representative government in the republic, namely a general annual meeting of deputies of all the primary Councils. It might be known as the National Congress. Its tasks would include: 1) choosing the head of state from one of two candidates proposed by the Mekhk-Khel; 2) an annual rotation of the Mekhk-Khel itself.

There were two main reasons why having a National Congress elect the president was desirable. On the one hand, it would stop a president from trying the voters' patience on the grounds that he had been elected for four or five years, and so should be considered untouchable until the end of that term, even if he was making obvious blunders. But on the other hand, it would stop the Mekhk-Khel from believing that, since it elected the head of state from among its members, it could regard him as its placeman, accountable to it in all his decision-making, which would paralyse initiative on the part of the executive branch. In my opinion, the structure we were proposing had clear advantages. Most importantly, it delivered a maximum degree of real democracy and prevented political parties and regional clans from being unduly dominant; at the same time, the organic inter-relatedness of all the branches of government ensured their dynamism and mobility. Any public controversy, any differences between the representative and executive branches of government would be resolved within the framework of the relevant councils. The possibility of being directly recalled by those who had delegated power in the first place would ensure an ongoing sense of answerability to public opinion. It would be possible for those who elected him to recall a deputy at any level, even one holding the highest office of the state. This consideration would safeguard those in power against corruption, conceit, and losing touch with their roots, which Chechens see as wholly unacceptable behaviour.

Because reform of the power of the state unquestionably affected every aspect of the life of the nation, we needed to explain our thinking succinctly on such issues as economic policy and the introduction of a national currency, the administrative division of territory, the power of the judiciary, law enforcement, and the organization of self-defence forces.

National Currency

Even before the First War, when the republic's huge economy was still intact and not a penny had to be spent on reconstructing everything that had been destroyed, there was a shortage of money for paying such items as benefits and scholarships. Factories were being closed, fields left unsown, again because of a lack of funds. It was obvious that the flow of foreign currency, including the Russian ruble, into the republic's Treasury depended entirely on the extent to which we could sell our goods and raw materials abroad. The export share of turnover, even in developed countries, is considerably lower than the domestic share. Accordingly, the financial and banking policies of the state, even without a blockade by Russia, doomed us to suffer an acute shortage of funds, which in turn generated a crisis which our society suffered for many years. Prevarication on the grounds that the time was not ripe for us to issue our own currency was unjustifiable.

Djohar understood this, and that is why he commissioned our national currency and wanted to bring it into circulation even before the First War. Despite all the destruction, the state owned and would in future own sufficient material resources, not least in the form of minerals and land, for the government to be solvent. In the second place, an entirely effective way to curb the predicted inflation was to link the issuing of money to sales of oil and oil-based products both within and beyond the boundaries of the republic. By retaining a monopoly in the oil sector, the government would ensure an uninterrupted inflow of foreign currency, which could be used to purchase modern technology. Without a doubt, the only way out of the economic impasse of the time was to issue our own national currency to finance, at the very least, our own, domestic Chechen production.

Administrative Division of Territory

Splitting the republic into regions (*'raiony'*) was inefficient, and there were no valid reasons for the Soviet regime to have done so in the first place. The socialist planned economy and authoritarian methods of governance were now history. Naturally, an economy based on private property and private initiative needs to plan on the basis of market supply and demand rather than of directives from the Communist Party and Soviet government, passed down and implemented by regional institutions. In post-Soviet society, particularly given the modest territorial size of the Chechen Republic, regional divisions of government were needless. Quite apart from the wasteful duplication of systems, the extensive bureaucracy in regional institutions was expensive. Under our proposed new model of governance, virtually every town and village would be directly represented through its own deputy in the top institution of political power, the Mekhk-Khel. There would still be a need for regional departments for certain public services, such as the police.

Power of the Judiciary

Since ancient times, the institution of the local magistrate had been well adapted to the realities of life in Chechnya. It continued even under the Soviet regime, although semi-clandestinely, and remained unchallenged during the years of independence. In each village, or shared between several hamlets, there was a figure of spiritual authority known as the Qadi, who dispensed Chechen or Muslim justice. Because the traditional Chechen laws, the Adats, have in the course of our history been brought into full compliance with Islamic, or Sharia, law, we could use the expressions 'Chechen justice' and 'Islamic justice' interchangeably. We were in no doubt that it was necessary to legally recognize this Chechen institution as the basis of the national court system, although the way it operated would need to be properly thought through and systematized. For example, each locality would have attached to its Yurt-Khel or Council of Deputies a suitably authoritative and educated Qadi. After becoming qualified and certified at national level, a candidate for the position of Qadi would need to be approved by the Yurt-Khel of the locality. In turn, the Supreme Court, chaired by the Supreme Qadi, would be approved by the Mekhk-Khel. The detail of the system would have to be spelled out by specialists in appropriate professional language.

The System of Law Enforcement

The basis for Chechen law enforcement agencies should be a police station attached to each local Council, with staffing appropriate to the number of people in the locality. A limited number of necessary and transparent institutions under the direction of the minister of police would be created at national and regional level to coordinate and control the police. They would work closely with the Councils of People's Deputies to which, at their various levels, they would be entirely accountable. Like any other civilized country, the republic should have an investigation and prosecution service. The Mekhk-Khel would also have an agency under its jurisdiction to deal with issues of national security.

The National Defence Force

Since the Chechen Republic could not today aspire to intervention in international or regional matters, our armed forces should be strictly defensive in nature, in accordance with our national military tradition. Every Chechen man would be obliged to perform military service. Upon coming of age, he would be awarded a certificate conferring the right to defend his homeland. The minister of defence too would be appointed from among the deputies of the Mekhk-Khel. The Chechen Army would have a professional officer corps which in peacetime. would provide military training to conscripts, and refresher courses to reservists. In time of war, it would command the National Defence Force.

All satisfactorily developing societies and countries have a model of government appropriate to their national mentality and traditions, and this was the analysis I and my colleagues arrived at during our discussions. It provided us with a basis for formulating policy statements to be made on television in the free airtime allocated to presidential candidates in accordance with our electoral law. I constructed my broadcasts around our main contention, which was that we needed to reform our system of government, and that this meant changing the principles underlying how state power was currently organized in the Chechen Republic. This should be done by the president and parliament elected by the people of Chechnya in the elections on 27 January 1997. Two years would be quite sufficient to implement the reforms, which were necessary if we were to create a legal framework respecting the national and historical traditions of Chechen society.

XIV

A False Dawn

Aslan Maskhadov is elected president, but alienates his opponents and promotes cronies. Zelimkhan Yandarbiev rushes through reforms to 'islamize' the republic before Maskhadov's inauguration. Huge ransoms are paid to kidnappers. In May 1997, Maskhadov and Yeltsin sign a doctored peace treaty, which the Russians immediately start undermining. Yeltsin is already preparing for the Second Russo-Chechen War. Chechens prematurely celebrate the ending of 300 years of conflict with Russia.

After we had issued this manifesto statement, and two days before the election, Kazbek Makhashev came to see me at home. He said Aslan Maskhadov wanted to talk and had sent him to fetch me. I got into Kazbek's car, taking Alu and Said-Khusein with me. Aslan was living at his mother's house in Pervomaisk in a Grozny suburb. As we were driving along, I asked Kazbek if he knew what Aslan wanted to talk about. I had not seen him for ten days or so. Kazbek smiled meaningfully and said he knew only that Aslan had asked him to find me as a matter of urgency and bring me to him. I decided to play along, and asked Kazbek in which capacity he had come to fetch me: as interior minister or as a friend. 'As a friend, of course!' he exclaimed. 'In any case, as a CRI presidential candidate you have immunity from arrest.' After 15–20 minutes of such banter we reached our destination.

I had visited Aslan before, but now his situation was different. There was a barrier at the entrance to the village and armed guards checking everybody driving in. They waved Kazbek and me through without any checks or questions, and I asked them to let through the following car with Alu and Said-Khusein. We passed through a further three checkpoints before reaching Aslan's house. Frankly, these security measures seemed over the top. We parked in Aslan's courtyard. By Chechen standards, the house was quite small, with only three or four rooms. Kazbek and I entered, to find that Aslan had a lot of guests. They included Vakha Arsanov, Islam Khalimov, Movladi

Udugov, Isa Umarov, Ruslan Alikhadzhiev, Turpal-Ali Atgireyev, and a few people I did not recognize.

Isa Umarov, as usual, was holding forth with some religious tale. For him, talking on religious topics was a tactic, because he could be sure his listeners knew nothing about these matters and so there could be no discussion. He was thus able to turn all present into obedient listeners, and himself into the teacher with unchallengeable authority to whom everybody had to listen respectfully. Chechens of our generation were very devout Muslims in their hearts, but had no knowledge of theological matters. The only experts in the area were those who had specialized in religious studies on the instructions of or under the watchful eye of the KGB. Umarov was one of those.

Isa Umarov was the older step-brother of Movladi Udugov. During the Soviet period he was a psychiatrist. The USSR had three professions controlled by the KGB: the clergy, revived by Stalin in the Second World War to manipulate believers; forensic pathologists, whose job was to give an opinion on the causes of death; and psychiatrists, who dished out a diagnosis of mental health or insanity depending on what the brutal machinery of the Communist regime was planning to do with the 'patient:' put him in prison or spirit him away behind the walls of a psychiatric clinic. All practitioners of these professions were either controlled by the KGB or secretly collaborating with that sinister organization. Often they were permanent members of its staff. I remembered Isa Umarov's television appearances during Perestroika, when he was trying to convince his public of the need to save the Soviet Union which, he told them, was a great boon for all Muslims.

In the 1980s, Mikhail Gorbachev in the course of his reforms announced the abolition of Article 6 of the USSR Constitution, which provided the legal basis for the 'leading role' of the CPSU leadership in every aspect of life in the USSR. It was not difficult for the secret police to anticipate that people disaffected with the Soviet regime who, up to that time, had been used to gathering in their kitchens for disgruntled discussions and who, as Perestroika progressed, had already begun organizing mass protest meetings, would as the situation developed begin organizing themselves into political parties and movements. These tended to be, on the one hand, people given to veneration of liberal values or, on the other, supporters of national and religious liberation. Following the rule that, 'If you can't beat them, lead them,' the KGB, that military wing of the CPSU, founded the Liberal Democratic Party for the liberals, under the leadership of their long-time agent, Vladimir Zhirinovsky; and for Muslims, the Islamic Revival Party. We have to credit Zhirinovsky's party with ensuring that to this day it has proved impossible to form a genuine democratic opposition in Russia to the ruling totalitarian regime. The Islamic Revival Party for its part, founded at a congress in Astrakhan in 1988, succeeded in every republic where it managed to set up its remarkably permanent offices, in inciting bloody strife between Muslims, dividing them into 'right Muslims' and 'wrong Muslims,' and paralysing in these petty squabbles and spats the entire creative potential of the Muslim peoples of the USSR and later of the former Soviet territories. These hothouse 'Islamists,' cultivated in the Lubyanka, had their greatest success in Tajikistan and, sad to say, among us in Chechnya. Isa Umarov was the unofficial leader of the party, although formally its leaders at the time were Bislan Gantemirov and later Adam Deniev. In the course of the Russo-Chechen conflict, Isa Umarov was to do more damage to the cause of national liberation of the Chechen people than all the Russian security agencies and the Russian Army put together. On the day we are describing, Umarov was one of the most trusted and authoritative figures in Aslan Maskhadov's entourage.

When Umarov had finished his tale, Aslan apologized to the audience and said he needed to talk to me in private. He took me through to his study. The setting was typical of the times and conditions in which we found ourselves. On the desk was a computer (not, of course, connected to the Internet). Aslan evidently used it to store some of his working documents and archives. There were two chairs and a sofa, the Chechen flag on one wall, and a carpet on the floor. Aslan sat in one of the chairs and invited me to sit on the sofa. I thought he probably wanted to talk about our policy statement, but I was wrong. He had not even seen my televised pre-election speeches.

Aslan began the conversation by condemning the campaign tactics of Shamil and Zelimkhan as unworthy of a Chechen. He expressed surprise that people could be in such haste to seize power or hold on to it that they discarded Chechen ethical standards and all propriety. He went on to say that his analysts believed that, as the political forces currently stood, a second round of elections might be needed. His information was that, if a winner did not emerge in the first round, forces interested in seeing the elections fail might succeed in disrupting them, and that he had consequently been advised to invite me to withdraw my candidacy in his favour. If I refused, a second round might be needed because I had drawn votes away from him. He wanted me to go on television to address my supporters, tell them I was withdrawing in favour of Aslan Maskhadov, and urge them to vote for him. That I simply could not do, because I had said from the outset that I would not side with any of the other candidates. That was why I and my team had entered the election in the first place.

I realize, of course, that readers may see me as a starry-eyed idealist, but that was not the case. We were certain that Maskhadov would be elected president and my 'pragmatic' idea was to remain neutral towards the three main candidates and try at the end to reconcile their positions. They had been allies yesterday, today they were opponents, but they had not yet crossed the line to becoming outright enemies. To some extent, and in the early stages after the elections, we did succeed in this. That day, however, I told Aslan that I was meeting many people, I could judge their mood, and had not the slightest doubt that he would defeat his opponents in the first round. I asked him whether, after the elections, he saw any place for me in his team. Aslan replied immediately that we were members of the same team; we had been through the war together, and it was incumbent upon us now to build our independent state together.

'In that case, Aslan, do not ask me to do what you have mentioned,' I said. 'For me it is a matter of principle. If, after the elections, we work together as a team, in the eyes of every Chechen, and especially of those with whom I will have to work, it will seem as if there has been a trade-off: I gave you the votes of my supporters, and in return you will have given me a job. With that knowledge, it would be impossible for me to work with you.'

As Aslan listened, his expression changed. Normally very restrained and discreet, during this period he had changed markedly. Clearly the whole election campaign had put him on edge. He said drily that I could do as I pleased, and stood up, making it clear that our conversation was at an end. I stood up too, walked out of the office, said goodbye to Aslan and his guests, and went out to the yard where Said-Khusein and Alu were waiting for me. They told me Kazbek had already left. I got in the car and we drove home. I must confess I was in a terrible mood. The next day I gathered my team at our headquarters and told them about yesterday's conversation. After much deliberation, we agreed that I should not make the statement on television which Aslan had asked for. The elections were held, as planned, on 27 January, and the next day, after the votes were counted, it was reported that Aslan Maskhadov had beaten his main rivals in the first round by a large margin. His analysts' predictions of the need for a second round were wide of the mark.

That same day, I contacted Aslanbek Ismailov and told him that, now this whole nightmare of the elections was over, in order to reassure our citizens and upset our enemies, Shamil and I should go to see Aslan and congratulate him on his victory, making it clear that this was the end of our disagreements. We did so, and images of the meeting were shown that evening on television, gladdening the hearts of the whole Chechen community.

Ernst Muehlemann, who headed a group of observers of our elections from the Council of Europe, returned to Strasbourg where he convened a full session of the Parliamentary Assembly and said that the elections in Chechnya had been admirably conducted, in full compliance with international standards. Describing the presidential candidates, whom he met several times, Muehlemann emphasized that Maskhadov was calm, modest, and had promised to abide scrupulously by the Khasavyurt Accord. Basaev, according to the Swiss deputy, was more nationalistic, demanded complete independence for Chechnya, and always had a lot of people with guns around him. Yandarbiev Muehlemann described as a religious thinker who would like to stand above the fray, and had intended if the ballot had gone to a second round, to transfer his votes to Basaev. Muehlemann also noted the positive role in the organizing of the elections of the OSCE Mission in Chechnya, which had been working in concert with Ivan Rybkin, secretary of the Russian Security Council.

'I am pleased Maskhadov was elected. He is a politician and a realist who wants not military confrontation but political cooperation, and knows that to resolve all the problems facing Chechnya there is no escaping its natural links with Russia,' Muehlemann said. He also stressed that, while the Council of Europe observers were in Chechnya, they had not felt under threat. 'An important step forward has been taken in the political resolution of the conflict in this region of the Caucasus,' he concluded.

With the elections over, a date was set for the inauguration of Aslan Maskhadov as the new president of the Chechen Republic of Ichkeria. However, until he formally became president, Zelimkhan Yandarbiev remained acting president, with Said-Khasan Abumuslimov as his vice-president. Every day the two of them issued decrees verging on violation of the CRI Constitution. They issued a decree dissolving the Supreme Court of the CRI, introduced a new Code of Criminal Procedure at the instigation of Shamsuddin Batukaev, also appointing him chairman of a Supreme Sharia Court. Twenty-three-year old Arbi Baraev was promoted to the rank of brigadier general and appointed commander of the Sharia Guard. By decree of Yandarbiev, everyone who had worked in the preceding months for his campaign headquarters received the highest state honours of the CRI, the Order of *K"oman Siy* (Pride of the Nation) and the order of *K"oman Turpal* (Hero of the Nation). Many members of the Resistance were awarded orders and medals and promoted in rank solely on the basis that they had expressed support for Yandarbiev during the election. In the process, the acting president and Said-Khasan began a process of discrediting state awards of the CRI and divided the rank and file members of the Resistance.

On the first or second day after the announcement of the election results, Yandarbiev expelled Tim Guldimann from Chechnya, declaring him persona non grata. That is, he expelled from the republic the head of the OSCE Mission, a man who had played a crucial role in bringing peace and who had organized all our meetings with the Russian leaders. Tim Guldimann had been the instigator and organizer of elections to the state institutions of Chechnya under the CRI Constitution of 1992. The official reason given was a statement by Guldimann that he recognized Russia's territorial integrity. For the Chechen leaders this was no news: we knew the OSCE Mission in Chechnya could only operate with the consent of Russia, and that Russia had the right under the statutes of OSCE to close the Mission in Chechnya if its members exceeded their mandate. The first condition for allowing the OSCE Mission to be present in Chechnya was recognition by the organization of the territorial integrity of the Russian Federation.

For us, the presence in the republic of such a prestigious international organization was extremely important. Tim Guldimann was an experienced politician and diplomat and had achieved something almost impossible, by getting Russia to recognize the CRI elections, held under our Constitution which specified that Chechnya was an independent entity in international law. Guldimann really had done more than we had dared to hope for. Now everything depended on us and whether we were prepared to build on this political success and establish diplomatic relations with Russia. Yandarbiev's act was not only politically illiterate and harmful to Chechnya but, in purely human terms, it was dishonourable. Guldimann was risking his life by being in Chechnya: there had been attempts to assassinate him. Despite formally enjoying diplomatic immunity, the OSCE Mission was fired at after Guldimann stated that the so-called election of Zavgaev as head of the republic had not met generally accepted standards of democracy. On another occasion, in summer 1996 Guldimann had a miraculous escape when there was an attempt to blow up the car in which he and Aslan Maskhadov were travelling. During the fighting in August 1996, he and his staff came under fire when they tried to leave Grozny. On the orders of Aslanbek Ismailov, our soldiers risked their own lives to escort them to Aslanbek's headquarters before accompanying them out to Ingushetia.

Yandarbiev's expulsion of Tim Guldimann was universally condemned by Chechens and seen as a sign of weakness on his part. There was general agreement that Zelimkhan was trying to vent his spite after losing the election. After our meeting in Moscow with Yeltsin on 27 May 1996, Chechens had been proud of Zelimkhan and his authority was very high. Everybody had seen on television the way he forced Yeltsin to get off his 'throne' and sit opposite the Chechen delegation. Later, however, by attempting to cling to power, Zelimkhan squandered all that respect. His decree expelling Tim Guldimann finally discredited him as a responsible politician. His actions from then on were extremist and, ultimately, he became just another political outsider.

Meanwhile, preparations were being made in the republic for the inauguration of the president. Numerous guests and delegations were expected. In the entire republic there was not a single building still standing worthy of accommodating this ceremonial event. Accordingly, repairs began at breakneck speed to the Palace of Culture in Chernorechiye, which had more or less survived. I was appointed head of the Organizing Committee, responsible for everything, including the reception, accommodation, feeding, and subsequent departure of the guests. Despite all the difficulties, the Organizing Committee did a great job and, of course, we could never have coped without the help of ordinary citizens of the republic. Our government institutions had no hotels, no transport, and no money. We found private houses for those visitors who had to stay overnight, mostly our guests from the neighbouring republics of Georgia and Azerbaijan. The Russian delegation had its permanent mission in the vicinity of Sheikh Mansur Airport. Overall, thanks to the Chechen community, we somehow coped with the task entrusted to us.

On 12 February at 10.00 am the ceremony began. A hall designed to hold 700 people miraculously accommodated some 1,000. Several thousand more gathered in the square in front. In accordance with the schedule, the event began with a speech by Zelimkhan Yandarbiev. He came out on to the stage and the upshot of his short speech was that he was presenting Aslan Maskhadov with a fully fledged Islamic state. At first nobody could work out what he was talking about, but then realized he was referring to the unconstitutional reforms he had pushed through in the two weeks before Aslan's inauguration. Later, Zelimkhan several times claimed to his friends to have 'laid a minefield all round Aslan Maskhadov.' That day, however, in his parting speech at the ceremony he described it as a 'fully-fledged Islamic state.' In conclusion, Zelimkhan said that he 'would now leave as there were people present in whose company he could not remain.' That day, Zelimkhan behaved in a thoroughly undignified manner, letting himself down both as acting president and simply as a Chechen citizen. He had no business insulting not only our guests but us, his comrades-in-arms. Most of those present were representatives of other republics and a Russian delegation also attended. Along with other representatives of the Council of Europe, Tim Guldimann was there. Perhaps Yandarbiev was referring to him, but in general he was just looking for an excuse to spoil the festivities. His rudeness was the news of the day throughout Chechnya, and unanimously condemned. Except for this tiresome incident, however, all the other aspects of Aslan Maskhadov's inauguration went well. Everybody was in a very positive mood and felt this day would see the beginning of a new life, which they were sure would be peaceful and happy.

Aslan Maskhadov, it transpired, had also not been idle. A day after the inauguration he announced the composition of his new Cabinet: Shamil Basaev became a deputy prime minister with responsibility for heavy industry; Ruslan Gelaev was similarly responsible for construction; Islam Khalimov for social welfare; Musa Dashukaev for the economy; Movladi Udugov became a deputy prime minister and head of the Commission for Negotiations. There was no explanation of my dismissal as head of the government's negotiating team, but none was needed. On the eve of the elections, Movladi had made a public statement urging everyone to vote for Maskhadov. For the time being I remained minister of culture and secretary of the National Security Council, and also a member of the Commission for Negotiations. The Commission also included Minister of the Interior Kazbek Makhashev; the president of YuNKO (Southern Oil Company), Khozh-Akhmed Yarikhanov; and Said-Khasan Abumuslimov took up a new appointment as presidential adviser on political affairs.

As if trying to outbid Yandarbiev, Maskhadov continued the newly instituted tradition of dishing out military ranks and government awards to his election supporters. More than 30 were promoted brigadier generals, more than 50 received the highest awards of Pride of the Nation and Hero of the Nation. For comparison, during the entire period of Djohar Dudaev's presidency he created four generals and nine Cavaliers of the Order of Pride of the Nation. Djohar took these matters very seriously. There was a provision that, on the entrance of a person awarded the Order of Pride of the Nation, even the country's president was obliged to stand up as a mark of respect.

I saw these decrees of Yandarbiev and Maskhadov not only as demeaning the top ranks of the army and insignia of heroism, but also as a departure from centuries-old Chechen traditions. The Chechens took the naming of national heroes very seriously, indeed scrupulously. In practice, it was only in exceptional cases that a person was honoured with this title during his lifetime. He had to have lived his life with dignity, strictly observing the Chechen code of honour and meeting all the stringent criteria for determining who was a K"onakh. After the death of every person who had won renown in war, his entire life was scrutinized and only if it was found to be beyond reproach in all respects did he have an illi, a heroic epic poem, devoted to him, recognizing him as a hero of the nation. In the course of three centuries full of wars only a small number of Chechens were admitted to the constellation of national heroes to whom an illi was devoted. There was great wisdom in this, because only after passing on into another world was the hero free of the possibility of committing some blunder or action unworthy of his status. Moreover, only the death of the hero could ensure that he would not become puffed up with pride because of national veneration, and hubris and arrogance are seen by Chechens as being among the most repugnant of human characteristics.

For a short time it seemed to me that, with the elections over, our differences had been left behind. Less than a week after the inauguration, however, I realized they were only beginning, and coming at us from several directions. Aslan decided that, since the people had supported him and Vakha Arsanov, they should wield absolute power. For a while, Aslan and Vakha were in complete agreement, and they began jointly trying to place their own people in key positions. Their main criterion was personal loyalty rather than professional competence. First, Aslan and Vakha wanted their man, Ruslan Alikhadzhiev, as speaker of the parliament. Shamil Basaev also wanted his man in that position, and put forward two names from his team: Aslanbek Abdulkhadzhiev and Isa Temirov. Both had participated in the Budyonnovsk Raid. Salman Raduev and Lecha Dudaev wanted to see their relative, Akhiad Idigov, ex-speaker of the parliament, reappointed. A majority of deputies supported the president, and Ruslan Alikhadzhiev became speaker. Isa Temirov and Selim Beshaev were elected his deputies.

Ruslan Alikhadzhiev had no experience in this area at all. A former corporal in the Soviet Army, he became close to Maskhadov during the war and was one of the people he felt he could trust. Even before his appointment, Aslan had promoted him to the rank of brigadier general and awarded him both the Orders of Pride of the Nation and Hero of the Nation. If Yandarbiev had tried to create a semblance of objectivity by establishing an Awards Commission and avoided making two awards to a particular individual, Aslan and Vakha had no such scruples and distributed military ranks and awards to lists of their cronies. Needless to say this, to put it mildly, companionable approach to important matters of state ultimately discredited all the government's institutions.

This was largely due to inexperience, but that is no excuse. The Chechen people had entrusted their fate and their future to us, and we had no right to fragment into factions and fritter away everything we had won, and for which our people had paid such a heavy price. After the elections, there was an opportunity to close ranks, just as the Chechen community did in 1944-57 during the years of the Deportation. The main obstacle to this was the split, already becoming visible, on the basis of religion. Wahhabi ideology was injected into Chechnya by the Russian intelligence agencies to destroy the national liberation movement, and was to cause far greater problems later.

On 18 February we learned, again from the Russian media, that the ORT correspondents abducted on 19 January had been released and were back in Moscow just on the eve of the presidential election. In an interview with RIA Novosti, Deputy Security Council Secretary Boris Berezovsky stated that 'in the freeing of the ORT journalists, Roman Perevezentsev and Vyacheslav Tibelius, held by Chechen rebels, an important part was played by the Chechen president, Aslan Maskhadov, First Deputy Prime Minister Movladi Udugov, and Minister of the Interior Kazbek Makhashev.' This abduction was unique, in that who was behind it, and who was paid the three million dollar ransom, remained a mystery to us. One thing is for sure: it started something that grew into a national catastrophe. No less certain is that neither Maskhadov, Udugov, nor Makhashev played any part at all in the journalists' release. In devastated and impoverished Chechnya there were people who saw kidnapping as an easy way to solve their financial problems.

On 21 February, a first official meeting between the Chechen and Russian negotiating teams was held at the country residence of President Ruslan Aushev of Ingushetia. The Russian representatives were Ivan Rybkin and Boris Berezovsky and on the Chechen side there were Movladi Udugov and myself. We agreed at this meeting that in future no ransoms would be paid for the release of kidnap victims, aware that, in all likelihood, abductions would continue.

In late February 1997, we attended a working consultation in Moscow to discuss a number of draft agreements. The Chechen side proposed an agreement on economic matters as a development of the Interim Agreement signed by Chernomyrdin and Maskhadov on 23 November 1996. We also proposed a draft peace treaty between the Russian Federation and the

Chechen Republic of Ichkeria which would prepare the way for an Intergovernmental Agreement on economic cooperation. This would draw to a conclusion the 400-year conflict between Russia and Chechnya. On this trip we came face to face for the first time with grave reservations on the Russian side about the wording of our draft agreement. We explicitly referred in the draft to the need to establish diplomatic relations. We knew perfectly well that the Russian side would not agree to that wording. It was just a tactic to include contentious matters in the negotiation process on which we could subsequently give ground without compromising our strategic objectives. In all the long history of conflict between Russia and Chechnya, there had never been a document which attempted to define the relationship between our two countries, and for us it was strategically important to have an agreement signed by our two heads of state. After the elections in Chechnya, whose results Russia had recognized, there was no reason for them to dispute the legitimacy of Aslan Maskhadov's presidency, as they always had the presidency of Djohar Dudaev. This treaty was to define the nature of Russo-Chechen relations.

The next day we had a scheduled meeting with the Russians, at which Rybkin requested a meeting with Aslan Maskhadov for direct talks to agree the draft peace treaty before submitting it to Yeltsin. In fact, during April 1997, Rybkin had several meetings with Maskhadov. The stumbling block in our negotiations was the second paragraph, which stated that Russia and the CRI would conduct their relations in accordance with the 'the generally recognized principles and standards of international law.' The Russian side offered more than twenty alternative formulations, including 'The Russian Federation and the Chechen Republic of Ichkeria conduct their relations in accordance with the Constitutions of the Russian Federation and the Chechen Republic of Ichkeria, as well as on the generally recognized principles and standards of international law.'

The Chechen side rejected all the options and insisted on the original wording. On our return from Moscow, we reported to Aslan Maskhadov on the disagreements with the Russian side and Rybkin's request to meet him. Aslan recognized that Rybkin wanted to meet him in the hope of persuading him to change the wording of that second paragraph. On 9 April 1997 they met in Grozny. During the meeting, the city centre and the route along which the Russian delegation travelled was heavily guarded by our police. The republic's leaders were well aware of many possible risks. At this period Salman Raduev had organized a standing protest against the possibility that the Russian president might come to Chechnya to sign a peace treaty. The protesters had occupied the entire square in front of the ruined Presidential Palace, and we knew for a fact that the whole business was being orchestrated by forces outside the republic. Simultaneously, kidnappings of journalists and foreigners became more frequent.

In the course of our talks, one of the options considered was that Yeltsin might sign the Peace Treaty in Grozny, supposing that, if he saw at first hand what the Russian Army had done in Chechnya, it might have a beneficial psychological impact and encourage him to be more positive about recognizing our independence. The Russian side opposed this proposal, citing security concerns. Raduev, as if to confirm their fears, declared that the 'Army of General Dudaev' would never let Yeltsin leave Grozny alive. With slogans along those lines, he rallied people to his permanent protest meeting. Everyone could see his unhelpful utterances were a ruse to discredit President Maskhadov. His actions were privately supported by his relatives Lecha Dudaev, the mayor of Grozny, and Akhiad Idigov. It was their family revenge for Aslan's wanting to replace Lecha Dudaev with Turpal-Ali Atgireyev as Mayor of Grozny, and for preventing Idigov being re-elected as speaker of parliament. If their intention was to let Maskhadov know they could make trouble, the result, deliberate or not, was to provide fuel for Russia's propaganda that the Chechens were incapable of governing themselves. At that stage, I was still underestimating quite how serious the forces were which opposed us, both within and outside the republic. We carried on haggling with our Russian negotiation partners over the wording, firmly believing that correctly formulating the position of the two sides in agreements and treaties was the way to the settle the relationship between Russia and Chechnya.

We saw the reason for the centuries-long continuation of our conflict as a lack of clarity about this relationship. The agreements we signed really were historic, and only this can excuse the fact that the CRI government showed excessive scrupulousness, uncharacteristic of modern diplomacy which is built on compromise. Let me adduce just one assessment of the agreements and treaties we managed to conclude with Russia. It comes from Vadim Belotserkovsky, a well known writer and human rights activist.

> Let us return from the elections back to the end of the war and Khasavyurt. We were all watching Lebed: Russian patriots with admiration, imperialistic chauvinists with indignation, but paid almost no attention to another miracle wrought by the Chechens. What peace terms they negotiated! What succinct, thought-through agreements they drafted, with never a word against their interests! This despite a truly

fraught situation, and the fact that they had not a single career diplomat or international lawyer. I am certain the texts of these agreements, laconic and tough as nails (like their language itself), will be included in future textbooks on diplomacy.[6]

For us, however, the issues surrounding the sovereignty of the CRI could not be vague or the subject of diplomatic bargaining and compromise: they were just too important for the Chechen people. We felt that the success we had had in previous agreements should be consolidated by a Treaty of Peace and principles of relations between the Russian Federation and the Chechen Republic of Ichkeria. During his meeting with Ivan Rybkin in 1997, which was attended by members of the delegations of both sides, Aslan Maskhadov made it clear that there could be no compromise on the issue of the independence of Chechnya, and that no wording which called into doubt the republic's sovereignty could ever be acceptable to us.

Our delegations continued to meet regularly to discuss the draft peace treaty. Simultaneously a draft agreement between our two governments, to be signed by Maskhadov and Chernomyrdin, dealt with purely economic issues. We also, of course, discussed issues related to the release of kidnapped journalists. Shortly after the mysterious disappearance and equally mysterious reappearance of the ORT journalists, reporters from the RTR television station and TASS news agency were abducted. No doubt this was precisely what those who pioneered the way with the first kidnappings (or staged kidnappings) of journalists and foreigners were hoping for. Our war-torn republic was full of unemployed, and armed, young people, and it was not difficult to guess that some of them would be eager to make a lot of easy money. The way to do so was helpfully suggested to them. For Russia these operations were a preparation of the ground so that, if unable to incline the CRI leaders to compromise as Moscow wished on the status of the republic, they would be able to declare Chechnya an area too dangerous for foreigners and journalists to visit. That is precisely what Russia subsequently did. Public opinion in the international community and in Russia itself, which, during the war had been predominantly in favour of the Chechens, was being readied for an abrupt change of direction.

---

[6] Vadim Belotserkovskii, 'Chechenskii fenomen' (Munich, 1997), republished by Chechenews, 17 November 2015 http://chechenews.com/вадим-белоцерковский-чеченский-фено/

The situation with kidnapping was additionally an effective means of putting the Chechen delegation under pressure. If we became too high-minded when discussing sensitive issues, our Russian colleagues would steer the discussion towards the topic of kidnapping and hostage-taking, reminding us that we bore responsibility for what was going on in our country.

By late April 1997 we had finally agreed the text of both the documents Maskhadov was to sign with Yeltsin and Chernomyrdin. On 30 April, meetings took place at the residence of the CRI president in Grozny between Rybkin and Maskhadov. At Rybkin's request, the meeting was held behind closed doors, one-to-one. At the end of the meeting, Maskhadov told reporters he was pleased with the results and also with the work the two delegations had done to complete the draft treaty. 'We have finally reached agreement. The two sides will hold a meeting in the near future at the highest level and put an end to many centuries of conflict in the Caucasus,' Maskhadov said. At a briefing in Moscow, presidential spokesman Sergey Yastrzhembsky said, 'Moscow and Grozny are finalizing preparations for a culminating meeting between the presidents of Russia and the Chechen Republic of Ichkeria. The meeting between President Boris Yeltsin of the Russian Federation and Aslan Maskhadov, President of the Chechen Republic of Ichkeria, is of the greatest importance for peaceful settlement of the Chechen conflict.'

At that time, relations between Russia and Chechnya were front page news in Russia. The CRI president's press office reported that Aslan Maskhadov had received an official invitation from the Russian president to come to Moscow to sign a Peace Treaty, agreed by the national delegations of the two sides for peaceful settlement of the Russo-Chechen conflict. The meeting was expected to take place in the first half of May. CRI Vice-President Vakha Arsanov, meanwhile, confirmed to Echo of Moscow Radio that Maskhadov had been invited to Moscow, but was emphatic that the Chechen side had yet to decide whether to accept the invitation or not. After Maskhadov's press office had already confirmed that the meeting of the Russian and Chechen presidents was scheduled to take place in Moscow in the first half of May, Arsanov's pronouncement was completely out of order. Such contradictory statements from the top Chechen leaders only paraded a lack of coherent political strategy. This was due not only to inexperience but also to an unhelpful streak of populism which had dogged us since the days of the protest meetings in Grozny in the early 1990s.

I first had it very diplomatically pointed out to me that the Chechens had no political strategy by Heidi Tagliavini, a Swiss diplomat who was a member of the OSCE Mission. 'Akhmed,' she said, 'the Chechen delegation has an amazing ability to present the lack of any strategy as a brilliant strategy.' The remark was made in 1995. I did not take it very seriously, because Djohar Dudaev was still alive and had around him people who had been there at the beginning of the liberation movement: Said-Khasan Abumuslimov, Zelimkhan Yandarbiev and many others who urged the Chechen people to rise and fight. I never doubted that these people were omniscient, had thought everything through and worked out a strategy which would lead us to independence and a joyous future. I heard them on television and they seemed very clever and judicious. Said-Khasan Abumuslimov would talk for hours about international law and the United Nations, calling for Chechens to go to protest rallies. He spoke about genocide of the Chechen people, cited figures on the natural resources which Russia was taking out of Chechnya, and people believed him. Hundreds of thousands of Chechens attended the rallies.

Only many years later, having passed through the First War, did I realize that these people had no strategy at all, and that everything was held together solely by Djohar Dudaev. Those I have mentioned, and others I have not mentioned, did not have a clue how to establish an independent state, let alone in the extremely difficult conditions created for us by Russia. I had to recognize that what they did at that time was no more than take a reckless gamble which was to cost the lives of hundreds of thousands of Chechens. Their fiery speeches were banal populist rhetoric, as Said-Khasan Abumuslimov later admitted in conversation with members of the Resistance. When he was asked if they had had any sort of strategy at all, any programme fit for the purpose of leading the Chechens to independence and recognition by the international community, Said-Khasan admitted they had nothing of the sort, and that personally at that time he could not stand the way some Chechens regarded themselves as a superior kind of elite. To this the young people gathered at the meeting retorted, 'You should be put on trial for what you did to the Chechen people!'

But to return to my history, despite all the rough edges and blunders, the peace process continued. On 11 May 1997, I flew to Moscow on behalf of Aslan Maskhadov to sign the protocol for a meeting between the CRI president, the Russian president, and the Russian prime minister. As always, I was accompanied by Alu Gaisumov and Said-Khusein Tazbaev. We stayed at the President Hotel where, with Ivan Rybkin, we signed the protocol.

At 10.00 am on 12 May, a plane landed at Vnukovo Airport with Aslan Maskhadov and the Chechen delegation on board. In accordance with the protocol, it was met by Ivan Rybkin and myself. When the steps were brought up, I went on board and explained to those accompanying Maskhadov that they should wait about ten minutes after our president went out as there were a huge number of journalists at the bottom of the gangway. This event had focused on it the attention not only of the Russian but also of the world's press. Several of Maskhadov's bodyguards had already been in Moscow for over a week. In collaboration with the relevant Russian agencies and in accordance with instructions for the protection of our head of state, they ensured the security of the Chechen leader and delegation members. At 12.00 noon, the official meeting of the presidents of the two states began. On the Chechen side the meeting was attended by Aslan Maskhadov, Movladi Udugov, and myself. On the Russian side were Boris Yeltsin, Ivan Rybkin, Boris Berezovsky and Valentin Yumashev, son-in-law and chief of staff of the Russian president. I noticed a big change in Yeltsin since our last meeting almost a year before. A lot had happened in that time, including the presidential race in Russia in summer 1996 and a major operation he had undergone. It had taken its toll. He was noticeably thinner and, despite a layer of makeup on his face, looked unwell. His behaviour too had changed: there was none of the ebullience I remembered from our last meeting.

This time we met in the Hearthside Room. After the official handshakes, Yeltsin invited us to be seated at the oval table. There were some small pieces of paper in front of him. He took the topmost one and began to read:

Allow me to welcome the president of Ichkeria, Aslan Alievich Maskhadov. The purpose of today's meeting is to complete an important stage in the systematic, peaceful settlement of relations between the institutions of government of Russia and Chechnya, to do away with confrontation between them, and sign a peace treaty. We have met with Maskhadov in order to confirm previously reached understandings and agreements, and to declare our commitment to renounce forever the use or threat of force. If this result is achieved, it will be greeted with approval and relief. Furthermore, there will be a realistic possibility of signing a specific agreement on economic, social and other sectors.

I noticed that the font used for the text was not particularly large but Yeltsin was able to read it without glasses. I had the impression this was not the first time he had done so, because he read the sentences very smoothly and without hesitation. Yeltsin continued:

It is within our power to put an end to terrorist acts. The Chechen authorities must ensure the security of journalists and representatives of other professions. All hostages who have been seized must be released. The delays in releasing persons forcibly detained in Chechnya are unacceptable. We shall consider this problem solved when every last hostage has been released and the leaders take a decision on an amnesty.

Yeltsin's mention of an amnesty referred to Russian prisoners of war held on the territory of Chechnya. When he had finished, Aslan Maskhadov responded. He spoke in his usual manner, very softly, enunciating every word with deliberation:

> Boris Nikolaevich, I thank you for your warm welcome. I fully support everything you have said. All wars end with peace talks and Russia and Chechnya have been no exception. I very much hope that today we shall be able to end the centuries-old confrontation between Chechnya and Russia. You and I did not start this war: we inherited it. The conflict has a long history. Yes, we have a shared, albeit bloody, history and we bear a historic responsibility to our people as to what kind of future they will have. We are destined to live next to each other and have the choice of whether to live in peace and friendship or in war and enmity. I am very glad that we have chosen peace, which is exactly what our people want us to do. The treaty which we are to sign today is of great importance for solving all the problems you have quite rightly mentioned in your speech. I am profoundly convinced that if we are sincere in our intention to establish a lasting peace between our peoples, there are no contradictions which we cannot resolve at the negotiating table.

Concluding his speech, Aslan again thanked all those who had participated in the negotiations and worked on the draft peace treaty. After that, Yeltsin proposed that we should go through the text of the Treaty. It had been prepared in two copies and in two languages: Russian and Chechen. Yeltsin asked Aslan Maskhadov about the translation from Russian to Chechen, 'Is it accurate? I have to sign it too.' He added, 'You, Aslan Alievich, have the better of me. You know both languages and I have to rely on your word of honour in signing the agreement in Chechen.'

It was a joke, of course, and all present took it as such. Maskhadov assured Yeltsin the texts were identical, so he could sign the Chechen version with no qualms. Yeltsin then suddenly turned to Maskhadov with a suggestion. 'Aslan Alievich, let's cross out of the preamble this line which says, "In confirmation of the Khasavyurt Accord of 31 August 1996."'

Without waiting for Maskhadov's response, Yeltsin crossed the line out. It was a technique he used in negotiations to catch his opponents off guard and insert an amendment to his advantage without their noticing. At the time we did not see it mattered in the slightest, especially since Yeltsin added, 'Why do we have to bring the Khasavyurt Accord and Lebed into this? Let's turn over a new leaf. We are two presidents, the president of Russia and the president of Chechnya.'

I did not at that time detect any political chicanery in this. Discussing the incident afterwards among ourselves, we thought Yeltsin struck out the mention of the Khasavyurt Accord from the Preamble because of hostility towards General Lebed. It was only after the Second War began in 1999 that the political significance of the amendment became clear. If that point had been retained in the Peace Treaty, all Russia's talk about our 'deferred status' would have made no legal sense. In effect, Yeltsin was signing a peace treaty while preparing for a new war. By the time we realized that, however, it was too late.

When the definitive text was finally agreed, Yumashev said that, in accordance with the protocol, the signing of the document was to take place in a different hall, in front of the television cameras. The protocol provided for the presidents to be left in private before the signing of the Treaty. Accompanied by Yumashev, we all went through to where the signing was to take place. This historic ceremony took place some twenty minutes later. The Peace Treaty concluded on 12 May 1997 remains the only document in existence which defines the relationship between Russia and Chechnya. It was an extremely important moment and, as Yeltsin and Maskhadov repeatedly emphasized in their comments, marked the 'end of the confrontation between Moscow and Grozny.'

Paradoxically, however, the moment the Treaty was signed, for the first time in 7–8 months of intensive discussion, the two sides to the negotiations began to interpret the content and meaning of the document quite differently. Sergey Yastrzhembsky called it 'a document of trust, concluding centuries of confrontation.' At the same time he stressed that the Treaty did not say, and that there had never been any talk of, Chechnya being recognized as an independent entity under international law. Russian Security Council Secretary Ivan Rybkin commented, 'The Treaty clearly states that an end has been put to the confrontation between Moscow and Grozny. Henceforth, their relationship is to comply fully with the norms and principles of international law. This and the other provisions of the document are wholly in compliance with the Russian Constitution.' In other words, he was making it emphatically clear that the document was not a treaty between equals. The Russian foreign minister, Yevgeny Primakov, was asked at a press conference, 'The document signed by the presidents of Russia and the Chechen Republic of Ichkeria implies de jure recognition of the CRI. What will happen if another country, following Russia's example, also recognizes Chechnya's independence and establishes diplomatic relations with it?' Primakov said, 'Russia's reaction will be to break off diplomatic relations with any country establishing diplomatic relations with Chechnya.'

Meanwhile, Chechnya's politicians were all saying as one that, by signing the Peace Treaty as it was worded, Russia had de facto and de jure recognized Chechen independence. Having fought a devastating war which had cost many thousands of lives and maimed several generations, we were back where we started. In 1991 Chechnya had, just as now, considered itself an independent state while Russia had considered it an integral part of the Russian Federation. We found we had made no real progress in safeguarding our sovereignty. Reference to international law providing the basis of Russo-Chechen relations could equally well be given an interpretation favourable to Russia, because the Russian Constitution stipulated that all domestic relationships in Russia are conducted in accordance with the provisions of international law. In other words, Russia, having declared in its constitution the primacy of international law over national law, had already formally pledged to respect the norms and principles of international law in respect of all domestic legal entities, whether a public society, an autonomous republic, a village administration, or a citizen of the Russian Federation. As the Russians were interpreting the Treaty, Chechnya was just another domestic legal entity on the list.

There were, however, a number of differences between the state of our affairs before and during the war and now, and unfortunately they were not in our favour. Our post-war situation was made worse by the fact that, before and during the war, the sympathies of the international community had been on our side, but now after 7–8 months of ceasefire, the abduction of journalists and foreigners on Chechen territory had enabled Russian propaganda to turn against us those who had previously morally supported us in our struggle for freedom. There was another important factor: the powers that be now also saw the Chechens as a danger to themselves. They saw us as having set a precedent that a small nation could stand up to a mighty nation with aspirations to superpower status. Nearly all great powers have their own problems with peoples trying to gain independence from them, and a sovereign Chechnya could give these nations new hope and a new incentive to struggle for national liberation. The Chechens by their heroic resistance to Russian aggression had dispelled the myth that great powers are invincible.

At that time, however, neither the Chechen leaders nor the Chechen people were aware of these subtleties. On 13 May our delegation returned to Chechnya and my first deputy, Makkal Sabdullaev, organized a great reception for President Maskhadov at Sheikh Mansur Airport. It was all very theatrical: the State Symphony Orchestra played the CRI national anthem and there was dancing and singing by children in national costume to greet the president. It was an event which gave expression to the sincere joy of the Chechen people that a peace treaty had been signed with Russia. There were a vast number of journalists at the airport and our delegation found itself the focus of many television and press cameras, but it was also noticeable that almost all the journalists were Chechens and Ingush. These were days when Chechens, not only in the republic but throughout the world, celebrated not a victory over Russia, but a long-awaited peace deal. By presidential decree, 12 May was declared Peace Day, and the intention was to celebrate it every year. The Cabinet of Ministers resolved to set up an organizing committee for celebrations to mark the signing of the Peace Treaty, which were to take place on 18 May. Inevitably, I was appointed chairman. Preparations began throughout the republic and, at my suggestion, it was decided the venue for the celebrations should be a field on the outskirts of Novye Atagi where, by order of Djohar Dudaev before the war, the Chechen National Cauldron from Nashkha had been installed on a high pedestal.

By tradition, the Chechen National Cauldron was one of the three most venerated relics of our people. The bronze cauldron had 63 shields attached to its surface, on which were engraved the names of the indigenous Vainakh Teips. Since ancient times it had been kept in the Castle of Motsarkh in Nashkha. The Cauldron could contain the meat of one fatted bull and was brought out of the castle only for festivities of national importance, such as a meeting of the Mekhk-Khel, a declaration of war, the conclusion of peace, or reconciliation of the two sides in a blood feud. Reconciliation of feuding parties was seen by Chechens as a matter of importance and concern for the entire nation. The other major relics of the Chechen people were the national Chronicle, the *Teptar*, and the national Seal, the *Mukhar*. The Chronicle and Seal were also kept in Motsarkh Castle.

It was explained to me that the Cauldron symbolized the unity of the Chechens in space ('We and our country'); the Chronicle denoted the unity of Chechens in time ('We and our ancestors'); while the Seal was the emblem of the Covenant of the First Fathers of the Nakh people with the Prophet Noah

(Peace be upon him), from whom the Chechens consider themselves to be in direct descent ('We and the Sacred Covenant'). The experts tell us that the Cauldron was broken on the orders of Imam Shamil, either in 1845 or 1846, by two local Chechen leaders of the Caucasian Imamate. Individual bronze strips from it survived and were kept by a number of Chechen families until the deportation of the Vainakhs to Siberia and Central Asia in February 1944. It is not known whether any of the remains of the original Cauldron have survived to the present day. Of the Chronicle we know only that its guardian disappeared without trace during the Deportation. The Seal, by some accounts, is still preserved by one of the families in Roshni-Chu.

The Mekhk-Khel did not invariably meet in Nashkha. Often the National Council would move to places where events of importance to the entire Chechen community were taking place. All these places are remembered by Chechens. One such, according to legend, was the field near Novye Atagi where Djohar Dudaev had the Cauldron Monument erected. I know that a group of Chechen intellectuals, prominent figures and businessmen in 1998 envisaged a project to restore the Castle of Motsarkh, the Cauldron and the surrounding towers and castles, including the Tower of Khaibakh where, during the 1944 Deportation, NKVD troops burned alive or shot some 700 Chechen civilians. The intention was to build a modern road there, and for this historic place to become a site where Chechens could celebrate national events with the parading of a reproduction of the bronze Cauldron. Alas, the Second Chechen War was to prevent this very imaginative project from being realized.

But let us return to 18 May 1997, when hundreds of thousands of Chechens gathered at the field in Novye Atagi around the Cauldron Monument. I felt that was the day a great national reconciliation occurred, because all Chechens were there irrespective of their political or religious differences. The majority of our people rallied to Maskhadov, and it was on that day that he truly became the leader of the nation. Everybody wanted to believe the worst was over. None of us present at that celebration ever imagined that our most terrible trials and sorrows were yet to come.

Djohar Dudaev, First President of the Chechen Republic, 1992.
(Sputnik / Alamy Stock Photo)

L to R: Aslan Maskhadov, Second President of the Chechen Republic of Ichkeria, AZ, Zelimkhan Yandarbiev, 1997. (Sputnik / Alamy Stock Photo)

1970. First and second from the right, Aindi, Akhmed. (Zakaev archive)

Akhmed as Hamlet, Khusein Guzuev as Polonius, 1979. (Zakaev archive)

Actors of Grozny Dramatic Theatre. AZ bottom row, centre, Moscow, 1982. (Zakaev archive)

Freedom or Death by Said-Khamzat Nunuev. L to R, Abdul-Mutalip Davletmurzaev as Imam Shamil, AZ as his Naib, Grozny Theatre, 1986. (Zakaev archive)

Akhmed, Radima, Naib, Shamil, Roza Zakaev, 1990. (Zakaev archive)

A Russian military column makes its way through the ruins of Grozny, March 1995. (© Jeremy Nicholl, 1995)

AZ, Minister of Culture, and Khozh-Akhmed Yarikhanov, Head of Education Department of the Chechen Republic of Ichkeria at peace negotiations in Russia, 1995. (Sputnik / Alamy Stock Photo)

Said-Khusein Tazbaev and AZ at the funeral of President Djohar Dudaev, April 1996. (Zakaev archive)

RF Security Council Secretary Alexander Lebed and CRI Armed Forces Chief of Staff Aslan Maskhadov meet in Novye Atagi, 17 September 1996.
(ITAR–TASS / Alamy Stock Photo)

L to R: Ivan Rybkin, AZ, Boris Berezovsky, Grozny, 1996. (Reuters)

Peace talks in Moscow, May 1997. L to R: Movladi Udugov, Aslan Maskhadov, AZ, Valentin Yumashev, Boris Yeltsin, Ivan Rybkin, Boris Berezovsky. (Alexander Sentsov; Alexander Chumichev, ITAR–TASS / Alamy Stock Photo)

Signing of peace treaty between Chechen Republic of Ichkeria President Aslan Maskhadov and Russian President Boris Yeltsin. Back row L to R: Movladi Udugov, Ivan Rybkin, AZ, Valentin Yumashev. Kremlin, Moscow, 12 May 1997. (ITAR–TASS / Alamy Stock Photo)

AZ, Shamil Basaev and Movladi Udugov mark Basaev's 32nd birthday in January 1997. (ITAR–TASS / Alamy Stock Photo)

L to R: Shaaman, Alu Gaisumov, Vakha Dushuev, AZ, Musa; in front: Ibrakhim Chimaev, Anzor. 1998. (Zakaev archive)

Part 2

I
Missed Opportunities in Europe

Chechen delegates behave crassly at an international conference in The Hague and are never invited back. Opportunities to move towards international diplomatic recognition of Chechen independence are consistently missed. The role of the FSB in manipulating the muftiate in Chechnya. Akhmad-haddzhi Kadyrov. Antelope hunting in the Kazakh steppe.

The spring and summer of 1997 were remarkable for a number of major events. On 22 May 1997 an international conference was held at the Peace Palace in The Hague on the restoration of relations between Russia and Chechnya. Participating in the conference were the European Union; the OSCE; academics and analysts from the United States and the Netherlands; Ruud Lubbers, former prime minister of the Netherlands; William Ury, director of the Program on Negotiation at Harvard Law School. On the Russian side, the conference was attended by Boris Berezovsky, deputy secretary of the Russian Security Council; Vladimir Zorin, chairman of the State Duma Committee on Nationalities; Emil Pain, adviser to the Russian president; and Boris Kolokolov, ambassador extraordinary of the Russian Foreign Ministry.

The Hague Initiative was first convened in 1994 after a proposal by President Mintimer Shaimiev of Tatarstan for settling conflicts in the former Soviet territories. The informal meetings held within its framework of political leaders and international specialists were not negotiations in the classical sense, not a forum for settling scores, but a means of arriving at the truth, a means of exchanging views and experience between the political leaders of the conflicting parties with the participation and assistance of international specialists.

The delegation from the Chechen Republic of Ichkeria at these consultations was led by Vakha Arsanov, vice-president of the CRI. It consisted of Said-Khasan Abumuslimov, presidential adviser on foreign affairs; Ilias Akhmadov, and several assistants of Vakha Arsanov. President

Shaimiev opened the meeting and, according to participants, said it was noteworthy that the conference was being held only a few days after the signing of a Treaty of Friendship and Cooperation between the Republic of Tatarstan and the Chechen Republic of Ichkeria, and ten days after the signing of the Moscow Peace Treaty between the Russian Federation and the Chechen Republic of Ichkeria. All the participants, both Russian and Western, noted with satisfaction that the Moscow Peace Treaty, in which Russia and the Chechen Republic of Ichkeria expressed their determination to permanently renounce the use of force in resolving disputes, was a breakthrough in relations between the parties which had ended a war and brought hope to the peoples of Chechnya and Russia. The participants stated that they considered it essential:

1. To provide full and comprehensive economic assistance in restoring the Chechen economy;

2. To develop an effective mechanism for ensuring peace, security and stability in the Caucasus;

3. To continue the negotiation process between the Russian Federation and the Chechen Republic of Ichkeria in order to further develop relations.

The Hague Initiative, despite the fact that the resolutions adopted at meetings of the Round Table were solely recommendations not binding on the conflicting parties, was exceptionally important for the Chechen side, which was not officially recognized by the international community and had no official voice in international institutions. It was an excellent forum from which to communicate the reasons for and disastrous consequences of the 400-year long confrontation between Russia and Chechnya. Regrettably, our delegation headed by Arsanov and Abumuslimov went out of its way to make sure the Chechen side was never invited back. This is how they went about it.

After the signing of the Peace Treaty, an official invitation was extended to President Maskhadov to participate in this forum. He decided to send a Chechen delegation headed by Vakha Arsanov, who was very jealous of any political activity by Maskhadov or the Negotiating Commission, who had signed some important agreements and treaties with Russia. As vice-president, he had no clear portfolio of duties and responsibilities in the institutions of the CRI, and decided he was entitled to act on behalf of the president, standing in for him in on every occasion. He was encouraged in this belief by his entourage, who assured him that, like Maskhadov, he had been popularly elected and had the same rights and obligations as the president. For the first year of his presidency, Maskhadov unwittingly played along with this, as is shown by his decision to send Arsanov to The Hague instead of going there himself.

I can only say with great regret that our politicians' lack of the experience and sophistication their positions demanded had tragic consequences for our nation. It presented the organizers of the Hague Initiative, who had invited us, with major problems and incidents which were entirely the fault of the members of the Chechen delegation. First, they refused to pass through border controls at the international airport in Mineralnye Vody in Russia. These are formalities which have to be observed by all officials arriving from abroad or departing to another country. The organizers of the Hague conference, in order not to see their event derailed, persuaded Ukraine to let the Chechen delegation pass through border controls at the airport in Odessa. At the last moment before departure, Abumuslimov announced that he refused to go to The Hague with a Russian passport and, gathering a press pack at the airport, publicly tore his up. Vakha Arsanov supported this impromptu initiative to assert the CRI's national sovereignty. The Chechen delegation hung around for several hours in Odessa Airport waiting for Russia to provide a new passport, which, we should note, had in any case to be issued to him by Russian officials, although this time it was a passport of the no longer extant USSR. The conference organizers had a few more anxious hours before the members of the Chechen delegation received Dutch entry visas in their obsolete Soviet passports.

Why do I consider the Hague Initiative was a failure for us, despite the adoption of resolutions which were helpful to Chechnya? Because subsequently the conference organizers wanted nothing more to do with us. No doubt the issues surrounding Chechen national passports and the international status of the airport in Grozny were highly relevant and important at that time, but they needed to be resolved not en route to The Hague but either before departure or after arrival, and certainly not at the airport in Mineralnye Vody or Odessa, putting the organizers in a ridiculous position.

Chechen passports, a Chechen national currency, and the patriotic spirit of the Chechens were described by Djohar as the Three Secrets of the Nation (*K"oman K"ho' K"aile*). Chechen passports and currency had by this time already been printed. The first attempt to have them printed in the United Kingdom ended in tragedy when the Utsiev brothers were brutally murdered on this mission in London. Their bodies were dismembered, put in black plastic bags, and dumped in various rubbish bins. Scotland Yard soon solved the crime and two Russian citizens, ethnic Armenians, were brought before an English court. Chechen passports and currency were subsequently produced in a different European country.

Several months before the Hague conference, I proposed a different approach to our passports. In March 1997, the CRI received an official invitation from the King of Saudi Arabia for 3,000 of our citizens to perform the Hajj to Mecca as his personal guests. This gave us a good opportunity to get our passports internationally recognized. The first thing was to work with our people to get droves of Chechens to refuse to make the pilgrimage with passports of the former Soviet Union. We would then ask the Russian government not to prevent our pilgrims from going to Mecca with Chechen passports. If Russia refused, we would appeal to the Council of Europe (at that time Russia was very proud of its membership of this organization) to complain that Russia, as a member of the Council of Europe, was obstructing rights and freedoms laid down in international conventions signed by all members of the Council of Europe, and specifically Article 9 which states: 'Everyone has the right to freedom of thought, conscience and religion; this right includes freedom (...), either alone or in community with others and in public or private, to manifest his religion or belief in teaching, practice, worship and observance.' Our case was a perfect fit: making a pilgrimage to Mecca is the duty of every Muslim and thus came under Article 9 of an international convention signed by all members of the Council of Europe, including Russia. I am sure that the European Community would have supported Chechens appealing to the European Convention on Human Rights and Fundamental Freedoms. The Council of Europe was still at that time able to exert influence on Russia, and the Chechen demand would have been considered in the context of law rather than of politics. Saudi Arabia would have found it easier to accept Chechen pilgrims with passports of an unrecognized state (the CRI) than of a non-existent state (the USSR). I still believe this was a time of missed opportunities. Aslan Maskhadov himself was going to visit Mecca. He said he would agree my proposal with Vakha Arsanov and the Muftiate, in other words, Akhmad-khaddzhi Kadyrov.

Before coming to the doings of the Chechen Muftiate, I would like to look briefly at this religious institution and its history in the Russian Empire. In Russia, the Muftiate was introduced, at first for the Muslims of the Volga region and later for those in the newly conquered Crimea (Tauris). It was established by a number of decrees of Catherine II. On the basis of these, 17 laws were drafted governing the observance of their religion by Muslims in the Russian Empire. It is worth noting that 13 of these laws relate directly to the appointment of Muslim clergy, their activities, responsibilities, awards, and privileges. Moreover, Muslim clerics, including imams and, of course, muftis were appointed by the governors of provinces with a Muslim population only after careful investigation of their political loyalty to the Empire. In short, Muslim clergy were members of the imperial bureaucracy, obliged to promote among the faithful whatever policies and propaganda the Russian government came up with. Like any other official, they were paid a salary from the Imperial Treasury for doing so.

Muftiates, along with all the religious institutions of other faiths, were eliminated by the Communist regime, which officially proclaimed atheism and materialism as the cornerstone of its ideology. Stalin restored these institutions during the Second World War in order to carry out 'patriotic propaganda' among believers, ensuring in the process that almost every lower order or middle-ranking cleric was an informer of the Soviet secret police. As for the higher ranks of the clerical hierarchies, they were usually full KGB officers and generals. For example, the late Patriarch Aleksiy II was called, almost to his face, 'General Drozdov' by Russian journalists during the liberties of the Yeltsin era. This was his pseudonym in KGB documents partly declassified at the time. Needless to say, Muslim clerics, just like their Christian counterparts, were rigorously controlled by the state and handled directly from the offices of the KGB.

Such was the imperial legacy in the form of the muftiate we inherited after declaring Chechnya an independent state. The muftiates were, and to this day remain, channels for inculcating state ideology in Muslim communities. Because the state, both under the tsars and the Communist rulers, was imperial and the Muslims were peoples conquered by the Empire, the Boards of Religious Affairs were unambiguously an instrument of Russia's colonial domination in its Islamic regions. From the 1940s, these institutions were, in the most literal sense, branches of the KGB, specifically employed in packaging atheistic Communist doctrines in Islamic guises. The day before yesterday, muftis were enjoining Muslims to to be loyal subjects of the Russian emperors who had enslaved them; yesterday they were calling on Muslims to be loyal to the 'Father of the Peoples, Stalin' and his Communist successors; today the muftis exhort Muslims to loyalty, love and devotion to 'Mighty Russia.' Since the muftis were accustomed to faithfully serving the state, we might have expected their loyalty to have been to the Chechen Republic of Ichkeria when it declared independence in the early 1990s and defended it in a brutal war. Subsequent events showed, however, that this was not the case. The Russian intelligence agencies had a stranglehold on Chechnya's official clergy.

The muftiate was an institution into which you could draft absolutely anyone. Chechens were inherently very pious, and completely innocent of knowledge as far as theological subtleties were concerned. Their attitude to religious matters could be childlike in its naivety. The Ichkerian national security officers, whose job it was to detect and stop the establishment of a network of foreign agents in the republic, were extremely cautious in their approach to the religious sphere. Abu Movsaev, our head of the Department of State Security, told me about the difficulties they faced. They were concerned that arresting a foreign agent concealed behind his religious status might bring down accusations of 'anti-Islamic behaviour.' This was the Achilles' heel of the Chechen state, a fact which our enemies skilfully exploited against us.

The fact that Chechens had little knowledge of religious matters was due to the slaughter back in the 1920s–1930s of almost all Chechen clerics by the NKVD. I say 'almost,' because some were spared, if they agreed to collaborate and become obedient conduits for Bolshevik ideology. They manipulated the Muslims of Chechnya, Ingushetia and the rest of the North Caucasus. In particular, they went to great lengths to preach against the anti-Stalinist insurgency in the mountains of Checheno-Ingushetia. Extraordinarily, these 'religious authorities' were not necessarily secret NKVD-KGB agents but might appear in public wearing the uniform of an officer of that blood-stained department. The veneration of Chechens for Muslim clergy was so strong that these people were not only left untouched, but people actually also listened to their thoroughly dubious teachings.

To return to the passports: I remain convinced to this day that we missed a great opportunity at that time to get our national passports into circulation. From then on, the attitude of the Chechen leaders to the problem was purely populist. Chechen passports would be handed out to members of the Cabinet in front of the television cameras, and this gave some people the impression that we were officially introducing national passports. In reality, the government succeeded only in turning them into souvenirs.

Accompanying these populist measures, decrees were issued mandating the introduction of Sharia regulations relating to women's clothing. The problem that in Islam a woman may not work, trade, or appear in public unless accompanied by her husband or close male relatives, while 90 per cent of Chechen women were literally their families' breadwinners, earning a living by trading in the markets, was blithely overlooked by the doughty champions of 'pure Islam.' Government institutions, instead of dealing with affairs of state aimed at developing Chechen sovereignty, economic recovery, restoration of the industrial infrastructure, and combating unemployment, as if competing with emissaries from Arab countries who by now had flooded the entire republic, started involving themselves in religious matters of which they had a very limited understanding. They gave great priority, for instance, to setting up Sharia committees in every town and village, in state institutions and organizations.

There was an episode in March 1997. When Aslan Maskhadov was performing the Hajj pilgrimage to Mecca, he delegated his duties to Vice-President Vakha Arsanov. It was probably the only time Aslan relinquished his presidential powers for a specified period of time. The moment he left for Mecca, Vakha dismissed by presidential decree all the heads of all the regions, which caused a final and irreparable rift among the supporters of independence. Almost all the regional prefects dismissed by Vakha were members of the Resistance and had been appointed to their positions by Acting President Zelimkhan Yandarbiev. Naturally, many had supported Zelimkhan in one way or another during the election campaign, and Vakha decided in March that the moment had come to replace them with people who had supported Aslan Maskhadov and himself in the presidential race. Vakha's second decree required women to wear a headscarf. The following day we were discussing these vice-presidential initiatives at work, and Said Khuscin Tazbaev, then working as director of the National Drama Theatre, told me they reminded him of a film he had seen about Fidel Castro and his comrades. When, quite unexpectedly, they came to power, they had no idea where to begin, so the Cuban revolutionaries issued a decree requiring all men to grow beards. Vakha Arsanov had evidently decided to mark his period in power by obliging women to wear headscarves, although this had been the rule in Chechnya since the dawn of time, even before the coming of Islam.

At about this time, an invitation was received in Maskhadov's office from the president of Kalmykia to come and celebrate the 75th birthday of the Kalmyk writer, David Kugultinov. The president ordered that a delegation of Chechen artists and intellectuals should be put together, and appointed me to head it. Even travelling to neighbouring Kalmykia was very time-consuming for our government. We had to arrange reliable transport, which none of our institutions yet possessed. My friends and acquaintances solved the problem by providing us with two Mercedes and a Land Cruiser. Alu Gaisumov, in charge of security, organized an escort of two vehicles and worked out the route. He chose a road through the steppe to avoid being held up at checkpoints by the Russian traffic police and having to explain to them who we were and where we were going, despite our having officially notified the

Russian Legation in the CRI of our trip and that we would have armed bodyguards. The route Alu took us along certainly was deserted and we encountered no police or Russian army checkpoints, only huge herds of saiga antelopes which periodically ran across the road in front of us.

I had only ever seen so many saigas in Kazakhstan when I was on *shabashka*, earning money by casual labour. It was in the mid-1980s. Our brigade consisted of 10 or 12 people, nearly all of them my relatives. In August 1986, during their month's break from the theatre, Khusein Guzuev, Gapur Aliev and Tavus Isaev came to join me. After graduating from the GITIS Theatre Institute, Khusein was working as a director, Gapur was in charge of stage management, and Tavus, a poet and writer, had graduated from the Gorky Literary Institute in Moscow. My brigade was split between two sites, one team working at a collective farm and the other at a stone quarry 190 km away from where we were building a cowshed. Half the time I had to be at the quarry where we were getting the stone, and the rest at the building site. When we had any free time, we went out into the steppe on a truck to hunt saigas.

Saigas are cloven-hoofed antelope found in Kazakhstan, Turkmenistan and Russia, particularly in Kalmykia and Astrakhan province. During certain seasons, saiga antelopes gather in large flocks in the steppe and semi-desert areas. They feed off a wide variety of vegetation, including some poisonous to other animals, and migrate over long distances. In the 1980s, saigas were not yet categorized as 'critical' in the endangered species list. The International Union for the Conservation of Nature did that only in 2002. In the years I am describing, almost all the building and harvesting brigades in the regions of Kazakhstan inhabited by saigas hunted them because they were free meat. The males have small, translucent, light-coloured horns with dark tips. Females do not have horns. The males weigh on average 45 kg and females 30-35 kg. Almost until the end of autumn, we hunted them too. In those years we found dozens, even hundreds, of abandoned saiga corpses in the steppe. They were killed barbarically, just for their horns. In the USSR, as still today in Russia, policies to protect the environment and wildlife are purely declaratory and for the benefit of the Western world, which takes these issues much more seriously. The same is true, of course, of the defence in the USSR and Russia of human rights and democratic principles.

The herds of saigas we encountered on the road to Kalmykia reminded me of an incident that occurred in Kazakhstan. Khusein, Tavus and I were setting off to drive to the quarry to bring the stone our lads had processed. We drove out in two lorries, a Gaz–52 and a Kamaz. I was at the wheel of the Gaz with Khusein sitting next to me in the cab. Tavus, instead of getting into the cab of the Kamaz with the driver, decided, as he said, to enjoy the breeze and climbed into the back of our truck. After about 40 minutes, however, he banged on the roof, I stopped, and he transferred to the cab of the Kamaz. We had taken a gun with us so that, if the opportunity presented itself, we could shoot a saiga. Khusein was holding it, with the barrel sticking out the window. After a while we saw a huge herd of saiga crossing our path.

I did not at first understand why saigas do that. Crossing the road in front of hunters, the herd divided in two. The hunters would usually rush after one half of the herd, enabling the other to escape. The half being pursued would then again divide in two, and this would continue until the hunters were chasing just a single lead stag which had drawn the hunters after itself. Later, when I had entered politics, I thought about the behaviour of the saigas in such an extreme situation and of how they had among them individuals prepared to sacrifice themselves for the sake of the herd. I could not help drawing parallels between human and animal behaviour. The latter, God endowed with instinct; the former with conscious thought.

Why am I reminded of the behaviour of the saigas? In their case the selection of a leader occurred in an emergency where his qualities of leadership were manifested naturally and, in following him, the animals were almost never wrong. In today's world, the choice of a leader often occurs in far more propitious circumstances, but people make mistakes and, as a rule, pay a heavy price for them. Of course, at that moment I was thinking nothing of the sort: we were so engrossed in the hunt and so keen to shoot at least one saiga that we forgot about everything else. Having no hunting experience, Khusein was finding it far from easy to aim a rifle out of the window of a truck hurtling along at 80 kilometres an hour. Our saigas executed their choreographed moves for our benefit, but we were so carried away with the pursuit that we quite failed to notice that the last, good-sized stag we were after had led us into an area where geologists were conducting their researches with the use of explosives. In an instant we found ourselves careering towards large pits two or three metres deep. I managed by wrenching the steering wheel to avoid one, only immediately to plunge into another. The impact was so violent that the windscreen flew out. Khusein was lucky that at the moment of impact he was sitting back in the cab, holding the gun out the window with his right hand. I managed to grab him just as he was about to fly out through the windscreen. It all happened in a matter of seconds, but I remember everything as if I had been watching it in slow motion: glass, bolts and spanners floated through the cab and, when they all just as slowly sank to the floor, there followed a dead silence. I looked at Khusein who was completely motionless. I shouted, 'Khusein, are you alive? Are you in one piece?'

Khusein was silent for a moment before patting his legs and giving his answer. 'Alive, definitely. In one piece, probably.'

After that I tried to open the door which something had blocked. I forced it open by bashing it with my shoulder and got out to inspect the truck. The impact was so strong that the front axle had sheared off and was lying in the pit we had flown over. The back of the truck had been severed by the pit and was half lying with its sides open on the ground. The sunglasses I had put in my front shirt pocket were lying in the back of the truck. Evidently, at the time of the first impact which knocked the windscreen out, they had flown up in the air and, by the time they fell, were above the truck. Walking round what was left of it, I found myself on Khusein's side and, talking to myself, said, 'We're up the creek!'

Khusein, still sitting in the cab, suggested with great optimism in his voice, 'Akhmed, perhaps not completely?' I invited him to get out and take a look for himself but he replied that his door would not open, and carried on calmly sitting in the cab. I said, 'Khusein, first press the handle down, then push the door.'

It opened at the second or third attempt and Khusein came out. We were both uninjured, incredibly lucky to have come out of such a serious accident without a scratch, and very relieved that Tavus had transferred out of the back of our truck into the cab of the Kamaz. If he had stayed with us, our antelope hunt could have ended tragically. The driver of the Kamaz had continued on his way, not following us in our pursuit of the antelope, and now Khusein and I had not the faintest idea where we were. Soon it started to become dark. I glanced at my watch and worked out that our pursuit of the saiga had lasted 40 minutes, all of which time we had been moving away from the road to the quarry. Then, when the darkness deepened, we saw some lights far away in the steppe. Our first thought was that it must be floodlighting from tractors. We knew that in this region, because the daytime summer temperature could reach 50 degrees and the machinery simply could not function in such heat, tractors often went out to plough in the night-time. We found our rifle not far from the truck, and it too proved to be in one piece. We had a sufficient supply of ammunition. We took all our things out of the cab and headed towards the distant lights in the steppe. Before we left, however, I turned on the sidelights so that, if need be, we could find our way back to the truck in the dark.

The summer nights in Kazakhstan are stunning! Bright, twinkling stars seem to be hanging directly overhead, so that you could reach out and touch them. The pure, fresh air, the night-time sounds and scufflings in the steppe which testify to the busy life of its inhabitants, the danger we had just experienced and our miraculous escape from death gave us a sense of jubilation as we walked unspeaking towards the lights. The closer we got, the less they seemed like floodlights, but I said nothing. For a long time our distance from them seemed not to be decreasing. I was timing us, and we had been walking for over two hours before they seemed any closer. It was becoming increasingly plain that these were not the headlights of tractors, and shortly after that we realized the steppe was on fire. We conferred briefly and decided to make our way back to the truck.

We had heard from local people that there were poisonous vipers in the steppe so, despite our weariness, could not lie or even sit to rest. Khusein doubted we would be able to find the truck, even with the sidelights on. Half an hour after leaving it, I had looked back and been unable to see them, and he had probably done the same. Before the accident, while we were careering through the steppe, I had noticed that, although at first glance it seems as flat as a tabletop, it does in fact have rises and dips. They are gentle slopes and from a distance almost unnoticeable, but on foot they were a very real feature of the landscape. I tried to reassure Khusein by saying I knew the direction we needed to go in. As we were walking, I had been mentally counting the boundaries between fields. On cultivated land these divisions are clearly visible even at night, but these fields had been long abandoned and were overgrown. Nevertheless, the ditches between them were visible. I pointed out the brightest star in the sky, and told Khusein that when we had been walking away from the crashed truck it was on our right, so now we just needed to keep it on our left.

There was another problem. From the moment we crashed we had been feeling thirsty, and as we walked towards the light I had been relying on the tractor drivers giving us water, which they always stocked up with before going out to the fields. Khusein admitted he had had the same hope. At this point I had a bright idea.

'When we we get back to the truck, we will have two important things: water from the radiator, which must have cooled by now, and a place in the cab where we can sleep without fear of poisonous snakes.'

My mention of the radiator water cheered him up no end. He congratulated me on my resourcefulness, even thanking me for holding on to him when we crashed. At just this moment we were illuminated by a dazzling yellow light, so bright I could clearly see Khusein's eyes and mouth wide open in amazement. I was overcome by fear. The light must have flashed several times for two or three seconds, but my sense of time had gone. All sorts of nonsense came into my head. Was it a nuclear strike? UFOs with alien life forms? Waves of light were coming from the ground and rising up into the sky, leaving behind a bright spiral of changing colours. I remembered we were in Kazakhstan, which meant the Baikonur Space Centre must be nearby. Perhaps a rocket was being launched into space with another sputnik.

Of course, after we overcame our fear, the spiral of coloured lights disappearing into the sky struck us as magical, but we soon had to come back down to earth and face the fact that we were out in the steppe at night without food or water, or the least idea as to our whereabouts. We had the hope, of course, that in a day or two our disappearance would cause alarm and our friends and families would come looking for us. The problem was, though, that our ill-fated hunting expedition was at the weekend. They would assume at the farm that we had gone to the quarry, as we had said, while at the quarry Tavus would tell them we had been hunting the antelopes and they might well conclude we had gone back with our booty to the farm, which was the only place with facilities for storing meat. It would probably be a day or two at least before anyone came looking for us. Of course, we could consider ourselves amazingly lucky not to have suffered injuries in the crash and be needing urgent medical attention.

With these reflections, we continued on our way. We hoped the bright star on our left would guide us back to the wrecked truck we had been in such a hurry to abandon a few hours ago, as if by abandoning it we could free ourselves of all the problems we had brought down on ourselves by our over-zealous pursuit of the saiga. Our hunting instinct had overruled our instinct of self-preservation and our common sense. Now we were trying to return to the truck as if it could save us from our predicament. As we made our way through the steppe, I saw a ray of light which seemed to be shining up out of the ground. I felt we had seen quite enough lights in the desert that night, but hoped it was coming from our truck's sidelights. Khusein asked,

'Why is it shining up into the sky?'

I confessed the exact answer to his question eluded me for the moment, but surmised there was a mound between us and the truck. It was also possible that, as the truck had parted company with its front axle and had its nose in the ground, the light might be being reflected back up. Khusein asked how many field boundaries I had counted on the way back and I had also to admit that I had lost count after our encounter with the 'aliens.' We decided, all things considered, to make for the ray of light, which soon resolved itself into two sidelights. We were as pleased as if we were already home.

The first thing I did was open the bonnet and feel the radiator. It was cold. Khusein found a plastic cup in the cab, something Soviet drivers always took with them. I opened the radiator's drain valve and filled the cup with water. Before offering it to Khusein, I thought I should test it. It tasted revolting, had a musty smell of petrol and rust, and was completely undrinkable. Khusein wanted nevertheless to try it but, after taking a sip, handed it back, spitting and frowning. We climbed into the cab, cleared the seat of glass, bolts and other detritus, and sat down shoulder to shoulder. It was probably the first time in my life I fell asleep so quickly.

I do not know what woke us first: an unbelievably loud roaring, the morning cold, or a combination of the two. I looked out shivering to see what was making so much noise and found our truck was surrounded by thousands of antelopes. This was wholly amazing, because wild saigas never come near people, or the vehicles from which they get shot at, yet here they were literally bumping against our truck. I said to Khusein, 'Look, our stag has brought his herd back to show them the idiots who failed to shoot him yesterday.' We laughed hysterically and the saigas roared too. When we finally decided to come out of the truck, they shied away and then began slowly retreating back into the steppe. The rifle was in the cab but we did not shoot at them, even though it would have been almost impossible to miss. We conceded defeat to the leader of the herd. Even the next day, when we were very hungry, Khusein and I did not regret our decision.

Then we noticed the tyre tracks of our truck, which stopped some considerable distance from where the cab was now. Khusein decided to measure it and made it 18 metres. That was how far our truck had flown through the air after its initial impact. The morning dew was weighing down the grass, so the tyre tracks in the steppe were clearly visible. We decided to follow them back before the sun dried the dew and the grass straightened again. We hoped to get back to, or at least close to, the road we had turned off in pursuit of the antelopes. We quickly gathered some earth and put it in a shirt. Khusein found a small plastic canister under the seat, I opened the radiator drain tap, and we began filtering the water. It passed through the earth and cloth and dripped into the canister. It was not perfect, but at least after filtering it was drinkable. We slaked our thirst, filled the canister, and wrapped it in the wet, muddy shirt to keep it cool. I had noticed Kazakh drivers wrapping their water canisters in damp wool felt and we decided to imitate them.

I will not describe all the details of our three-day adventure, except to say that we had to spend a second night out in the steppe. This time we set fire to the grass where we were planning to stop in order to clear it of snakes and poisonous insects. We could have faced a serious threat from steppe wolves, which were active at this time. Although we had a rifle, we had no wish to tangle with them. First, we gathered grass to lie on, then set fire to the steppe around us and went to sleep.

This night too was not without incident. Past midnight we were awakened by the sound of vehicles and gunfire. These came from hunters pursuing the saigas with bright spotlights to dazzle them. Blinded by the light, the antelope froze where they were and the hunters just mowed them down. The hunt was proceeding not too far from where we were, but as the steppe around us was still on fire the antelopes did not come our way and led the hunters in the opposite direction. I fired in the air just on the off chance, but the hunters did not hear. That was a disappointment, but these nocturnal hunters gave us hope that we were not too far away from a settlement or the camp of some harvesting brigade. I told Khusein that tomorrow we should head in the direction they had come from, and in the morning that is what we did. After a few hours, we heard the roar of an engine, and saw it was coming from a large-wheeled Kirov tractor. We were so pleased to see it we became overly demonstrative, waving our arms and yelling. We failed to anticipate how the tractor driver might react to a couple of yelling strangers jumping up and down with a rifle in their hands. He evidently decided not to tempt providence and to steer clear of us. We realized what was happening, but just had not the strength to run after him. We tried shouting in Chechen and Russian that we were Chechens builders from the third site of the Pskov Collective Farm, lost in the steppe and in need of help, but he did not stop.

Now we needed to decide which direction to take, whether the one the tractor had come from, or the one it had departed in. It might have been coming from a village out to a team working in the fields or, on the contrary, from a brigade to the outpost of a state farm. These were scattered throughout Kazakhstan, but a long distance apart. In the end, we decided to follow the tractor. After an hour or so, we saw the Kirov in front of us. We could see that a hose had broken on it and leaked oil. The driver was nowhere to be seen. I could not be sure it was the same tractor, but Khusein had no doubt it was the one which had abandoned us in the steppe, and that God had punished the driver for his wickedness. Khusein climbed into the cab and found a water canister wrapped in the way described above, but there was little water in it. We decided this meant the tractor had been driving back to base because otherwise the flask would have been full. We were very pleased we had decided to follow it and, after a rest in its shade, continued on our way in the same direction.

That third day was tough. We were almost exhausted and the heat was unbelievable. We began to regret not having remained by the tractor but, elated by the unexpected discovery of water, had not thought more carefully about our strength. I was just deciding we would need to go back, because whoever had left the tractor in the steppe would sooner or later have to go back for it, when Khusein thought he was beginning to hallucinate. He told me he was seeing palaces and cities in front of him. I started helpfully explaining the difference between a hallucination and a mirage. In the heat of the Kazakh steppe you do seem to see palaces, castles, and entire cities of extraordinary beauty in the far distance. Khusein had been in Kazakhstan only a few days and did not know that. At just this moment, however, I myself seemed to see, far away to the right, two yurts and a large cow pen. I could not believe my eyes and asked Khusein to look in that direction and tell me if he could see anything. He looked and said that now, instead of palaces and cities, he was seeing tents and cows. I cried, 'Khusein, we've made it! Let's head for the cows. We are saved! I can see them too, and we can't both be seeing the same mirage.'

We soon reached the yurt, and made straight for the watering place for the cattle. There was a borehole from which you could pump water, but it was so cold we could not drink it. The owner came out to us. His name was Abai and he and his family were living out at this *gurt*, as the Kazakhs called the summer pasturage for their cows. It was some 50 kilometres from the outpost of the farm we were working at and to which Abai too was attached. I did not recognize him, because last summer he had been out at a pasturage with the cows, and by late autumn when he returned to the farm I had already gone home. Last summer, however, it was his house we had been repairing, and the new stone cowshed we were building now was for his cows. Abai fed us and gave us Kazakh tea to drink. Kazakh tea is special and the Kazakhs have a special way of drinking, only half filling the cup. They nevertheless drink a great deal of it. After a big meal, Khusein and I fell asleep. We were awakened by the voice of Tavus. He had come out looking for us that morning and called in here to make enquiries. Tavus told us off and said we were behaving like children, dozing here in the coolness of this yurt without a care in the world while everyone was worried and out searching for us. He was older than us and considered it his duty to berate us for the alarm we had caused. He had no idea how delighted we were to see him, knowing that now our nightmare in the steppe was over.

This was the story I was telling Dik-Magomed and the others in the car when our motorcade encountered the column of vehicles sent to meet us and headed by the deputy prime minister of Kalmykia. The president of Kalmykia was, of course, as good as his word, and received the Chechen delegation with all the honours he was able to as the head of a territory which was part of the Russian Federation. They accommodated me, as head of the delegation, and my security team in a villa in the country, and the other members of the delegation were given rooms in the main hotel of Elista. That same evening I had an official meeting with President Kirsan Ilyumzhinov at the Presidential Palace. After half an hour of conversation, the president invited members of his government in and instructed them to give all possible assistance to the Chechens. He told the prime minister and his deputies not to wait for us to ask for help, but to offer whatever they could, 'because the Chechens have nothing, and anything you can give will be helpful.'

A delegation came from Moscow, headed by Nationalities Minister Mikhailov. David Kugultinov was a figure of national importance in the days of the USSR and had many friends in all the former Soviet republics. Today these were independent states, with the consequence that numerous state delegations arrived in Kalmykia. After the official ceremonies, the president gave a banquet in honour of the writer. You could still feel the Soviet legacy in celebrations of this kind. All these people were celebrities from the Soviet era: Makhmud Esambaev, Rasul Gamzatov, Chingiz Aitmatov, Olzhes Suleymenov and many other pillars of Soviet literature and art were present. Even though they had by now long been living in different states, they had not lost their sense of a shared culture, and they also shared a nostalgia for Soviet times past or, more probably, for the years of their youth which they had spent together. That evening, one by one, they rose to their feet to propose toasts and recall episodes from the past. The banquet went on until very late.

We had a busy programme in Kalmykia. Besides the birthday celebrations, we had a meeting on the morning of our third day with First Deputy Prime Minister Valeriy Kazaev. We discussed what help Kalmykia could give Chechnya. Kazaev told me President Ilyumzhinov had instructed him to donate 30 Volga cars to the Chechen government. That was greatly appreciated. On that trip, too, I had a meeting with the Chechen diaspora in Kalmykia. As a rule, at such meetings our compatriots expressed full support for the Chechen government and offered help to restore the republic.

II

Learning Statecraft

May 1997, successful diplomatic visit to Georgia to establish good neighbourly relations. Prospective mediation in Georgian-Abkhazian relations. Improving the lot of Chechens living in Georgia. Meetings with Eduard Shevardnadze. Hostile Russian reaction. Inept Chechen ministers mar Georgian-Chechen relations. Official visit to Georgia by President Maskhadov.

In May 1997, after the signing of the Moscow Peace Treaty, I undertook another important and very sensitive trip, this time to Georgia. Aslan Maskhadov and I had often discussed how to neutralize everything that had soured relations between Georgia and Chechnya and marred the traditional friendship and understanding between our peoples. Relations had been seriously undermined when Chechen volunteers fought in 1992–4 on the Abkhaz side in their conflict with Georgia. The Georgians had caused offence by allowing the Russians to mount air raids on Chechnya from bases in Georgia, as well as by statements from President Eduard Shevardnadze to the effect that 'Georgia, like Russia, has been compelled to take up arms to defend the integrity of its state.' This created considerable psychological barriers to restoring good neighbourly relations. We knew, however, that because of our geography and history, Georgia more than any other country in the Caucasus should be a strategic ally of Chechnya. The recently signed Peace Treaty, in which Russia de facto recognized our independence, gave us every opportunity of obtaining the same recognition from Georgia. Zviad Gamsakhurdia, Shevardnadze's predecessor as Georgian president, had already recognized Chechnya's independence, and this had been ratified by the Georgian parliament. Recognition of Chechen independence by the government of Eduard Shevardnadze, if it could be achieved, would be a diplomatic precedent leading to recognition by other countries.

Using my old ties with cultural figures, I made contact with the political leaders of Georgia and received an official invitation from Nugzar

Sajaia, secretary of their National Security Council, to participate in the 25 May festivities to mark Georgia's Independence Day. After agreeing the route with the Russian Legation, I travelled on 23 May, accompanied by Said-Khusein Tazbaev, Alu Gaisumov and several bodyguards, along the Georgian Military Highway, through Verkhniy Lars, to Georgia. At the Chechen-Ingush border we were met by officers of the Ministry of the Interior of Ingushetia, who escorted us to the Ingush-Ossetian border. There the baton was passed to officers of the North Ossetian Ministry of the Interior, who accompanied us to the Ossetia-Georgian border, and there we were met by the CRI representative in Georgia, Hizir Aldamov, and an assistant of Nugzar Sajaia. They accompanied us to Tbilisi. I was only too aware that this was an important moment in the history of Chechen-Georgian relations. We and the Georgians understood that classifying my visit to Tbilisi as 'cultural contacts' was a pure formality. In reality we were talking about resumption of political cooperation between our two countries. This added to the weight of responsibility I felt.

I had not been in Georgia for five highly eventful years, during which the country had endured a civil war and the death of President Zviad Gamsakhurdia, who was buried in Chechnya. At the beginning of the First Russo-Chechen War, during the massive air and artillery strikes on the Chechen capital, his burial site faced total devastation and, on Djohar Dudaev's orders, his remains were reburied in secret. The fact that Zviad Gamsakhurdia was buried in Chechnya aroused mixed feelings in Georgia. Some Georgians blamed us Chechens for all their troubles, while others, for whom Gamsakhurdia was a national hero, were grateful to us for giving him refuge in our land and burying his remains with the highest state honours. As for the 'Abkhaz problem,' all Georgians were in agreement that the central role in their defeat in the war with Abkhazia had been played by Chechens. At the time of my visit, there were around 300,000 Georgian refugees from Abkhazia in Tbilisi, people who had lost their homes, property, and often family members, and this gave an extra edge to the charges levelled against Chechnya.

The Chechens, of course, also had grudges against the Georgians. Every Chechen schoolchild knew that the long and bloody Caucasian War stemmed from the Treaty of Georgievsk, concluded in 1783 between Russia and the East Georgian kingdom of Kartli-Kakheti. Under this treaty, East Georgia became a protectorate of the Russian Emperor and Russia, in order to secure access to its new Transcaucasian possessions, went to war with the independent peoples of the North Caucasus. Chechnya became the primary arena of the war, which officially lasted from Sheikh Mansur's movement in 1785 until the capture of Imam Shamil in 1859, a period of 74 years. According to historians, this war led to the killing of up to 65 per cent of all Chechens and 45 per cent of Avars. Other North Caucasian peoples also suffered huge losses from the war and subsequent deportations to the Ottoman Empire. Some peoples were totally annihilated. Such was the fate of the Ubykhs, who lived where the Russian cities of Novorossiysk and Sochi now are. In fact, all the blood-drenched wars in the Caucasus, including the two latest Russo-Chechen Wars, have to varying degrees been consequences of the Treaty of Georgievsk.

Given this historical and political background, I was fully aware that it would be no simple matter to promote dialogue between Chechnya and Georgia. I also knew that gaining acceptance of reconciliation with Georgia would be particularly difficult in my own country, not least because such respected Resistance commanders as Shamil Basaev, Ruslan Gelaev, and Turpal-Ali Atgireyev had been among the volunteers on the side of the Abkhaz. There were even rumours that Shamil Basaev was to be awarded Abkhazia's highest honour, the Order of Honour and Glory. These commanders were still certain they had acted correctly, so my conciliatory role was not going to be easy. I could look forward to occupying the no-man's-land between my comrades in the Resistance and the leaders of Georgia, trying to bring their positions closer while preventing mutual recrimination.

The blame for 'Abkhaz separatism' did lie largely with Georgia which, proud of its genuinely long and glorious history, could not easily free itself of imperial complexes in respect of its 'autonomous' regions, and it was this that prompted the Chechen volunteers to side with the weak against the strong. There was plenty we could reproach Gamsakhurdia's supporters with too. The first president of Georgia had been in no hurry while in power to afford political and diplomatic assistance to Chechnya. Zviad Gamsakhurdia's Presidential Decree recognizing the independence of the Chechen Republic was issued on 13 March 1992 and ratified the same day by the Supreme Council of Georgia only after Gamsakhurdia and the Georgian parliament were in exile in Grozny. The second point of the Decree noted that the exchange of instruments of ratification of the two countries' mutual recognition would take place in Tbilisi 'after the restoration in Georgia of constitutional government.' This had not been fated to happen.

All this was in my mind as I and my companions proceeded along the Georgian Military Highway, built by the Russian colonialists as a symbol of their subjection of the Caucasus. When we reached Tbilisi we were immediately taken on to Metekhi, where the government complex and accommodation for foreign visitors were located. The complex was inherited from the Soviet Union and is a secure area where the Georgian president also lives. There we were met by Anzor Burdjanadze, a friend and adviser of President Eduard Shevardnadze and the father of Nino Burdjanadze, today a well known politician in Georgia. That same evening, Nugzar Sajaia, secretary of the Georgian National Security Council, came and we discussed my planned formal and informal meetings. We decided to start the official visit on 24 May with a meeting with the minister of culture and representatives of the arts. I had a very full programme: on 25 May, after the Independence Day celebrations, I was to meet the heads of the country's security agencies in the office of Nugzar Sajaia, who said he would invite the ministers there so I would not have to visit their offices separately. I asked him to postpone my meeting with the speaker of parliament, Zurab Zhvania, to 27 May because on 26 May I was planning to go to the Pankisi Gorge to meet the Chechens living in that part of Georgia. I already knew from the Kistinian representatives (as Chechens born in Georgia are called) that they had problems which needed to be addressed at the highest level. I thought it best to gain an oversight of these directly at a meeting with our compatriots before discussing them with the speaker of the Georgian parliament. In their government hierarchy, the speaker was the second most senior office-bearer in Georgia, so Zhvania was an extremely powerful figure.

During our discussion, Nugzar commented that combining the positions of minister of culture and secretary of the CRI National Security Council was a very ingenious arrangement. It enabled us to play down the political significance of my visit, which might otherwise irritate our 'northern neighbour.' Georgia had its own internal problems with Abkhazia, South Ossetia, and Adjara and had to be very careful, because Russia had strong influence in these regions. He told me frankly that there had been protracted discussion at the very top of the possible consequences of my visit before it was agreed. It was obvious that Tbilisi was monitoring the situation in Chechnya closely. After all our official meetings in Moscow and the signing of the Russo-Chechen Peace Treaty, the Georgian leaders had decided it was time for them too to take an active role in politics in the Caucasus and look beyond their own domestic problems.

After discussing the matter of the programme, Nugzar invited me and those accompanying me to dinner. Right there in the residence was a banqueting hall. I found he had not come alone, but brought several ministers with him: of the Interior, of State Security, and even the head of the Foreign

Intelligence Department. Nugzar introduced them all to me before we sat down. After these courtesies, he invited us, as he put it, 'to the repast.'

A Georgian feast is truly an art form. In addition to an abundance of the most exquisite cuisine, a Georgian Tamada, or master of ceremonies, initiates the guests into the history and culture of his country. By tradition, the first toast is dedicated to the guests. The second toast is raised to their forebears. The third toast is to Georgia. After these three initial toasts, the Tamada gives the floor to those present, first introducing the person about to propose the toast. The Tamada will be sure to relate a story about the person's life, designed to illustrate his virtues. These stories alternate between the comical and the touching. After a single feast with Georgians you will know almost all there is to know about the country and its history, along with many details about the various nationalities living there. The merits of each will be extolled, and their shortcomings touched on with such sparkling wit that no one feels the slightest offence. Despite the abundance of wines and brandies, no one at a Georgian feast gets drunk or becomes loose-tongued, and nobody is overlooked. Of course, the Georgians, like the rest of us sinners, are ordinary human beings. They can take a dislike to each other, feel jealousy, have conflicts. When they are dining, however, these feelings are not evident, people exchange only generous compliments, and the Tamada takes great care that every guest at table enjoys his share of the limelight.

It is widely agreed in the Caucasus that the Georgians are unsurpassed masters in the art of feasting and, in my opinion, that reputation is richly deserved. Georgians sing beautifully and, admittedly, do a great deal of drinking. It is said that the day after a feast, they tell each other at work how much they drank the night before, and in the afternoon agree where to hold the next feast that evening. Many Chechens believe that, if the Georgians were not such great wine lovers, they would have embraced Islam. In fact, however, centuries of proximity to Turkey and Persia have led to a significant proportion of Georgians adopting the Muslim faith. Thus, Adjara, which borders Turkey, has a population of Muslim Georgians and many mosques. There are mosques in Tbilisi and other Georgian cities. I do not know how true it is, but Zviad Gamsakhurdia once said in Grozny that, out of respect for their Muslim neighbours, Christian Georgians in mixed neighbourhoods do not keep pigs or hold lavish feasts during the Muslim fast.

This was not the first time I had enjoyed such a feast, because before all the military upheavals in the Caucasus I often visited Georgia and had many friends and acquaintances there. Accordingly, I already had a fair idea of how to behave and could, when necessary, explain some of the finer points to my companions.

The next day, on 24 May, I had a reception at the Ministry of Culture, to which Hutevari Buba, the producer and artistic director of the Cinema Studios, came, as did Georgiy Dolidze, vice-rector of the Theatre Institute, and many other friends and acquaintances in the theatre. After the reception, we held a joint press conference. The Georgian press were taking a great interest in our trip and covered all my meetings in detail. On the first pages of Georgian newspapers and magazines there were intriguing articles about the prospects for Chechen-Georgian relations. The Russian press also took an interest through its correspondents in Tbilisi.

The following day, 25 May, I was involved in the celebration of Georgia's Independence Day. Simultaneously, our representative in Georgia sent people to Pankisi to warn them I would be visiting the following day. Early in the morning on 26 May we set off in several cars to Pankisi, accompanied by the Georgian ministers of state security and nationalities. (Nugzar had decided against my going there alone.) For both ministers this was their first visit to Pankisi.

The Kistinians living in Georgia are an organic part of the Chechen people. Research by ethnographers tells us that the Kistinians consist of the following indigenous Chechen Teips or clans: Maistoy, Melkhiy, Terloy, Dishniy, Khildekharoy, Nashkhoy, Khacharoy, and Sharoy. There are over 20,000 Kistinians in Georgia, and a total of about 40,000 in the world. Georgian historiography suggests that the Chechen-Kistinians in Tushetia appeared only in 1840-70, but this is not entirely accurate, because long before the nineteenth century, when hundreds of Chechen families from the upper reaches of the River Chanti-Argun, led by the renowned military leaders Dzhakolo and Dui, migrated south, there was already a Vainakh population living in the Pankisi Gorge. We also know from the Georgian chronicles that the second Kartli tsar, Saurmag, 'of a Chechen tribe' as several historians call him, at the turn of the third–second centuries BCE gave the entire mountainous part of Georgia to the Durdzuk-Vainakhs for settlement. Tsar Saurmag did so not only in gratitude for military support they had provided for him and his father, Parnavaz, but also in order to have a bulwark to deflect internal and external threats to the young Georgian state.

The Kistinians are recorded as living in their current location in the oldest extant Armenian and Georgian manuscripts. This people is mentioned in the *Armenian Geography* dating from the seventh century, and Georgian historical sources mention the 'Kists' from the thirteenth century onwards.

The name 'Kists' or 'Kistinians' comes from the Chechen geographical name 'Key-Yist,' which combines the name of one of the Chechen Teips, the Key, and the term *'yist,'* meaning land or country. These names are typical Chechen toponymy, for example, Ma-Yist (Maiste), Terk-Yist, Malkh-Yist, and so on. In Georgian pronunciation, Key-Yist became Kist. At the end of the nineteenth century, the Kistinian Chechens were living in the villages of Omalo, Duisi, Dzhibakhevi, Dzhokolo, Birkiani, Khalatsani (Shua-Khalatsani), Zenamkhari, Artana and Akhmeta. After their Georgian rulers attempted to impose Christianity on them, some Kistinians adopted the religion and assimilated with the Georgians, while others left the Pankisi Gorge and migrated to Chechnya. Most Kistinians, however, continued to live on their own lands and to profess Islam. In 1944, in order to avoid the deportation which the Stalin regime had decreed for all Vainakhs, the Kistinians began writing their names in the Georgian fashion, adding the suffix '-*shvili*' ('child').

Such, in outline, is the history of the Kistinians I went to meet on the morning of 26 May. They gave us a tremendous reception. Beyond the village of Duisi there is a seemingly very ancient amphitheatre where the Kistinians traditionally celebrated important events in the life of their community and conducted large public meetings. The elders and heads of village administrations met us at the regional centre of Akhmeta. The official Georgian administrative name for the Pankisi Gorge is the Akhmeta region. Accompanied by Chechens who had come out to meet us and the head of the regional administration, we drove to the amphitheatre to find several thousand people waiting. There were not only Kistinians, but also Tush and Khevsurs from the area.

All along the road to the amphitheatre, Chechen and Georgian flags were flying from posts and in archways and, as our mixed delegation approached, the Kistinians played the Chechen national anthem. We and our Georgian colleagues addressed the gathering alternately. In my speech I talked only about positive aspects of the centuries-old relations of Chechens and Georgians, focusing the attention of my audience on examples of good neighbourly and brotherly interaction between our ancient peoples. I reminded them that during the deportation of the Vainakhs in February 1944, many Chechens and Ingush who made their way through mountain passes to Georgia were saved from persecution by the secret police by being issued with Georgian passports.

After the speeches, the organizers put on a concert of Chechen and Georgian dancing and singing in our honour. My visit to the Pankisi developed into a major event for the people of the region, and of course it was accompanied by a lavish Caucasian feast. The celebrations were overshadowed for me by what I had been told on arrival by the heads of the regional and village administrations. It was clear that the Akhmet region was being seriously neglected by the Georgian authorities. A lack of jobs, a complete lack of funding for education, health care, culture, pensions, and sport, – in short, every aspect of social provision was being denied to the residents of Pankisi. After the collapse of the USSR, they had been deprived of support by the Georgian state. The head of Akhmet region said at our meeting that his administration was unable to cope with needs in any of these areas. I invited the administrative heads to write a letter outlining the issues to the president of Georgia and the speaker of parliament, undertaking to deliver it to Zurab Zhvania at my meeting the next day. I had that letter in my pocket when we took a warm farewell from the hospitable Kistinians and returned to Tbilisi.

The next day, on 27 July I had my meeting with Zurab Zhvania. I had first seen him in 1988 when he spoke at the Checheno-Ingush State University in Grozny at a conference on 'Russia in the Caucasus.' It was the period of Perestroika, when political processes were afoot in the region and political parties and movements were being formed. Zhvania was the leader of Georgia's Green Party, heading the environmental movement in what was at that time still one of the 15 union republics of the USSR. I remember he said in his speech that 'by signing the Treaty of Georgievsk, Georgia stabbed in the back the Chechens and other peoples of the North Caucasus who were leading resistance to Russia's colonial expansion.' That was an extremely frank assessment of what happened, which is also to be found in *Eliso*, a novella by the classic Georgian writer, Alexander Kazbegi. Zurab Zhvania, however, was the first modern Georgian speaker and politician to give such an unflattering assessment of the treaty. It was that which caused me to remember Zhvania, and now I was wondering whether the years and his impressive political career would have changed him since then and, if so, how much. It was obvious that, at the time Zviad Gamsakhurdia was overthrown, he had been on the side of the acting president, Eduard Shevardnadze.

After the usual exchange of courtesies, I reminded Zhvania of what he had said about the Treaty of Georgievsk in his speech in Grozny, and added that if he had not changed his views, as one of the top leaders of Georgia, he was in a position to put right a historical injustice by recognizing the independence of the Chechen state. I then suggested that the Georgian parliament might ratify Zviad Gamsakhurdia's decree, or at least officially acknowledge its existence. Zurab Zhvania had, of course, changed a lot and was no longer the revolutionary firebrand implacably criticizing the Communist regime. Instead, he was an experienced politician and diplomat who knew how to move gracefully away from controversial topics, which he duly did, without saying 'no' but just smoothly steering our conversation towards other matters. He asked me for my impressions during the visit to the Pankisi Gorge, and said he knew the trip had been interesting and useful. I did not try to press the issue of recognition of the CRI, having achieved my main aim of raising a subject which was very delicate for Georgia but very important for Chechnya. This had created an opening for further diplomatic discussions, and I had no doubt it was a topic to which we would return.

While we were discussing the problems of Pankisi, Zhvania took me by surprise by inviting me to meet President Eduard Shevardnadze. I gave no sign that this was unexpected and said I thought that would be useful. Zurab Zhvania immediately dialled a telephone number and began talking to someone. The conversation was in Georgian, so I had no idea what was being said, but when he hung up, Zurab said he had been speaking to the president and to Nugzar Sajaia. Thus ended my first meeting with the speaker of the Georgian parliament, whom I was to meet often after that, and with whom I established an amicable working relationship.

That evening I was facing another challenge, having been invited to appear live on Georgian television to answer viewers' questions. The programme had already been announced as *A Guest from Chechnya*. I arrived at the studio at the appointed time. The idea was that people would telephone me questions live, but there were almost no questions, only comments, and very emotional comments at that. Some expressed their respect for the Chechen people, their admiration for its heroism, and their congratulations on our victory over Russia. Others accused the Chechens of being responsible for all Georgia's troubles and cursed us roundly. As mentioned, there were some 300,000 Georgian refugees from Abkhazia living in Tbilisi, and I could see the harsh words were coming from them. For an hour and a half I had to respond to some very unpleasant accusations, although most were based on unfounded rumour. Thus, the Chechen volunteers who fought in Abkhazia were accused of having played football with the severed head of a Georgian, raping elderly Georgian women and underage girls, and various other pieces of nonsensical black propaganda in circulation were repeated.

Having lived through a brutal war in Chechnya, I could understand only too well the bitter sense of loss and pain of these people, who had experienced all its horrors. I tried to convey to viewers that the participation of Chechen volunteers in the war in Abkhazia had not been sanctioned by the Chechen government and their actions had not been condoned by the Chechen people. I drew a parallel between the Chechens and those Georgian volunteers, who also participated in the war on the side of the Abkhaz. Eight of the Georgian volunteers were even awarded Abkhazia's highest military honours. I brought up the fighting on the Russian side of Georgians in the recently ended war against Chechnya, and recalled how painful it was to Chechens to know that Russian aircraft were flying to bomb our towns and villages from airfields in Georgia.

Of course, we knew why they had done that. Basing Russian military aircraft on Georgian territory had cost Moscow an extraordinary amount in financial terms, but the Russian leadership had gone ahead, in pursuit of their policy of 'Divide and Rule.' Having said all that, I continued that I had come to Georgia, not to rake up the past and trade hurts and grievances, but to propose to Georgia that we should put behind us the darker episodes of our history and re-establish the good neighbourly, brotherly ties that had bound our two peoples since ancient times. By the end of the broadcast the mood of the television viewers had changed markedly, and large numbers were phoning the studio to express sympathy for the Chechen people and call for us to put our differences behind us. On this friendly note, the broadcast ended. When I got back to Metekhi that evening, Nugzar Sajaia came round to say he had watched the programme and felt it was not only interesting but also very helpful for restoring a climate of friendship between our peoples. Then he added that my meeting with President Eduard Shevardnadze was scheduled for the next morning at 11.00. After he left, I phoned Aslan Maskhadov and told him I had an appointment to meet the president of Georgia tomorrow, and that the meeting was at the initiative of the Georgian side. President Maskhadov did not raise any objection, and the following day I was received by the Georgian leader as planned.

After exchanging greetings, we got down to our conversation. The President was interested to know how the situation in Chechnya was after such a devastating war, and asked how negotiations with Russia were going. He rated the Russo-Chechen Peace Treaty, signed just two weeks previously, very highly, and added that he believed the way forward for us Chechens was through diplomacy. Before the meeting, I had thought through the threads of conversation I needed to follow with him, and steered our discussion towards the situation in Abkhazia and South Ossetia. I asked what stage had been reached in negotiating with the leaders of these republics, and where Georgia felt the solution lay. I also, however, expressed the hope that Georgia was not thinking of resorting to military force. Shevardnadze categorically rejected the idea of using force, particularly against South Ossetia. He said the war in South Ossetia had been a mistake, 'comparable to a crime.' This had been the most peaceful region of Georgia, a place where Georgians and Ossetians had lived in peace as good neighbours for centuries, and that they had all long ago intermarried. He added that he was confident a peaceful solution to the situation there would be found soon.

I could see why Eduard Shevardnadze preferred to focus on South Ossetia. The military operation there began during the rule of Zviad Gamsakhurdia, and the present Georgian leader was keen to lay the blame for the difficulties in Georgia's autonomous regions squarely on his ousted predecessor. He was in less of a hurry to remind me that military action against Abkhazia, which had had far more serious political and economic consequences for Georgia, had been his initiative. Accordingly, he did not comment on the Georgian-Abkhaz conflict beyond saying that the main problem now was how to enable the hundreds of thousands of Georgian refugees to return there. After a short pause, he suddenly said it would be very helpful if I could meet the Abkhaz president, Vladislav Ardzinba, and try to persuade him not to place too much reliance on the Russians. He added that he believed Chechnya could play an important role in facilitating a peaceful settlement of the Georgian-Abkhaz conflict, because the Abkhaz had great respect for the Chechens.

I replied that I was entirely willing to meet President Ardzinba, although I would need to agree the matter with President Aslan Maskhadov. I immediately made a proposal I had up my sleeve, by suggesting it would be very good for our relations if President Maskhadov paid an official visit to Georgia. I could see from Shevardnadze's reaction that this was unexpected and that he was not in a position to respond immediately. I guessed he was concerned about how Russia might react.

As if responding to these unspoken reservations, I pointed out that, since the presidents of Russia and Chechnya had signed a peace treaty, a visit by Maskhadov to Georgia would be justifiable in terms of political and diplomatic etiquette, particularly since Georgia had over 10,000 ethnic Chechens living on its territory. A visit by the Chechen president could contribute to stabilizing the political situation in Georgia itself. I briefly told Shevardnadze about my trip to Pankisi and the problems there. He replied that he had already received a report on the situation in the Pankisi Gorge and had discussed the issues with Zurab Zhvania that morning. They had decided to put the social problems of the Akhmet region on the agenda of an enlarged meeting of their National Security Council. Shevardnadze then summoned Nugzar Sajaia over the intercom and, in my presence, asked him to organize a visit for me to Abkhazia tomorrow, and to begin preparations for an official visit by Aslan Maskhadov to Georgia. Needless to say, this was a major political success for the CRI and a brilliant realization of my hopes. After my meeting with Shevardnadze, I gave Aslan Maskhadov a detailed report.

The following morning, the Georgian minister of state security came to collect me and, with Said-Khusein and Alu, we departed for Abkhazia. The minister accompanied us to the Russian peacekeepers' checkpoint, escorted us through it, and on the far side we were met by the deputy prime minister of Abkhazia. After an hour's drive we were in Sukhumi, where President Vladislav Ardzinba immediately received me.

He gave me a very warm welcome, and spent the next half hour or so explaining why it had been impossible for Abkhazia to help us in our war. I assured him the Chechens held no grudges against the Abkhaz and fully understood their predicament. Russia was their only ally in the confrontation with Georgia, and naturally they could not fight on the Chechen side against Russia. At the same time, I stressed, I believed the Abkhaz needed to appreciate that in the Georgian-Abkhaz conflict Russia was furthering its own interests and not defending the freedom of Abkhazia out of altruism. It was just using the situation to pressurize Georgia and retain its imperial status in the Caucasus. I said, 'Not only does Russia not want you to be free, it is opposed to anybody's freedom. A state, which for centuries has denied freedom to its own people, cannot allow any of the peoples subjugated by its empire to be free. The Russians treat Caucasians like natives, and they do that because we cannot get along with each other and our history has taught us nothing.'

Vladislav Ardzinba agreed, but observed that Georgia, as one of the states of the Caucasus, could have been a focus for Caucasians and a base for liberating them but, having been granted formal independence by Russia, was denying it to others, and specifically to the Abkhaz. As a full member of the United Nations, the president said, Georgia could recognize the independence of Abkhazia and Chechnya, and we could start thinking about a Caucasian confederation or united Caucasian state.

'Incidentally,' Ardzinba added, 'all the Caucasians came under Russian rule because of the treachery of Georgia, which voluntarily accepted domination by the Empire, and many territories in the Caucasus which Tbilisi nowadays claims have 'always' been Georgian were in fact awarded to them by the Russian tsars and Communist leaders as payment for their treachery.

Abkhazia, for example, never was part of Georgia. Georgia brought Russia into the Caucasus, so Georgia is complicit in the Russians' extermination of hundreds of thousands of Caucasians and the complete eradication of many Caucasian peoples, including our kindred Ubykhs.'

I had once read *The Last of the Departed*, a heart-rending novel by the Abkhaz writer, Bagrat Shinkuba, so I knew about the fate of the courageous Ubykh people, all of whom, refusing to accept domination by Russia, were killed or emigrated to Turkey. For me, Haji Kerantukh Berzek, who for twenty years led the Ubykhs' struggle against Russia's colonial empire, was a hero as important as the heroes of my own people: Sheikh Mansur, Taimin Biybolat, Boysangar Beno, and the dozens of other heroes of the Caucasian War. So I could fully understand the indignation and pain with which Vladislav Ardzinba related the history of the unprecedentedly tragic history of the Caucasians, for which the Abkhaz president held Georgia directly answerable. Nevertheless, from my conversation with him I gathered that Abkhazia was prepared to sign a treaty of confederation with Georgia, ceding responsibility for defence and foreign policy to Tbilisi.

It was important that President Ardzinba was prepared not only to talk about the principle of confederal relations with Georgia, but also to discuss the issue with Tbilisi and translate his words into practical solutions. Vladislav Ardzinba saw the main obstacle to a political compromise as being Tbilisi's insistence that the 300,000 Georgian refugees from the republic should be allowed to return to Abkhazia. The problem was that there were only 80,000-90,000 Abkhaz there. That meant they would be outnumbered more than three to one by Georgians, which would make meaningless all talk of sovereignty. Interestingly, the president of Abkhazia, without realizing, it repeated almost word for word what the president of Georgia had said about Chechnya being able to play an important role in facilitating a peaceful settlement of the Georgian-Abkhaz conflict.

President Ardzinba told me he was far from happy at having to rely on Russia in his conflict with Georgia, and well aware that Russia had its own agenda. Our meeting ended with a Caucasian feast in a dacha which had once belonged to Lavrentiy Beria, the head of Stalin's secret police. The dacha became famous throughout Abkhazia because, during their war with Georgia, the Abkhaz had very nearly captured Eduard Shevardnadze there. A Russian helicopter had to be sent, and the Georgian president was evacuated barely half an hour before the arrival of the Abkhaz volunteer militia. I had already heard this tale, which the Abkhaz leader told me with considerable relish, from Ruslan Khasbulatov who, as chairman of the Russian Supreme Soviet, gave the order for a military helicopter to be sent. The Georgian president, who had been in no hurry to take his country into the Commonwealth of Independent States, was obliged while in the helicopter to make a handwritten application to Yeltsin for Georgia to be admitted to membership. I knew from Khasbulatov that this had been the condition on which the Russians agreed to save Shevardnadze from ignominious captivity. For me, the whole saga was just further confirmation that Moscow never does a favour without an ulterior motive.

That evening I and my companions returned to Georgia. In Tbilisi, Nugzar Sajaia was waiting, and told me that tomorrow, before returning to Chechnya, I was to have a further meeting with President Shevardnadze. This took place in the morning, and I gave the president an account of my conversation with Vladislav Ardzinba, softening the tone, of course, of some of his more caustic remarks. I told Shevardnadze I believed it was perfectly possible to persuade the Abkhaz side to accept a reasonable compromise, providing Georgia abandoned its imperial ambitions, which were wholly alien to the Caucasian mentality. Shevardnadze thanked me for my mediation and said we must certainly continue with such meetings in the future. He added that Nugzar Sajaia would shortly come to Chechnya to discuss the date for an official visit to Georgia by President Aslan Maskhadov.

After my meeting with Shevardnadze, our delegation returned to Chechnya. The Georgians accompanied us to the Russian border, and four hours later we were back in Grozny. Journalists were waiting there for me. I held a press conference and spoke about the trip. It was given wide media coverage, readers and viewers taking a great interest in the results but, like all our leaders, I made a mistake at this point. I said I was very pleased with the trip and my meetings with the presidents of Georgia and Abkhazia. I said I now firmly believed that all our states in the Caucasus needed to develop a common strategy, and that we were able to resolve our conflicts by ourselves, with no outside interference. To achieve this we needed to continue with direct talks between the countries of the Caucasus. By so saying, I needlessly alerted Russia and, of course, it immediately started taking countermeasures.

Moscow was greatly irritated by my efforts to organize direct dialogue between the presidents of Georgia and Abkhazia without Russian involvement. Russian television showed documentary footage of Yeltsin taking Shevardnadze and Ardzinba by the hand and literally forcing them to shake hands with each other. The accompanying commentary was, 'Zakaev would do well to remember that it was not he but the Russian president who established peace between Georgia and Abkhazia.' Within a few days, retracing my route, Boris Berezovsky, as deputy secretary of the Russian Security Council, was flying out 'to mediate.' He met first with Shevardnadze, then with Ardzinba, and at the end of his trip announced he had been visiting Tbilisi and Sukhumi to acquaint the leaders of Georgia and Abkhazia with a new Russian peace plan. He added that it was possible that he would shortly arrange a meeting between the Georgian president and the leader of Abkhazia. After Berezovsky's visit, the Russian Foreign Ministry got in on the act, Yevgeny Primakov announcing that they were working to arrange a meeting of the leaders of parties to the conflict, with Russia mediating.

This was nothing more than a knee-jerk reaction to my trip to Tbilisi and Sukhumi, plus, of course, a signal that Russia had the situation in the Caucasus entirely under its control and would not allow anyone to challenge it. Georgia was officially seeking an alliance with the United States, however, and our official contacts with Tbilisi were maintained. Two weeks after my trip, Nugzar Sajaia flew to Grozny to discuss Aslan Maskhadov's visit. His flight was delayed at Mineralnye Vody in Russia, and I had to phone Ivan Rybkin to have the plane allowed to fly on to Grozny. After protracted negotiations with the leaders of the various security ministries of Russia, the plane eventually landed at Sheikh Mansur Airport. I met our Georgian guest there, and we drove together to the Presidential Palace. Our route from the airport necessarily took us through the whole of the city, and Nugzar was shocked by the destruction. After greeting Aslan Maskhadov, he immediately began talking about what he had seen on his way from the airport. He said, 'The television pictures which international news agencies have shown of the destruction in Grozny were terrible enough, but the reality of what I have seen is beyond belief. It is obvious that most of these ruins were residential buildings, and I simply cannot imagine how, at the end of the twentieth century, anyone could have given the order to raze residential neighbourhoods to the ground.'

Of course, in addition to protocol issues relating to Aslan's visit to Georgia, we had prepared a number of other issues to discuss. The first was the matter of searching for people who had gone missing without trace during the Georgian-Abkhaz War. After the showing on Chechen television of a documentary, *Gamardzhoba, Georgia!*, about my trip to Georgia, I began to receive visits from Chechens whose relatives had gone missing at that time. The second issue concerned the building of a road from Chechnya to Georgia along the course of the River Argun to the village of Shatili. The third was an agreement for cooperation between our two countries' security and law enforcement agencies. Nugzar took all these questions on board and said he would forward them to President Shevardnadze and that, specifically, these and other questions could be discussed during my next visit to Tbilisi. We drafted a letter on behalf of Aslan Maskhadov to the Georgian president expressing gratitude for the invitation and stating that the Chechen leader would find it a pleasure and a great honour to visit Georgia. There followed a dinner, after which Nugzar returned to Tbilisi, and a new chapter had begun in Georgian-Chechen relations. The same day, Aslan Maskhadov signed a decree appointing me the CRI presidential representative for relations with Georgia.

At the end of July 1997, I had another meeting with Eduard Shevardnadze at which we agreed on all the matters the parties would discuss during the meeting of their presidents. At that meeting, I told him that Chechnya had already begun laying the road to Georgia. Moscow reacted sharply to our efforts to mediate in the Abkhaz-Georgian conflict, but made no attempt to obstruct the building of a road to Georgia, and did not even issue any barbed statements. I was puzzled that Russia seemed not to be reacting to this, but the reason became clear in 1999 with the outbreak of the Second Russo-Chechen War. The road became crucially important to us at that time, and was actually the most important aspect of our cooperation with Georgia, providing access to the outside world.

The signing of the Russo-Chechen Peace Treaty gave the Georgian government the opportunity to put relations between the security forces of Georgia and Chechnya on an official, legal footing, and this they were in principle prepared to do. The prospects were dashed, however, by misconduct on the Chechen side. After my latest trip to Tbilisi, I reported to President Maskhadov on progress in agreeing arrangements for formal cooperation in the fight against crime with the Georgian government. He convened a meeting of all the heads of our security and law enforcement ministries and agencies at which I explained the political importance of the proposed agreements with our Georgian colleagues. Maskhadov instructed them to prepare draft agreements, and send them to me for further discussion with the Georgians and to establish a date for signing them.

A week later, I was in Moscow for talks with the Russians on banking and customs agreements when I got a call from Tbilisi. I was told the head of the CRI National Security Service, Apti Batalov, and CRI Deputy Prime Minister with responsibility for security and law enforcement Turpal-Ali Atgireyev had arrived in Georgia and said they had come to sign the agreements. I replied that I knew nothing about their trip, and asked our representative in Georgia, Hizir Aldamov, to pass the phone to one of them.

Apti Batalov took the receiver, and I asked, 'What is going on? What are you up to?'

He said they were not up to anything. They had been in Baku meeting some of their Azerbaijani colleagues and decided to stop off in Tbilisi for the same purpose. President Maskhadov was aware of their trip. I called Nugzar Sajaia and got an entirely justified earful of criticism to the effect that this was no way to handle affairs of state. I apologized and said it was my fault for forgetting to warn him about the visit of our two officials. We agreed that Batalov and Atgireyev would have a working meeting with their Georgian colleagues. Nugzar asked me to ensure that in future our officials did not turn up in Georgia without prior notice.

In accordance with Caucasian tradition, the Georgians gave these visitors from Chechnya a very hospitable welcome and, after the formal meeting, invited them to the dinner table. During the feast, I was later told, Turpal-Ali rose to his feet and started telling everyone how much he respected and loved Georgians. During the Georgian–Abkhaz War, he went on, he had been fighting on the Abkhaz side, and had saved the lives of Georgian prisoners by not allowing the North Caucasian volunteers to humiliate and shoot at them. At this, the Georgians rose as one and walked out. The next day, the Georgian security officials said they were busy and that the negotiations were being postponed indefinitely. The day after that, I was phoned by Nugzar Sajaia, who said that we had made a serious mistake by sending an individual with Georgian blood on his hands to negotiate with official representatives of Georgia.

A few days later, I again went to Georgia, after agreeing the trip with Tbilisi. I had to make immense efforts to get our relationship back on the rails. It would have been impossible without the political will of President Shevardnadze who, unlike our Chechen politicians, eschewed populist gestures and followed a course dictated by political expediency and the interests of his country. During my trip, the Georgian president signed a decree on 'Urgent measures to improve the socio-economic situation of the inhabitants of the Pankisi Gorge.' We also finally agreed all the issues relating to the official visit of the president of the Chechen Republic of Ichkeria to Georgia. We agreed there would be a meeting of the two presidents on the day of his arrival in Georgia. On the second day, Aslan Maskhadov, Eduard Shevardnadze and those accompanying them would fly to Telavi, and then proceed by car to the Pankisi Gorge. On their return, the presidents would hold talks at the Georgian president's country residence. On the third day, there would be a joint press conference and we would return home.

My main topic for discussion was matters of protocol for the visit. The Chechen president would be met at the airport by the speaker of the Georgian parliament, Zurab Zhvania. There would be a red carpet and a military guard of honour, but the Georgians adamantly refused to raise the Chechen national flag. They proposed to raise three: Georgian, Chechen, and Russian, but I objected to this option. We finally agreed as a compromise not to have any flags at all. Ten minutes before Aslan Maskhadov's plane landed, airport officials discreetly lowered the Georgian flag. I was shocked, but see now that they were simply proceeding from the interests of their state. They wanted to avoid provoking Russia, but at the same time did not want to annoy their Chechen neighbours. As for the red carpet and guard of honour, they explained these away as being simply characteristic Caucasian hospitality. Hardly anyone noticed the lowering of the Georgian flag for a few minutes. Georgia's top officials were very pragmatic.

President Maskhadov's visit to Georgia began a new chapter in the history of the relationship between our two countries and peoples. For the first time in the many centuries of history of the Caucasus, Georgia officially received the leader of a Chechen state. The meeting between Aslan Maskhadov and Eduard Shevardnadze went according to the protocol, as did all the planned events and meetings. At their discussion, Shevardnadze expressed Georgia's determination to 'draw a line under the dark events in our recent history and set about reviving all that united our two nations for many, many centuries – the best traditions of good neighbourliness, friendship, and good relations in every sphere.' In turn, Aslan Maskhadov called the intervention by Chechen volunteers in the conflict between Georgia and Abkhazia, 'a black page in history which ill served our peoples.'

The main focus of the talks was on ways to strengthen peace and stability in the Caucasus. It was agreed to hold regular consultations to further the ideal of a 'peaceful Caucasian home.' Maskhadov noted that the problems of the Caucasus should be resolved by the Caucasians themselves. Shevardnadze said that, 'the visit of the president of Chechnya to Georgia should come as no surprise to anyone in Moscow, because everything that leads to stability in the Caucasus is in the interests of both Russia and Georgia.' On returning from Tbilisi, Aslan Maskhadov spoke of the 'productiveness of this friendship visit,' and added that 'the Chechens need friendly and fraternal relations with the Georgians more than with any other people.'

President Maskhadov's official visit to Georgia was a great political success, and further opened the way to official contacts between the two countries.

III

Funding Fanaticism

Tripartite commercial agreement signed between Russia, Azerbaijan and Chechnya. Rybkin and Berezovsky dismissed and replaced by Vladimir Putin, to protect the Yeltsin 'family' from future criminal prosecution. Misrepresenting Russian aggression against Chechnya as part of George W. Bush's 'war on terror,' Russia supports Islamist factions in Chechnya, and CRI law enforcement agencies cannot cope. Maskhadov is seen as ineffectual. Chechnya's European satellite telephone system is to be independent of Moscow. Three British and one New Zealand telephone engineers are beheaded. Zakaev names the culprits. Putin funds detachments of Islamist fanatics. Chechnya is torn between imported 'Pure Islam' and more easy-going traditional Chechen Islam.

Another important political development in summer 1997 was the signing in Moscow on 11 July of agreements on banking and customs arrangements. After that, Khozh-Akhmed Yarikhanov and I flew with the Russian delegation from Moscow to Baku to sign a tripartite agreement on the transportation of Azerbaijani oil. The Russian delegation was headed by First Deputy Prime Minister Boris Nemtsov. On arrival at Baku airport we were met by the Azerbaijani first deputy prime minister, Abbas Abbasov, and driven to the country residence of the president, where Geydar Aliev met us personally. Aliev first held talks with the Russians, then with the Chechens, and after that we continued with trilateral negotiations.

For us, this tripartite agreement was primarily of political importance. It was another step towards the recognition of Chechnya's independence, not only by Russia but also by Azerbaijan. For Russia, transportation of Azerbaijani early oil was an obligation under an interstate agreement, and Moscow was prepared to sign a bilateral agreement with us on almost any conditions we cared to name. It hated all suggestion of our participating independently in an international project. The Chechen government took a principled stand on the issue. Azerbaijan was demanding that Russia should fulfil an existing commitment to transport Azerbaijani oil via the Baku-Novorossiysk pipeline, which was due to begin in August 1997. Some 150 kilometres of this pipeline passed through the Chechen Republic, and in the time remaining Russia simply could not get a new oil pipeline, bypassing Chechnya, built. Accordingly, the Kremlin had no option but to accept the need for a trilateral agreement on the matter. We saw this as a further political success.

After the ceremonial signing of the agreement, the president of Azerbaijan announced at a press conference 'The document signed today between the Russian Federation, the Chechen Republic of Ichkeria and Azerbaijan removes the last obstacles to exporting the republic's black gold to our foreign European partners.'

Despite the fact that Russia did make some concessions to us during the signing of agreements at ministry level, which were concluded in almost all spheres, in reality nothing was changing. Russia was not fulfilling the obligations it had signed up to in social or humanitarian matters, or in respect of the Russian Ministry of the Interior. The CRI state prosecutor repeatedly requested the extradition to Chechnya of Adam Deniev, suspected of organizing the murder of Red Cross workers in Novye Atagi. The Russian Prosecutor's Office simply ignored our requests. To add insult to injury, the Russian law enforcement agencies, I later learned, continued regularly to distribute throughout the Russian Federation bulletins listing members of the Chechen Resistance forces they wanted for questioning, some of whom were even members of our government with whom the Russian leaders had several times met at official functions. Despite the Russian side having declared a full mutual amnesty for participants in the Russo-Chechen War, Moscow continued to seek to exert pressure on the Chechen government.

The turning point in relations between Russia and Chechnya came, arguably, in August 1997, after the second meeting between Presidents Maskhadov and Yeltsin. I was later told by Ivan Rybkin that Movladi Udugov and Said-Khasan Abumuslimov had been to Moscow on several occasions with proposals for a summit meeting between the two. They argued that, despite the signing of the Peace Treaty and a succession of ministry-level agreements, the Russian side was simply not abiding by them, and a meeting between the two presidents could move the process forward and oblige Russia's executive institutions to honour their commitments. Our negotiating partners on the Russian side, and in particular Boris Berezovsky, persuaded Yumashev of the need for such a meeting. It was organized after a number of matters at issue had been ironed out. During the meeting, however,

Maskhadov brought up with Yeltsin our proposal to sign a further Intergovernmental Agreement, acknowledging Chechen independence, which came as a complete surprise to him. Yeltsin, very well versed in the ways of politics, did not refuse outright, and very diplomatically told Maskhadov that they would need to establish two groups to work through all the matters relating to it. This was to prove the last meeting between the two presidents.

Later, Ivan Rybkin chided us informally for violating an agreement our two delegations had reached during our first meeting in Nazran. We had agreed then not to try to outwit each other and only to issue jointly agreed statements. Rybkin saw Maskhadov's raising of an issue not previously considered by the negotiating delegation and not included in the protocol for the summit as breaching that agreement. Movladi Udugov tried to get himself off the hook by claiming he had not known Maskhadov was going to make this proposal, but of course he was lying. Udugov and Said-Khasan Abumuslimov had themselves prepared the proposal for Maskhadov.

Aslan Maskhadov was influenced by rumours widespread at the time that Yeltsin was no longer in control of the situation since his entourage were not keeping him abreast of the real situation. That is why Maskhadov decided to have a go at persuading him in a personal conversation to recognize the sovereignty of Chechnya. Of course, this was a complete nonstarter. Regardless of Yeltsin's physical and mental condition, Russia had a functioning state apparatus which regulated all issues of importance. The real problem was that neither Maskhadov nor Udugov nor I, none of us, had any real experience of diplomacy, and there were no state institutions to monitor what we were planning to do. What happened was not malicious, but it was a blunder. There were no further meetings of our delegations to continue work on drafting an intergovernmental agreement.

In early November 1997, Boris Yeltsin signed a decree relieving Boris Berezovsky of his post as deputy secretary of the Russian National Security Council 'in connection with his transfer to other work.' In 1998, Ivan Rybkin himself was dismissed as secretary of the Security Council. Berezovsky was appointed executive secretary of the Commonwealth of Independent States, and Rybkin became deputy prime minister with special responsibility for CIS relations. At least on paper, their transfers were not punishment but promotion. It was well deserved from Russia's viewpoint, because they had won what Russia most needed: time. The totally unknown Vladimir Putin was appointed director of the FSB and later additionally became secretary of the National Security Council. Prime Minister Viktor Chernomyrdin was also removed and replaced by Sergey Kirienko. In effect, all the key players with whom we had worked, negotiated and signed agreements had been replaced.

It is, alas, a long-established tradition that Russian leaders maintain continuity only in matters they see as being in their own interests, or which fit in with the policies being pursued by the new leaders. This is true even of international obligations, and Chechnya they viewed entirely within the legal framework of the Russian Federation. Accordingly, they felt no compunction about abandoning inherited obligations relating to Russo-Chechen relations or reneging on existing agreements. Indeed, the earlier political concessions made by the Russian government when signing agreements with us were made with no expectation on their part that they would be honoured. Moscow was merely playing for time, seeking systematically to undermine the popular Russian and international perception of a heroic Chechen people fighting in an unequal struggle with Russia for their national freedom. Within a year of the end of a terrible war, that favourable opinion had become negative as a result of black operations undertaken by the Russian security services, in most cases manipulating Chechens to do their dirty work.

The situation in the republic was steadily deteriorating, with increasing numbers of people dissatisfied with our government. Kidnappings were becoming more frequent. There was animated discussion in the press about a supposed 'leak' that the kidnapped ORT television reporters had been released in return for a ransom of US$ 3 million. From that moment a hostage-taking industry developed, which took off solely because of the enormous sums being paid in ransom. These greatly excited local criminal gangs, which had already fused with the so-called jamaats, created by former members of the Resistance under the patronage of emissaries from the Middle East. The latter, after the end of the First Chechen War, all but turned Chechnya into a place of pilgrimage. The process was, of course, under the supervision of Moscow, since all these envoys had visas issued by Russian embassies in their home countries and openly flew in via Moscow. From there they were transported on to the North Caucasus, mostly Dagestan and Chechnya. This, too, as later became clear, was part of a campaign to discredit the Chechen state and its leaders. The presence of these individuals in our republic provided Russian propaganda with 'proof' that the CRI was a 'theatre of operations of international terrorist organizations.'

In fact, in the period between the two wars, the Chechen leaders did not even know of the existence of such extremist international organizations as al-Qaeda. It was only when the second invasion of Chechnya began and the Russians started claiming they were engaged in a 'war on terrorism' that it became clear to us why they had been funnelling these people into Chechnya without hindrance. I can confidently state that all the extremist religious associations and criminal gangs specializing in abduction were entirely under the control of the Russian intelligence agencies. It is, of course, more than likely that there were gangs they did not control, since many individuals with criminal inclinations saw kidnapping as an easy way to make large amounts of money. If any of them had qualms of conscience, or began to fear they might have to pay for their shameful crimes in the afterlife, the newly appeared sheikhs from the Middle East and their local followers hastened to reassure them, issuing special fatwas and interpretations, tailored to the occasion, of religious sources sacred to Muslims.

From reports of the heads of our own security forces, we knew the Russian Federation's intelligence agencies were in close contact with the kidnap gangs. The immediate handler was Vladimir Rushailo, Russia's deputy minister of the interior, who subsequently became the minister. The intermediaries between the Russian Ministry and the kidnappers were the minister of the interior of Ingushetia, Daud Korigov, and a nephew of Akhiad Idigov. Money was paid to the criminals through them. It has to be said, the whole business was organized down to the last detail. One gang was directly involved in the kidnapping, another detained the hostages, while a third conducted the negotiations with Russia's representatives. Our own law enforcement agencies were powerless to break this criminal chain, mainly because the Russian side continued paying ransoms.

This not only enabled the Russian intelligence agencies to score an ideological victory over us, but provided them with profitable business opportunities. The source of the ransom money deserves particular mention. Deputy Minister Rushailo had a special unit under him which, whenever the Chechen kidnappers' negotiators demanded a certain sum as ransom, would coerce Chechen businessmen living in Russia, particularly in Moscow and St Petersburg, to come up with the money. This was done quite openly. Men in military uniform would stop the car of a businessman in the street, or men wearing masks would burst into his office. In both cases they would plant a pistol cartridge or a package of drugs in his pocket, arrest him, and then offer him a choice between going to jail for a considerable term or producing a large sum of money. The businessmen naturally preferred to pay. In addition, the amount demanded by kidnappers could be contributed 'voluntarily' by Russian oligarchs. Needless to say, the Russian agencies involved in 'special operations to free hostages,' i.e. paying the ransoms, frequently made as much for themselves as did the kidnappers. Russia's most senior leaders were fully aware of what was going on, but the Kremlin not only failed to stop these criminal activities but gave them every encouragement. The West too was aware at the highest diplomatic levels that the Russian government was continuing to pay ransoms for the release of hostages, but no steps were taken to oblige it to desist. At meetings with our Russian negotiating partners we urged them to stop the payment of ransoms, but the situation only got worse. Eventually, President Aslan Maskhadov publicly complained to the Russian side that their intelligence agencies were in cahoots with the criminals behind the kidnappings. It had no effect. The situation was close to being out of control. Even members of the Resistance were sucked into these subversive gangs in substantial numbers.

Among the first abducted foreigners were citizens of Great Britain, Poland, Turkey and other countries sympathetic to the Chechen liberation struggle which were giving us political and moral support. Moreover, the kidnappers' victims were people who had directly helped us during the First War. Here are a few examples.

On 2 July 1997, two British citizens, Camilla Carr and Jon James, were abducted. They were employees of a British charity which had worked in Chechnya during the First War to help orphans. This was the only humanitarian organization to continue working in Chechnya after the shooting of the Red Cross workers in Novye Atagi. Camilla Carr and Jon James were held hostage for over a year. Vladimir Rushailo, under his streamlined arrangement, held talks with the kidnappers behind the backs of the Chechen government and ransomed them for US$ 3 million. According to the official version, the ransom was paid by Boris Berezovsky, with the implication that he had used his own money.

There was another case. On 17 December 1997, five Poles were abducted in Chechnya. They were Marek Kurzyniec, Paweł Chojnacki, Krzysztof Galiński, Dominik Piaskovski and Marcin Thiel. All were members of a humanitarian aid convoy in support of Chechnya organized by the Polish-Chechen Friendship Society under the patronage of the Archbishop and Municipality of Gdansk. The Polish-Chechen Friendship Society set up an information centre in Kraków, which covered events in Chechnya from 1994 to 1996. This Centre was virtually the only source of information in Europe on the crimes committed by the Russian Army in Chechnya. The Russian government exerted diplomatic pressure on Poland to suppress the Kraków Information Centre, but to their credit the Poles did not give in to it and allowed the Centre to continue. Activists of the Society went on to establish a student association called 'Freedom for Chechnya.' The organization sent convoys of humanitarian aid, two of which got through to territory controlled by the Resistance forces, where all previous attempts had been blocked by Russian troops. In 1996, Marek Kurzyniec, Paweł Chojnacki and Jerzy Dobrowolski arrived in the Chechen Republic with one of the convoys which did reach its destination. President Djohar Dudaev met them. He thanked them, and through them all the people and the government of Poland, for their moral support of the Chechens in these difficult and testing years. At this meeting, Djohar Dudaev also conferred honorary citizenship of Chechnya on Marek and Paweł. These were the people captured and held hostage in Chechnya after the end of the First War for 53 days, and freed on 18 February 1998 by fighters from the Counterterrorism Centre of the CRI.

Another of the first kidnap victims in Chechnya was Ali Djunid, a Turkish citizen of Chechen origin. During the First War he set up committees in support of Chechnya in major Turkish cities, which collected money to support the Chechen Resistance and conducted educative and ideological work among the Turkish population. The committees published and distributed magazines in Turkish which had illustrated stories about what was happening in Chechnya, about Chechen heroes and leaders. Ali Djunid, the founder and director of these committees, was taken hostage in Chechnya and held in captivity for several months.

These examples make clear enough the targeted nature of the kidnappings of foreigners in Chechnya in the early stages. As regards Russians, the most symbolic was the kidnapping of Russian journalist Yelena Masyuk, who became world famous for her truthful reports from war-torn Chechnya, shown in Russia on NTV. This was the television channel whose criticism of the Russian government largely turned Russian public opinion in favour of the Chechens fighting for their freedom. Yelena Masyuk was also a personal friend of Shamil Basaev. Her kidnapping by Chechens was not only a terrible shock and tragedy for this courageous woman, but also did great damage to the reputation of our government. It later transpired that one of the organizers of her abduction was a senior figure in our law enforcement agencies. This was discovered after Yelena Masyuk was released, or more precisely, ransomed. That individual died the same day, when he was accidentally shot in the head by one of his accomplices, who mishandled a specialist weapon. Then, on 1 May 1998, Valentin Vlasov was kidnapped on the Rostov-Baku Highway near the village of Assinovskaya. Vlasov was the first deputy of Ivan Rybkin, plenipotentiary representative of the Russian Federation in the CRI. There were persistent rumours in the republic that the abduction was the work of Baudi Bakuev's gang, which was under the control of Vakha Arsanov, vice-president of the CRI. Be that as it may, the kidnapping was not so much a criminal as a political crime, and it dealt a crippling blow to the prestige of the Chechen state and of President Aslan Maskhadov personally. Vlasov was subsequently ransomed for US$ 7 million.

The crime wave in the republic was spiralling out of the control of our official government institutions. In early 1998, President Maskhadov attempted to crack down on it. He sacked the entire Cabinet of Ministers by decree, appointed Shamil Basaev acting prime minister with the rank of first deputy prime minister, and asked him to form a new Cabinet. In the new government, the post of minister of Sharia State Security was filled by Islam Khalimov, who was renowned as a 'Wahhabi ideologist.' Movladi Udugov, who was already openly advocating Wahhabi ideology, was appointed foreign minister. I was appointed deputy prime minister and minister of culture, information, press and communications. At first I had hopes that the new government would be able to bring the crime situation in the republic back under control, and initially Shamil Basaev took his job very seriously and acted responsibly. Of course, there were problems because of his lack of essential education and experience but, by appointing appropriate officials, these could have been compensated for by his personal authority and organizational skills. His first mistake, however, was to appoint his brother, Shirvani Basaev, to the post of minister of fuel and energy.

Shamil Basaev had later to introduce some very unpopular reforms. In order to balance the national budget, he raised taxes, lowered the wages of certain categories of civil servants, and ordered that the Central Market, the largest in the republic, on which tens of thousands of residents of Grozny relied for their livelihood, be moved to another location and that vendors should be required to buy new market pitches from the state. This raised furious objections from women trading in the market and there were spontaneous protest rallies. Protesters gathered in front of Government House and angrily broke the windows. The protesters shouted that Basaev had 'sat his brother on the oil pipeline' and was 'pumping all the republic's wealth into his own pockets.' They claimed he had built palaces for himself and his relatives, and made other unflattering allegations.

Shamil Basaev's most important policy announcement while he was acting prime minister was a promise that the government would, by the end of the year, complete construction of the road through the Argun Gorge to Georgia as far as Shatili. After the announcement I again went to Georgia to discuss with Nugzar Sajaia details of the 60-kilometre stretch of the road from Shatili to Tbilisi. It was essential to widen this section if it was to remain passable throughout the year. In its current state, it was unusable during the winter. We had great hopes of this Transcaucasian Highway and planned to equip it with all the necessary infrastructure, including a customs and border post. Without agreement on the Georgian section, it could not function properly. During our discussion, I learned from Nugzar that Moscow had asked the Georgian government to allow Russia to place border guards on Georgian territory. President Shevardnadze had refused. I had no doubt that Moscow would be planning to take action of some kind against Georgia, which was adopting an increasingly independent line in its political treatment of Chechnya.

Sure enough, shortly after my return from Georgia, on 9 February 1998, the media reported that another attempt had been made on the life of Eduard Shevardnadze. That same night, Salman Raduev sensationally claimed responsibility for this act of terrorism. The Russian media instantly trumpeted this statement, with which Raduev had just jettisoned all the positive results we had achieved in the past year and a half in our relations with Georgia, our strategic partner in the Caucasus. Almost everybody in the republic was appalled by his assertion. At the same time, the Russian media reported that documents found in the pockets of a terrorist killed in the attack indicated he was a Chechen living in Dagestan. The next day, Shamil Basaev and I told Raduev in no uncertain terms that he must retract his lie about having organized the assassination attempt, and he reluctantly agreed to do so. Shamil and I called a press conference in my ministry at which Raduev confirmed to reporters that he had had nothing whatsoever to do with the incident in Tbilisi.

A few days later, a Georgian investigation team arrived in Chechnya to enquire into the circumstances of this attempt on the life of their head of state. In addition to meeting the heads of our security and law enforcement agencies, the Georgian investigators wanted to meet Raduev to question him about his statements. At this meeting, Raduev claimed Russian journalists had taken certain phrases out of context in order to misrepresent him as appearing to be claiming responsibility. The Georgian side were satisfied that the Chechen government had done everything in its power to assist in the investigation of the crime. I avoided all contact with Raduev after that.

This was all possible, of course, largely because of the firm line Shamil Basaev took on the matter. Those former members of the Resistance who were beginning to oppose Aslan Maskhadov refrained from openly attempting to thwart Shamil Basaev. In late April 1998, the so-called Congress of the Peoples of Chechnya and Dagestan was held in Grozny, and was to play a calamitous role in the fate of Shamil Basaev and of the entire Chechen nation. During the organizing of the congress, Movladi Udugov, one of its instigators, regularly reported to the president on the preparations, the aims and objectives of the forum. He constantly assured Maskhadov he would be elected president of the congress and that this would give him extra political standing in the eyes of Russia. Through Udugov, Isa Umarov was aiming to use both Maskhadov and Basaev. Maskhadov was to give the congress an aura of legitimacy through his participation, while Basaev was elected 'Imam of Chechnya and Dagestan' in order to give a dramatic boost to his growing challenge to the Chechen president.

Maskhadov made one further attempt to retain control of the situation. On 22 June 1998, he declared a state of emergency in the republic. A curfew was introduced in Grozny, and Aslanbek Ismailov was appointed commandant of the city. All the republic's security and law enforcement services were made directly subordinate to the president, as were state television and radio. All private television channels were taken off the air. The truth of the matter was, however, that Maskhadov and his supporters by now lacked the power to take decisive action against extremist and criminal groups.

Let me give an example. Despite the Emergency Decree's prohibition, inter alia, of all non-governmental television channels, the station controlled by Salman Raduev continued broadcasting until our security forces closed it down and impounded its equipment. In response, on Raduev's orders, members of his gang seized state television and, during the firefight to get them out, Lecha Khultygov, the head of the Chechen National Security Agency, and three members of Raduev's gang were killed. That day, I had just arrived back from Germany where I had been meeting members of the Bundestag and negotiating for them to visit the republic. Just one week before, I had met Lecha Khultygov in the president's reception room. He had told me about the difficulties he faced due to the fact that senior civil servants or people close to them were involved in kidnappings and other crimes. He was preparing a report for Aslan Maskhadov with proposals on how to address the problem.

When I flew in from Germany, Ibrakhim and Alu met me at the airport and told me about the circumstances of Lecha's death. I drove straight from there to see the president. In his office I found Vakha Arsanov, Akhiad Idigov, and Shamil Basaev all trying to persuade Aslan to withdraw from the television station and release Raduev's gang members. Aslan asked my opinion and I told him that today was a major opportunity to show that the

Chechen government was in control. He needed to have the gang members disarmed and send them, along with Raduev, to prison. If they refused to surrender, they must be killed. Akhiad and Vakha rounded on me: 'You want bloodshed! These are young people there who are only 18 or 19 years old!' I retorted, 'What are you talking about? They have already shed blood. They have killed the director of our National Security Agency, and if they get away with that today, others will kill the president and anyone they feel like tomorrow.'

I was absolutely convinced there could be no question of Raduev walking away from there scot-free, although it seemed entirely probable that he had already made his escape. State television was housed in the same building as the Mayor's Office and it seemed certain that, before seizing the building, Raduev would have made his intention known to Lecha Dudaev, the mayor of Grozny, and his relative Akhiad Idigov. Without their consent, he would never have moved in. Lecha Dudaev and Idigov may not have been expecting bloodshed, but that they were aware of Raduev's intentions I had not the slightest doubt. I cannot imagine why President Maskhadov failed to give orders that day for the attackers to be disarmed and arrested.

The following day, Raduev was summoned to appear before the Sharia court and, needless to say, did not turn up. The State Prosecutor's Office then issued a warrant for his arrest, and the Sharia court, for failure to appear before it, sentenced him in absentia to four years' imprisonment. Aslan Maskhadov signed a decree reducing Raduev to the ranks, stripped him of his right to a state bodyguard, and ordered the officers of the Ministry of Sharia State Security to arrest him in accordance with the decision of the Sharia court. Raduev was not arrested, the main reason being that Shamil Basaev, having meanwhile resigned from the post of deputy prime minister, took him under his wing.

Shamil resigned because he had realized that, without extensive economic assistance from the outside world, he could never set the republic on the road to recovery. Given Russia's hard line on Chechnya, there was very little prospect of that, so Shamil looked for a pretext to resign, but in such a way as to ensure that the blame for it fell on President Maskhadov. He demanded that Aslan promote him from 'acting' to full prime minister. Maskhadov refused, citing the Constitution, according to which the office of prime minister was inseparable from the presidency. Of course, this was only an excuse. Basaev finally gave an ultimatum that, if the parliament did not separate out the powers of president and prime minister, he would resign. I discussed it with Maskhadov and suggested he should put forward a legislative initiative to delimit the powers of the president and the prime minister, while adding an article to the Constitution that the president was the head of state. At that time, Maskhadov could have got that through our parliament but he flatly refused, asking pointedly, 'Are you trying to turn me into a stuffed dummy?'

I replied, 'No, Aslan. I want you to remain our national leader, above criticism. You could be that if you were not tied up with issues over pensions, payment of salaries, and other social needs. You can sack the prime minister and the entire government every six months and appoint replacements.'

I gave the example of President Aushev in Ingushetia, but Aslan was having none of it. He believed that, if he lost the powers of the prime minister, he would be weakened. Basaev resigned. Aslan Maskhadov was again head of the government and, at the first meeting of the Cabinet of Ministers, said he was glad Basaev was gone because now everyone could see how incompetent he had been. I suspected Shamil Basaev's resignation might come back to haunt the government. He had not gone off 'to keep bees,' as he had previously talked of a future apart from politics. By his very nature this man could never be a passive observer of events in the republic. I had no doubt that if Shamil was not in the government he would be opposing it, and that that would be a big headache for the republic's leaders. Maskhadov was confident, however, that, after his disastrous premiership, Basaev was no longer a threat to his power.

Crime, the gradual impoverishment of the population, corruption within the government, the economic crisis, all were due mainly, of course, to Russia's failure to honour its obligations to restore the republic's economic infrastructure, destroyed in a war it had unleashed. Ultimately, however, in the eyes of the public the person to blame for all our troubles and economic difficulties was President Aslan Maskhadov. His approval rating began to fall catastrophically. When I became minister of culture, press, information, and communications, I also discovered that the mobile telephone communications network Russia had donated to Maskhadov's government had been misappropriated by my predecessor in the post, Movladi Udugov. Before his departure, he transferred the entire system to a private company. More precisely, he helped himself to it. In the name of this private company, Udugov began charging the Chechen government billions of rubles for its use of the network. I reported this to Maskhadov, and submitted all the documentation relating to my predecessor's illegal dealings. Maskhadov instructed one of his assistants to look into it, and there the matter rested. The communications network remained Udugov's private property, and he was effectively receiving that money directly from Moscow as payment for a debt owed to the Chechen government. Nowadays, controlling your own communications is one of the most important attributes of national independence. The above shows just where we stood in that respect.

At this moment, my friend Movladi Akhmetkhanov came back from England with a proposal to establish wireless communications in Chechnya. Movladi was not only a friend, but also a business partner. We had worked together in the theatre and then, when new economic freedoms appeared in the Perestroika era, he left and went into business. In the so-called 'heady nineties' we had several joint business projects. When Djohar Dudaev asked me in 1994, on the eve of war, to head the Ministry of Culture, I transferred all my assets to Movladi. When the war began, he came home to join the militia but I urged him not to, because he could be a lot more help if he carried on bringing in money for our military needs. Movladi was a patriot and an unswerving supporter of our independence. I can say with confidence that he was the only Chechen businessman who altruistically put 30 million dollars into the Chechen economy after the First War.

Movladi told me he had held talks with Granger Telecom, a British company which was prepared to invest US$ 300 million to develop communications in the Chechen Republic and that, for a start, we needed to establish a company in Chechnya and obtain permission to use frequencies. I asked Movladi, 'What do they need from our government?'

He said they wanted nothing other than that there should be no bureaucratic obstacles put in the way of overcoming the technicalities of registering the company. It was also necessary to get the government's permission and agreement that, in addition to taxes required by law, the company would donate 20% of its profits to the republic's budget. I talked to Aslan Maskhadov about this. Understandably, he did not believe anything would come of the project, but gave permission for us to work along these lines. We did.

A few days later, we registered Chechen–Telecom, a closed joint-stock company, at No. 6, Pushkin Street. The Ministry of Culture, Information, Press and Communications commissioned Chechen–Telecom to prepare a plan to develop a telecommunications system for the Chechen Republic, to be approved by the government of the CRI. For the work, we employed highly skilled professionals. The telecommunications system which existed in the CRI before the war had been built in conformity with standards and technologies adopted in the USSR under the plan for a 'Unified Automated Communications Network.' The system was obsolete. Moreover, in terms of such aspects as signalling and digitization, it had not been in compliance with international norms and standards even at the time it was introduced. This meant there was little point in trying to restore the pre-war system, which had in any case been almost totally destroyed. It was decided to design a new system from scratch.

Very soon, Movladi submitted for the Cabinet's approval a completely new plan for the CRI's telecommunications. It laid out the basic principles for setting up and developing a network designed to operate independently on the territory of a sovereign state. The principles were developed specifically for the Chechen Republic and in full conformity with international standards. Soon, specialists arrived from the United Kingdom to carry out the technical work. I was very impressed by the speed with which British investors operated. In literally one and a half or two months they had done so much it was unbelievable. This was just the way they did business. They knew they were working for themselves and, the sooner they had the system up and running, the sooner they would see returns on their investment and be able to start similar projects in other regions of the Caucasus. We found out later that the efficiency of the British telecommunications engineers pleased the Russians far less than it pleased me.

The British were not, however, the only foreign 'investors' in our republic. After Putin became director of the FSB, Chechnya was inundated with emissaries from the Middle East, who brought large sums of money with them. Except that they brought their money not to the government of Maskhadov but to those who opposed him. Very soon, armed detachments of 100-500 men were appearing in the republic. There were several dozen such detachments, and all of them opposed our government.

The influence of ideological 'Pure Islam,' imported by these 'investors' from the Middle East, increased dramatically. It was in opposition to 'Traditional Islam,' which was propounded by the Mufti of Chechnya, Akhmad-khaddzhi Kadyrov. Both parties escalated the conflict. Every evening, Mufti Kadyrov was appearing on state television to preach against the evil brought in by the ideologists of Wahhabism, and to tell his audience that the Qur'an instructed that they should be destroyed. On Udugov's Kavkaz TV the preachers of Pure Islam were broadcasting constantly, accusing supporters of Traditional Islam, in other words, Sufism, of apostasy and proclaiming that if they did not come to their senses and renounce their errors, they too must be physically destroyed. The situation in the republic reached an explosive level, and it became clear that it was a matter of time before there would be clashes.

We know only too well from world history that clashes between members of a single religion which has split into different denominations are often more vicious and merciless than conflicts between members of different religions and nationalities. We have only to recall the massacres which Catholics and Protestants inflicted on each other in France in the sixteenth century, culminating in the infamous St Bartholomew's Day Massacre in Paris. The fact that after such a rift both parties believe their opponents to be heretics, apostates, people who have 'betrayed God,' explains the intensity of their hatred for each other. In such a situation, what is needed is urgent measures to cool passions and seek compromise, but the preachers on both sides did the exact opposite, inciting hatred and loathing of their ideological enemies with ever-increasing vehemence. It needed only one spark for a fratricidal conflict to break out in the republic. I knew the principal ideologues on both sides, and I can state categorically that, although they stirred up fanaticism in their followers, they themselves were by no means blind fanatics. That being so, the only possible conclusion is that they had some other reason for pushing the republic towards a civil war whose flames would consume the Chechen state we had succeeded in establishing at such terrible cost. Subsequent events showed this to be the case, and it became obvious that these ideologues were not only serving the interests of Moscow but being managed from there.

The spark which lit the powder keg came in the summer of 1998 from a trivial incident in Gudermes. The city was under the control of the so-called Wahhabis, but the two Yamadaev brothers, loyal to Akhmad-khaddzhi Kadyrov, lived there. The Wahhabis set about introducing Sharia rules in the city and, more specifically, banned trading and consumption of alcohol. The guardians of the Sharia rules happened upon three young men drinking vodka in a cafe. A quarrel broke out, and the Wahhabis called for backup to arrest these violators of Sharia, who could expect the next day, when they sobered up, to be sentenced by the Sharia court to forty strokes of the cane on the back and buttocks. Now, for Chechens any punishment of that sort would be considered a very serious insult, even without publicity, and in this case the intention was to broadcast the punishment as an example to others on television.

Although centuries ago our ancestors voluntarily converted to Islam and became faithful followers of the religion, because of the national psychology of the Chechens this punishment was never generally accepted. Being beaten, both in the Caucasus and its neighbouring countries, was the lot only of the servant classes. Chechens so jealously guarded their dignity and personal freedom that even a sneer or a sideways glance could be grounds for serious retaliation, and to strike a man was considered a deadly insult calling for retribution. A major reason for the Chechens turning away from Imam Shamil in the nineteenth century was his attempt to impose norms of behaviour which were inimical to our traditions. Practices Imam Shamil had no trouble introducing in other parts of the Imamate, where the population were accustomed to social hierarchies and corporal punishment, encountered fierce resistance in Chechnya and led to armed rebellion against his Murid Army.

Even the Communist regime, which brought to bear all its resources of blanket propaganda and state terror, failed to eradicate the Chechens' attitude to matters of honour. In the 1980s, on the eve of the collapse of the USSR, Chechnya was probably the last place on the planet where duels were being fought with pistols in the presence of witnesses. It is not difficult to imagine the reaction of Chechens to public flogging. In fact, the practice of corporal punishment for certain offences had been introduced in Chechnya during the First War of 1994-6 by none other than Akhmad-khaddzhi Kadyrov. At the time, the members of the Resistance voluntarily accepted this as a necessary way of strengthening discipline in time of war, particularly since it was rarely used. The population as a whole, however, were not ready to accept it, let alone in peacetime.

The episode in Gudermes was a flashpoint which led to bloodshed. The lads in the cafe refused to go back with the Wahhabis to their premises and a fight broke out. Due to the fact that the guardians of Islamic order enjoyed numerical superiority, the delinquent vodka-drinkers were viciously beaten up. They belonged to a group controlled by Sulim Yamadaev, who summoned all the troops under his command and, with the full support of Akhmad-khaddzhi Kadyrov, set about hunting down Wahhabis, shooting several of them and plundering their stores. The latter blockaded themselves in one of the buildings at the railway station and summoned reinforcements. Islam Khalimov was minister of Sharia state security and had appointed Wahhabi supporters as the heads of all the regional offices of the MSSS. They went to the aid of their brothers in Gudermes. Sulim Yamadaev, however, was the deputy commander of the National Guard, with the result that one CRI state institution was now in armed conflict with another. All the local residents who rejected the Wahhabis' ideology also rose up against them, and the most fanatical supporter of these reprisals was, unsurprisingly, Mufti Akhmad-khaddzhi Kadyrov.

He was not alone. The majority of the Chechen population were demanding exactly the same from Aslan Maskhadov. The republic was teetering on the verge of civil war, the passions on both sides being fuelled by Russia's agents. By now we had obtained a secret document prepared by the Russian intelligence agencies, Army, and Ministry of the Interior. I present it here:

Confidential

For Official Use

Special Measures to Neutralize Pockets of Separatism in the North Caucasus

Protracted negotiation between the Russian Federal government and that part of the Chechen population favouring separatism, based on a policy of appeasement and seeking by incremental steps to draw the rebel territory back towards the centre, is not producing tangible results. The trend of global political processes, a shift of global interest towards new energy centres in the zone of our direct national interests, the lack of a strategic decision on the issue of 'Power 2000' in Russia, together with the unresolved issue of Chechnya, constitute a threat to the national security of the Russian Federation and make it impossible for the current political elite to continue to remain inactive, something which is increasingly regarded by society as a crime against Russia.

Geopolitical processes which have engulfed huge areas of the globe are ever more clearly marking out a line of confrontation between the civilizations of Christianity and Islam. The Caucasus will be at the forefront of this global rift in the twenty-first century. It will be the site of major political and military battles. Objective reality is pushing the Catholic–Protestant world towards alliance with Russia in the face of the Islamic threat which is increasingly evident in various parts of the globe. Chechnya is our problem. We must make it a problem for our potential allies. Our task is to explain and demonstrate the dangers of a terroristic Islamic entity which is aspiring to independent statehood. It is clear that the emergence and consolidation of such a state would also be a problem for the West, whose policy of dollar expansionism into Transcaucasia and Central Asia is a preparation for further strengthening its political presence in these regions. Clearly, investors are averse to politically unstable regions. We may therefore anticipate understanding and support from our Western partners for operations in Chechnya to stabilize the situation and manage the processes occurring in the North Caucasus.

First of all, without deceiving ourselves, let us face the realities:
- Russia lost the military campaign in Chechnya.
- The authority of Russia in the Caucasus has fallen to a critical level.
- Dagestan and Ingushetia have become susceptible to Chechen influence and attraction.
- Russia has limited military capabilities in the Caucasus.
- Consolidation of the so-called Chechen state will lead to Russia losing Dagestan and Ingushetia and a change in the ethnological complexion of the North Caucasus. In this event, Russia's borders will move back 400 km from the Caucasus-Caspian transportation arteries.
- Today, Russian interests in the Caucasus are largely dependent on the situation in Chechnya.
- Tomorrow, the situation in Moscow (the 2000 election) may also become largely dependent on Chechnya.

Is this not rather too much influence for a collection of separatists and criminals? A number of drastic military and psychological measures are needed on our part to have an impact on them. The aim is to prevent the appearance on the world map of a so-called State of Ichkeria.

We do not need to be squeamish about the means. We need to remember morality in this situation only in the context that it would be immoral for us to lose Russia. Defending the power of our state is the supreme moral priority of the Russian people and its political elite. Failure to defend Russia on the grounds of the immorality of a number of actions which it is necessary for us to take in Chechnya would be a crime, because it would deal a fatal blow to Russia itself.

Our actions:

1. At all costs, split the ruling elite of Chechnya. Maskhadov must hate Basaev, Basaev must hate Arsanov, Arsanov must hate Udugov, Udugov must hate Gelaev, and so on. They must all be at each other's throats.

2. The Chechen quasi-parliament, where yesterday's thugs sit in state in their new suits without the faintest idea of how to behave in a parliament, must be used in a struggle for power and influence against the Maskhadov government. It has long been known that the Chechens have a weakness for posturing and ostentation. We must exploit their base instincts. A couple of high-profile interviews on Russian television for the so-called speaker of the Chechen parliament or Raduev will be quite sufficient to make them see themselves as the saviours of the nation.

3. We need to make full use of our media. All the main Russian television channels are watched in Chechnya. We need to work on the subconscious of the Chechen mob and their leaders. The press should give more attention to those ambitious for power. Maskhadov must feel he has competitors breathing down his neck.

4. Make better use of black propaganda. Rumour is one of the most important elements in Chechen society. The extreme impressionability of Chechens was always exploited by tsarist generals, and later by the Soviet authorities, as a lever for influencing their behaviour. So, more circulation of damaging rumours. People are inherently susceptible to fantasies and exaggerated perceptions of reality, so the more extraordinary the rumour the better. The rumour mill should be relentless. Today, let them be talking about Maskhadov being ill; tomorrow, about a quarrel between Basaev and Udugov; the next day, about Arsanov's incredible income. Occasionally, we can toss in a rumour about Maskhadov planning to flee the country, which could usefully restrict the Chechen president's trips abroad, or about a plot being hatched by Gelaev and Yandarbiev.

5. We need to exploit religion as the most fertile soil for black propaganda. Religious factionalism is widespread in Chechnya, with little love lost between the sects, and sometimes outright hostility. Islamic fundamentalism consolidated its position during the war. We need to exploit the differences between these movements and play them off against each other. It is important to understand that if we can get all these religious groups at loggerheads, we will be able to take control of the situation in Chechnya for the long term. Large-scale indoctrination needs to be accompanied by specific black operations in Chechnya.

The first stage is to isolate Chechnya in terms of news reporting.

The second stage is to isolate it totally.

The first stage is easily achieved. In a poor country there is no difficulty in finding people who want money, and the more they can make and the faster they can make it the better. That means abductions. Here journalists and international aid workers can make themselves useful by being the commodity. The next step is to extend this to anyone who has money. Obviously, the impact can be optimized if those targeted are Chechnya's neighbours.

Implementing the proposed special operations will give the Federal government time to prepare more detailed measures to disintegrate Chechnya, divide and discredit the separatist leaders. Chechnya should be split into zones of influence of the various Chechen leaders and groupings. Our task will then be to organize hostilities on the part of the leaders and factions against each other. The most effective way to arouse passions is by causing offence to religious beliefs and physical elimination of religious opponents.

Options:

Arson attacks on places of religious significance (mosques, cemeteries, shrines), public disputes between the leaders and mutual insults at rallies and in the media, followed by claims that these were caused by quarrelling factions.

Our media, while retaining the appearance of neutrality, need constantly to provide coverage of new hostile acts being prepared by one group or leader against another, or to give conflicting accounts of events.

Example 1. 'Many people in Chechnya are inclined to see the desecration of this sectarian site as the handiwork of the Wahhabis.' Followed immediately by a brief account of Wahhabism's intolerance of sects.

Example 2. 'The explosion in the Sharia court building is retaliation by relatives of a fighter in Raduev's Army who was sent to prison for an act regarded as minor by Chechen standards but severely punishable under Sharia law.' Then, complain that Sharia laws restrict the freedoms of Chechens, who are unlikely to willingly surrender liberties they defended even in the time of Shamil.

The special operations proposed for Chechnya have the aim of ultimately returning control over the breakaway territory to Russia. Under any necessary pretext, negotiations should be drawn out to 2001 while thorough preparations are made for decisive action.

It needs to be emphasized that all our efforts and plans may be ineffective in the absence of adequate funding. Given the current situation of constant reorganization of the security institutions, it is important to establish a dedicated, inter-agency group on Chechnya to take full responsibility for preparing and implementing strategic measures to restore Russia's control of this rebellious territory.

(The document dates from 1997.)

In summer 1998, Magomed-Ali Magomedov was to be inaugurated as the president of Dagestan in Makhachkala. The new Russian prime minister, Sergey Kirienko, would be attending. President Maskhadov was also invited and it was intended that, after the inauguration, they would meet for the first time. Aslan summoned me and Khozh-Akhmed Yarikhanov, then minister of education, and instructed us to go to Dagestan and congratulate the new president on taking office. We should also meet Prime Minister Kirienko in Makhachkala to discuss current issues in the Intergovernmental Agreement negotiations. We had to agree a later date for Kirienko's meeting with Aslan Maskhadov in view of current problems in Chechnya.

Khozh-Akhmed and I set off in early morning. There was fighting in Gudermes for a second day and the city was on the Rostov-Baku highway to Makhachkala. We proceeded to Dagestan along minor country roads and rejoined the highway at Novogrozny, east of Gudermes, avoiding the section under fire. We arrived in time for the beginning of the inauguration ceremony and I gave a speech on behalf of President Maskhadov, congratulating Magomed-Ali Magomedov, and adding that the destruction of Chechnya was unlikely to be to the benefit of Dagestan.

After that we had a meeting with Kirienko and Sergey Stepashin, who was now Russian minister of the interior. Kirienko said he well understood why Maskhadov was unable to attend, and that they were following events in Chechnya with great concern. We also discussed the release of Valentin Vlasov, first deputy of Ivan Rybkin. Vlasov had been kidnapped in Chechnya several months previously. Now when we met Russia's representatives, they held all the trump cards. Although we knew perfectly well that all these incidents had been stage managed by the Russian intelligence agencies, that did not absolve us of responsibility. I firmly believe that nobody in our situation could have managed the situation any better in such a short period of time, and that no other people would have endured as much as the Chechens did. We were facing a fiendish adversary for whom nothing was off-limits and which, to achieve its ends, did not care how high the cost was in casualties.

The main campaign of black operations began after the second meeting between Maskhadov and Yeltsin, when it became clear to the Russian government that it would be unable to persuade him to sacrifice the principle of Chechen sovereignty. At that, the Russian intelligence agencies activated all their agents in Chechnya, including those they had infiltrated into the government institutions of the CRI. Their top priority was to discredit Maskhadov and the institutions he headed, in order to demonstrate to the world that Chechens were incapable of running their own state. First and foremost, they wanted to persuade the Chechens themselves of that.

Our meeting was brief, and we parted with an agreement that Kirienko would return to the North Caucasus in a week's time, probably to Pyatigorsk or Nalchik, for talks with Maskhadov. Khozh-Akhmed and I returned home that evening and reported to the president on our meetings and discussions. He in turn told us what had been happening in Gudermes, and said he had not expected so many people to come out in support of him and to demand that he should sort out the Wahhabis once and for all. He asked us for our opinions. Khozh-Akhmed and I were of the same opinion: that it was essential to separate the opposing forces. I cannot today claim that this was the decisive factor, but on the third day of the conflict, peace mediators were brought in, the main role being played by Abdul-Khalim Sadulaev. Also involved were Vice-President Vakha Arsanov, Salman Gazuev, and Magomed Vakhidov. The latter two were from Urus-Martan. The mainstay of the jamaat opposing the CRI government in Gudermes was from Urus-Martan. Abdurakhman, the emir of the jamaat after the mysterious death of Sheikh Fathi, was the individual who had given the order for all Wahhabis to take action against CRI government institutions in Gudermes.

In order to understand the forces opposing President Maskhadov, we need take a look at the main culprits behind the attempt to destabilize the situation in the republic, who ultimately succeeded in leading Chechnya into a Second War. First on the scene in Chechnya in the early 1990s was Sheikh Fathi, a Chechen from Jordan. His ancestors had emigrated to the Middle East after the Russians captured Imam Shamil. They were among the tens of thousands of Chechens who could not resign themselves to the foreign occupation of their country and had no wish to remain under the regime of the conquerors. Fathi belonged to the Zandak Teip. His full name was Magomed Fathi the Zandak but people called him simply Sheikh Fathi. His appearance in Chechnya caused no surprise. After the fall of the Iron Curtain, many descendants of Chechens who had emigrated to the Middle East in the mid-nineteenth century began returning from Arab countries and Turkey to their homeland. This was not seen as suspicious in their, or Fathi's, case, although the CRI Department of State Security opened a case against him on a charge of being a CIA collaborator. The reason for this was that he had fought for eight years in Afghanistan against the Soviet occupation forces. The Afghan mujahideen had been comprehensively supported by the United States and the CIA. No prosecution was brought against Fathi in Chechnya and nobody hampered his preaching.

In addition to the Islamic Revival party, there was the Islamic Ar Risalah organization, whose members included Isa Umarov, Islam Khalimov,

Movladi Udugov, Adam Deniev, and Supian Abdullaev. This organization taught young Chechens the basics of Orthodox Islam, the Qur'an, and later provided military training. Initially Sheikh Fathi was a member and opened a small Islamic school in Argun, but he later distanced himself from them and began preaching on his own. At the outbreak of the First Russo-Chechen War, Ar Risalah established an Islamic battalion under the command of Islam Khalimov, and Sheikh Fathi organized his own armed jamaat. These units consisted entirely of young Chechens and, although not officially part of the CRI Armed Forces, they fought the Russian invaders with great dedication.

At just this time there was talk among Resistance fighters of a Chechen from America who wanted to depose Djohar Dudaev and declare himself Imam. These rumours evidently reached the ears of Fathi, and he insisted on having a meeting with Djohar. This was organized by Salman Gazuev, a Chechen patriot and campaigner, and Abdulla Artakhanov , the former prefect of the Urus-Martan region. The meeting was held at the house of the CRI military prosecutor, Magomed Dzhaniev, and I also attended. Fathi explained his position to Dudaev. He said he had come to Chechnya on his own initiative, to make himself useful to his people and, in the name of Allah, to devote the rest of his life to the liberation of Chechnya. He had no other aims than those. He took Bay'at from President Dudaev, the act of swearing allegiance, and from then on served within the framework of the CRI's national defence forces. President Dudaev later made him a member of the State Defence Committee.

After that meeting, I often met with Fathi, we became friends, and I had great respect for him. He was a profoundly God-fearing and decent person. I would invite him to talk to the men under my command. Despite having been born and bred in a foreign land, Fathi was Chechen through and through, very knowledgeable about our traditions, and spoke Chechen well. He expressed himself tactfully, trying not to offend the national feelings of his listeners, about the contradictions between the Chechen Adats and the Sharia rules, but Fathi never set Islam against our traditions. He said that time was needed to smooth out the contradictions. He was categorically against confrontation between Chechens over matters of religion, and said that if it came about, the fault would lie with those more highly educated in Islam. He was well aware that the Chechens, having lived for seven decades under the rule of atheists, could not suddenly become perfect Muslims or preachers of Islam. Fathi never condemned the saintly evliyas, but said rather that through them God had preserved Islam on Chechen soil and it was due to these holy martyrs that today all Chechens were Muslims. After each meeting with him, my fighters would give up various bad habits: one would stop smoking; another who did not perform namaz would start. This was exactly the kind of *daavat* or sermon Chechens needed. Fathi enjoyed great prestige not only among the fighters but among the population at large.

There were, however, other representatives of the Middle East in Chechnya. In 1995, Hattab appeared. He did not engage in any sort of missionary work but devoted himself exclusively to military matters, training the men in his group in the arts of warfare. Hattab was subordinate to Shamil Basaev and specialized mainly in sabotage, attacking and destroying Russian military convoys. Also, after the end of the First War, during the so-called 'time of peace,' Abdurakhman of Syria came on the scene. He was a young man of Chechen origin who presented himself as an expert in Islam. He was radical and aggressive and, because he had considerable financial resources, managed to gather round him a fair number of young Chechens. After the war, groups like that of Abdurakhman were gradually activated by the Russian intelligence services and began interfering in government business and demanding that Aslan Maskhadov should introduce radical political changes. This meddling became particularly obtrusive with the arrival in the republic of Abu-Umar, an Arab from Saudi Arabia who was notable for having huge amounts of money which he freely dispensed. All these radical factions found themselves confronted by Sheikh Fathi with his enormous prestige. He was totally opposed to all clarion calls and ideologies which led to conflict among those who only recently had been brothers in the fight against Russian aggression, and this discountenanced all these Middle East emissaries and their local supporters.

In autumn 1997, Fathi, aged 60, died suddenly from a heart attack. He was replaced by the young and virtually unknown Abdurakhman of Syria. From that moment, the jamaat turned into an armed opposition to the democratically elected government of President Aslan Maskhadov. Bagautdin of Dagestan and his jamaat now joined forces with Abdurakhman. It was Abdurakhman who ordered the commander of the Sharia Guard, Brigadier General Abdul-Malik Mezhidov, and Commander Arbi Baraev of the Islamic Special Operations Regiment to attack government forces in Gudermes, although both were commanders of official units of the CRI Armed Forces.

The conflict in Gudermes was contained without major casualties. Abdul-Malik Mezhidov and Arbi Baraev were discharged from the armed forces. All the jamaats which had opposed government forces were provided with a corridor through which to leave Gudermes. They redeployed to Urus-Martan, and that city then became a no-go area for the government. The clashes in Gudermes left a total of about twenty dead. Although the conflict was considered to be over, this was in fact only the beginning of armed insurrection. Islam Khalimov was dismissed as minister of the interior and replaced by Aslanbek Arsaev. President Maskhadov signed a decree classifying Wahhabism as an extremist ideology and banning its propaganda in the republic. The chiefs of the security ministries were instructed to arrest and deport from the republic Abu-Umar, Abdurakhman, and other emissaries from the Middle East who were promoting Wahhabi ideology. Aslanbek Arsaev, the newly appointed minister of Sharia state security, announced in a television broadcast that his department was beginning the disarmament of illegal armed groups, by which he meant the jamaats. He warned that if they resisted they would be physically eliminated.

IV

The Threat of Democracy

Yeltsin commends Wahhabi extremism just as the CRI government attempts to outlaw it. Saudi nationals in Chechnya condemn Maskhadov as an apostate from Islam who must be assassinated. In summer 1998, Berezovsky warns that Russia will find failure to compromise on Chechen independence intolerable, fearing a chain reaction in other republics. A decision to restart the war is taken in March 1998. The pretext is an incursion by Shamil Basaev into Dagestan, secretly encouraged by Berezovsky. Russia's leaders consider Islamist extremism less dangerous than Western-style democracy. A new war will make the unknown Putin a credible presidential candidate. Chechnya prepares for war.

At just this moment, Yeltsin's administration in Moscow was hosting a meeting of the Presidential Commission to Combat Political Extremism with the participation of three ministers: of justice, nationalities, and of the interior, as well as the director of the Federal Security Bureau. The Commission resolved that Wahhabism was not in fact extremist, but a peaceful branch of Islam.

Shortly thereafter, Minister of the Interior Sergey Stepashin visited several towns in the so-called Kadar Zone of Dagestan, met the local Wahhabi leaders and, on his return to Moscow, reported to President Yeltsin that 'these amiable beardies,' as he called them, were neither terrorists nor extremists. He noted that in the area where they had established Sharia law there was no drunkenness or stealing, and the overall crime rate was down. Yeltsin responded that Russia was a democratic country and 'if the people there want to live under Sharia law, then let them get on with it!' All this was broadcast on the national channels of Russian television.

A few days after the events in Gudermes, a meeting of the armed opposition, led by Abdurakhman as the emir of the jamaat, was held in Urus-Martan. The meeting was attended by Abu-Umar, Abu-Djunid, and other Middle East representatives who, under President Maskhadov's decree, were due to be deported from the republic. At this meeting Aslan Maskhadov was declared an 'apostate' who must be executed. This verdict was pronounced in the presence of Chechens who had fought together with Aslan Maskhadov against the Russian invaders, none of whom spoke out against a verdict delivered by outsiders of whom they knew nothing except that they could speak Arabic and read the Qur'an. The young people duped were as sincere in their Muslim faith as they were ignorant of the Islamic religion, a fact skilfully exploited by these emissaries – or rather, agents of Middle East intelligence agencies which were furthering the interests of Russia. I have evidence of this, which I shall present below.

At 9.45 am on 23 July 1998 an attempt was made to assassinate President Maskhadov as the presidential motorcade was driving along Staropromyslovsky Highway. Two officers of the Security Service were killed and eight people seriously injured. A UAZ truck parked on the verge and packed with explosives was detonated. I was told by Ruslan, one of the surviving bodyguards, that they had left the house as usual that morning. Before departing, the prospective route was always checked by two cars with security officers. If they noticed anything suspicious or if a traffic accident had occurred which might obstruct progress, they would report it and a different route would be chosen. That morning the route was reported clear. When the motorcade reached Staropromyslovsky Highway, they noticed the UAZ ahead, parked by the roadside in the direction of travel. An escort car changed position and drove between the UAZ and the presidential car. At this moment there was an explosion, the main force of which was taken by the escort, but the shock wave hit the armoured presidential limousine, which rolled over and caught fire. The guards pulled the president from the burning vehicle, put him in another car and quickly drove away. Aslan suffered only minor scratches.

Information about the attempted assassination spread quickly, and within half an hour Russian television was broadcasting the details, explaining to its viewers that the Wahhabis had tried to kill the Chechen president. This information was accompanied by commentary about the events in Gudermes, and viewers were also reminded of Maskhadov's decree deporting the Middle East emissaries from the republic. The assassination attempt was directly linked to these events. That evening it was reported on local television that the Sharia court of the republic had summoned former Acting President Zelimkhan Yandarbiev, former Commander of the Islamic Regiment Arbi Baraev, and Ramzan Akhmadov, emir of the Urus-Martan Jamaat to give evidence in respect of the attempted assassination attempt. Representatives of the security ministries stated that, if the suspects failed to attend voluntarily, they would be brought to the court by force. Zelimkhan Yandarbiev was among the suspects because, after Gudermes, he appeared on Udugov's anti-government Kavkaz TV channel and accused Maskhadov of 'violating the God-given rights of Muslims' and calling him an 'enemy of Islam.'

All three arrived at the court and swore on the Qur'an that they had had nothing to do with the assassination attempt. Later when, after the start of the Second Russo-Chechen War, we were together in besieged Grozny, Arbi Baraev talked contritely about this episode and said they knew perfectly well about the planned assassination. Indeed, according to Arbi, they were intending, after Maskhadov's death, to kill all his supporters. When he was asked how, then, they had been able to swear on the Qur'an to have known nothing about it, Arbi said they had been given permission to do so by their religious mentors. The actual fatwa for the murder of Aslan Maskhadov was issued by Abu-Djunid. The young man who detonated the explosives died in a car accident a few days after the attack. His accomplice was later arrested by our law enforcement officers.

At the end of September, Shamil Basaev and Salman Raduev convened a congress of participants in the war and charged Maskhadov with usurping power and making unacceptable concessions to Russia on crucial matters of the sovereignty of the CRI. This was a blatant lie. The supporters of Basaev and Raduev demanded that the president should resign. The accusations against Aslan Maskhadov were supported by his vice-president, Vakha Arsanov, and ex-Acting President Zelimkhan Yandarbiev. On 30 September 1998, a permanent protest rally by opponents of Maskhadov began in Grozny, which the organizers described as 'national,' although the protesters numbered fewer than a hundred. The organizers of the rally were, in any case, not interested in trying for large numbers. All they needed was television pictures of slogans calling for the resignation of the president. The Russian government had already decided in March to reintegrate Chechnya into the Russian Federation by force, and found the political label of 'democratically elected president,' firmly attached to the person of Aslan Maskhadov, very inconvenient. This protest, though it had few participants, stayed there until the beginning of Russia's Second War: its members moved only after Russian bombs began falling on Grozny.

Maskhadov's supporters convened their own forum, which they named the National Congress of the Chechen People to emphasize its continuity with Djohar Dudaev's National Congress which functioned in 1990-93. The delegates expressed their support for the president, condemned the misdeeds of the opposition, demanded that illegal armed groups should be disbanded, and advised Aslan Maskhadov to deport all foreign Wahhabi preachers. In this they had the wholehearted support of the CRI mufti, Akhmat-khaddzhi Kadyrov. In his speech he excoriated the Wahhabis as 'enemies of Islam and the Chechen people.' The mufti also declared that the main Wahhabi organization was the Congress of the Peoples of Chechnya and Dagestan, headed by Shamil Basaev and Movladi Udugov.

At the end of October, Aslan Maskhadov issued an ultimatum ordering all armed groups not integrated within the CRI Armed Forces to disarm. In his speech, the Chechen president described as criminal gangs Hattab's Kavkaz military base at Serzhen-Yurt, the centre in Vedeno where Shamil Basaev's detachments were deployed, and the jamaat led by the Akhmadov brothers in Urus-Martan. Aslanbek Arsaev, the head of Sharia security, filled in the detail. He made it clear that the national law enforcement agencies were prepared to undertake a large-scale operation against the criminal gangs, and that this time it was not a matter of releasing hostages or confiscating weapons but of eliminating criminals.

While the representatives of the security agencies limited themselves to loudly protesting their determination, the gangs did not bother to reply with words but with acts of defiance On 20 October, General Shadid Borshchigov, the chief of the Anti-Abduction Squad, was assassinated in the centre of Grozny as he was driving out of his headquarters. The following day an attempt was made to assassinate Mufti Kadyrov. He was uninjured but some of the relatives guarding him were wounded. Nobody in the republic was in any doubt that the perpetrators of these crimes were Wahhabis making money out of kidnappings. It was only too clear that Aslan Maskhadov must now finally move from words to resolute action against the criminals, or admit his Administration was impotent. The third option was to attempt to negotiate with those Wahhabi leaders who were at least not enmeshed in the abduction business. Kazbek Makhashev and I, with the president's approval, initiated negotiations with Shamil Basaev and Zelimkhan Yandarbiev, and reached agreement for them to have a meeting with Maskhadov. This duly occurred on 18 November in Grozny.

In addition to Yandarbiev and Basaev, the meeting was attended by Said-Khasan Abumuslimov, Movladi Udugov, Ruslan Gelaev, Vakha Arsanov, Turpal-Ali Atgireyev, Kazbek Makhashev, and myself. The meeting lasted seven hours, with everyone fully aware that the republic was on the verge of a full-scale civil war. Those now opposing Maskhadov were not minor gangs but an army many thousands strong, well-trained and armed to the teeth. I have no doubt that in terms of numbers that army exceeded all the security agencies of the CRI put together. This could only be a war with no winners.

The meeting culminated in agreement to set up an advisory council to decide domestic and foreign policy, to introduce a law to purge office-holders in the republic who had collaborated with the Russians, and to establish courts of honour. Alas, the very next day Basaev and Raduev at a meeting in Grozny of their supporters called for the resignation of Maskhadov and the entire CRI government. Anti-government organizations stepped up their activities drastically. The Wahhabi press, controlled by Udugov, accused the president and his supporters of having usurped power. Here are some quotations and samples from the press:

'The current government are self-confessed *mankurts*, devoid of memory. Today Russia is closer and dearer to Maskhadov than his own unhappy, war-ravaged Chechen people' (*Nation of Islam*).

'Today, the Maskhadov gang are in opposition to their own people, openly planning to collude with Russia' (*The Path of Islam*).

Caucasus Confederation, a newspaper under the direction of Zelimkhan Yandarbiev, claimed that 'It is entirely (Maskhadov's) fault that Russia continues to call Chechnya part of Russia.'

The Wahhabi jamaats made outright threats to the CRI government. The 'Islamic Union of Journalists' also demanded that Maskhadov should resign and hand over his presidential powers to the field commanders. Today, after all the time that has passed, I believe that responsibility for what happened in Chechnya during this period lies squarely with Zelimkhan Yandarbiev and Said-Khasan Abumuslimov. The reforms they instigated while acting president and vice-president of the CRI, after which they proclaimed the creation of a 'fully-fledged Islamic state,' provided abundant space for the Russian intelligence agencies to manoeuvre. When the laws proclaimed by a government are completely at odds with reality, they create a dangerous dichotomy in the public mind. If society sees that what the government says is unrelated to the actual state of affairs in the country, its authority plummets.

President Maskhadov could not rescind the vacuous declarations of Yandarbiev and Abumuslimov without being accused of apostasy and seeking to undermine the Sharia. Neither, however, could he in purely practical terms implement these laws, which he had never introduced; the Chechen state was thoroughly secular, in structure and in the minds of the population, and mere declarations could not turn it into a theocracy. Such was the 'legacy,' fragmenting both the Chechen state, Chechen society, and public opinion itself into hostile fractions, that Yandarbiev and Abumuslimov passed on to Chechnya's democratically elected President Aslan Maskhadov as a result of their irresponsible 'Sharia reforms.' Of course, the Russian government with its vested interest in seeing the Chechen state fail, could hardly be expected not to take advantage of this situation by using its intelligence agencies to stir up trouble. However, this in no way absolves Chechens of their share of the blame. Indeed, it was our own senior field commanders who carried out all the Russian-inspired mischief making and sabotage designed to destroy the Chechen state.

When the Russian intelligence agencies and generals made their preparations for the first Russo-Chechen War, they were thinking in purely quantitative categories and confident of victory. With absolute superiority in material terms, Moscow overlooked Djohar Dudaev's warning about the strength of Chechnya's national spirit. The Russian Army invaded Chechnya and, a year and a half later, skulked away with its tail between its legs. The Kremlin seemed to learn from that experience, and now set out to misdirect Chechen determination. They wanted ordinary Chechens to give up their aspiration to state sovereignty. The Kremlin ideologists saw the mechanism for achieving this as being to subject the Chechens to a further nightmare, perpetrated this time by the very people who had led the fight for independence. Their aim was to turn the Chechens not only against those individuals but against the ideal of state sovereignty they had stood for. The Kremlin's strategy was to face the Chechen people with a typically Russian historical choice between two evils: on the one hand, subjugation by Russia, and on the other a Chechen state so dysfunctional as to make the first prospect seem the lesser evil. A second invasion of Chechnya should change the minds of those still inclined to cling to the ideal of Chechen sovereignty. This was precisely what Boris Berezovsky was hinting at when he said in an interview, 'I am quite certain that the Russian government is not simply going to barge in again. If we are talking about military intervention, you do not first send in the tanks against your own people and subsequently explain why you did it. That is plain stupid. I think this time will be quite different, especially given the radical change in the situation that has occurred in the past year in terms of public perceptions.'

Remarks of this sort were made by Russian politicians both publicly and in private. In summer 1998, on my way back home from Berlin, I passed through Moscow. My trips were invariably official and the Russian National Security Council, which had oversight of all matters related to Chechnya, also made the arrangements for my movements on Russian territory. Boris Berezovsky was by then executive secretary of the Commonwealth of Independent States and, when he heard I was in Moscow, proposed a meeting through Boris Agapov, the deputy secretary of the Security Council. When we met, Berezovsky said openly that, if by the year's end we had not found a way to formalize our relations with Moscow which did not violate the principle of Russia's territorial integrity, all that would remain of Chechnya would be a big hole in the ground.

Berezovsky said Russia could not accept not being taken seriously even by countries in the CIS, which, he added, was precisely the situation at present. He said that in the course of his duties he met all the presidents of the CIS countries, and all of them made it clear that, after its military defeat in Chechnya, Russia's international status too had suffered a major setback. Boris now, for the first time, stated he knew that, if war broke out, 'the Chechens' would blow up apartment blocks. That was in the summer of 1998. When I got back to Grozny, I reported this conversation to Aslan Maskhadov. I know that, after that, Aslan asked Ruslan Aushev to arrange a meeting with Berezovsky, but I do not know what they talked about.

As further evidence that the actions of Russian politicians and the statements and actions of the Chechen oppositionists were synchronized and complementary, I offer this example. On the eve of a meeting between President Maskhadov and Russian Prime Minister Kirienko, four prominent Russian politicians, – Viktor Chernomyrdin, Alexander Lebed, Mintimer Shaimiev and Boris Berezovsky, – reminded Kirienko that Valentin Vlasov, the Presidential Envoy to Chechnya, had been held hostage in Chechnya for some three months. 'The Wahhabis, sensing their impunity, are raising their heads right across the North Caucasus, and the government simply must respond to events in the south of the country,' they said. The signatories demanded that the government should clearly and publicly state its position in respect of the Chechen Republic.

After his meeting with President Maskhadov, Kirienko talked to reporters and said the Russian government considered Chechnya an integral part of the Russian Federation, just as the four signatories had demanded. Kirienko's statement was broadcast on Russian TV, and seized upon by the armed opposition, which blamed Maskhadov for it, even though Yandarbiev and Movladi Udugov knew full well that Maskhadov had never compromised on the principle of independence. The fact of the matter is that at this time they behaved, not as political opponents of Maskhadov, but as enemies of the Chechen people. Unlike many of the young people who had no understanding of politics or religious matters, both were perfectly well aware that all the processes they had set in train might lead to an incursion of Russian troops into the republic and the start of a second war.

And in fact, we were now already doomed to a new war with Russia. To initiate a full-scale military operation against the armed opposition was certain to lead to the bloody slaughter of a civil war, which would provide Moscow with a pretext for sending troops into the republic. If, in order to avoid that, Aslan agreed to stand down, as the opposition demanded, that too would give Russia a pretext to invade, on the grounds that Islamic radicals had overthrown the legitimate government in one of the republics of the Russian Federation with the intention of proclaiming a Caucasian caliphate from sea to sea. Maskhadov did not, therefore, resign the presidency and, despite the fact that a majority of the population were demanding firm action against the armed irregulars, continued to try to avoid the shedding of the blood of one Chechen by another. Our enemy had, however, a third strategy of which we were unaware, and to which I will return. At this stage the armed stand off in Chechnya gained new momentum with the murder of three British citizens and one New Zealander.

In spite of all the intrigues and unrest being fomented in the republic by outside forces, we made great efforts to achieve something meaningful and lasting for our nation. Our top priority was to complete an independent telecommunications network and we made this a high-profile project. President Maskhadov featured in several television broadcasts, one of which showed him attending the opening of the head office of Chechen Telecom. He inspected the new equipment, as experts explained the technical specifications and pointed out that Chechnya was the only republic in the Caucasus with this cutting-edge technology.

The project was seen as having historic importance. Our holy evliyas had foretold that Chechnya would become truly free only when a road to Georgia was built through the Argun Gorge and England extended its protection to Chechnya. This first British investment by Chechen Telecom was popularly seen as fulfilment of those prophecies, as was an imminent contract with Omni Petroleum to buy two million tons of Chechen oil, with prepayment of some US$ 150 million as an interest-free loan from the United Kingdom. For the Chechen government, cooperation with British businesses was of great economic and political importance, and there were plans for President Maskhadov to visit the United Kingdom before the end of the year. We in the government had great hopes of this initial investment, which we were sure must have the tacit backing of the British government. London had after all been taking a strategic interest in the Caucasus since the eighteenth century. Alas, our hopes were not to be realized at this stage in our history.

At 10.00 am on 2 October 1998, Rustam, the managing director of Chechen Telecom, brought four engineers from Granger Telecom to take their farewell. They had finished the job and at 08.00 hrs the following morning they would be connecting Chechen Telecom to a European satellite. From that moment our republic would have a telephone network independent of Russia. I thanked them and presented them with souvenirs bearing the state insignia of the Chechen Republic of Ichkeria. They were to fly back to Moscow at noon the next day, and I told them I hoped to see them next time in London. Movladi Akhmetkhanov told me he and our British friends were arranging an invitation for me to visit the UK.

The next time I saw them, however, was not in London but driving through the centre of Grozny in Rustam's car, which overtook mine, without any security escort. I asked my driver to catch up and stop them, and reprimanded Rustam for his irresponsibility. If he was short of people to protect his guests he should tell Movladi or me. A few days previously there had been an attempt to abduct foreigners in the middle of Grozny, even though they were accompanied by an armed guard. Two of the would-be kidnappers had been killed.

Given the progress our republic was making, it was obvious that the Russian intelligence agencies would stop at nothing to punish businessmen who defied Moscow's official position by investing in Chechnya. Rustam assured me he had plenty of people, and that the car with the accompanying bodyguards had only just stopped to drop someone off at his office. I remained very dissatisfied with the situation. I called Movladi, who was in Moscow with our minister of fuel and energy, and told him about the incident and my concern for the engineers' safety. All these matters were interrelated, because a contract with Omni Petroleum was due to be signed on 3 October at the Radisson Slavyanskaya Hotel in Moscow. The company's CEO, Fred Bonn, was already in Moscow and Movladi, at whose initiative this deal had been struck would, be attending the signing.

After my call to Movladi, already quite late at night, Rustam called and again assured me I need have no worries about the safety of the engineers, which was his responsibility. He told me everything was under control. Early the next morning, however, on 3 October he called yet again. This time his voice was trembling as he reported that about an hour previously, at about 3.45 am, the house where the engineers were staying had been attacked and all four of them had been abducted. He told me one of their bodyguards had been wounded and one attacker had been shot in the leg.

I shall not repeat what I said on hearing this news, only that I never spoke to Rustam again. In the republic at that time such an abduction could have happened to anyone, but the fact that the perpetrators found it so easy was clearly Rustam's fault. He showed a lack of rigour untypical of Chechens, who take such responsibilities very seriously. The fact that the republic was in a state of lawlessness does not exonerate him and his family from failing in their duty to protect his guests, who were living in their house and for whom they had assumed responsibility. Under Chechen tradition, even a verbal slight to a guest is regarded as an unforgivable insult to the host and, certainly in the past, not infrequently led to bloodshed. What then are we to say about the abduction or murder of guests? In purely practical terms, Rustam was the managing director of Chechen Telecom and being recompensed by the company at the top rate for his visitors' board, lodging and security. Quite apart from our traditions, it was his duty to the business to guarantee the safety of his foreign guests. He was well aware of the mayhem prevalent in the republic, and he and his relatives should have enhanced their security measures accordingly. I am quite sure that if they had not been so lackadaisical this would never have happened.

In the event, blame for the disaster fell not only on the republic's government but on the entire Chechen nation. Journalists, who until this moment had written passionate reports about the heroic, unequal struggle of the Chechens for their freedom, now reported a Chechen state too weak to rein in rampant criminality. This was precisely the kind of reputational damage those who instigated all these blood-soaked incidents wanted to inflict on the Chechen state.

When I got in touch with Movladi, he was already aware of what had happened. I asked him to instruct Rustam to issue a statement on behalf of Chechen Telecom about the abduction, and in return he told me that the oil contract had been signed at 3.00 am on 3 October. He added that our foreign partners were not yet aware of what had happened, and that he would need to accompany them on their flight to London that morning. He would be back in Grozny within two days.

Despite the early hour, I reported what had happened to President Maskhadov, and first thing that morning he called an emergency meeting of the heads of our security agencies, ordering them to find and free the kidnapped engineers at all costs. I was present at the meeting, at which the president warned, 'The future of our state depends on how successfully you cope with this task. If we fail to free the hostages and punish the criminals, nobody in the world will want any dealings with us.' The president explained the importance of contracts with the British, and said he had no doubt the abduction was directly linked to the agreement signed that morning with the oil company and the fact that this was the day Chechnya's independent telecommunications network was to become operational.

After the meeting I went to the scene of the kidnapping with representatives of our security agencies. Witnesses told us there had been about 15 assailants. The visitors had been staying in a large house in a typical Vainakh courtyard in the RTS district of Grozny. A smaller house next to it was occupied by the bodyguards. At around 3.45 am the kidnappers climbed over a fence, opened the gate, and drove two vehicles into the yard. One group dealt with the bodyguards, of whom that night only two were on duty, both asleep. They woke to hear the foreigners shouting as they were attacked by the other group, and found their rifles, which had been stacked in a corner of the room, already in the hands of the criminals. One of the guards had a pistol and fired, wounding an assailant in the leg. They returned fire and he was seriously wounded. The second guard was warned not to move. They quickly collected their wounded accomplice and drove off with their captives.

In the two months after the attack, the kidnappers only once contacted Granger Telecom, by phone in London, claiming that the hostages were in Chechnya and demanding US$ 10 million for their release. They gave no contact number for any response, and made no further attempt to contact British representatives in the United Kingdom or us in Chechnya.

Movladi and I appealed to all our powerful commanders, including Shamil Basaev and Vakha Arsanov who had good relations with the emirs of the jamaats. The jamaats were really just armed gangs. Movladi and I had a suspicion that there was a particular gang from Urus-Martan behind the abduction. It was impossible for me to have any contact with this jamaat. As a colleague of President Maskhadov, in their eyes, I was an enemy. We also knew that Yandarbiev had, or at least claimed to have, influence with them. After the presidential campaign he and I were barely on speaking terms so, as Movladi knew him well, it was he who asked for help in getting the hostages released. Zelimkhan promised that if this gang was responsible he could guarantee the hostages would be released. The next day, however, he told Movladi the hostages were not in Urus-Martan.

We announced a reward of US$ 50,000 for any crucial information about the incident, and guaranteed to keep the informant's identity secret. Very soon, a man came forward who was prepared to give information on those terms. Movladi met him, handed over the reward, and in return learned the name of the leader of the group behind the abduction. Movladi told me the culprit was Apti Abitaev, a native of Urus-Martan who led a gang subordinate to Arbi Baraev. Baraev was under the control of Zelimkhan Yandarbiev, who had once promoted him to the rank of brigadier general. A few days later Movladi told me that the security division of Chechen Telecom had Apti Abitaev under surveillance and were waiting for a suitable opportunity to detain him.

When I came home from work that evening, I learned to my surprise that Abitaev himself, together with another person I did not know, was waiting to see me. My son and nephews had been at home and, when Abitaev heard I was not there, said he had something very important to tell me and wanted to await my return. My family members invited him and his companion in.

I went through to the living room, greeted them, and asked what had brought them here. Abitaev seemed ill at ease and immediately asked if I had a copy of the Qur'an in the house. I told him I had and asked what he needed it for, but before I had finished he said he knew I had been told he had organized the kidnapping of the Englishmen. He wanted to prevent our taking action against him by swearing on the Qur'an that he was innocent.

'*Wallahi billahi tallahi,*' he continued. 'I did not have anything to do with the kidnapping!'

This was tantamount to an oath on the Qur'an, but frankly I did not believe him. Indeed, my suspicions of his complicity were only reinforced. Like many other Chechens, I was aware by this time that the new Islamist ideologists gave their followers permission to swear false oaths on the Qur'an. My suspicions only deepened when Abitaev said he was sure one of his associates had told us about his supposed role in the abduction. Obviously our informant would not have told him that, and Movladi and I had not passed the information on to anyone. Abitaev was assuming that an insider would betray him to get the reward. As Chechens say, 'What two people know, sooner or later, everyone will know.' Apti's crime was known not to two but to dozens of people. My guess was that he had decided to try to cover his back by perjuring himself.

That same evening I contacted Movladi and he agreed with me. We decided nevertheless that he should meet our informant again and tell him of the conversation with Apti Abitaev. Two days later Movladi came to see me in my office to say he retained full confidence in his informant, who indeed had now provided further evidence to corroborate his claim that the engineers had been abducted by none other than Abitaev. Movladi and I now faced a dilemma: should we have the suspects detained through official channels, or act on our own initiative? We were concerned that, if we used the security agencies, information might leak out and put the hostages' lives at risk.

There had been a precedent of this kind, when officers from our Anti-Terrorism Squad, led by Khunkar Israpilov, were ambushed during an operation to free hostages held in Urus-Martan, resulting in the death of two of the squad's officers. Khunkar believed the kidnappers had been tipped off by people in President Maskhadov's confidence. Islam Khalimov, a close ally of Isa Umarov, was also a close friend of Maskhadov. Movladi and I decided it would be best to arrange Abitaev's arrest ourselves, through the security division of Chechen Telecom, get information from him on the whereabouts of the hostages, and after that hand him over to the forces of law and order. The only person we told of this plan was the president.

On 2 December 1998 on Pervomaiskaya Street in Grozny, security officers of Chechen Telecom boxed in the car in which Apti Abitaev was travelling. He made no attempt to resist arrest or being disarmed. With him in the car was his young wife. The officers let her go, a tragic mistake which cost the lives of the engineers. She immediately went and told his accomplices what had happened, and they quickly moved the hostages.

Abitaev, realizing that those detaining him were not from the official state agencies and that he would have to answer for his actions directly to the people he had offended by endangering the lives and liberty of their guests, decided to reveal everything. He told us all we needed to know without anyone laying a finger on him: the address in Urus-Martan where the hostages were being held, how many people were guarding them, who had taken part in the abduction, and so on.

Abitaev also told us who commissioned him to commit the crime. This was a certain Yunadi Elmarzaev who lived in Urus-Martan. He left for Moscow the same morning Abitaev's gang kidnapped the engineers, ordering him not to communicate with anyone until told to, and promising that Abitaev personally would be paid US$ 10 million for 'the job.' Abitaev also described their preparations for the abduction, and said it was their second attempt. They had earlier spent a night near where the engineers were staying, but decided not to attack because that night there were more guards and the guards did not go to sleep. He said they had kept the engineers under constant surveillance for the past month, and had established that they never had more than five guards.

Movladi told me our suspicion that one of the guards might have been a traitor had proved unfounded. The fact that there were only two on duty that night was simple negligence. Abitaev said that Yunadi Elmarzaev had warned them this was their last opportunity, because the next day the foreigners would be flying to Moscow.

Now our top priority was to rescue the hostages. They were no longer at the address Abitaev had given. Despite the huge amount of effort we had put into saving them, that single mistake by Chechen Telecom's security division in letting Abitaev's wife go free meant that they were now at the mercy of criminals and gangsters. Movladi told me a tape had been sent to Arbi Baraev, in which Abitaev begged for the foreigners to be set free because otherwise he was likely to be killed for abducting them. Baraev convened a 'Shura,' or 'Ulama Council' in the vicinity of Urus-Martan to decide what to do next. This Shura was presided over by Abu-Umar, the emissary from Saudi Arabia, and as 'experts on Sharia' there were present also Abu-Djunid, Abdurakhman Shishani, and Bagautdin of Dagestan. Others present were Magomed Vakhidov, Ramzan Akhmadov, and Arbi Baraev. The meeting lasted several hours, and throughout Abu-Umar was on the telephone to some sheikh in Saudi Arabia. Abdurakhman translated from Arabic to Chechen and Bagautdin translated from Russian to Arabic for Abu-Umar. None of the Chechens present spoke Arabic.

We already had evidence that the jamaats were being handled by the Russian intelligence agencies through their residency in the Middle East, inherited from the USSR. When FSB Director Vladimir Putin came to power in Russia, these secret links were revived and Middle East agents began to be used in Chechnya. This information was confirmed a few years later by Alexander Litvinenko. Further confirmation was provided by the fact that Abu-Djunid, well known throughout the Caucasus as a leader of the fundamentalist Wahhabi movement, was arrested by Russian intelligence during the Second War and, without any attempt to put him on trial, deported to Denmark. This was despite the fact that, according to his diary, part of which was published on the Internet, he had been involved in many crimes, including the barbaric murder of the engineers.

About Abdurakhman who, after the mysterious death of Fathi, headed the jamaats in Chechnya, I knew the following. Salman Gazuev, a close friend of Sheikh Fathi, asked me to arrange a business meeting with Khusein Chechenov, the prime minister of Kabardino-Balkaria, with whom I was on good terms. I did so, and Gazuev and his two companions were provided with a security escort by the government for their return from Nalchik. On the way they began discussing the situation in Chechnya, and the officer-in-charge told them a curious story of how Abdurakhman Shishani, a

Syrian citizen, was detained at a checkpoint by officers of the Kabardino-Balkarian Ministry of the Interior. When they inspected his documents, the visa was found to have expired long before and he was arrested. This was reported to Moscow, and within a couple of hours the Russian Foreign Ministry was demanding that he should be released immediately. Not only that, Valeriy Kokov, the president of Kabardino-Balkaria, was ordered to personally supervise Abdurakhman's release. On instructions from Kokov, his intelligence officers escorted Abdurakhman to the border of Chechnya to ensure he had no problems in transit through North Ossetia and Ingushetia. Salman told me this when he got back to Chechnya, and the information was confirmed privately by a senior figure in the government when I was on a visit to Kabardino-Balkaria.

I should explain that the initiative to have him released was taken by the Russian Foreign Ministry rather than the Federal Security Bureau because its diaspora committees provide good cover for espionage. As secretary of the CRI National Security Council, I and my assistants set up an analogous organization for relations with our diaspora in Russia.

After this, Salman began talking of the need to exhume Sheikh Fathi's body for forensic examination. There had been no post mortem at the time because it is customary for Muslims to bury their dead before sunset, and everybody had assumed the cause of death was cardiac arrest. Salman took this matter up very seriously. A few days later 'unidentified assailants' sprayed his car with bullets and he died from multiple wounds. I should make it clear that Salman did not directly accuse Abdurakhman of murdering Sheikh Fathi, but he no longer trusted him and managed to have him dismissed from his post as emir of the jamaats. Nevertheless, Abdurakhman remained influential within them. It was this same Abdurakhman who translated the fatwa issued by Abu-Djunid, ruling that the kidnapped Britons and New Zealander should be beheaded and their heads left on the main Rostov-Baku Highway at the border between Chechnya and Ingushetia as a warning to anyone else thinking of assisting the government of Aslan Maskhadov.

On 4 December 1998, the severed heads were found at the side of the highway. This was a triumph for the Russian intelligence agencies, as the dreadful images were flashed all round the world and, I believe, fatally undermined faith in the Chechen state's ability to curb criminal activity. Since then the Kremlin has had a free hand to do whatever it pleases in Chechnya, without worrying how the West may react.

It was a humiliating defeat for the Chechen government, and more was to follow. The gangsters guilty of this crime demanded that the republic's leaders should release Apti Abitaev from prison, together with another criminal jailed on a charge of plotting to assassinate President Maskhadov. This was the moment at which Vakha Arsanov, vice-president of the CRI, and Zelimkhan Yandarbiev, former acting president of the CRI, saw fit to issue statements almost simultaneously, the former on television and the latter in the press. They claimed that the murdered engineers had been British spies, thus exonerating the criminals who murdered them. These absurd pronouncements were made by leading Chechen politicians against a background of condemnation of this act of savagery by almost all the global news agencies and international organizations, and demands that the leaders of the CRI should bring the criminals to justice.

Meanwhile the criminals were living openly within 30 kilometres of the Presidential Palace and issuing ultimatums. Our government found itself powerless and was forced to accept the gangsters' demands. Apti Abitaev and the other prisoner were released in exchange for the bodies of the murdered foreigners, so that their remains could be returned to their families in the United Kingdom and New Zealand.

V

Destabilization

President Maskhadov, in an attempt to forestall an Islamist coup, decides to introduce overnight 'full Sharia law' and rapidly loses credibility. Mufti Akhmad-haddzhi Kadyrov persuades Putin he is the real power in Chechnya, and willing to compromise on independence. Treachery flourishes, with Udugov plotting with Berezovsky to overthrow Maskhadov. Shamil Basaev contributes to the destabilization.

People in Chechnya were profoundly shocked by these events. Many sensed an impending catastrophe, conscious that the evil deeds being openly perpetrated in the republic would not go unpunished. Our people had sacrificed their sons in a war against aggression, but many of our young men, duped by the preachers of Pure Islam, joined these gangs and turned their weapons against their own state. Our people, still reeling from the atrocities of a genocidal war, had no more strength, no more sons to give to bridle this pernicious force.

The Chechen people have extraordinary reserves of energy, but these are not infinite. For all that, tens of thousands gathered in a spontaneous protest in the centre of Grozny to demand that Aslan Maskhadov should take firm action against the criminal gangs growing more brazen by the day. Over 5,000 reservists came out to bear arms in support of the president. These events spurred him to action. He announced he was mobilizing reservists of the CRI Armed Forces and former members of the Resistance to fight the gangs. In a matter of days, more than 1,000 citizens with combat training reported to the Khankala military base. In total, throughout the republic over 5,000 people joined units to fight crime.

Deputy Prime Minister Turpal-Ali Atgireyev, who had oversight of the security ministries, announced on television that the government would punish the criminals and put an end to the gangsters' business of trading hostages for ransom. He was followed by Magomed Khambiev, commander of the CRI National Guard, who announced, also on television, that the Guard had completed its combat training and stood ready to carry out the president's orders. In mid-December 1998, many thousands assembled for a national rally, at which they passed a resolution authorizing the president to take the most stringent measures against armed groups which refused to recognize the legitimacy of the republic's government. The rally also called for order to be restored in the Urus-Martan region and for the resistance of illegal armed groups there to be crushed. Everybody watching events in Chechnya, and all Aslan Maskhadov's supporters, assumed that with this level of popular support our head of state would take resolute action against the criminals and rebel groups. The president, however, now went on television to say he had no wish to see civil war break out, and would give the rebel leaders one final opportunity to resolve their differences through negotiation. From this moment, Aslan Maskhadov was seen as ineffectual, and many of his supporters became disillusioned. The gangster groups responded to his goodwill with acts of terrorism, attempting to assassinate the minister of Sharia state security, Aslambek Arsaev, and Mufti Akhmat-khaddzhi Kadyrov. In the Urus-Martan region, rebel fighters clashed with government forces.

In early February 1999, Kazbek Makhashev and Dalkhan Khozhaev came to my office to tell me they had been instructed by Aslan Maskhadov to prepare, together with me, a presidential decree introducing full Sharia law in the republic. They said the CRI's National Security Service had reliable information that the following day the armed opposition were planning a coup d'etat, with proclamation of Sharia law. I understood from what they said that, on the advice of his friend and adviser on religious affairs, Islam Khalimov, President Maskhadov had decided to do this in order to pre-empt the coup and split the adherents of the arch-conservative Salafi movement. This ideology strictly forbids opposition to a leader imposing Sharia precepts. We spent an hour drafting the text of the decree and took it to the president's residence, where a meeting was in progress at which I heard the details of the coup plot. Those present included Ruslan Alikhadzhiev, the speaker of parliament; Mufti Akhmat-khaddzhi Kadyrov; and the ministers in charge of the security agencies. The president had information that a week previously a so-called Shura had been convened in Urus-Martan to plot the overthrow of Maskhadov's 'regime of idolatrous *mushriks* and apostate *murtads.*' The main grounds for representing Maskhadov and his associates as enemies of Islam was the fact that the 'infidel Russian President Yeltsin' was not opposing the introduction of Sharia in Dagestan, while Maskhadov was resisting its imposition in Chechnya. The Russian president's mischievous intervention was designed specifically to undermine Maskhadov by encouraging those opposing him and calling for immediate introduction of Sharia law.

The Shura sent two emissaries to Zelimkhan Yandarbiev, proposing that he should become head of the republic after Maskhadov was overthrown. They were Vakha Ibrakhimov (killed in Baku in September 2003 by an unidentified hitman) and Uvais, the elder of the Akhmadov brothers. Zelimkhan replied that he would need several days to consider their proposal. President Maskhadov's information was that the coup was planned for the night of 2 February 1999, but he did not make clear whether or not Zelimkhan Yandarbiev was known to have accepted the conspirators' offer. Our meeting resolved that a presidential decree should be read out on the evening news introducing full Sharia law in the Chechen Republic. The decree stated also that parliament was being stripped of its legislative powers and spoke of the need to establish a Security Council (Islamic Council), to function as a regulatory authority. My understanding was that the decree made specific mention of the parliament because the parliament building, together with the Presidential Residence, were the putschists' two main targets.

A congress of all military commanders, including the opposition leaders Zelimkhan Yandarbiev, Vakha Arsanov, and Shamil Basaev, was convened to form the Islamic Council. The presidential decree on introducing total Sharia rule was read on the evening television news. The night passed without incident and the next day, 3 February, a meeting was held in the national theatre of those in charge of the security ministries and the leaders of the armed opposition. Maskhadov there announced the creation of a state commission to prepare a Sharia constitution, and appointed me to head it.

That same day, Kazbek Makhashev and I made one more attempt to reconcile Vakha Arsanov with Aslan Maskhadov. I say, 'one more' because we had made many attempts to do so before, but Arsanov had categorically refused to make any move towards reconciliation. This time, however, he himself expressed a desire to meet Aslan and Kazbek, and I persuaded the president to receive the three of us. Vakha Arsanov could have been very valuable in enabling the government's agencies to operate effectively. He stood at the head of a powerful military force numbering about 1,000 men. During the meeting, Vakha assured Aslan that from now on he would be like a younger brother and be Aslan's faithful *naib* (aide), carrying out his every order. Aslan was extremely pleased. His plan had worked. Rank-and-file Chechens in the jamaats, hearing that the president had decreed the introduction of Sharia law, had refused to oppose him. That day, the four of us – Aslan, Vakha, Kazbek, and I – performed a joint namaz. When we left

Aslan's office, Vakha Arsanov went upstairs to the vice-president's office, where he had not been seen for a long time. We were all very satisfied. I thought that from now on the situation would improve.

That evening, however, as I was driving home after work, Kazbek phoned to say that Mairbek Vachagaev, Maskhadov's spokesman, had just read a presidential decree on television relieving Vakha Arsanov of his duties as vice-president. We later discovered that earlier in the day, when Kazbek and I were urging the president to make peace with Vakha Arsanov, the decree had already been drafted and signed, but Maskhadov gave no indication of that. Needless to say, I thought then and still think that the decree was a political blunder. It was unwise in the extreme to push Arsanov back into the arms of Udugov, Isa Umarov, and Shamil Basaev. Vakha Arsanov, with his very considerable military forces, was a powerful and influential player on the political scene, and it would have been much more advantageous for Aslan to have numbered him among his allies and friends than leave him in the camp of his opponents and enemies. Aslan appeared, however, to be convinced that he had just outplayed them all, and continued in the same wise with the evident intention of persuading the rank and file of the jamaats to defect to his side. He sent Islam Khalimov to the Urus-Martan Jamaat with a video cassette in which he offered the members of the relevant gangs an amnesty and his favour and told them he needed their help to create an Islamic state and establish Sharia law. I know for a fact that there were fighters in the Urus-Martan Jamaat who, after watching the video, were prepared to respond to his appeal.

At the time, Maskhadov's decree on introducing Sharia rule was widely seen as an attempt to hijack the religious slogans of the jamaat leaders, but I could see myself that it was not merely declarative: Aslan sincerely intended to introduce Sharia reforms, although he was not knowledgeable about what exactly that involved. This was both a practical problem for him and the source of an error of judgement. The reforms would oblige him to rely on learned alims, or Islamic scholars. Unfortunately, the alims in the republic were so divided and irreconcilably hostile to each other that to rely on some would be automatically to alienate the others, who would inevitably accuse him of apostasy from the 'true teachings' of Islam.

All his tactical manoeuvring with Islamic reforms posed a deadly danger at this stage of our national development. We were not recognized as an entity in international law, which would have ensured that our actions and reforms were viewed by the international community as the internal affair of a sovereign state. Given our situation, Russia could use all this zigzagging to accuse us before the court of world public opinion of extremism. Aslan Maskhadov had emphasized in his video address that he needed the jamaats in order to build an Islamic state. It was only too obvious he believed he could win them over to his side, blissfully unaware that they were not capable of taking independent decisions because they were heavily influenced by their patrons. Only too predictably, the leaders of the jamaats convened a Shura headed by the same miscreants as had been plotting the overthrow of President Maskhadov. This Shura duly ruled that Maskhadov was an apostate, and it was impermissible to have anything to do with him. He had declared Sharia rule because he feared losing power. He was insincere in his thoughts and there could accordingly be no faith in him. At their meeting, they decided to make public his video appeal 'so that all who support the president may see his hypocrisy.'

In his address to the young men in these units, Aslan condemned certain statements Mufti Kadyrov had made against the Wahhabi Salafits. We were already in possession of intelligence that a criminal boss by the name of Atlangeriev had organized a secret meeting between Kadyrov and the director of the Federal Security Bureau, Vladimir Putin. After this, Kadyrov changed his stance dramatically. He now missed no opportunity to urge Maskhadov to declare a religious war on 'those Wahhabi gangs.' At one of the meetings of our National Security Council, I asked Kadyrov why he was so insistent that this was the only correct policy. I said, 'The people currently engaged in kidnappings and other crimes have nothing to do with any religious ideology or movement, not even with the Wahhabis you keep talking about.'

I asked him how many times he had been to Saudi Arabia, the ideological homeland of Wahhabism. Then I asked if he had seen the severed heads of foreigners on the streets of the Arabian cities, or people performing collective prayers in jamaats on top of cellars in which Muslims were languishing after being taken hostage for ransom. Kadyrov replied that he had seen nothing of the sort. 'Well,' I continued, 'what is happening in Chechnya is not called Wahhabism but gangsterism, and what we need in the republic is not a religious war in which, in the name of Allah, Muslim Chechens kill each other, but the declaration of a war on crime.'

To give Kadyrov Senior his due, he was not only a very stubborn man but entirely familiar with the issues I had raised. He countered that the war against gangsterism was a matter for government agencies, without involving the public. However, the current situation in Chechnya was so serious that government agencies alone would be unable to cope with the crime wave without the help of the population at large. 'And we can mobilize the population at large,' Kadyrov went on, 'only by declaring a holy war.'

Kadyrov took advantage of the fact that many of the president's supporters saw his address not so much as a sign of hypocrisy as of weakness. The Mufti assembled at his home all the commanders of reservists and the acting heads of the security ministries, declared himself the Imam at this meeting, and declared a holy war against the Wahhabis. He did everything very neatly, not attacking Aslan Maskhadov but arguing that, not being a cleric, the president could not declare a holy war. He, Kadyrov, was prepared as mufti of the republic to assume that responsibility in the eyes of God and the Chechen people if those assembled would support him and take Bayat from him as the Imam declaring jihad against the Wahhabis.

One interesting detail about all this has remained little known. When at that meeting the Yamadaev brothers, Commander of the Presidential Lifeguard Ilias Talkhadov, Commander of the National Guard Magomed Khambiev, Minister of Sharia State Security Aslanbek Arsaev, and National Security Chief Ibrakhim Khultygov and others took Bayat from the Mufti, the whole proceedings were being recorded on video. When asked what the video was for, Kadyrov said it was for history. In fact, however, as later became known, the video cassette was forwarded to Vladimir Putin at the Federal Security Bureau, as proof that all the 'warlords,' as the Russians called us, supported Akhmat-khaddzhi Kadyrov. From this moment on, Putin decided irrevocably to sort out the 'Chechen problem' by force of arms, and to bet his money on Kadyrov.

President Maskhadov, and indeed the whole republic, heard about this meeting almost immediately. Many of the participants came to report on it to him, explaining that they had only gone along to find out what the Mufti was up to and pass the information on to Maskhadov. In reality, what took place in Gudermes was treason by trusted senior officials in Aslan Maskhadov's immediate circle. I believe the president should have forced them to resign. His bodyguards later told me that Aslan just mildly rebuked them and left it at that. They retained their positions until the start of the Second War when, almost all who were not killed defected immediately to Kadyrov, who was appointed head of the Russians' puppet regime.

Indeed, before that Aslan Maskhadov had even promoted them. Magomed Khambiev was appointed minister of defence and promoted to the rank of major general. The same rank was conferred on Minister of Sharia State Security Aslanbek Arsaev. This was taking place in the midst of all the anarchy engulfing the republic. Just a week before his promotion to this high military rank, Aslanbek Arsaev had presided over a mass jailbreak from the investigative detention centre in Grozny of prisoners accused of the most heinous crimes. It was universally expected that this would result in the dismissal of officials at the Ministry of Sharia State Security, starting with Minister Arsaev, but nothing happened. Instead, perversely, President Maskhadov went to the ministry and started handing out awards and promotions. The Chechen public took an extremely poor view of all this and, at a meeting of deputy prime ministers, I expressed my opinion forthrightly and listed what I saw as the president's mistakes.

Firstly, he should never have offered to collaborate with people who had brutally executed the foreigners. Secondly, it was not good policy to promote to high military rank heads of ministries and agencies who were incapable of adequately ensuring law enforcement and the security of citizens of the CRI. Finally, it was not appropriate for the deputy prime minister and key ministers of the Chechen government to fly home at the weekend to Moscow, the capital of a country which was preparing to wage war against us. Aslan took great exception to my remarks. It was a characteristic of Chechen politicians that they did not, and do not, take kindly to criticism.

Aslan Maskhadov had another problem: he quarrelled with or alienated everyone who could exercise real influence in the republic. I told him that was a very big mistake. The fact that he gave Shamil Basaev and Vakha Arsanov grounds to go over to the opposition proved disastrous, because these were major political and military figures in Chechnya between the wars. Those Aslan brought into his team because they belonged to his Teip or family or because of their personal loyalty were people with no weight in society whatsoever. They had no influence or authority with the people at large. These, however, were the people Aslan chose to rely on. Even worse was the fact that these individuals kept falling out with each other, so they were not even members of a coherent presidential team. They were constantly devising petty intrigues against whoever was currently in the president's favour. The tales of all this infighting became common knowledge outside the Presidential Palace and further undermined Maskhadov's credibility. While he was vainly trying to shore up his authority with the aid of these no-hopers, the leaders of the armed opposition were publicly refusing to join the State Council, and declaring Maskhadov had forfeited his constitutional legitimacy when he 'illegally imposed Sharia law.' It would have been laughable if it had not been so sad. These were the very individuals who had put Maskhadov under intolerable psychological pressure by accusing him of being opposed to Sharia law, but when he buckled under the strain of their moral blackmail and introduced it, they argued he could no longer be recognized as president because, by doing so, he had violated the Constitution. It was only too obvious that what was principally bugging the opposition was Maskhadov's position as the republic's legitimately elected president. It was no coincidence that at just this time President Maskhadov's unassailable democratic credentials did not suit Russia either.

The opposition began setting up their own alternative government institutions, with Shamil Basaev as their chief. In other words, they went ahead with what they had planned at the beginning of February before Aslan introduced Sharia law. The only difference was that they did not bother to take over the existing state institutions, and the new 'government' was headed now not by Zelimkhan Yandarbiev but by Shamil Basaev. Movladi Udugov was appointed Basaev's deputy, but the real power in these upstart institutions lay with Vakha Arsanov, former vice-president of the CRI, and Shamil Basaev, former acting prime minister of the CRI. They had very substantial armies supporting them, but in fact the reputation and authority of Arsanov, Basaev, Yandarbiev and the other opposition leaders had been severely damaged. The Chechen public accused them of deliberately seeking to provoke a civil war which would lead to a new invasion by Russian troops, in other words, a second war. By early 1999, our enemy had achieved every objective outlined in the 1997 plan of 'Special Measures to Neutralize Pockets of Separatism in the North Caucasus.' These special measures involved terrorism, sabotage, psychological and ideological warfare, and had just one strategic aim: to prevent the appearance on the world map of an independent Chechen state.

All the major Russian and Chechen officials were aware that annexation of Chechnya to Russia by force was scheduled for autumn 1999. As already mentioned, in 1966 General Lebed, as secretary of the Russian Security Council, had sent to the General Headquarters of the Russian Armed Forces and the Russian Ministry of the Interior a proposal to form a 50,000-strong legion 'to crush the Chechen separatists.' Back then he received a reply from General Kolesnikov, chief of Russia's GHQ, and Lieutenant General Maslov, commander of Russia's Interior Troops, that his order could be implemented only by late 1999. We also had intelligence that resources had been allocated in the Year 2000 budget for a so-called 'counterterrorist operation' in the North Caucasus. This all pointed to the instigation of a second Russo-Chechen War.

By midsummer 1999, Russia was ready, in terms of news manipulation, ideology, and military preparation, for war and needed only a convincing pretext to initiate hostilities. We were not only aware of the

Kremlin's plan to take revenge, we also knew of two tactical options: a civil war in Chechnya, or the overthrow of the elected president of the CRI. Aslan Maskhadov did what he could to thwart these two scenarios, but we were to discover that Russia had a third option which we were powerless to prevent. That was a military incursion into a neighbouring republic of the armed jamaat gangs which had been massing on Chechen territory. Chechen and Dagestani gangs operating under the ideological umbrella of the 'Congress of the Peoples of Chechnya and Dagestan' energetically set about implementing this third option. The ideologues of the congress concentrated their efforts on raising the peoples of Dagestan to 'a holy jihad which will be the final stage in liberating the Caucasus from Russia's colonial oppression.' Isa Umarov and Shamil Basaev started convening all manner of conferences in Dagestan, and Dagestani alims began to call the people to jihad. Not only that, they asserted that it was the duty of every Muslim to embark on jihad against the Russians. Thirty-three well known alims issued a fatwa declaring that the Jihad in the Caucasus, and specifically in Dagestan, was 'fard-ain,' that is, compulsory for Muslims.

It is worth noting that, during all this activity on the part of the ideologists of jihad, Russia kept their military forces well out of the way, even the border guards, which effectively left the border of the Russian Federation wide open. Not only that, Russian artillery destroyed the Chechen government's border outpost on the frontier with Dagestan's Kizlyar region. It was not repaired. There were a number of instances of armoured fighting vehicles based in Russia's Stavropol Territory mounting raids into the Chechen Republic of Ichkeria and attacking farmers in Naur District. There was even an attempt, coming from the territory of Ingushetia, to move the Russian checkpoint to the village of Sernovodskaya in Chechnya. These were deliberately provocative incidents, sometimes involving armed clashes. Long before the incident in Dagestan, there was fighting between Russian and Chechen military units, invariably provoked by the Russian side. Not a word about this appeared in either the Russian or Western media, because by now there was not a single foreign journalist or international humanitarian organization left in the Chechen Republic of Ichkeria. Moscow could do anything it pleased in Chechnya, and put whatever spin it cared to on the report of what had happened.

In early August 1999, I went on a mission for Aslan Maskhadov through Georgia to Turkey, and on the way back stopped in Tbilisi. From a Georgian television broadcast I learned that Shamil Basaev and Hattab had entered Dagestan, and that there was fighting in the mountainous Botlikh region. I went back home the next day. Returning through Verkhniy Lars meant I had to pass through a Russian border post. This time it took longer than usual, about an hour rather than the usual five minutes. We took this as an indication that Russo-Chechen relations were again under strain. Arriving in Grozny, I went to see Aslanbek Ismailov and asked what was happening. He said he had no idea, but offered to arrange for me to meet Shamil Basaev who, he understood, was returning that night from Dagestan to Grozny. I went on then to see Aslan Maskhadov and report the results of my visit to Turkey. Aslan did seem particularly disturbed or depressed.

Immediately after Basaev and Hattab's invasion of Dagestan, the Russian prime minister, Sergey Stepashin, whom everybody was predicting would succeed Yeltsin, made a statement to the effect that 'Russia has lost Dagestan.' Literally the next day, Yeltsin read a decree dismissing Stepashin as prime minister and appointing to the job the director of the FSB and secretary of the National Security Council, Vladimir Putin who, for good measure, Yeltsin also announced was to be his successor. I have to admit that I knew nothing of all the unseen grappling going on among the Kremlin leaders and thought all the reshuffles were just the usual Russian bungling, with decisions being taken on the hoof rather than in accordance with anyone's plan of action. It was only years later, when I got to know well people who had had a part in almost all these intrigues, that I realized the Kremlin had been following a carefully thought out plan, and that for several years Putin had been systematically groomed to take over the presidency. This becomes evident if you examine the successive stages of his career. Yeltsin finally made up his mind about who was to succeed him when Putin provided him with evidence that Stepashin had been meeting with Yury Luzhkov and Yevgeny Primakov, who were implacable and very dangerous political enemies of Yeltsin and his family. Stepashin decided to err on the side of caution and agree with Luzhkov and Primakov that, if he became president, he would not prosecute them and would enable them to retain all their political influence. If Primakov became president, he would do the same thing and not pursue Stepashin. This was the information Putin was able to present to Yeltsin, and it was the main reason Stepashin was sacked and Putin appointed prime minister in his place.

Stepashin's announcement that 'Russia has lost Dagestan' was, of course, deliberately misleading and intended to provoke the armed units to even greater efforts and ensure that the incipient armed conflict should escalate out of control. Movladi Udugov and Isa Umarov assured their followers that Russia had neither the means nor the men to fight for the

Caucasus, and Stepashin's statement seemed to show they were right. It later transpired that the Udugov brothers had earlier reached some agreement with representatives of the Russian leaders. Before the incursion into Dagestan, in late July, Movladi Udugov had met Boris Berezovsky and invited him to participate in what he described as 'the new political movement in the Caucasus,' of which he was virtually the leader and which, Udugov assured him, would define future relations between Russia and the North Caucasus. If Berezovsky wished to come on board, he should contribute half a million US dollars. Udugov said this association included all the well known Chechen commanders and religious authorities of the entire North Caucasus and enjoyed great respect among Muslims. Perhaps as an earnest of good faith, Movladi told Boris Berezovsky about an event in the pipeline, namely the planned campaign in Dagestan, and also about agreements reached with the Russian leaders about relations between them and the Congress of the Peoples of Chechnya and Dagestan.

I have already mentioned the cosy relationship which Stepashin and Udugov had enjoyed since 1996. Udugov thought that, in order to open relations between the leaders of Russia and the supposed leaders of the Congress, Aslan Maskhadov should first be removed from the CRI presidency and replaced by someone acceptable to the Kremlin. The force able to effect this change, Movladi assured Berezovsky, was the armed jamaats. He went on to say that for them, unlike for Maskhadov and his government, national independence was not a high priority. For them, what mattered most was that the Russian government should not prevent the Muslims of the North Caucasus establishing Sharia law, as had been done in the Kadar Zone of Dagestan for a year already.

Udugov assured Berezovsky that an alliance with the leaders of the Congress of the Peoples of Chechnya and Dagestan would be more advantageous for Russia in every respect than cooperating with Aslan Maskhadov, who was following in the footsteps of Georgia and focusing on the West, that is, on the enemies of Islam. This was as unsatisfactory for true Muslims as it was for true patriots of Russia, and in this way the interests of Russia and of the Congress were aligned. Neither wished to see any strengthening of a Western alliance with the Caucasus. Udugov's plan anticipated that the incursion into Dagestan would provoke a crisis in relations between official Moscow and Grozny and give the Russian government a pretext to strike against Chechnya and then to renege on all the peace agreements signed by the Russian and Chechen presidents. The second phase of Udugov's plan would see Russia invade the northern regions of Chechnya as far as the River Terek, before opening negotiations with the leaders of the Congress which was 'the only effective political and military force in the North Caucasus.' In Udugov's view, this would lead to the fall of the 'pro-Western Maskhadov regime' and politically strengthen the hand of 'pro-Russian Muslims' in Chechnya. The latter would, for their part, renounce the ideal of independence and restore order not only in Chechnya but throughout the North Caucasus, and also contribute to strengthening Russia's position in Georgia and Azerbaijan. Berezovsky responded that he had long ago ceased to influence Russian policy on Chechnya but, although he disagreed with what they were planning, he would have to report it to Prime Minister Stepashin and FSB Director Putin. It would have been highly imprudent of him not to pass on what Udugov told him, because he suspected the whole episode had been got up specifically for the purpose of compromising him personally. Boris Berezovsky duly told Stepashin and Putin what Udugov had said, and both told him they had the situation fully under control and he should not interfere.

Although Berezovsky later claimed never to have supported the plan, the facts and the way events subsequently developed suggest the opposite. There are two reasons for believing that he was involved in this operation from the outset. First, it was Boris who persuaded Putin that Russian troops should not advance further than the Terek, and that negotiations should be conducted 'with all political movements and forces, including Basaev and Udugov,' rather than only with Aslan Maskhadov. The second is that, after Stepashin was fired, it was Berezovsky whom Udugov phoned to remind him of the agreement that there would be 'no bombing from the air.' Many people will remember this conversation, a recording of which was broadcast by NTV. We should not lose sight, however, of an important detail, which is that the recording was made and broadcast on NTV not by agents of the Russian intelligence agencies, as many assumed, but by people employed by the owner of NTV, the oligarch Vladimir Gusinsky, who was supporting the candidacy for Russian president of Grigoriy Yavlinsky and had made pungent criticisms of Putin.

I am fairly sure Aslan Maskhadov was no better informed than I was about what was going on in Moscow. He believed Putin was an inexperienced official with little understanding of the intricacies of politics, and that there would be no difficulty talking to him on any topic. Aslan Maskhadov instructed me and Kazbek Makhashev to meet Vyacheslav Mikhailov, due to visit Ingushetia from Moscow the next day, and communicate to him our position in respect of all the events currently taking place. More importantly, we were to suggest that Mikhailov should arrange for Aslan Maskhadov to meet the new Russian prime minister, Vladimir Putin.

After leaving Aslan, I went with Aslanbek Ismailov that night to see Shamil Basaev. Shamil was already at home and in good spirits. He immediately began telling us about his exploits in Dagestan, how they had shot down several Russian army helicopters, and so on. I asked him why he had allowed himself to be used in this way, what on earth he was doing there, and who needed a war for its own sake. Shamil took umbrage and said I was insulting him. He was not some adventurist who would start a war just for the hell of it, and their campaign in Dagestan was no more than proffering assistance to fellow believers. He claimed the peoples of Dagestan had risen up in a sacred jihad and we should not deny them what we ourselves had fought for in the recent war, namely, trying to liberate themselves from Russia. That evening, Shamil assured us that the whole of Dagestan was in rebellion against Russia and that he and Hattab had only gone to their aid. He told us also that in the past year more than 7,000 Dagestanis had undergone military training at a camp in Serzhen-Yurt in Chechnya. I knew from our experience in the First War that, if even half that many people were really able to fight, they would constitute a huge force capable of wearing down any army, including the Russian Army. I asked why they had started fighting in the highland region of Dagestan, and Shamil explained that the intention was to liberate the mountains of Dagestan within three months to provide access to the frontier with Azerbaijan, creating a corridor for support for jihad in the Caucasus from abroad.

'The only problem,' Shamil said, 'is that we have too few commanders involved in Dagestan whose names are known to the outside world.'

He very convincingly explained that a war in Dagestan was the only way to avoid a new war in Chechnya. By now, we knew for a fact that Russia was preparing to launch a new war against us, but it was equally clear that it could not undertake a large-scale military campaign in Dagestan and Chechnya simultaneously. That meant it was in our interests for the war to continue in Dagestan. I told Shamil, 'If everything is as you say, we must do everything we can to ensure the war is fought in Dagestan. We can regard it as historical justice. In the Caucasian War the Dagestanis fought Russia for nearly 20 years in Chechnya, and now Chechens have a chance to fight Russia in Dagestan.'

That evening, Aslanbek and I promised Shamil that, if the picture he had presented reflected the real state of affairs, we would resign our government positions and augment his list of commanders fighting in Dagestan whose names were known to the outside world. We also agreed to conduct a Congress of Resistance Veterans of the First War within the next three days. With those undertakings, we took our leave.

The next morning, Kazbek Makhashev and I travelled to Ingushetia to meet Nationalities Minister Mikhailov. As usual, one of Ruslan Aushev's assistants met us at the border and we drove to the Ingush president's official residence in Magas. The appearance of Mikhailov as the Russian government's representative was an unwelcome sign of the likely renewal of armed conflict between Russia and Chechnya. After the introductory formalities, Mikhailov launched into a tirade.

'Admit it! The Chechen Republic has violated the Peace Treaty and committed an act of aggression against Russia.'

On behalf of Aslan Maskhadov, we assured Mikhailov that the Chechen side remained committed to observing the Peace Treaty, despite all the provocative incidents Russia had been responsible for. We handed him a list of all the violations committed by Russian government institutions against Chechnya. Regarding the events in Dagestan, we told him the Chechen Republic was formally declaring its policy as non-interference. The fact that Chechen volunteers had turned up in a conflict zone in Russia did not reflect the official position of the Chechen state. The leaders of Chechnya called upon all parties to the conflict to resolve their disagreements by political means at the negotiating table.

Even after so many years have passed, there are still people who assert that Aslan Maskhadov, by failing to publicly condemn the invasion of Dagestan by Basaev and Hattab, gave Russia a pretext to restart its war against Chechnya. Those people accuse the Chechen president of inaction at a time of terrible events, and thereby of doing nothing to prevent the new war. The whole problem was, however, that any such statement from the president would have been tantamount to an admission that there had not been a large-scale spontaneous uprising in Dagestan, which would lend credence to Russia's claim that Chechnya had violated the Peace Treaty. Needless to say, this was precisely what the authors of the new military strategy wanted, since it would have given the green light to the Russian 'hawks' who, all these years, had been smarting for revenge. In Russia, the head of state remained, at least officially, the same President Yeltsin as had signed the Russo-Chechen Peace Treaty. Aslan Maskhadov, while not publicly acknowledging aggression on the part of Chechnya, nonetheless strongly condemned the efforts of Shamil Basaev to place himself at the head of an uprising of the peoples of Dagestan.

Indeed, Maskhadov did everything in his power to avert this armed provocation. Our intelligence services had had information that an invasion of Dagestan was in the making, and on 16 July 1999 President Maskhadov sent Turpal-Ali Atgireyev, the CRI's minister of state security, to Moscow to pass on information about an impending attack on the republic to his Russian colleagues. Atgireyev was detained for three days by members of the Russian intelligence agencies: further evidence that the FSB and its director Putin had no interest in preventing this incident in Dagestan. Indeed, as later became evident, the Russian intelligence agencies were managing the whole process.

As we were speaking to Mikhailov, we had no idea that the enemy was beating us hands down. We were the dupes on the receiving end of one of the FSB's biggest black operations, later to become known as Operation Successor. After Mikhailov, we several times had meetings with representatives of Putin. We insisted that they should arrange a meeting between Russia's new prime minister and the Chechen president, but Putin evaded direct contact with Maskhadov. The Chechen president then tried to arrange a meeting with all the heads of state of the North Caucasus region, which Ruslan Aushev undertook to organize. The leaders provisionally agreed to the meeting, including Magomedali Magomedov of Dagestan. The intention was for those attending to appeal to Aslan Maskhadov to intervene in the events in Dagestan and get all the rebel forces, including the Chechen volunteers, to withdraw from the republic. The leaders of these states actually had good, even friendly, personal relations with Maskhadov, understood his predicament, and tried at first to do all they could to help him.

By this time, the Congress of Veterans of the First War had already been held in Grozny. The situation in Dagestan was discussed. I spoke, and said the events there were nothing other than a national liberation movement, and the peoples of Dagestan had every right to freedom and independence from Russia. The right to revolt against oppression was recognized by all civilized states as being in accordance with natural justice and required no further legal basis. Accordingly, the Dagestanis' rebellion against colonial oppression was entirely legitimate, as was assistance to their rebellion on the part of volunteers. In my speech, I also commented that the attempt by Russia's rulers to blame the participation of Chechen volunteers in Dagestan on the CRI government was just another example of their campaign to whip up anti-Chechen hysteria. I recalled how Russian television had been used to sign up volunteers to go to Yugoslavia to fight in support of the Serbs, without NATO feeling obliged to bomb Moscow or accuse the Russian government of interfering in the affairs of a foreign state. The same thing had happened in

1992, when Russia officially sent volunteers to Abkhazia to fight against the Georgian Army. As regards the participation of Chechen volunteers in a war against the Russian Army in Dagestan, I went on, it was entirely understandable and justified: the wounds Russia had inflicted on Chechnya had still not healed and, instead of showing repentance for its misdeeds and recognizing our independence, Russia was continuing to commit provocations against our country. The Russian intelligence agencies were behind all the horrors the Chechen people had endured over the past two years, so few people in Chechnya felt any great sympathy for Russia.

This speech was subsequently invariably cited by those accusing me of having supported and even almost of having organized the Dagestan incursion. In fact, I was trying as far as possible to counter Moscow's claim that Chechnya had violated the Peace Treaty and was committing an act of aggression against Russia. There is a major difference in law, as I stressed in my speech, between volunteers joining an existing conflict and an attack on a foreign country with which you have a peace treaty. The Congress was also attended by Akhmad-khaddzhi Kadyrov and the Yamadaev brothers. The Mufti was intending to make a speech, but after mine he left the Congress, saying this was no place for him. It was his last appearance at any event organized by the CRI government. Shortly afterwards, he turned up in Moscow and had a meeting with Prime Minister Putin.

As for Aslan Maskhadov's meetings with Putin and the regional leaders of the North Caucasus, neither took place. Two days before the planned meeting in Pyatigorsk, all Chechen units left Dagestan. Islam Khalimov told me later this was done because he had asked the leaders of the Dagestan campaign, and in particular Shamil Basaev, Movladi Udugov, and Isa Umarov, to remain there for a few days more 'to separate the parties to the conflict' after Maskhadov's meeting with Putin, so that their departure could seem to be in response to an order from the Chechen president. I understood from Khalimov that he met them at Maskhadov's request. However, the leaders of the Congress of the Peoples of Chechnya and Dagestan had not the slightest intention of bolstering Maskhadov's authority and made haste to withdraw their troops from Dagestan before the Chechen president's meeting with Russian representatives. Immediately afterwards, Udugov's Kavkaz TV channel announced that 'the Joint Armed Forces of the Congress of the Peoples of Chechnya and Dagestan, after conducting a successful military operation in Dagestan, have returned to their permanent base in Chechnya.' That same evening, this TV station began showing monstrous videos of the beheading of captive Russian soldiers and, moreover, almost all those providing commentary on the events in Dagestan were Chechens. Against these televised reports, our attempts to represent the campaign of Basaev and Hattab as 'Chechen volunteers going to the assistance of the rebelling peoples of Dagestan' looked ridiculous. I had no further contact with Shamil Basaev until the outbreak of the Second Russo-Chechen War. Virtually everything he had said when Aslanbek and I met him proved to be untrue. I believed then, and still believe, he provided Putin with the pretext he needed to start a new war against the Chechen state.

Aslan Maskhadov made one further attempt to meet President Magomedali Magomedov of Dagestan and was driving towards Makhachkala when Dagestanis in the vicinity of Khasavyurt blocked the route of the Chechen president's motorcade. The protest was, needless to say, orchestrated by Moscow, but the man on the spot organizing the action was Akhmad-khaddzhi Kadyrov. The evening news on Russian television stations featured reports in which those blocking the road cursed President Maskhadov and sang the praises of Kadyrov. From that moment, it was clear that Kadyrov was working hand-in-glove with the Russian intelligence agencies to bring Russian troops back into Chechnya. I believe it was a big mistake that no steps were taken to isolate him, although Sultan Makhomadov, the then chairman of the Sharia court (who is now working as a mufti in Chechnya), sentenced Kadyrov to death. However, our government took no action to prevent further subversion on his part as he recruited Chechen fighters to the Russian cause under the pretext of 'fighting the Wahhabis.' On the contrary, Vakha Arsanov personally met Akhmad-haddzhi Kadyrov's uncle and asked him to restrain his nephew, to which the man replied that he could not do so because that would get him killed. I later had confirmation of this from Umar Khambiev, who said when he himself spoke to the man, the uncle said he understood what his nephew was doing was wrong, but could not attempt to influence him because he believed he might be killed for his pains.

Meanwhile, Moscow was maintaining informal contact with President Maskhadov. The conditions for a meeting between Prime Minister Putin and President Maskhadov to initiate talks for arriving at a peaceful settlement of the situation in the North Caucasus were the following, issued to us in the form of an ultimatum:

1. The Chechen government must acknowledge that the events in Dagestan were an act of aggression, but also acknowledge that the CRI was a bridgehead for aggression against Russia.

2. Aslan Maskhadov must publicly condemn the Dagestan campaign.

3. The Chechen president must announce his readiness to place himself at the head of all the armed forces of the CRI and, jointly with Russian troops, initiate military action against the Chechen volunteers who had taken part in the Dagestan events.

Needless to say, it was completely out of the question for the Chechen president to comply with these demands, and obvious that a second war was inevitable. President Maskhadov divided the republic into sectors, fronts and directions. At a meeting of the State Defence Committee, the president read out a decree proposing that I should be appointed commander of the Urus-Martan direction. I told Aslan that this appointment was unrealistic because the jamaats based in Urus-Martan would never agree to be subordinate to me. I suggested he should instead appoint Ramzan Akhmadov who, since the death of his brother Khuta, was the effective leader of the Urus-Martan groups which had opposed the CRI government. Now the situation had changed, we were at war, and nobody doubted the need for us all to join forces. Shamil Basaev was even appointed commander of the Eastern Front, which produced howls of outrage from Russia's rulers. President Maskhadov had, of course, foreseen that, but believed that if Russian aggression was to be deterred it was essential to demonstrate that Chechnya was ready to fight. For us, that meant showing that our forces were as one. Shamil Basaev had in any case stopped talking about the Congress of the Peoples of Chechnya and Dagestan, and his appointment as commander of the Eastern Front confirmed that he was back on board. Aslanbek Ismailov was appointed deputy supreme commander. As regards the Urus-Martan direction, all present supported my proposal and Aslan appointed Ramzan Akhmadov as commander.

Dalkhan Khozhaev and I had prepared a draft decree for this meeting, providing for the creation of a separate Special Operations Brigade, which President Maskhadov immediately approved. I was appointed brigade commander, with Khusein Isabaev as my deputy and Dalkhan Khozhaev as chief of staff. The decree was read out that evening on television, and from that moment fighters who been under my command in the First War began arriving. Within ten days we had more than 500 men in the brigade. Among the volunteers were many young people with no military experience, and we set up a fast-track training programme for them. We set up a barracks for the trainees in the basement of the Manual Sports Stadium, and appointed one of the veterans of the Resistance as head of the training centre. We also appointed instructors, selecting experienced fighters who taught the new recruits everything, from how to use small arms and grenade launchers to how to lay mines and defuse them, as well as how to dig trenches and construct bunkers.

In just two or three weeks these young newcomers had become almost professional fighters.

In early October, we put the brigade on parade. I invited the newly appointed Mufti of Chechnya, Bai-Ali Tepsaev, who spoke to the brigade's fighters about the sacred nature of a defensive jihad, the duty of every able-bodied Muslim. On that day, Mufti Bai-Ali Tepsaev received from the soldiers of my Special Operations Brigade an oath of preparedness to sacrifice their lives for Allah in the defence of their homeland. The brigade was now a fully staffed and equipped combat unit of the CRI Armed Forces and was deployed to positions in my area of responsibility, the Chernorechiye Defence Sector. Everybody immediately set to work constructing our defences. My fighters dug trenches and built bunkers and hidden passageways. Our brigade headquarters was in the Chernorechiye region. At the same time, issuing an internal order as minister of culture, press, information and communications, I set up a coordinating council which included the heads of all departments and social ministries under my control. I appointed Makkal Sabdullaev head of the council which, in accordance with martial law, was described as a staff headquarters. We did what we could to prepare to repel another Russian invasion, which no one now doubted was imminent. Putin's final touch, to raise his approval rating and prepare public opinion for a second Russo Chechen War, was the blowing up in September 1999 of apartment buildings in Moscow, Buynaksk, and Volgodonsk, blaming this villainy on the Chechen government.

Martial law was introduced in the republic, and a plan for the defence of Grozny and the rest of the country was devised. Aslanbek Ismailov was appointed chief of the Headquarters for the Defence of Grozny. The capital was divided into five sectors, one of which I was to command.

VI

Gambling on Putin

Threats of criminal proceedings against Yeltsin's entourage lead him to 'gamble on Putin and declare him his successor.' The FSB blows up apartment buildings in Moscow, Buynaksk, and Volgodonsk, blaming 'Chechen terrorists,' and presenting Putin as the only strong man capable of protecting Russian voters.

We need to say a few words about what was going on in the late 1990s in Russia itself. Under the Russian Constitution, if for any reason the president became incapable of performing his duties, the prime minister automatically became acting president until new elections could be held. This explains why, in less than a year, Russia had five changes of prime minister. The members of the Family, as Yeltsin's inner circle headed by his daughter Tatiana Diachenko was known, were frantically looking for a successor to whom they could entrust not only the money they had stolen during the Yeltsin era, but also their freedom and, perhaps, even their lives. They finally settled on Putin after he proved his unquestioning loyalty to them. When he was appointed director of the FSB, it was he who carried out a black operation to discredit the Russian prosecutor general, Yury Skuratov, who had opened an investigation into the Family's involvement in the embezzlement of money from an International Monetary Fund loan. Some US$ 4.3 billion had been loaned to Russia. The Prosecutor General's Office was also investigating allegations of bribery in Yeltsin's immediate entourage. Mabetex, a Swiss construction company, was renovating the Kremlin. The prosecutor general was alleging that it had paid Yeltsin's administration a bribe for the US$ 300 million contract. The head of the Presidential Administration was Valentin Yumashev, the husband of Tatiana Diachenko. In 1999, at the request of the Russian prosecutor general, Swiss prosecution investigators searched the head office of Mabetex in Lugano for evidence. Shortly afterwards, Carla del Ponte, the prosecutor general of Switzerland, came to Moscow and passed the

Mabetex file to Skuratov. A report appeared in the media that Tatiana Diachenko was among those accused of bribe-taking.

Of course, everyone knew Skuratov would never have dared to initiate such a high-profile investigation if he did not have the support of Yevgeny Primakov, who was prime minister at the time. In May, Yeltsin fired Primakov, violating an agreement with the Communists who had a majority in the Duma. The agreement was that Yeltsin and Primakov would both resign in 2000, handing over power to the young reformers. Primakov was replaced as prime minister by Sergey Stepashin, previously minister of the interior. The Communists, despite their Duma majority, confirmed Stepashin's appointment because Yeltsin had the right to dissolve the Duma, which he was entirely likely to do if they proved refractory. Yeltsin ran into problems with the Federation Council, however. He signed a decree dismissing the prosecutor general, but the Council voted to rescind his decree. At the time, the Council consisted of the heads of the Russian regions and, under the Constitution, the prosecutor general could be appointed or dismissed only with its consent. Primakov and Luzhkov set about creating their own political party, and almost all the regional leaders supported them. Many people were sure they would be victorious at election time.

As always in Russia's internal political conflicts, the antagonists played the 'Chechen card.' I personally heard comments Yury Luzhkov made about Chechnya. He said, 'We are realists, and if we come to power we shall recognize Chechnya's independence. That is, we will separate Chechnya from Russia.' There was, however, another party in Russia, the War Party, which was backing Putin and played the Chechen card quite differently.

Putin finally won the trust of the Family and the Russian revanchists when he battered the Federation Council into endorsing Yeltsin's decision to dismiss Skuratov. He managed this by secretly filming intimate scenes involving, as the Russian media cautiously put it, 'a person resembling Prosecutor General Yury Skuratov.' These videos were shown on Russian television and lethally undermined Skuratov's reputation. One of the people who were numbered at that time among the members of the Yeltsin Family told me that FSB Director Putin had a meeting with Skuratov and gave him the option of voluntary resignation before handing the compromising tape over to ORT, but he refused. At that they went ahead with the dirty tricks which so recommended Putin to the Family as someone they could rely on. When he then provided Yeltsin with the material compromising Stepashin, the president of Russia, at the prompting of Anatoly Chubais and Tatiana Diachenko, finally decided to gamble on Putin and declare him his successor.

Contrary to a widespread belief that Boris Berezovsky was the kingmaker behind Putin, I can confidently state that he was simply used. More precisely, the media empire of Berezovsky was used, and care was taken to make sure he did not prevent Putin being shoe-horned into the presidency. The decision to push Putin forward was made without the knowledge of Berezovsky, who was backing General Lebed. It was Berezovsky who invited Alexander Lebed back to Moscow at the time of the Dagestan events and Stepashin's declaration that 'Russia has lost Dagestan.' Berezovsky put Lebed on television commenting on Dagestan and claiming that, by signing the 1996 Khasavyurt Accord, he had saved the honour of the Russian Army, which would otherwise have been paraded through Grozny just as the captive German soldiers were paraded through Moscow in World War II. 'The Khasavyurt Accord,' Lebed said, 'was only an outline agreement and did not imply recognition of the independence of Chechnya.'

That was the first time Lebed talked publicly about 'Chechen wolves' and the need for a force of 50,000 Russian wolfhounds. He recalled that back in 1996 he had given orders for the heads of the security ministries to create a legion of 50,000 men, but they had failed to do so. This legion therefore needed to be created now. He added that he had been waiting, confident that his time would come. Lebed's interview is evidence that Russia had been thirsting for revenge ever since 1996. He was sure he would be appointed prime minister of Russia, which in the current situation was almost tantamount to becoming president, and he was encouraged in that belief by Boris Berezovsky. Berezovsky, as time was to show, had never been a member of Yeltsin's inner circle, and the Family instead of General Lebed chose as his successor Lieutenant Colonel Putin, who had doggedly proved his loyalty to them and to Yeltsin personally. Alexander Lebed made no more appearances on Russian television after that, and it was only after the blowing up of apartment buildings in Russian cities that, while in Paris, he issued a statement that the explosions were the work of the Russian intelligence agencies, as he would shortly prove. After those bombings, Putin had no serious political rivals. All Berezovsky's media outlets were now promoting him. Sergey Dorenko over at ORT 'Public Television' mounted ferocious attacks on the presidential aspirations of Luzhkov and Primakov, dishing the dirt on them in every one of his news analysis programmes. The muck gushed out at such a rate that Luzhkov and Primakov simply could not keep up with refuting all the allegations. After the bombings, they finally abandoned their attempts to oppose Putin. We know today that all three presidential hopefuls, Primakov, Stepashin, and Putin, were stooges of the Russian state security apparatus, the War Party, so when Putin emerged as the undisputed front runner, the other two put up little resistance and threw in their lots with the favourite. Stepashin, when Boris Berezovsky visited him, wept and asked plaintively what he had done to be so cruelly treated. Berezovsky told him it was his own fault for running to Primakov, who was a serious opponent of Yeltsin and Berezovsky himself.

The apartment bombings in Moscow, Buynaksk and Volgodonsk made Putin the undisputed leader and he had overwhelming public support for his so-called 'anti-terrorist operation' in the North Caucasus, unleashing yet another war against Chechnya. Officials in Moscow immediately accused Chechens of being responsible for the crimes. Moscow Mayor Yury Luzhkov was quick to announce to reporters that there were 'Chechen fingerprints' all over these attacks and to detail measures which would be taken against Chechens living in Moscow. Many Chechens in the hope that, as in the First War, they would be able to sit out the war far from Chechnya, had taken their families to Russia, well away from the bombs and artillery bombardment. Now, however, a campaign of persecution of Chechens began not only in Moscow but the length and breadth of Russia.

After the explosions, Aslan Maskhadov chaired a meeting of the CRI's State Defence Committee and a working group was formed to investigate the bombings since Chechens were being accused of them. President Maskhadov condemned the attacks and expressed his willingness to assist in the investigation and in bringing the perpetrators of this terrible crime to justice. By now, however, nobody in Russia was listening. Anti-Chechen propaganda flooded from all the Russian television channels. A video showed Russian military convoys heading towards Chechnya to the accompaniment of a famous song from the Second World War, 'Arise, vast land....' Russia was unambiguously going to war against Chechnya as an enemy state.

Aslanbek Ismailov and I met Hattab and I can testify that neither Hattab nor Shamil Basaev had anything to do with the apartment bombings. Russian official spokesmen at the time and subsequently claimed that Chechens, and more specifically, those two, had blown up the apartments in revenge for their defeat in Dagestan. In fact, organizing, preparing, and carrying out any such operation would have taken an extended period of time, which Basaev and Hattab simply did not have, since the explosions occurred immediately after their departure from Dagestan. Obviously, too, any such large-scale operation would require cover from the law enforcement agencies, because without that it would be impossible to send trucks loaded with explosives from the North Caucasus to Moscow and the other Russian cities, when there were police and army checkpoints almost every kilometre of the way meticulously inspecting all vehicles.

At that moment, however, nobody gave a moment's thought to these very obvious facts. Understanding came only after a fiasco in Ryazan, when the local police detained people packing the basement of an apartment block with sacks of cyclonite. Those arrested proved to be FSB officers. Various bumbling and contradictory statements from Russian officialdom attempted to explain away this fiasco, but nobody was taken in, with the exception of Yuliya Latynina, a popular journalist. In my opinion, Latynina was allowed to criticize the Russian government and Putin personally – on economic and political matters – only to enable her to gain a reputation as a journalist opposed to the Kremlin and win the trust of the liberal segment of Russian society. She could then be used more convincingly to whitewash Putin and the FSB over the small matter of these explosions in Russian cities in autumn 1999.

After the debacle of the Russian intelligence agencies in Ryazan, it became obvious to everyone in Russia and around the world that the earlier apartment bombings had been the handiwork of those same secret Russian agencies. By inertia, independent mass media were still functioning in Russia, and a number of newspapers and NTV conclusively proved on the basis of facts that the murder of hundreds of Russian citizens had been the work of the Russian intelligence agencies. By now, however, the war machine was geared up, and the voices of honest journalists and human rights activists like Anna Politkovskaya and members of the Memorial Historical and Human Rights Centre were drowned out by the ultra-nationalistic hysteria with which Kremlin propagandists infected the bulk of the Russian population.

VII

The Second Russo-Chechen War

On 23 September 1999, missile strikes are launched against civilian targets across Chechnya, accompanied by a barrage of disinformation from Russia. The subsequent military operations are genocidal. A secret Russian document states, 'We do not need to be squeamish about the means.' Chechnya's Resistance forces are now contaminated by externally funded Islamists not averse to collaborating with the FSB. Unexplained and unauthorized withdrawals of Chechen units from crucial sectors follow. The Russians retake Grozny.

On 23 September 1999, Russian warplanes began missile air strikes across Chechnya. Chechen villages in the Vedeno and Nozhai-Yurt regions on the Dagestan border had been subjected to heavy Russian bombing and artillery fire during the fighting in the Dagestan villages of the Kadar Zone. After resistance there was crushed, Russian warplanes started indiscriminately bombing the entire territory of Chechnya. The first victims of this bombing campaign were the villagers of Elistanzhi. Human rights activist Natalya Estemirova presented journalists with a list of 48 people killed instantly or fatally wounded during this air raid. Grozny and its suburbs were also subjected to bombing and artillery bombardment. Staraya Sunzha, Argun, Gudermes, Serzhen-Yurt, Vedeno, Zandak, Benoy, Zaman-Yurt, Pravoberezhnoye, Keni-Yurt, Naur, Naur Station, Goragorsk, Samashki, Achkhoy-Martan, Urus-Martan – the list goes on of Chechen towns and villages where Russian bombs, missiles, and shells killed and injured hundreds of civilians, women, children, the elderly. All the claims made by the Russian Military Command that these were 'pinpoint strikes on terrorist bases' were very far from the truth.

At first I thought the Russian Command was committing these indiscriminate massacres of civilians because they lacked reliable information about where Chechen army units were located. Only gradually did it become apparent that this was a deliberate tactic on the part of Putin to terrorize the entire Chechen population, and to make clear to every Chechen that Russia had returned to its traditional method of waging war in the Caucasus, expressed in the words, 'Subjugate or exterminate.' Any lingering doubt was dispelled when Putin gave orders to use weapons of mass destruction in Chechnya: tactical ground-to-ground missiles. Initially, these were used to attack Urus-Martan, but they fell not on the bases of jamaats returning from the Dagestan campaign but on people's homes. Among other residents killed during this strike was my brother-in-law, Ibrakhim Umalatov, aged 50. My sister Leila was seriously wounded.

I am not a superstitious person, but I was surprised by one strange coincidence. I remember Ibrakhim urging people who were preparing to flee to Ingushetia, not to leave their homes because, he assured them, it would all be over on 20 October. He had, he said, a premonition. It proved accurate for him at least. He was killed during the night of 19 October and buried on the morning of the twentieth. My sister was admitted to the hospital, and on 21 October I went to Urus-Martan to see her and my mother. That evening as we returned to Grozny and drove out from Minutka Square on to Avtorkhanov Prospekt, travelling in the direction of the Presidential Palace, I saw three missiles explode in the vicinity of the Central Market, Maternity Hospital, and Main Post Office.

In all, five missiles exploded that evening in the sky above Grozny: the other two exploded in the townships of Kalinin, near the mosque, and in Staraya Sunzha. My driver, Ibrakhim, immediately slowed down and suggested we should take cover in a nearby house. We got out of the car and waited for three minutes or so. No aircraft were to be seen or heard, and we decided to go to our headquarters, which was in the offices of the Department of Postal Services. The ChechenPress agency had its offices in the same building.

When we reached headquarters, Makkal told me that, among others, Said-Khusein Tazbaev had been wounded by shrapnel. He and I immediately went to the National Maternity Hospital, where a missile had exploded in the courtyard killing 13 women and 15 newborn babies. A further seven people were killed at the bus stop for the hospital. It was already dark when we drove to the Central Market. Their families had already come to take the dead home and the wounded to hospital. In order to cause maximum casualties, the missile strike had been timed for the evening, when people had come to buy food after their day's work. The entire market area had been destroyed. From there we went on to Municipal Hospital No. 9. I will never forget the atrocious sight. It was indescribable. The ward floors and corridors were swimming with blood. People with severed limbs were lying in the corridors. The doctors simply could not cope with the number of wounded, and more were constantly being brought in. The staff were asking for the wounded to be taken to other hospitals. People were dying right there in the corridors.

The following day there was a lot of comment on the use of missile strikes on the Chechen capital. A preliminary report from the Memorial Human Rights Centre listed 137 dead and over 250 injured. The list was far from complete because, in accordance with Islamic custom, relatives immediately took their dead for burial and nobody kept count of those casualties. The head of the intensive care unit in Hospital No. 9 warned that the civilian death toll was certain to rise significantly, as many of the wounded were in a serious or critical condition.

The next day, 22 October, Russia's officials trotted out their statements. Some of these deserve to be quoted. Alexander Mikhailov, director of the Russian Information Centre, said in an interview on NTV that 'not a single combat mission was flown by Russian aircraft over Grozny, and there was no use of tactical ground-to-ground missiles.' Mikhailov went on to claim that the explosion at the Central Market in Grozny was 'a terrorist act committed by Chechen fighters.' This was followed by comments on Radio Russia by the director of the Federal Security Bureau's Public Relations Centre, Alexander Zdanovich, who stated that the FSB had had no involvement in the explosions in central Grozny and the city market. He declared that the Federal Security Bureau had information that militants, believing that the crowds of people would shield them from an airstrike, had stockpiled a vast quantity of weapons, ammunition and explosives at the market. 'We cannot therefore exclude the possibility that a spontaneous explosion of ammunition may have occurred and led to loss of life.' On ORT television, Alexander Veklich, director of the Joint Press Centre of the Federal Armed Forces in the North Caucasus, stated, 'A special operation against arms dealers was conducted in Grozny on 21 October. According to intelligence, a market was discovered in Grozny where arms and ammunition were being sold to terrorists. As a result of the special operation, the market, along with arms, ammunition, and also the arms traders, was destroyed.' Veklich went out of his way to emphasize that the operation did not involve the use of troops, artillery, or aircraft. In response to a reporter's question as to whether there had been any civilian casualties during the raid, Veklich replied, 'Well, you know, civilians do not go out in the dark to a market where weapons are being sold to terrorists, so if there were casualties, they were among people selling arms and ammunition to gangsters.'

At a press conference in Helsinki, Prime Minister Vladimir Putin was asked about the missile strike and replied, 'I can confirm that there was indeed an explosion of some sort in Grozny, at a market, but I wish to draw the attention of representatives of the press to the fact that we are talking here not about a market in the usual sense of the word. We are referring to the Arms Market, as this place is known in Grozny. It is a base where arms are stored and it is the headquarters of criminal gangs. We do not exclude the possibility that the explosion which occurred there resulted from a clash between rival factions.' One of the journalists present said that there was information that a special operation had been conducted in Grozny, and cited Veklich. Putin replied: 'Yes, such operations are conducted regularly and there is reason to believe that such an operation was carried out yesterday, but it was completely unconnected with the events which occurred in Grozny.'

I give these examples to show how Russian officialdom, in trying to conceal the crime, contradicted itself. The final Russian version was articulated by Valeriy Manilov, first deputy chief of the General Staff. Speaking on NTV, he said, 'If we turn to the latest operations, like the one on 21 October, this was a no-boots-on-the-ground special operation carried out in Grozny. As a result of this swift special operation a clash occurred between two large, rival gangs which had been warring with each other for a long time. This conflict between the two gangs entered an acute phase, culminating in the vicinity of one of the very large depots of arms and ammunition. This depot is located, or now we should say, was located close to an area where arms and ammunition had been traded for a long time. Operational intelligence indicated there was a huge quantity of many different types of arms in this depot, including missiles. So, anyway, as a result of this intense firefight which we reported earlier probably one of the bursts of fire or tracer ... something hit this arms and ammunition depot and there was a massive explosion.' As we see, Manilov simply put together all the statements made by Russian officials and presented his compilation as the last word of the rulers of the Russian Federation on the missile attacks they launched on Grozny.

The first person to dismiss Russian lies about a supposed explosion at an arms and ammunition depot was President Ruslan Aushev of Ingushetia. In an interview with Savik Shuster on Radio Liberty, he said, 'I have seen fires at military depots. Even when extremely large depots in the Far East of Russia exploded, there might be one or two people injured. Here there was a direct hit, and so many dead, so many wounded, that to me as a military man it is obvious that this was a deliberate tactical missile strike.' According to

Aushev, people living in North Ossetia and Ingushetia heard these missiles flying overhead, most probably launched from the 58th Army base in Tarskoye, North Ossetia. He doubted that the decision to launch a missile attack on Grozny could have been taken at the level of a regional or army commander. 'No, this was authorized at the highest level,' Aushev said unambiguously. 'Everything is decided at the highest level ... Ground-to-ground missiles were being used ... These are the kind of missiles which carry nuclear warheads, so, when the matter was being discussed, what capabilities were to be employed ... when the operation was being planned, the go-ahead came from the top. I think the president knows all about it. Who would take responsibility for bringing in missile units without the knowledge of the president?'

Finally, on 26 October 1999 on Yevgeny Kisilyov's NTV programme *The Voice of the People*, Major General Vladimir Shamanov, commander of the Western Russian Army Group, admitted the explosions in Grozny on 21 October had been a missile attack launched by Russian troops. Here is the dialogue between Kisilyov and Shamanov:

Shamanov: Evidently use was made of the senior commander's resources.

Kisilyov: What does that mean?

Shamanov: It can be missile strikes launched by aircraft or ground troops, or precision-guided weapons.

Kisilyov: Who had the right to order the use of such weapons?

Shamanov: That is not a question for me to answer, it is a question for my superiors.

Kisilyov: Do you have authority to give such an order?

Shamanov: No, I do not have such resources at my command.

Yevgeny Kisilyov summed up the conversation:

'This makes it clear that the most senior office-bearers of Russia and the highest officers of the Russian High Command have not only been lying in order to try to hide the cause of the explosions in Grozny, but they also bear direct personal responsibility for the mass murder of civilians.'

From then on, the intensity of missile strikes throughout the republic increased, and so did the flood of people trying to flee Chechnya and get their children away from the line of fire. However, as the Memorial Human Rights Centre later discovered, already from 29 September the ministries and directorates of the interior of several republics, territories and provinces belonging to the Russian Federation had been sent telegrams ordering them to close their administrative borders to prevent refugees escaping from

Chechnya. Memorial includes in its report a copy of one such telegram, sent to North Ossetia's minister of the interior, Major General Kazbek Dzantiev:

'In view of the deteriorating situation in the North Caucasus, Major General Shamanov, Commander of the Western Joint Command of Federal Forces, has ordered closure of the border for the passage of vehicles and civilians from the Chechen Republic to the Republics of Ingushetia and North Ossetia-Alania through control and monitoring points and police checkpoints.' The order bears the decision of the deputy minister of the interior of North Ossetia: 'Totally rigorous enforcement. No vehicle to pass through. None!'

The only regional leader in the North Caucasus who refused to comply with this order was President Ruslan Aushev. Everybody who wanted to get out of Chechnya began moving to Ingushetia, but on 22 October Russian troops advanced to the Chechnya-Ingushetia border and closed it, setting up the Kavkaz–1 checkpoint on the Rostov-Baku Highway. On 26 October, state-controlled Russian media broadcast an announcement that a special 'humanitarian corridor' would be opened to enable refugees to move from Chechnya to Ingushetia, passing through the filtering Kavkaz-1 checkpoint. Official representatives of the security agencies involved in the war said that all those not availing themselves of the corridor and remaining in the republic would be considered criminals or accomplices.

People began leaving Chechnya en masse, in cars, buses and trucks. Thousands decided to take this opportunity, and hundreds of cars with refugees headed for Ingushetia. Within two days there was an 11-kilometre long traffic jam. At the same time, Russian military convoys moved unhindered towards Grozny, driving along the verges of the highway blocked with refugees and through the adjacent fields. The Command of the Russian troops used the refugee columns as human shields to protect themselves from attack by Chechen units. Our men began retreating eastwards towards Urus-Martan and Alkhan-Yurt, leaving their positions without a fight. Alkhan-Yurt is virtually a suburb of Grozny.

When on 29 October it was announced at the Kavkaz–1 checkpoint that nobody would be allowed through that day, vehicles with refugees began turning and moving back. According to eyewitnesses, planes then appeared in the sky and began bombing the column of vehicles which were, for the most part, carrying women, children, and the elderly. Much has been written about this Russian Army atrocity. There is the testimony of witnesses and people caught in these air strikes who survived. The massacre of the refugee columns proceeded from every direction. Attacks from the air and from ground forces were directed not only at civilians moving towards Ingushetia, but also at those heading for Georgia, Dagestan and Stavropol Territory. The bombing and shelling killed hundreds and wounded thousands of civilians attempting to flee the war-ravaged republic. Russian pilots pursued vehicles heading for the borders. It was systematic genocide.

At the same time, the Russian media, freely available for the Chechen population to watch, featured the Russian rulers' official spokesmen talking of the qualitative difference between the first and current military campaigns in Chechnya. They stressed that using selective tactics and smart weapons enabled them to 'destroy the terrorists' with few losses of Russian soldiers and minimal civilian casualties. Speaking on ORT television, Prime Minister Putin expressed his 'admiration for the training and skill of the pilots' and spoke with especial warmth of the Russian armourers who had 'created high-precision weapons, enabling us to strike directly at the bases and concentrations of militants while avoiding unnecessary casualties among the civilian population.' Meanwhile, the television presenter Mikhail Leontiev declared on ORT that 'the tactical missile strikes on the centre of Grozny are actually not barbaric as is being claimed around the world. Indeed, news of bombing and civilian casualties in Chechnya is good news, because it will cause the Chechens themselves to bring us the heads of Basaev and Maskhadov and ask, "What else can we do to stop the bombing?"' Leontiev was conveying a message to the Chechen people from Russia's rulers, in other words, Putin. The TV presenter was making clear that the Kremlin rulers had embarked on their 'Final Solution of the Chechen Problem.' Let us not forget that, when Yeltsin proclaimed Putin his successor, he named among the principal tasks of the future president the 'final solution of the Chechen problem.' Putin promised to accomplish this task, but the Almighty denied him the power to exterminate the Chechen people, despite barbarity and mendacity with few parallels in history.

In consideration of the fact that, under international law, the Russian troops and security agencies committed war crimes, which have no statute of limitations, I testify that the events of the Second Russo-Chechen War which I have described above actually happened. At that time I held the post of vice-chairman of the CRI Cabinet of Ministers and was present in the Chechen Republic. Analysis of the bombing and artillery strikes on Chechen populated areas entitles us to categorize them as a wilful act on the part of the Russian Armed Forces to effect mass destruction of Chechen civilians. This has been testified to also by victims and witnesses, as well as journalists and human rights activists. These murderous actions were aimed, apart from annihilating the population of the republic, at driving the surviving population of Chechnya to Russia, in order then to instigate a persecution of Chechens through all the vast expanses of that country, exterminating the insubordinate and assimilating the rest. The authors of this plan intended that the Chechen nation should cease to exist.

The Russian army leaders began a methodical and systematic bombing and shelling of the perimeter of the republic so that the largest possible number of refugees should concentrate in the Chechen capital. This was followed by tactical missile strikes on the centre of the densely populated city. Even that, however, was not the peak of their wickedness. That came when, with unbounded cynicism, refugees were first granted a 'humanitarian corridor' to leave the republic and given hope that they were a stone's throw from safety, only then to have death rain down on them from the air and ground. Concentrating the refugees in one place, Russia's criminal war machine carried out an unambiguous policy of genocide. History knows no more evil and cynical instance of the extermination of innocent people, and it took place on the eve of the new millennium. Russia's rulers attempted to manipulate world public opinion into believing that, after their army had carried out these acts of genocide, anyone remaining on the territory of Chechnya could be classified as 'terrorists and gangsters' for whom there should be no mercy and every last one of whom should be destroyed. Since the only people remaining in the republic were supposedly terrorists, in the light of the new exigencies of the 'War against Terror,' international conventions should not apply to them as they would to combatants in conventional hostilities.

To some extent they succeeded in this. It took long years of bloodshed before the horrifying extent of the crimes committed by the Russian Army in Chechnya became known to the international community. That this did eventually happen is because honest, courageous journalists and human rights champions made it happen. I wish particularly to pay tribute to the staff of the Memorial Human Rights Centre, to Amnesty International, and Human Rights Watch, who undertook the enormous and extremely dangerous task of documenting the war crimes committed, with the blessing of the Kremlin, in Chechnya by the Russian military and the Russian intelligence agencies. We must never forget what happened. Those guilty of these inhuman crimes must receive the severest punishments. The principal criminals are Putin, Yeltsin, Patrushev, Rushailo, Sergey Ivanov, Gryzlov, Shamanov, Troshev, and all the rest who are guilty of mass genocide. Their names are known. It is vital that they should be prosecuted if such crimes are not to be repeated. I very much hope that the day will come when, as Alexander Litvinenko, a true patriot of Russia and Chechnya, said, the Chechen and Russian people will put Putin, Yeltsin, and the entire political and military establishment of Russia on trial in the centre of Grozny. Even those of them who do not live to that day must be judged posthumously. The most important thing is that this trial should take place.

Returning to the events, I have to say I have no doubt that Putin decided to completely flatten Chechnya, without bothering to divide Chechens into 'good' and 'bad.' The negative reaction of the international community, and in particular of the Council of Europe and the European Union, was one reason he had to change his tactics. In early November 1999, the Parliamentary Assembly of the Council of Europe passed a resolution calling on Russia to desist from aerial bombing of civilians, institute a ceasefire, and enter a peace dialogue with the elected government of Chechnya. This obliged Putin to resort to differentiating between 'good' and 'bad' Chechens.

It later emerged that he had been unsure initially whether the Family had finally settled on him as Yeltsin's successor. When asked by Natasha Gevorkyan in an interview whether he had not been afraid he might be cast aside like his predecessors, Putin replied that he had had concerns, and that was why wanted to 'to deal with the Chechens in short order.' This is the explanation of the brutality he showed and the mass murder of people in Chechnya on his orders at the start of the Second War. Putin adjusted his policy in Chechnya after he knew he was definitely going to be Yeltsin's successor. He was shown a draft decree to the effect that Yeltsin would retire on the eve of the New Year of 2000 and hand over supreme power in Russia to him. This changed Putin's attitude to the Chechen question. He was aware that in future he would be personally responsible for everything happening in Chechnya, and that also he was not going to be able to achieve a Final Solution of the Chechen problem. He changed his approach to exterminating all rebellious Chechens and decided to unite all malleable Chechens under the Russian flag.

For a start, he pardoned Bislan Gantemirov, the former mayor of Grozny, who was convicted in 1996 of embezzling budgetary funds. A huge amount of money was allocated after the First War to rebuild Grozny. The Russian press spoke of a sum in the region of a trillion rubles. The money disappeared but Grozny was still in ruins. That was the formal charge against Gantemirov, although everyone knew that not a single ruble in the republic would have disappeared without Zavgaev knowing all about it. The real reason for Gantemirov's arrest and imprisonment was that in 1996 he had begun negotiating to sign up with the Chechen Resistance. He regretted having sided with Russia and decided to rejoin those supporting an independent Chechnya. Djohar Dudaev was still alive at the time. I was present at a conversation when Vakha Arsanov told Djohar that Gantemirov had been in touch and wanted to talk about switching to our side. The information evidently reached the Russian intelligence agencies and Bislan Gantemirov was duly arrested. His defection to the Resistance would have had a considerable impact and been politically damaging to Russia, because he had been much hyped by Russian ideologists before the First War. He believed Russia had cheated him because, when their troops invaded, they first decided to hand the republic over to Salambek Khadzhiev and then, staging a spoof election, finally gave power to Zavgaev. Zavgaev hated Gantemirov, believing he had played a key role in his overthrow in 1991 after the failed coup in Moscow. The result was that Gantemirov was sentenced to six years' imprisonment and was serving time in Moscow. Now, suddenly, he was again needed as the main Chechen collaborator. Putin met him personally and appointed him chief of the 'Chechen Police.' From a prison cell Gantemirov moved straight into the job of minister of the interior.

At this same time, the FSB began recruiting criminals in Russian prisons and labour camps to fight in Chechnya on contract, promising them money and freedom at the end of their contract. For the Russian Command these men were entirely expendable, like the penal death battalions during the Second World War. Hastily dressed in military uniform, the criminals were unbelievably brutal towards civilians during punitive search and destroy operations in Chechen villages. Their superiors not only did not punish them for manifesting their criminal tendencies but actively encouraged them. When it was time to pay these mercenaries at the end of their contract, they would be thrown into the thick of the fighting. The Russians well knew that the fighters for Chechen independence would kill this thieving, murderous rabble without pity. Any who survived were often finished off by Russian air attack. Not all contract troops were recruited from the prisons, but 'free' mercenaries very soon learned criminal ways from them. If alcoholism and drug addiction had become the scourge of Russian society at this time, it is not difficult to imagine how widespread these vices were among the contract criminals.

At the same time, the Kremlin announced it was resuscitating the so-called 'Zavgaev parliament,' which Putin decided to rename the 'State Council.' He appointed Malik Saidullaev, a Chechen living in Moscow, to lead it. Saidullaev was one of the few Chechens who became successful businessmen during the Gorbachev thaw of the 1980s. His core business was gambling and, in particular, 'Russian Bingo' on television. I made Saidullaev's acquaintance in 1995 during the First War, and we subsequently met on several occasions during the presidency of Aslan Maskhadov. He often came to Grozny, negotiated with Maskhadov, and said he could arrange the investment the republic so desperately needed. Malik was one of only two wealthy Chechens who publicly announced their intention of investing some of their capital in Chechnya and, indeed, attracting additional investment to rebuild the war-ravaged economy. I think it was as a punishment for that that his brother and sister were kidnapped and held for ransom. Most unfortunately, our law enforcement agencies were unable to help him effectively, which was probably what changed his attitude to the Ichkerian government in general, and to Aslan Maskhadov's administration in particular.

I do not condone his behaviour, but at the same time I believe it was the ineffectualness of our law enforcement which turned a large proportion of Chechens against Maskhadov and our government, and made many overtly hostile. The situation had been deliberately provoked, and there can be no doubt that behind the gangsters terrorizing the Chechen people, frightening away our wealthy compatriots, and deterring others who were not compatriots but intended to help restore our economy, stood the Russian intelligence agencies. Subsequently, these set about turning the victims of the terror and crime wave they had themselves inspired into a 'political opposition' to Maskhadov.

Malik Saidullaev is a case in point. Like many other Chechens, he became a prey of the Russian intelligence agencies. By nature he was very ambitious. At the start of the Second War, Putin played skilfully on that by appointing him chairman of the State Council. The Kremlin recognized they could not back Akhmad-haddzhi Kadyrov at the very beginning of the invasion because he would be unacceptable to Chechen society. By appointing Saidullaev, Putin succeeded in hoodwinking a number of Chechens, including even some who had fought for independence in the First War. These people fell for Saidullaev's pseudo-patriotic stance and saw him as potentially a leader who could stop the new war, enable the economy to recover, and provide security for the civilian population.

Putin needed to transform pro-Russian 'Moscow Chechens' into 'representatives of the Chechen people' who could endorse his actions in Chechnya for the benefit of the international community and, in particular, the Parliamentary Assembly of the Council of Europe. This institution was monitoring the situation in Chechnya and demanding that Russia should stop using disproportionate force in its military operations in the Caucasus. For this ignominious role, Putin found a few Chechen-speaking individuals. Abdul-Khakim Sultygov was one of them. He became the United Russia party's nationalities policy coordinator. Sultygov had been an aide of Shamil Basaev when he was acting prime minister of the CRI. At a government meeting, I once had to listen to a report Basaev invited him to give. The gist was that Russia had no future, was about to fall apart, and we should do our best to accelerate the process. Such lectures evidently had an effect on Basaev when the Udugovs were trying to persuade him Russia had neither the men nor the resources to defend Dagestan and wage a second war against Chechnya at the same time. Let us recall a passage in the document quoted above which states:

> We do not need to be squeamish about the means. We need to remember morality in this situation only in the context that it would be immoral for us to lose Russia. Defending the power of our state is the supreme moral priority of the Russian people and its political elite. Failure to defend Russia on the grounds of the immorality of a number of actions which it is necessary for us to take in Chechnya would be a crime.

I can testify that Putin followed the recommendations contained in that document to the letter. He was certainly not squeamish about the means he used, and personally met Gantemirov, Sultygov and Malika Gaziliev, a woman of uncertain ethnic origin who was appointed mayor of Gudermes and who, I was told by Anna Politkovskaya, startled even Russian officers with her phenomenal capacity for drinking and swearing. It was these people, and others like them, that Putin sent off, together with Dmitry Rogozin, to the PACE session in Strasbourg as 'representatives of the Chechen people.' There they attempted to persuade the European parliamentarians that Putin was not waging a war against the Chechen people but against 'international terrorists who have occupied Chechnya.' Although the Europeans were not particularly inclined to trust these political camp followers, it was important to Putin to parade them in front of the Western parliamentarians as living proof that there were people in Chechnya who supported his policies. By playing on their ambitions, Putin managed to bring together for a time Akhmad-haddzhi Kadyrov, Bislan Gantemirov, and Malik Saidullaev, and this paid dividends. All those who before the First War were opposed to President Dudaev were drawn to Gantemirov; all those who had a score to settle with the Wahhabis lined up behind Kadyrov; while Saidullaev appealed to those disillusioned with Aslan Maskhadov. Separately, these three individuals did not add up to much, but jointly they proved more effective than Putin could have hoped, as he himself later admitted in his annual speech to the Federation Council.

In Shali in the latter half of November 1999, we had the last joint meeting I was to attend of the government and parliament. It was to prove also the last time I saw Aslan Maskhadov, Ruslan Alikhadzhiev, and many other comrades-in-arms and friends. Turpal-Ali Atgireyev reported to the assembly that the Yamadaev brothers had defected to the Russian side. We had already lost Gudermes. We discussed the overall military situation. Aslanbek Ismailov reported on preparations for the defence of the five sectors into which Grozny had been divided. Ruslan Alikhadzhiev said he had been contacted by representatives of the Russian regime and, more specifically, of Putin, who had talked about possible negotiations with the parliament of Chechnya.

This was entirely typical of Putin's policy towards Chechnya, which was constantly to initiate negotiations with individual 'warlords,' in this way emphasizing that Russian officialdom did not recognize the legitimate CRI government. Those contacting the parliament had far-reaching plans to cause a rift between the legislative body and the president of the CRI. The Kremlin did ultimately achieve this, but only later. At this meeting it was resolved that the CRI president was the sole person entitled to speak on behalf of the Chechen people and state, while members of the government and parliamentary deputies could only comment on the situation. Aslan Maskhadov called upon all the ministers and parliamentary deputies present to form militias and prepare for a long war.

Three members of his entourage promptly refused. Ruslan Alikhadzhiev, the speaker of parliament, said he was a politician and did not consider it appropriate for him to 'run around with a gun.' Apti Batalov and Turpal-Ali Atgireyev followed his lead and decided that they too were politicians for whom it would be unseemly to fight in the trenches. Maskhadov warned them that, with that attitude in the present situation, they would end up bringing dishonour on themselves, and so it was to prove.

There was already fierce fighting in Alkhan-Yurt. The capital was subjected to massive bombing and shelling but had not yet been surrounded. The fighters of the Special Operations Brigade under my command took up positions from Alkhan-Yurt to the traffic police post and held back the advance of Russian troops along the Rostov-Baku highway. If Alkhan-Yurt fell, we would have no option but to fall back to the second line of defence in the sector of Grozny for which I was responsible. Well aware of how important Alkhan-Yurt was for our brigade's lines of defence, I kept a close eye on the situation there. The problem was that, in early November, Ramzan Tsakaev, the commander of the Alkhan-Yurt Jamaat responsible for defending the village, had been killed. Dalkhan and I had known Ramzan and many fighters in his group from the First War, when they were under my command. After his death, the unit all but collapsed, although the remaining two dozen fighters stayed at their positions in Alkhan-Yurt. One of them contacted Dalkhan and asked for support because they no longer had the strength or the means to hold their ground. I reported this to Aslanbek Ismailov and, on his orders, sent a group there under the command of Said-Khusein Tazbaev. I went along. We needed to find who exactly was responsible for defending the village. A local fighter told me their headquarters was in a school basement and we went there.

After Ramzan Tsakaev's death, overall command of the defence of Alkhan-Yurt had passed to one of the Middle East volunteers whose loyalty was to the Congress of the Peoples of Chechnya and Dagestan and was formally subordinate to Shamil Basaev. For the previous six months, Ramzan Tsakaev had also owed allegiance to the Congress and participated in the march on Dagestan. I introduced Said-Khusein to the Alkhan-Yurt fighters and told him to take up position with his group opposite the Bashlam Restaurant complex on the highway in order to control the road to Grozny and the bridge. It would have been suicidal to return to the fighters' earlier positions, because the enemy had found their range and its shells were landing right in the trenches.

That night we transferred a few of Ramzan's fighters who had survived, and one who was severely wounded, to Goyty. I returned to Grozny and reported the situation to Aslanbek Ismailov. He said he would need a few days to send replacements, but at lunchtime the next day Said-Khusein Tazbaev radioed me to say the Russians had entered Alkhan-Yurt from the direction of Yermolovka. They were almost behind his group and he had had to fight his way out of encirclement. Said-Khusein said he had some wounded and they were retreating to Grozny by Route 1. This was code for a route we had identified for redeploying to Grozny if the situation deteriorated. There were several of these, and I knew which way he was headed. I sent reinforcements to meet him, cover their retreat, and help with the wounded, who included Musa Khaddzhimuradov. Said-Khusein's group got back to Grozny without losses, apart from a few fighters with minor wounds. The wounded were transferred the same day to hospital in Chiri-Yurt. Said-Khusein prepared a report outlining the events in Alkhan-Yurt from the moment he had arrived there. He found that, without warning me, the commanders charged with defending Alkhan-Yurt had withdrawn their troops in preparation for abandoning the village. The following morning local collaborators guided a convoy of Russian troops into the village from the direction of Yermolovka, which was how the invaders came to be to the rear of Said-Khusein's group.

Shortly after that retreat, Bislan Gantemirov made a sensational announcement that in the next few days they would be taking Urus-Martan. I have to say I assumed this was just propaganda for the benefit of the average Russian watching the war on television. Urus-Martan was a major city with some 2,000 fighters defending it, most of whom had had their baptism of fire in Dagestan. This direction was under the command of Ramzan Akhmadov, a commander battle hardened in the First War. At the end of October, I had met him to agree some issues about the line of defence. A unit of the Special Operations Brigade commanded by Khusein Isabaev was occupying positions between Tangi-Chu and Urus-Martan. Fighters from a jamaat subordinate to Ramzan were between Urus-Martan and Alkhan-Yurt and covering the road to Grozny. We agreed these two units should change places as this would be more convenient for both of us. That day Ramzan Akhmadov's headquarters were full of leaders of groups of fighters, or emirs of jamaats as they preferred to style themselves. They were reporting to him on possible directions along which the Russian invaders might stage their assault on Urus-Martan.

Almost the entire population of Urus-Martan, certain there would be a battle, had fled the city, leaving it in the hands of Ramzan Akhmadov's fighters. There were ample supplies of food and livestock in Urus-Martan and practically no civilians, so nobody took Gantemirov's declaration seriously. Greatly to our surprise, however, Russian television was soon broadcasting pictures showing columns of enemy troops marching into Urus-Martan exactly at the time Bislan Gantemirov had predicted. This happened literally the day after we withdrew from Alkhan-Yurt. Dalkhan Khozhaev and many others felt sure there had been treachery. I can say nothing definite about Alkhan-Yurt, but I made it my business to investigate Ramzan Akhmadov and rumours about how Urus-Martan came to be surrendered without a fight.

I talked to many people who were in the headquarters of the Urus-Martan Jamaat when the decision was taken to abandon the city. Ramzan was virtually forced to give the order to retreat and redeploy to the highland Shatoy region. The emirs at the meeting reported that Russian troops were advancing from two directions: from the direction of the foothill village of Martan-Chu to the south, and from the direction of Gekhi to the west. The enemy's first advance was repulsed, but Urus-Martan was almost surrounded, leaving open only a corridor in the direction of Alkhazurovo, that is, towards Shatoy. All the emirs who spoke at the meeting argued that if the corridor was closed, they would be surrounded and cut off from outside help. The enemy was hoping that Ramzan Akhmadov's fighters would decide to avail themselves of this corridor. It was a tactic they had used during the First War, surrounding a centre of population on three sides and leaving a way out along which the Chechens could retreat. We can also safely say that among those urging Ramzan Akhmadov to abandon Urus-Martan without delay were some who had an understanding with the Russian Army Command through the agency of Bislan Gantemirov, and who were later awarded positions under the Russian regime of occupation. Whatever the truth, the invading army took Urus-Martan and almost the entire lowland region of the republic, with the exception of Grozny.

In late November, entrenched in Alkhan-Yurt, and by then also in Urus-Martan, Russian troops began attempting to break through to Gudermes, also under their control, along the section of the Rostov-Baku highway which we were defending. Our soldiers repulsed several of their attempts, the invaders retreating with the loss of men and armour. The enemy called in massive bombing of our positions and a barrage of artillery shelling. From my experience of the First War, I had anticipated this and stood my fighters down from their positions, so that all this firepower caused us no harm. In reality, after the Russians had occupied Urus-Martan, continuing to defend this stretch of the road made no sense: the enemy could bypass us and rejoin the highway from Goyty, completing the encirclement of Grozny. By agreement with Aslanbek Ismailov, I decided to redeploy the fighters of my brigade to the second line of defence of the capital. On 2 December 1999, Russian troops, as expected, completed the encirclement of Grozny by coming out on to the Rostov–Baku highway by way of Goyty.

That day, 2 December, I and several of my fighters were outside the encirclement. In the morning we transported Khusein Isabaev and a small group of fighters out of Grozny to Shatoy. We decided to keep one of the brigade's units outside the encirclement, in the highland part of the republic, to prepare a camp in the mountains for us so that, if the capital were lost and we had to switch to guerrilla warfare, we would have a base of operations. Establishing bases in the mountains was provided for in the war plan developed by our General Headquarters and approved by President Maskhadov, which devolved responsibility for preparing such bases to commanders of detachments. My chief of staff, Dalkhan Khozhaev, and I decided to entrust the task to my deputy, Brigadier General Khusein Isabaev.

Khusein was reluctant to leave Grozny, but I ordered him to do so. A small detachment of fighters from my brigade had previously been sent to Shatoy to support fighters holding the road leading to Shatili in Georgia. With these fighters, Khusein Isabaev was to prepare a base in the mountains and set up delivery of arms and ammunition from Georgia, for which we had already sent a group of young fighters.

We returned to Grozny that afternoon in thick fog. Near Novye Atagi, a few kilometres from the intersection on the Rostov–Baku highway, a young man literally jumped out on to the road and stopped us. He warned that Russians were stationed at the crossroads and had opened fire on a passenger car carrying civilians about half an hour ago. The boy told us the Russians had made no attempt to check who was in the car. He did not know how many people had been shot, only that no one had emerged. He and his elder brother had been driving behind this vehicle. They too had come under fire, but managed to turn and get away. His brother had left him at the roadside to warn anyone heading into danger, and had himself gone to the village to call people to help block off the road.

At this time I was contacted by my brigade headquarters with a report that Russian troops had completely surrounded Grozny and that I should not proceed along my present route. We waited for the people to arrive from Novye Atagi to set up the roadblock. They told us that, if we wanted to get into Grozny, we needed first to make for the village of Belgatoy, from there to Chechen-Aul, and from there through the foothills to Prigorodnoye, which was almost in Grozny. We took their advice, reached Chechen-Aul without incident, and performed evening namaz. There were a lot of people at the mosque who, like us, were intending to go into the capital. We left our car there and handed the keys to a local man as our Lada–6 would never make it up the road we had to drive. We split into twos and climbed into Niva off-roaders which were taking food supplies into the city. Before reaching Prigorodnoye, we saw a column of vehicles approaching. When we met, they stopped to ask about the situation ahead. I recognized the questioner as Vakha Arsanov's bodyguard and asked how Vakha was doing. Vakha recognized my voice and got out of his car. I got out too and he told me his men were insisting he should leave Grozny. I said they were right to do so. Vakha had a serious problem with his spine and, although he had had an operation in Georgia, time was needed for him to recover. That was to prove our last meeting. We said goodbye and drove off in different directions.

We made it safely to brigade headquarters but, within a day or two, Grozny had turned into a seething cauldron. There were still a lot of civilians in the city. I gave our staff officers instructions to check which basements in the sector we controlled had civilians in them. We soon found out: in most cases they themselves took the initiative. Their representatives came to see us and, with the help of local residents, we set up a small bakery at Okruzhnaya. I instructed our support staff to ensure that all these civilians were fed too. We also set up a medical centre for emergency care both of our fighters and civilians. I want to stress that, in the interwar period, despite all the chaos in the republic, the civilian population of Chechnya fully supported the Resistance. It could hardly have been otherwise, because the Resistance consisted of members of the public. We did not have a professional army. The residents of Chernorechiye, Aldy, Okruzhnaya, Voykova, Districts 20 and 12, and indeed everybody in the area for which I was responsible, supported us and, to the best of their ability, did what they could to help.

I was struck by the life-affirming energy of Chechens. There was no despondency or bewilderment. On the contrary, each person was self-possessed and prepared to overcome dangers and hardships, which our national psychology perceived as an inevitable part of the life of every generation. Our fathers lived through the brutal Deportation to Central Asia. Our grandfathers had to endure a period of bloody mass repression as Bolshevism gestated. Before that our distant forebears lived through the endless Caucasian War. Every Chechen, no matter how different in age, education or wealth, understood one indisputable truth: these wars and calamities all proceeded from a single source: Russia. They would continue for as long as we lacked independence. Or until we become 'Russians' not only in name but in spirit, which would be a national catastrophe. The battle cry of 'Liberty or death!' was for us not mere rhetoric but an integral part of our lives. That is why all Chechens, with the exception only of a few faint hearts, supported us, the army of their people, in spite of all the mistakes we made in the interwar period.

Not only our positions on the line of defence but the entire city was subjected to constant bombing from the air and artillery bombardment In spite of the horror, people began adapting to life under such circumstances. One incident really took me aback. I saw a convoy of cars driving under fire across the dam from Aldy to Chernorechiye. The cars had their headlights on and were sounding their horns. I thought it must be our fighters showing off how tough they were, and went to reprimand them for exposing themselves to needless danger with such crazy antics. I met the convoy when it drove in behind some apartment blocks, only to discover when I got out of my vehicle that it was a wedding procession. They were civilians, residents of

Chernorechiye who had gone to Aldy to collect the bride. The young people had set the date for their wedding in peacetime, and the families of both bride and groom saw no reason to change it just because a war had broken out. When I commented that this was not the obvious time for a wedding, one of them replied, 'Akhmed, if our young people postponed getting married because of wars, the Chechen nation would have vanished from the Earth long ago.' I acknowledged that I was out of order and wished the newlyweds happiness and long life. After saying goodbye, I reflected that neither Russia nor anyone else could defeat these people. During the two or three months of the initial phase of the Second War there were more than a dozen weddings in the area I was responsible for. These were absolutely genuine marriages, arranged with due observance of all our rituals and traditions.

That year winter arrived very early. We considered that the Almighty was coming to our aid, because most of our fighters, unlike the Russian soldiers, had proper shelter, and those who were in trenches on the front line were regularly replaced. This applied to the fighters in my brigade and the volunteers who joined us in the course of the hostilities, including autonomous militia groups whom the war caught in the area of my responsibility. Our headquarters calculated that the brigade numbered 900 fighters, including commanders. Among the militias there were some people who had not participated in the First War, and they could cause trouble. One case involved Supian, the 40-year old commander of a smaller unit which became attached to my brigade.

The first time we talked, he told me he had not chosen to remain in Grozny, but found that Russian troops had blocked all the ways out. He lived in the October region, in a large new house with an enormous courtyard. There they had been joined by a group commanded by a certain Isa, and since there were a lot of old buildings in the yard, which Supian had been planning to demolish, there was enough room to accommodate everyone. It was Isa who suggested to Supian that he should join my brigade because, he said, he had known me since the First War. I did remember Isa. In the First War he belonged to a militia group who came mainly from Tangi-Chu, but he himself was from somewhere in the Terek area. Isa had a weakness for chocolate biscuits, for which the men nicknamed him Bacchus. He confirmed to me everything Supian had said, and indeed introduced the latter as the overall commander of their joint detachment. The unit also included several fighters from Martan-Chu.

Later the detachment split again over some internal issues, and this led to tragic consequences. Our headquarters knew about it and designated the fighters under the command of Supian and those under Isa as two separate detachments. They considered the matter too insignificant to report to me, and I learned of the split only after a crime was committed. In Isa's group there was a young woman of Nogai nationality who was about 25 years old. In Supian's group there was a young Chechen man aged 16. He was called Timur and in love with this girl. Timur was a skilled operator of rocket propelled grenade launchers, an important asset for any unit. Knowing Timur's feelings for the young woman, Isa began trying to entice him over to his unit, assuring him that if he came, the girl could be persuaded to marry him. Supian was very upset when Timur told him he was planning to do so. He said later he had words with the girl and asked her not to toy with Timur. Supian's 15-year-old son was also in his detachment and friends with Timur. Supian, showing paternal concern, tried to shield Timur from the bad influence of Isa and his frivolous friend. He talked to them and asked them to leave the boy alone. Isa and his lady friend ignored the request. When she again appeared to tempt Timur, Supian shot her.

We had a Special Department in the brigade, under the direction of an experienced officer called Alik (I will not mention his surname). The officers of the Special Department arrested Supian and accused him of premeditated murder. After completing their initial investigation, during which Supian was held in custody, they referred the case to the Sharia court. Throughout the whole time Grozny was under attack, a Sharia court chaired by Lema Goytinsky was functioning. It considered not only military but also civilian cases. There were still a lot of civilians in the city and situations arose which required a judicial hearing. Looting occurred, as I know because the Special Department officers succeeded in neutralizing three groups of looters operating in my area. These groups came out at night and, despite the unceasing air and ground attacks, would transport their booty to other areas so that people did not identify property stolen from their neighbours. That was usually when they got caught. The court was situated in the Zavodskoy region, and ruled in the case of Supian that the relatives of the murdered women had the right to demand satisfaction from him. Given the fact, however, that there was a war on, that Supian was an active member of the Resistance, and that none of the murdered woman's relatives had come forward, the court ruled that he should be released so that he could continue the Jihad. It commented, however, that the case remained open and that if, after the war, Supian was still alive, the case would be reviewed with the participation of the murdered woman's relatives. If the relatives so required, and if there were three witnesses confirming that the crime had been committed, Supian would have imposed on him the Sharia sentence for premeditated murder of a Muslim. Supian went back to his unit as an ordinary private soldier and had the weapons returned to him which were confiscated at the time of his arrest.

After this, I met Isa and Timur, who was determined to avenge the murder of his beloved. I briefed them on the court decision and warned that, if they did anything contrary to that decision, they would appear before it themselves. While we were in Grozny there were no clashes between them but I heard later that, when we left the city, Supian was shot dead in Yermolovka by persons unknown, who took away his personal Stechkin pistol and rifle.

In encircled Grozny, people both civil and military were dying every day, either at their posts or when moving around. Far more fighters were killed in the latter circumstances, because at their positions they were constantly strengthening and improving their cover, but when they were on the move everything was a matter of luck. At the Headquarters for the Defence of Grozny it was decided to bury dead fighters in Caucasus Park (formerly known as Kirov Park), so that after the war there could be an Avenue of Shahids there. All commanders of defence sectors were urged to have their dead buried there. For me, however, this was all but impossible because the park was far from my sector. We decided to bury our fallen fighters in Aldy. In this we were very greatly helped by the imam of the local mosque, Sheikh Khadzhi, and by Turk-Magomed. They did more than just help: they assumed responsibility for all the melancholy details of caring for our dead. They came to me and explained they had remained in Grozny specifically to render assistance to the defenders of our Fatherland and, in the name of Allah, to take care of burying the fallen. Sheikh Khadzhi said he would like to work within our official government institutions, and I appointed him my deputy for religious matters. He and Turk-Mohamed buried more than forty people, Sheikh Khadzhi personally digging the graves and performing the appropriate rites for the fallen. May the Almighty reward him for that! I remember this man with great gratitude.

Late in December 1999, Russian troops occupied Grozny Airport. The area was manned by the National Guard, and Magomed Khambiev, minister of defence and commander of the National Guard, was responsible for it. In fact, however, from the moment the enemy began advancing along the Sunzha Ridge, positions on this height were manned by fighters of the Presidential Guard. During the Second War, some Russian commanders modified their tactics. In the First War, the enemy had given high priority to trying to take every halfways significant height, even at the cost of enormous casualties. Our Command supposed that this time too Russian troops would try to take the Sunzha Ridge in order to advance along it towards Grozny. We fortified the heights, but the invaders did not in fact assault them, moving on Grozny below the Sunzha Ridge and leaving the Chechen units in their rear. This was unexpected and caused consternation, not to say panic, among our troops in their fortified positions on the Ridge. Ilias Talkhadov, commander of the Presidential Guard, reported on the situation at a meeting at the Headquarters for the Defence of Grozny. He asked for reinforcements to stop the Russians getting past. The occupation forces moved cautiously, sensing that they might find themselves trapped if they faced resistance ahead. In that case, their column could find itself under heavy flanking mortar fire both from above and below. It was a bold and risky move on their part.

Aslanbek Ismailov instructed Magomed Khambiev to use his men from the National Guard to support Ilias Talkhadov and strike at the advancing column, which would have caused panic among the invaders and they would have been routed. This did not happen, however. Minister of Defence Khambiev, commander of the National Guard, failed to carry out the order and made no move. As a result, Ilias had to withdraw his troops from the ridge and move back to the second line of defence, taking up positions in RTS region. The enemy then took Sheikh Mansur Airport and Khankala. Aslanbek Ismailov removed Magomed Khambiev from his post as commander of a defence sector of Grozny and replaced him with Ilias Talkhadov. From then until our retreat from Grozny, Khambiev lay low in the basement of a 9-storey building on Pervomaiskaya Street.

Despite the fact that both the Grozny airports were occupied by Russian troops, Putin decided against coming to Grozny for New Year's Eve as had been planned. On 31 December 1999, when Yeltsin announced his resignation and the transfer of power to Putin, those who had written the decree, the Family, intended that Putin should have been not in Gudermes but in Grozny. I learned this many years after the event when I was already in England. That New Year I listened to Yeltsin's speech in my staff headquarters using a small television set and an NTV satellite dish. He spoke about the successes and failures of his period of rule, and said his biggest mistake had been the war in Chechnya from 1994 to 1996. He tearfully begged the Russian public to forgive him. The sheer cynicism of this statement was that, at the very moment of Yeltsin's public repentance at having unleashed the First Russo-Chechen War, people on both sides were again being killed in Chechnya in a new war he had instigated only a few months earlier. The individual Yeltsin was proclaiming his successor and to whom he was transferring his powers was that same night in Gudermes, now occupied by Russian troops, handing out knives to paratroopers and enjoining them to put them to good use. Frankly, I was revolted, but in no doubt that all the evil currently being perpetrated would continue for a very long time.

VIII

With Friends Like These ...

The Chechen retreat from Grozny is mishandled, with absurd commands issued by Ruslan Gelaev which cause major loss of life. On the eve of the evacuation Zakaev is, for the second time in two days, involved in a car crash in the blackout and has his pelvis broken. His surviving troops are demobilized and urged to find their way back to their homes.

A month and a half previously, Umar from Prigorodnoye had insisted that my family must be evacuated to Georgia through Shatili. He first brought them from Urus-Martan to his home in Prigorodnoye. Before the ring of encirclement closed around Grozny, I went to say goodbye to them, and to assure my mother we would soon be reunited and that in a few weeks' time I would be able to bring them back to Chechnya. My mother believed me and got into the car with the words that she would not be able to bear being in a foreign land for longer than that. My wife quietly asked me what I really thought, and I replied equally quietly, 'Be ready for it to last ten years, and after that we will see.' Listening to Yeltsin that New Year's Night, I knew my prediction about the duration of the Second War was accurate. Hopes that Yeltsin might dump Putin before the presidential election and that hostilities might cease proved unfounded. It was obvious now that the war in Chechnya was integral to Putin's election campaign, and we had to do something dramatic if we wanted to change the situation. I believed that was entirely feasible, if we could shift military operations to the territory of Russia. If the events in Dagestan, got up by Moscow, had been the springboard for Putin's rise to power, then bringing the war to Russia would spell sudden political death for him. In Russia, human rights activists were already sounding the alarm. NTV, still independent of the Kremlin, was screening damning documentaries about events in Chechnya and the apartment bombing in Russian cities. Many independent Russian analysts were predicting that the war might spill out beyond the North Caucasus and into Russia proper. These analysts in effect suggested a way for us to turn the situation round. In an NTV programme featuring four former Russian prime ministers, Sergey Stepashin admitted in public that the decision to restart the war in Chechnya had been taken in March 1998. An e-publication, *Subbota* (*Saturday*, No. 11, 11 March 2004), rebroadcast excerpts from an interview Stepashin gave in 2000, in which he stated that 'The intervention was planned to begin in August-September.' 'It would have gone ahead even if there had been no explosions in Moscow.' 'I was preparing active intervention. We were planning to be to the north of the River Terek in August-September 1999. Putin, who was director of the FSB at this time, had that information.' In other words, Stepashin's statements dispelled the myth that what provoked the outbreak of full-scale hostilities were events in Dagestan and the apartment bombings. He made it unambiguously clear that those events were used purely as a pretext for a new war.

This was further confirmed by Russia's deputy prime minister, Nikolai Koshman, head of the occupation regime in Chechnya. In a programme titled *Hero of the Hour* broadcast on NTV at 7.40 pm on 2 November 1999, Koshman admitted that funds for a new war in Chechnya had been allocated in the previous year's budget, in 1998.

Our experience of armed conflict with Russian troops had shown that they panic when things do not go according to plan. This was clearly demonstrated by our August 1996 operation to liberate Grozny and the rest of the republic. Events did not develop as the enemy expected, and this led to disorientation and defeat. I shared my thoughts on taking the war to Russia with Aslanbek Ismailov, and we began quietly to make preparations. First, we talked to Shamil Basaev to secure his agreement to assume command of the Headquarters for the Defence of Grozny. We also kept Aslan Maskhadov informed. Before the city was sealed off, Mumadi Saidaev and I discussed a plan to strike at the rear of the Russian troops, but did not want to reveal the details to anyone. Shamil Basaev initially gave his consent, and we set a day for leaving Grozny. The day before withdrawing our fighters from their positions I coordinated the matter with Aslanbek and he confirmed the date as the first stage of the operation. Dalkhan and I also agreed that he would remain in the city and assume command of the part of the brigade staying behind. I ordered the fighters leaving the city to bring with them provisions for 5–6 days, which was the amount of time Aslanbek and I calculated was needed for us to get out and join the main group involved in this operation at the agreed place in Russia. Aslanbek and I had previously sent trusted people to muster volunteers. I received confirmation from Khusein Isabaev that he and other commanders were ready to act, and he indicated a total of more than 700 fighters. I was to bring about 400 men with me from Grozny. Aslanbek Ismailov had around 200 men and was relying on being joined by as many again after leaving the capital. Thus, we were counting on having up to 1,500 fighters at our disposal for the operation. For comparison, the size of the team which carried out the Budyonnovsk Raid was only 195 fighters. I appointed Said-Khusein Tazbaev as my deputy for the duration of the operation. I also divided the men into groups of 20 and appointed a commander for each group.

At the agreed time, I brought my men to the venue. This was a pedestrian subway at Minutka Square. When we arrived, there was no one to be seen, although it was already time. I waited ten minutes and then went to the headquarters, which was nearby in the basement of a nine-storey building. We did not use radios in such situations, and so Ibrahim and I walked there. I appointed Said-Khusein Tazbaev to command the fighters during my absence. This constant chain of command was essential, because the situation could change drastically in seconds and call for immediate decisions and orders. Additionally, given the shelling which continued day and night, any of us commanders could be killed at any moment, so the system of deputies was no formality. When I walked into the headquarters, Aslanbek was sitting at a desk and I could immediately see he was very upset. Anticipating my questions, he said,

'Akhmed, I am sorry. It is all off. It seems the operation was of interest only to you and me.'

Shamil Basaev came from the other room, greeted me, and said that he could not assume responsibility for the defence of Grozny.

'I have weighed everything up,' Shamil said, 'and come to the conclusion that if tomorrow the defenders of the city hear a rumour that Ismailov and Zakaev and their men have left Grozny, there will be a panic and I will be unable to tell them the truth.' He paused, and added: 'Everybody will abandon their positions and leave the city and the situation will get out of hand. I will be seen as responsible for the fall of Grozny. So I cannot stand in for Aslanbek. I refuse. Your operation must be cancelled and instead we must strengthen the line of defence all round the perimeter of the positions we hold.'

I believe our failure to go ahead with that operation was a mistake, but Aslanbek was indispensable. He had worked out all the detail during the First War, before the Budyonnovsk Raid. He knew the terrain, the passageways, the environment. Aslanbek had outstanding qualities as a commander and I found him a unique person. He was well versed in politics, economics, construction, and military matters, an erudite, well read man. He was also one of the very few people with a good understanding of how to build a new state. After the First War ended, he made the mistake of going into opposition against Aslan Maskhadov, but quickly realized that was an error and thereafter was one of the Chechen president's most trustworthy supporters. No less indispensable was Shamil Basaev, the only person at that moment capable of replacing Aslanbek as chief of staff for the defence of Grozny. Shamil, however, had said he could not do it. There was some logic to what he said, but I felt then and think today that he was being less than straight with us when he claimed he could not take over the defence of the city for five or six days. Aslanbek and I were intending that, by the end of those five or six days, Grozny would be the last thing on Putin's mind. Once again, though, history does not recognize the conditional tense. We did not go ahead with the planned operation, we did not take the war to the enemy, and this had tragic repercussions. Unfortunately, we made only too many such errors. That night I returned the fighters of my brigade to their former positions, explaining to them that the march on Russia had been indefinitely postponed. Soldiers do not usually ask questions, and I explained to the commanders that not all the details of the planned operation had been fully worked through. I returned to brigade headquarters, where Dalkhan and my other comrades were delighted to see me.

Shortly afterwards, Shamil Basaev, who had none of his own fighters in Grozny at that moment, left the city with Arbi Baraev's group and headed for Yermolovka. Arby was born in that village and told Shamil his information was that the occupying troops seemed to be feeling very relaxed there. Nobody was giving them any trouble, so it should be possible to hit them with a surprise attack to remind them they were unwelcome guests in someone else's country. Shamil went along with the idea, not least, I suspect, because he was feeling a bit guilty at not having let Aslanbek and me leave the city. Shamil and Arbi and their group left Grozny along a corridor we kept open for such purposes. The next day, Russian television reported that Chechen insurgents had attacked a military command post in the village of Yermolovka and that 'retaliatory fire had destroyed all the outlaws.' Shortly afterwards, Shamil reappeared at our brigade headquarters in Chernorechiye and told me they knocked out one armoured personnel carrier and a truck it was escorting to the outskirts of Yermolovka for water. There had been a brief firefight, the enemy was destroyed, and none of the Chechens were injured. Shamil added that Arbi and his men were still in Yermolovka but he had decided to come back before the Russians blocked the corridor they had used.

The Russian troops never succeeded in blocking all the ways in and out of Grozny. During the First War, the adversary deliberately left some ways out of the city in order to reduce the determination with which their advance was opposed. In the Second War, their Army Command set out to completely blockade Grozny, but failed and the city retained several ways out in different directions. These were also used by Chechen women bringing food into Grozny. Right up until the day we withdrew, the city had several outlets where you could buy everything from batteries and electronic components to chocolate bars and toothpaste. Russian pilots deliberately bombed these places, killing or wounding many women, but those who survived just moved to a different place and carried on trading there. It was a feature of these mobile markets that they operated in open areas, and that particularly annoyed the enemy but also raised the spirits of the city's defenders. I am confident that these women were motivated not by greed or purely a desire for profit: it was a protest against what the invaders were doing in Chechnya. Many of the women had close relatives among the defenders of the city. At first they bribed the occupying troops to let them in, explaining they just wanted to make a living and the Russian soldiers did not obstruct them, hoping to glean information about the situation in Grozny from them as they left. However, we soon gave the women one of our secret corridors, and they used that as their only route for entering and leaving the city.

Soon in Staraya Sunzha, on the frontline between our and the Russian forces, we found the positions opposite our fighters occupied by Gantemirovite collaborators, and these women became the first mediators between the collaborators and our Resistance fighters. Our women used the new route to enter and leave Grozny, and the Gantemirovites used them to contact the Headquarters of the Command for the Defence of Grozny and propose a meeting. They asked to be allowed to shoot a video in one of the apartment buildings of Micro-region 6, near Staraya Sunzha, and in exchange offered us a large quantity of 7.62 calibre ammunition, which we were desperately short of, a pile of single-use grenade launchers, and shells for multi-use manual grenade launchers. Aslanbek Ismailov put this proposal to a meeting of the Command and, after a brief discussion, it was agreed. We added a condition that the Gantemirovites must also evacuate our wounded to a place of safety, which they accepted. They really did evacuate some 30 of our wounded fighters, telling the Russians they were their own wounded, and provided us with the ammunition and grenade launchers. The Gantemirovites briefly entered Micro-region 6 and filmed a Russian flag on one of the high-rise blocks.

Subsequently, announcers on Russian TV exultantly announced the 'news' that Russian troops had 'taken control of the city of Grozny,' adding that 'at the present time reconnaissance and search operations are ongoing in the city to destroy the remnants of armed gangs.' This news report, presented in the pompous and emotional tones common in the Stalin era, was illustrated with the Gantemirovites' video. In the same report, Bislan Gantemirov was shown announcing, as he had in the case of Urus-Martan, that he and his 'Chechen rebels,' as he called the collaborators, would have Grozny completely under their control in early February. I saw this report on television, and no doubt everyone following events in Chechnya at that time will remember it. This time I was alarmed. For a month and a half there had been fierce clashes with Russian troops all along the frontline around Grozny. After the enemy had occupied Sheikh Mansur Airport and the military airfield at Khankala, had become entrenched in the fields near Districts 12 and 20, and occupied the area between Alkhan-Yurt and Grozny, they began carpet bombing of the city one square sector at a time. Continuous, intense shelling forced the Chechens to retreat from their positions back to the next line of defence. The invaders consolidated themselves in the positions abandoned by our fighters, brought up vehicles and artillery, and began massive bombing of the new Chechen positions.

There was fighting round the villages of Michurin, RTS, and Chernorechiye, and in Districts 12, 20, and 30. Russian troops occupied the entire Staropromyslovsky region as far as Grozneftyanaya and, very slowly and suffering heavy losses, moved towards the city centre. They occupied all the strategic high ground dominating the city: the Grozny Ridge, Karpinsky Kurgan, and Syuir-Kort. From these heights the invaders directed artillery fire at anything that moved and incessantly bombarded the nine-storey block housing Aslanbek Ismailov's headquarters. This had caused many of those visiting the headquarters over the past week to suffer shrapnel wounds. In order to safeguard his staff and commanders coming to the headquarters, Aslanbek was forced to move from Minutka Square to another place, four people remaining at the Minutka building to redirect commanders to his new headquarters location. A few days later, the building of the old headquarters collapsed from the shelling. The four fighters were buried alive in the basement and it was only in spring 2000 that their families were able to recover their remains from the rubble and bury them.

On 24 January 2000, I received a message from headquarters to attend an urgent meeting that night of all commanders defending the approaches to the capital. Because of the shelling, we drove only at night and with doused headlights. For my own brigade, the open area between Chernorechiye and Okruzhnaya was particularly vulnerable because the enemy troops had the precise range of the road running through it. When darkness fell, four of us decided to make a dash across it in a small Lada. Anzor was driving, with Shaaman in the front passenger seat, and Said-Khusein Tazbaev and me in the back.

There are two roads from Chernorechiye to the city centre. One option was for us to follow a gully to the left of the Grozny Reservoir dam and, if all went well, come out at Okruzhnaya. The alternative was to drive across the dam to Aldy and go on to Okruzhnaya from there. Nearly everybody chose the first route, because there was little chance of making it over the dam in one piece. Anzor turned left into the gully and put his foot down.

As we were coming up in the darkness out of the gully towards Okruzhnaya, a UAZ off-roader suddenly appeared in front of us and we crashed into it. No one was seriously hurt and we were all able to get out of the vehicles but, before we had time to speak, there was a massive explosion. It was so deafening that at first we did not understand what had happened. The lads who had crashed into us managed to start their UAZ and drove off, but our Lada just would not start. We pushed it over on to the verge and continued on foot. When we came up to the railway hospital we saw a huge crater caused by a blockbuster bomb, at the bottom of which another UAZ was lying on its side. We called to its occupants, hoping someone might have survived, and I was surprised that within a few minutes quite a crowd gathered. I and my companions were only too aware that, but for our minor accident, the bomb would have landed on us.

In war you do come to believe in Providence, and that makes you, not so much brave as confident that no bullets or shrapnel or fire can harm you unless, by the will of the Almighty, they are destined for you. Conversely, however, you believe that there is no escape in this world from what is fated. Commenting on the failed Russian-backed assault on Grozny of 26 November 1994, just before the official outbreak of the First Russo-Chechen War, Djohar Dudaev said that in war only the first 15 minutes are frightening. At the time the words of our founding president puzzled me, but later, when myself under heavy fire, I understood. If a fighter is not killed in those first 15 minutes, he undergoes a kind of psychological rebirth. War engenders a strong belief in predestination. That is the only explanation I can find for the fact that, in spite of the continuous shelling and bombing of the city, at any time of the day or night you could meet fighters and civilians moving around Grozny, going about their business.

Seeing that any occupants of the vehicle who had survived now had people to take care of them, we lost no more time at the crater and went on. As we headed into the city centre we several times came under shellfire and had to take cover. The blanket bombardment, with the enemy firing from different locations, was continuing. The din from explosions was incessant and had a major psychological impact. As far as the Russian military were concerned, Grozny was an enemy city they were going to raze to the ground, destroying every living thing in the process. Probably no other city in the world has been subjected to such total destruction twice within the space of five years. Everything we had endured in the First War was now nightmarishly repeated: the ruins of housing blocks black against the grimy snow, lit up at night by flames and the bursting of flares; the grey twilight days beneath a smoke-laden sky. The only difference from the First War was that now there were no dogs running wild, and no corpses for them to feed on. While the city was under our control, the dead were buried without delay.

To get from Okruzhnaya to headquarters took us several hours. I went in and found Abdul-Malik Mezhidov and Shamil Basaev still there with Aslanbek, but Ruslan Gelaev and Ilias Talkhadov had already left. Aslanbek explained why he had summoned all the city's defending commanders. Gelaev had approached him, saying he had had a bad dream and urging that we should withdraw from Grozny and redeploy to the mountains. He believed we would suffer very heavy casualties, losing most of the forces of the Resistance, if we did not move out within the next few days. The Russian leaders were aware the main Chechen forces and nearly all our senior commanders were concentrated in Grozny. They might resort to anything, including the use of nuclear or chemical weapons. This had already been proposed by the right-wing politician Vladimir Zhirinovsky, and rumours that they might be used against us had been circulating since the time of the First War. We found it disturbing that the Russian media had recently been claiming Chechens had excavated the radioactive waste site at the Radon plant in Grozny and were also using chemical weapons against Russian troops. Needless to say, there was not a word of truth in this, but we suspected the enemy was preparing to use these weapons against us and, with their usual cynicism, would blame their crime on those against whom they were perpetrating it.

In the light of this, Gelaev believed we needed to withdraw our units and disperse them throughout the republic. He supported this by arguing that, if we did withdraw from the city, the Russian generals would consider they had won a victory and decide there was no need for the extreme measure of using weapons of mass destruction.

There was some force in this argument, but I reminded those present of the recent appearance on Russian television by Bislan Gantemirov, the deputy representative of the Russian Federation in Chechnya, in which he had promised he would be in full control of Grozny by early February. Aslanbek replied that they had discussed that issue before I arrived, and a majority of the commanders were in favour of keeping to our previously agreed plan. This was that we should continue to defend Grozny until after the Russian presidential election in March, and then conduct an orderly withdrawal from the city, occupying instead all the plateau and highland regions of the republic. The Russian military were constantly claiming they had all areas 'under complete control' and, of course, our taking over these towns and villages would be a conspicuous military and political success for us.

We were additionally planning large-scale military operations on enemy territory. These were to be operations which Putin and the Russian propaganda machine would be unable to present as acts of terrorism. There would be no hostage-taking, and attacks would target strictly legitimate military targets, as well as dual purpose strategic targets with both civilian and military uses. That evening Shamil Basaev remained conspicuously silent on the subject.

Soon Abdul-Malik and I said goodbye to Shamil and Aslanbek and left the headquarters. Aslanbek gave me a car with a driver who took us safely back to Chernorechiye. Upon arrival, I told Dalkhan Khozhaev everything we had discussed. He was very suspicious, not of Gelaev but of some members of his team, in particular, of Suleyman Aslambekov. Dalkhan believed Aslambekov and several others in Gelaev's inner circle were potential traitors and manipulating him. At the time I put his words down to the fact that in the interwar period he had had a public argument with Suleyman Aslambekov in the Chechen media. In fact, however, Dalkhan was correct: Suleyman Aslambekov played a crucial role in getting Gelaev to withdraw his troops from the defence sector for which he was responsible, without agreeing this action with the Headquarters for the Defence of Grozny, and thus forced withdrawal from the city. When we met in Poland some years later, Aslambekov confirmed to me the part he had played in Gelaev's abandoning of his positions.

The following day I was again contacted by the Headquarters for the Defence of Grozny and asked to come back that evening. I asked Sulambek, the commander of one of our detachments, to find me a driver and vehicle.

My own driver, Anzor, was suffering chest pain from the previous night's collision, when he had impacted with the steering wheel. Half an hour later a UAZ arrived for me from Sulambek. The driver was called Ruslan. Once again the three of us got into the car, but this time Said-Khusein sat next to the driver while Shaaman and I took the back seat. When darkness fell, we drove out along the same route as the day before, with the lights switched off. When we reached the filling station, I saw a car coming towards us. Yesterday's accident was still fresh in my memory, and a sixth sense told me we were about to crash again. I just had a fraction of a second to brace myself. I felt a blow but no pain, just a flash of light in my eyes and then lapsed into unconsciousness.

I do not know how long I was unconscious, but finally I heard the weak echo in my head of someone calling my name. I opened my eyes and saw Vakha, one of my commanders, whom Shaaman had radioed. I realized I was lying on the ground and tried to get up but, apart from my arms, my body did not obey me. I was lying on white snow and saw my right leg twisted at an unnatural angle. I tried to move it but could not. Repeating the attempt, I felt such acute pain that I fainted again. When I recovered consciousness, I heard voices and called out. Several people came and leaned over me, among them Shaaman. I asked what had happened. He told me there had been an accident, and I immediately remembered who I had been travelling with and why, and the last moments before the collision. Shaaman's head was bandaged. I asked him about Said-Khusein and Ruslan and he said they were both alive. He had sent them to hospital and I was about to be taken there myself. I looked back at my legs, and they were already in a normal position. I could move the toes of my left foot, but could not feel my right leg at all, as if it had been torn off.

I was lifted up, put in a vehicle, and Shaaman and Vakha came with me. I did not know the lad who was driving and do not remember his name, although he introduced himself and told me he drove to the Chernorechiye spring to fetch water and that his detachment was stationed somewhere in Voykova. We soon reached the hospital, which was situated in a bomb shelter in Zavodskoy region. This was its third location because the Russians deliberately targeted it for shelling. Previously, the shelter had been home to Baudin Bakuev's group, but he had vacated the basement in favour of the wounded. The Russian Command somehow managed to find out quickly where our wounded were being treated and targeted those places for massive shelling and bombing. The car stopped before reaching the entrance. About ten metres from the descent to the shelter was what seemed to be a trench. I was dragged along it and then we were inside the makeshift hospital. It was hot and packed with people in white coats and bearded men in military uniform, of whom the latter were definitely the majority. When we entered a buzz went round the cellar, 'They've brought Zakaev in. Zakaev has been wounded.' It was only then I noticed that Shaaman and I were both covered in blood. Although his head was bandaged, he had obviously been bleeding profusely before that and his clothes, like mine, were soaked in blood.

Umar Khambiev immediately appeared in the corridor and asked what had happened. Shaaman explained we had been in a road accident and Umar had us moved to a room where I was put on a metal table. He began to examine me from the head down, dictating to a nurse: 'Wound to the back of the head, nasal septum broken, jaw and neck vertebrae undamaged, three lower ribs broken on the right hand side, right leg dislocated, possible hip fracture. We would need an X-ray to be sure.' Umar called the anaesthetist, a nurse came, gave me an injection and, after a short while, began asking me my name, where I lived, what I did for a living. I confess I was a bit surprised because all the talk in the hospital seemed to be about the fact that 'Zakaev has been brought in.' Noticing my puzzlement, Umar said, 'Akhmed, she knows who you are. She just wants to know when the anaesthetic has kicked in.'

Then I found myself hurtling through a narrow maze at very high speed. I saw a bright light in front of me which was getting larger as I approached. I had a sense that when I reached that bright place I would be at peace. After what seemed like just a few seconds, I heard Umar asking, 'Akhmed, can you hear me?' I replied that I could and asked, 'What was that?' Umar said they had done everything they could, and asked me to move my legs. I tried, and succeeded. I could wriggle both my right and left feet. Umar said my hip had been dislocated and they had put my leg back in place. He had had a lot of trouble with the leg muscles and that had meant the operation took several hours. An X-ray would be needed to check out my hip. Umar said that, even if there was no fracture, there was certainly a crack. He said he had reset my nose and told me not to pull out the wads of cotton wool in my nostrils. He continued talking, but I was suddenly so drowsy I could hardly hear him.

When I woke up, I found Isa Astemirov, Ruslan Gelaev's chief of staff, looking down on me. He said there had been three of their fighters in the car we crashed into. Fortunately none were killed, but they all had fractures to their arms or legs. The only person in the two cars not to have broken a limb was Shaaman. Said-Khusein had an open fracture of his right leg above the knee. Ruslan, our driver, had broken both legs and one arm. They were all in the same hospital as me. Umar came and told me that in the past six weeks more than 150 people had been injured in car accidents, and a third of them had died.

Shortly after Isa Astemirov left, Ibrakhim, Shaikhi, and Dalkhan came in to tell me he had just been killed. As he was driving away from the hospital, his car was riddled with shrapnel. They dragged him back to the hospital, but it had remained only for the doctors to pronounce him dead. Dalkhan also told me that, at the meeting we had failed to reach at the Headquarters for the Defence of Grozny, it had been decided to leave the city at the beginning of February. The decision had to be taken because Ruslan Gelaev had withdrawn his men from their positions in District 30 and Michurin, with the result that the enemy was already in the Minutka region. Russian troops had broken through Grozny's defensive ring and, to avoid a disorderly withdrawal, it had been decided to retreat. After the abandonment of Urus-Martan, this was the second time in a row that our soldiers would be abandoning their positions on the precise date publicly predicted by Bislan Gantemirov. To this day, I do not know whether this was coincidence, the result of treachery, or collusion on terms favourable to both sides. Possibly Bislan Gantemirov knew that Moscow was preparing to use weapons of mass destruction and warned Ruslan Gelaev and Shamil Basaev, both of whom he had known since the early 1990s when they were effectively fighting on the same side. That is a question only Bislan Gantemirov can answer, as the other two are no longer alive. It remains a mystery to me.

Dalkhan told me that, if Umar Khambiev would allow it, they would like to take me to our own infirmary in Chernorechiye. Many of the commanders wanted to visit me and moving around the city was extremely dangerous. Many people were being killed on their way to visit the hospital.

At this moment, we heard Umar Khambiev out in the corridor. He was scolding our fighters in Russian and Chechen at the same time, and also trying to comfort someone. We heard loud laughter. Dalkhan looked out and asked him to come to our ward. Umar and Dalkhan both belonged to the Beno Teip, as Dalkhan jokingly emphasized by calling him *'taipan vash'* ('Teip brother'). We asked him what was going on out there. It turned out that a Russian conscript who had been shot in the head was in the same ward as Chechen fighters. He was already recovering and the Chechens, who were lying there with limbs torn off, decided to wind him up by discussing in Russian whether it was permissible for Muslims to use Christian body parts for a donor transplant. They had a lively debate on the issue, eventually coming to the conclusion that the religious rules did allow it during jihad. They then began debating how they should share out the Russian soldier's limbs among themselves. As the Russian did not have enough arms and legs to go round, they started throwing dice. They wrote their names on scraps of paper, and grouped themselves on the basis of which particular limb they were missing, each group throwing dice to win the arm or leg they lacked. It was all being done very seriously, the participants congratulating the winners of each arm or leg, and consoling the losers that they would get their needful limb when new prisoners arrived. When the casting of lots came to the soldier's last limb, his left leg, he decided they were serious and, seeing Umar Khambiev in the doorway, shouted, 'Doctor, help me! They want to cut off my last leg!'

There was Homeric laughter in the ward. Umar at first thought someone was actually intending to kill the prisoner and began reprimanding our soldiers. When he saw it was all just a joke, he reassured the conscript and came in to see me.

I asked Umar to discharge me, as there was no more they could do for me, and all the more so because I learned that the nurses had given up their living accommodation to provide me with a private ward. Umar said he would give me some painkillers, adding that there really was no more they could do. I asked how long it would be before I would be back on my feet. He replied that without X-rays he could not say for sure but, from what he already knew, he thought it would be at least three months, and that full recovery would take a year to eighteen months. That was not what I wanted to hear and I mentally questioned his prognosis. I thanked Umar for all he had done, and the same day my friends took me from the hospital. Our brigade headquarters had moved to a new location near the southern bus station, in the grounds of a chemical factory.

That night Shamil Basaev and Aslanbek Ismailov came to see me. They talked about the military situation in Grozny, told me that Ruslan Gelaev had withdrawn his fighters from all their positions, and confirmed what Dalkhan had already said, that they were organizing an orderly retreat from the city. The moves we had planned for March were being brought forward to the beginning of February. I did not express my suspicions that this forced decision was related to Bislan Gantemirov's announcement, and Aslanbek immediately moved on to practical issues. Given the changed circumstances and the state of my health it was obvious that I could not participate in these operations, so Aslanbek suggested I should appoint someone as commander of my unit who would report directly to him. He also told me that the withdrawal was scheduled for 30 January. Before coming in to see me, he had made arrangements for the hospital to be closed and for all the wounded to be evacuated from the city. Aslanbek said Bislan Gantemirov had agreed he could take all our wounded out through Staraya Sunzha, and only I would be taken out by the same route as our fighters. Shamil Basaev elaborated that we would withdraw along the corridor we had kept open in the direction of Yermolovka. He added that after his raid with Arbi Baraev, Russian sappers had mined one of the sections of the corridor, so he and a few other people were beginning mine clearance today and he hoped they would have completed the job by the thirtieth.

When Shamil and Aslanbek had said goodbye, I had a meeting with the commanders of detachments of our brigade who had came to the headquarters to see me. Neither of my deputies, Khusein Isabaev or Said-Khusein Tazbaev, could take command of the brigade because Khusein was away in the city, and Said-Khusein had been injured at the same time as me. I told the commanders that command of the brigade was temporarily assigned to our chief of staff, Dalkhan Khozhaev. We discussed plans for our future operations in detail at this meeting. Dalkhan would coordinate all actions with Aslanbek Ismailov, deputy commander-in-chief. Dalkhan had been deputizing for me for several days at meetings of the Headquarters for the Defence of Grozny.

The three days remaining before 30 January were spent preparing to leave the city. Although I am calling it a withdrawal, it was in fact intended to be the first phase of the full-scale military operation already mentioned. On 30 January 2000 at 21.00 hours I conducted a last inspection of my brigade in Chernorechiye. Over 1,000 fighters were listed as present at the parade, and I asked Dalkhan how it was that we had had a brigade of 900 men, of whom more than 70 had been killed or wounded, and yet now our ranks numbered more than 1,000 fighters. He explained that the 'recruits' were civilians and fighters who had been holed up somewhere, even though they had weapons. They had not manned our positions but, when there was talk of withdrawing from Grozny, had started turning up at our headquarters asking to be enrolled. Dalkhan had allocated them to units which had suffered the worst casualties. I advised him not to rely on them too much. He agreed, and added that the decision to enrol them in combat units had been taken at the Headquarters for the Defence of Grozny.

Including this remarkable bolstering of numbers, the total list of fighters leaving the city was over 7,000 men. The line of defence around the perimeter of Grozny had been held all this time by just over 3,500 fighters. It seemed a similar number of armed men had just been sitting it out in cellars, taking no part in the fighting. I am sure that if the Headquarters for the Defence of Grozny had had 7,000 fighters at its disposal, we could have taken military operations to Russian territory without having to withdraw from the city. Be that as it may, the decision to leave Grozny had been taken and our brigade was ready to carry out any mission our Command might order.

Remembering my brigade, I have only great gratitude and admiration for those young fighters and their commanders. These were courageous Nokhchi, true patriots ready to give their lives, as many of them did, in the name of Allah and for the honour and freedom of the Chechen people. They had little cause to be grateful to those in authority over them, but they were fighting not for particular individuals or big names, but for a free Chechen nation.

I was seeing most of them for the last time that evening. Shaaman, Ibrakhim, Anzor and Muslim put together a wooden sledge for me and brought me on it to where my fighters were lined up on parade. I told them that no matter how this war might end, they were already the victors and now their first priority must be to survive. I said that in all sincerity, because these lads were the best stock of our nation, and if they were lost we would cease to exist as a viable ethnic group. That really would have been a final, irreversible defeat in our long war against an empire bent on destroying the Chechens as a people and determined to eradicate our love of freedom. The spirit of freedom cannot exist without brave men and women willing to sacrifice their lives for humanity's highest ideals. In support of that claim I quoted Djohar Dudaev, the first president of the Chechen Republic of Ichkeria. When asked how long the war would last, Djohar said he believed two warrior peoples, the Russians and the Chechens, were in a confrontation which would last fifty years, and the victor would be the nation which managed to survive and retain its national identity and honour.

I still remember the faces of those fighters, young, not so young, and even elderly, with their faith in the rightness of their cause and their ultimate victory. These were people who had defied the most feared army in the world, which never counted how many men and women it lost, and never shunned sadistic brutality against a defenceless civilian population. These fighters had, with full knowledge of what they were doing, risen up against an army a hundred times more numerous than our own. I saw no shadow of fear or despondency on their faces, although many of them were destined to die within the next few hours.

That evening, I gave my final order to the brigade and we were on our way. Elsi from Gekhi led the way, Ibrakhim was at the centre, and Sulambek brought up the rear. After an hour or so we joined up with the main column, which was moving towards Yermolovka. As we advanced, we could heard explosions and shooting. The column slowed down. Elsi contacted us to report that the path ahead had not been completely cleared of mines. After the first explosions as our fighters trod on them, the enemy intensified their shelling of this stretch. A little later we received a report from Elsi's deputy that Shamil Basaev had been blown up by a mine and lost both legs. After that Aslanbek Ismailov and Abu Movsaev came to me from where the mine had exploded to say we had lost some 40 men dead or wounded. These were major losses, but we stood to lose many more fighters if we failed to enter Yermolovka by dawn. Accordingly, Shamil Basaev had addressed his fighters and called upon them to use their bodies to clear this stretch of the path of mines, and had been the first to march forward. He trod on a mine almost immediately and the men dragged him back. Then, one by one, other fighters went out. When one was killed or injured, he was dragged back and another walked forward. So it continued until we had passed that stretch of the path.

Shamil's wounding seriously impacted on our plans, but Aslanbek reassured me by saying he would replace Shamil with Khunkar Israpilov. Aslanbek went back into the city to make sure that no unit under his command had been left behind, and was himself the last person in the column. As he departed, Aslanbek said that we would now be able to move forward more quickly, adding that he would see me in Yermolovka, so we did not bid each other farewell.

The column moved in single file, each man following in the footsteps of those who had used their bodies to provide safe passage through a minefield to 7,000 of their fellow fighters. By the time we reached this place, dawn was already breaking. We passed through a ravine, climbed up out of it, and again began descending into the gully with the minefield. As we came down, I heard the voice of Ruslan Gelaev. He had halted the column and was passionately urging that, as it was already light, we should return to the city and fight to the last, to give our descendants an example of how to carry out jihad. I knew what Gelaev was proposing was completely contrary to our plans, and that to drag our withdrawal from Grozny out for several days would be catastrophic. The success of our operation was highly dependent on the element of surprise. In the three days it would take the Russian Command to respond to our unexpected retreat, it was essential for us to reach the towns and villages we were planning to liberate. Gelaev's proposal was tantamount to sabotaging the entire operation. I told Shaaman to go and tell Gelaev that was not on. On the contrary, we needed to advance as quickly as possible before it was completely light. Shaaman, much younger than Gelaev, could not bring himself to interrupt him. When Gelaev finished his peroration, Shaaman asked what they should do with Akhmed Zakaev, to which Gelaev replied that they should take me back with them to Grozny. Through Shaaman I passed a message to Sulambek, who was bringing up the rear of our brigade, to continue to follow us to Yermolovka. Gelaev led the rest back into the city, yet another fatal blunder for which Chechens paid a heavy price.

As we were passing through the minefield, I was struck by something I had not seen in the course of the two wars. I heard voices calling for help and, looking more closely, saw several men in white camouflage suits lying in the snow. They had evidently tried to overtake the column which was moving slowly along the narrow corridor cleared of mines, and had been blown up. I was shocked that everyone was walking silently past these wounded soldiers without attempting to help. These people were probably from the ranks of the Redskin malingerers. Our fighters did not stop to help them for two reasons. First, stopping would have held up the entire column, putting at additional risk the lives of thousands of men. It was by now light and the Russian Command might well be aware that this column was on the move, because forward detachments had entered Yermolovka where the enemy had a command post. Although the garrison did not take any action itself, it would certainly have reported our arrival to the Russian Command, which meant that at any moment aircraft and helicopters might appear on the scene and be able to annihilate our units in these open minefields. The second reason, of course, was more personal. The men in our combat units had no time for Redskins who, all these weeks of fighting, had been safely hiding in basements while many of our positions were acutely short of fighters. They had made the situation today more dangerous by finally emerging. By doubling the size of the column they had greatly increased the time needed for our march towards Yermolovka. It was precisely because of them that we were still under way when dawn broke and made us vulnerable to air and artillery attack. For all that, I found the situation horrifying. I had those plaintive cries for help ringing in my ears for a long time afterwards, and remember the sight to this day. It was in glaring contrast to my understanding of how Chechens behave, and I firmly believe it could never have happened in the First War. It was one more result of what happened after the war, when we all split into political and religious factions and lost our sense of solidarity.

When we entered Yermolovka, we were billeted in people's homes. Shirvani, whom I had known since the First War, came and offered me his hospitality. I declined it, but asked him to organize people to rescue the wounded Redskins left in the minefield. After lunch, he came and told me it had all been done. They had thrown ropes with hooks to the wounded from the cleared path and had dragged them over. One was unlucky and got blown up by another mine. Three others had survived. Shirvani and his helpers brought them to Yermolovka and put them in the local hospital. He later brought Dr Khasan Baiev to see me. He examined me and said that in the current circumstances there was nothing he could do beyond changing the bandage on my head. Khasan did a tremendous job caring for the wounded and his work made him world famous. He wrote a book about it titled *The Oath: A Surgeon Under Fire*.[7]

That day, the mothers of young men in my brigade came to Yermolovka from all over the republic. Praise be to Allah, all the young people who joined our brigade in the autumn and underwent training came out of Grozny alive and in one piece. One group we had sent to the border with Georgia for weapons was stranded there because the enemy had blocked the gorge the road passed through. From Ingushetia the occupation forces cut a clearing through the forest to the border with Georgia, cutting off the road to Shatili. It was clear now why Russia had not prevented us from constructing that road, and had even financed the work. Ibrakhim told the mothers their sons were safe in Tbilisi and that, when conditions allowed, they could go there to collect them. He explained they were with my family, and gave a phone number where they could be contacted. The women were delighted, and I too was very glad these young people had survived. Except for Akhmed Chitaev from Vedeno, none of them were injured. Akhmed suffered a shrapnel wound during shelling and lost his right arm. We immediately sent him home via Staraya Sunzha. All the other young fighters, as I said, were alive and well and their mothers took many of them home. I had told Dalkhan to talk to the boys beforehand and ask them to obey their mothers and go home with them. In order to stop them objecting, Dalkhan was to assure them we would be needing them later.

---

[7] Khassan Baiev, *The Oath: A Surgeon Under Fire*, London: Simon and Schuster, 2003.

IX

Hors de Combat

Refusing to be evacuated, Zakaev is eventually forced to recognize he is now no longer useful and is endangering the lives of those entrusted with his security. A traitor tries to deliver him into the hands of the Russian army but his bodyguards enable him to escape to Urus-Martan. Eventually, by bribing Chechen police and FSB agents, he is spirited across the frontier to Ingushetia.

To my surprise, the occupying army did not bomb Yermolovka, but brought up armour and resumed laying mines on the path by which we had reached the village the previous night. Dalkhan and 'Big' Aslanbek Abdulkhadzhiev came to tell me this, and report that they had sent people to warn Aslanbek Ismailov and the other commanders in Grozny about the re-mining of the route, which indicated that this time the enemy would be on the alert. Dalkhan and Aslanbek also told me they had had a meeting with the commanders and decided that the main forces concentrated in Yermolovka should leave during the night and move westwards towards the villages of Kulary and Zakan-Yurt. The group of 400 men of my brigade under Aslanbek Ismailov's command remained in Yermolovka, but Dalkhan led the rest towards Zakan-Yurt. Shaaman, Ibrakhim, Anzor, and Muslim remained with me. They spent the day repairing the sledge, which had all but fallen apart on the exodus from Grozny, and Shirvani took us by bus to the village outskirts where they lifted me out on to it.

Before we set off, Ibrakhim gave me an injection of painkiller and we headed out into the snowy fields in the wake of our brigade. Shirvani sent one of his relatives to guide us. On the whole journey we rested only once, and within a few hours reached Zakan-Yurt. We were greeted by local people on the outskirts, who saw us into the village. They took it in turns, anticipating that our fighters would be arriving all night. We were taken to a detached house in a courtyard. The owner came and asked me about the situation and prospects for the future. Many people believed that a commander of my rank must have all the answers. They supposed we had thought through every step. What they really wanted to know was when all these horrors would end, and none of us had the answer to that. Only a profound faith in the Almighty gave people the strength to endure all their sufferings without losing their minds or their faith. Everyone I talked to was hoping that Russia would soon open negotiations and the war would end. I did not disillusion them. We were given a delicious meal and the owner left, wishing me a swift recovery. All this time we could hear the rumble of artillery fire, but the village was not attacked that night, the enemy only shelling the outskirts and the fields. The Russian Command had a fair idea, and probably knew for a fact, where we were because they had informers in every locality reporting our movements. Mainly, however, as became evident, the enemy was concentrating its main forces at the point where those of our fighters who had returned with Gelaev would have to leave Grozny. The commanders, despite our warning, decided to leave by the same route as before. This decision, taken on a great wave of emotion, was another huge blunder which led to our first major losses in either of the wars. More than 200 fighters were to die, and many more were wounded.

When Gelaev led over 3,500 people back into the city, which included a large number of civilians, Aslanbek Ismailov charged him with disrupting our planned operations. Without going into the details of their discussion, I have to say that our leaders failed to analyse the situation in the light of the information that were given by Dalkhan Khozhaev and Aslanbek Abdulkhadzhiev. I believe the decision they took the following day to leave by the same route was dictated by Aslanbek Ismailov's determination to initiate the planned operations at the time previously agreed with the commanders. Khunkar Israpilov was appointed in place of Shamil Basaev to take responsibility for the lowland territory of Chechnya from the Ingush border to Saadi-Kotar (Komsomolskoye). Responsibility for the highland regions of Chechnya from this point to the border with Georgia was entrusted to Ruslan Gelaev. Aslanbek Ismailov remained responsible for conducting operations on the territory of Russia. Yermolovka was a convenient spot for all three commanders to move on to their areas of responsibility.

I mention all this because, when the following day the Chechens suffered heavy casualties in the withdrawal from Grozny, the enemy began claiming some fictitious operation by the Russian intelligence agencies had 'lured the Chechen insurgents into minefields.' This was a barefaced lie. Our commanders did commit a serious error in taking the fighters back along this route, but the enemy had no part in that decision. On the contrary, in again laying mines on the path to Yermolovka, the Russian Command was aiming not to lure our fighters in this direction but to block the route. The main reason for the fateful decision was not any cunning operation on the part of the Russians but the bravado of young Chechen commanders who did not want to lose face in front of each other and, to an even greater extent, in front of those under their command. None of the commanders who took this decision wanted to appear cowardly by being the first to state the very obvious fact that proceeding along this route for a second time was extremely dangerous.

There was a fundamental difference between the Chechen military Command and the Command of the Russian Army. The commander of a Chechen armed detachment holds his post not as a consequence of a military career in the conventional sense, where promotion is decided on such factors as military training or the number of years served. To be a Chechen commander indicates a kind of social status in time of war. That is acquired as a result of personal qualities demonstrated in extreme situations and assessed more by rank-and-file soldiers than by superiors. The Chechen Army did, of course, also have more academic rules for appointing the officer corps. For example, our first presidents and commanders-in-chief, Djohar Dudaev and Aslan Maskhadov, had been serving officers in the Soviet Army, educated in Soviet military academies. They tried to form the Chechen Armed Forces into an army in the classic sense, but I was an eyewitness of how, when appointing commanders, they were obliged to take account of unwritten rules. I remember several occasions when Djohar and Aslan appointed someone commander of a unit or gave them command over a direction, only to rescind the appointment when their appointees were not accepted by the troops.

The most important difference between Chechen and Russian commanders was, of course, that the former led their troops from the front, never sitting out danger in a safe place like their Russian counterparts. A Chechen commander could not put his subordinates in harm's way if he was not prepared to share the danger with them. These traditions, rooted deep in our history, meant that a Chechen commander was very sensitive to anything affecting his honour, and most of all feared being suspected of cowardice. Most of the time, these qualities brought us victory, but sometimes they could have negative consequences, because in war a commander's courage must be tempered by prudence. The negative consequences were only too evident in the episode we are describing.

The following night of 31 January 2000, as our troops again began withdrawing from Grozny, we were in Zakan-Yurt. I listened in on the radio to what our soldiers coming out of the city were saying to those in

Yermolovka. I heard them say Mansur had been killed. This was Aslanbek Ismailov's codename. I did not believe the news and decided it was deliberate misinformation of a kind which spread like wildfire in Chechnya. It would reach the enemy, immediately find its way into the media, and be officially confirmed by the Russian Command, with much imaginative embellishment. They seemed little troubled that it would subsequently be disproved by the facts. We often exploited our enemy's enthusiasm for confirming uncomfirmed rumours about the death of well known Chechen commanders to score points against them on the information battlefield. This had been the case with Salman Raduev in 1996, whose death was officially proclaimed by the enemy and whose reappearance enabled us to show the Russian public how little reliance they should place on official announcements made by the Russian Command. I took the news of Aslanbek Ismailov's death to be an example of this. After the Russian generals had crowed to reporters about their latest achievement in killing a top commander of the Chechen Armed Forces, his appearance at the head of a thousand-strong battalion in the heartland of Russia would be particularly effective. That was what I wanted to believe, although knowing that our troops were repeating their withdrawal from Grozny along yesterday's route, I had a bad presentiment.

The withdrawal went on almost until morning. I did not turn off the radio and all night heard gunfire and the thunder of explosions. This was not a battle, because the enemy was well out of reach, as I could tell from what the Chechens were saying among themselves. The occupying army just fired incessantly at a column of fighters advancing through a minefield using all manner of weaponry, so the casualties were on the Chechen side. Russian generals gloated over that, embroidering their tales with all sorts of claptrap. One myth had a Russian FSB officer selling the Chechens a map showing all the minefields and safe passages through them. The Chechens were supposedly so stupid that they bought the map for several hundred thousand dollars and walked into a trap. There were various other no less improbable fantasies in circulation. Like almost everything else the Russian Command put out about the war, this was not information but misinformation intended to dupe the Russian man-in-the-street who believes everything he sees and hears on television. For us, however, the bitter truth was that during the night we suffered the worst casualties of either of the wars. Among the dead and wounded were many civilians who, knowing that our units were leaving Grozny, decided to come out with them.

The enemy had a major military success which had nothing to do with the propaganda claims flooding the airwaves. That night and in the preceding few days, many of the most senior Chechen commanders were killed or wounded. Isa Astemirov, Gelaev's chief of staff, was killed. Shamil Basaev lost a leg. Lecha Dudaev, the mayor of Grozny, died. Musa Dadaev was wounded. The death of our deputy commander-in-chief, Aslanbek Ismailov, was confirmed. He and Dokka Umarov were bringing up the rear of the column when a shell exploded nearby. Aslanbek and a young fellow, whose name I do not remember, who ran errands for him and was universally known as the Little Lad, were killed and Dokka Umarov was seriously wounded. Khunkar Israpilov also died. Like Shamil Basaev, he had been at the head of the column and was among the first to deliberately walk on to the minefield. Khunkar was a fearless fighter and talented commander. Over the years we had become friends. He had a very effective fighting force and Aslanbek Ismailov constantly sent him to hotspots where our fighters needed support. I met Khunkar several times at headquarters and when I asked, 'How are you?' he would reply, 'Despite Aslanbek's best efforts to kill me off, I am still alive.' He continued, 'He is relentless. 'Go here, Khunkar, the Russians have been trying to storm us there for several days.' 'Go there, Khunkar, relieve that group who have had no respite for two weeks.' I just wish he would give me a defence sector of my own so I could take it easy.' 'You can take it easy when you are dead,' Aslanbek replied.

The deaths of Aslanbek Ismailov and Khunkar Israpilov were an irreparable loss, not least because these two commanders were to lead the counteroffensive which we believed could turn the situation round. That was the enemy's real victory, not the fact that it had shelled several hundred Chechens, including a large number of civilians, with long-range artillery.

The next day, Dalkhan and two of his deputies, Ali and Abbas, came and gave me the details of the withdrawal. In the light of the changed situation we needed to amend our objectives. It was obvious that the operations we had planned could not now be realized, which meant that the period of head-on confrontation of the enemy was over. We needed time to regroup and work out a new strategy. Right now we had to decide what to do with our brigade. After conferring with Dalkhan, I decided to stand the brigade down and send our men home to await orders from the commanders of their units as to when and where to regroup. Those who did not want to return home could join Khusein Isabaev in Shatoy. Our brigade included fighters from towns and villages all over the republic. The unit commanders' details were held at headquarters, but we knew that after dissolving the brigade it would be virtually impossible to reassemble it. Our experience from the First War suggested we would be lucky to bring back even 20% of the current strength.

Despite this, we had little option but to release the fighters in order to minimize casualties.

Dalkhan said he had just come from a meeting with the commanders of other units at which they had discussed further action and a route for moving on: from Yermolovka to Zakan-Yurt to Shaami-Yurt to Katar-Yurt to Valerik to Gekhi-Chu to Roshni-Chu to Saadi-Kotar to Shatoy. From there they planned to move on to Vedeno and Nozhai-Yurt. It was obvious that the enemy would soon find out about this route, if it had not already done so, and that it would be only too easy to bomb and shell our fighters on the march. The enemy was bound to avail itself of such an easy success on a scale it had not managed in either of the wars. Our fighters terrified the enemy precisely because they could appear without warning, and for that the Russian soldiers called them 'ghosts,' which was the name Soviet soldiers gave the guerrillas in Afghanistan for their similar ability. Now, for the first time, Chechen fighters would be sitting targets. I told Dalkhan to invite the commanders of our brigade's units to choose whichever routes for moving on they found most convenient and safe. They were under no obligation at all to join the general column marching towards Shatoy. Fighters from Shatoy, Vedeno or Nozhai-Yurt had no alternative, but those from other regions could make their own way home or remain for the time being in Achkhoy-Martan region, where we were now, or in Urus-Martan region nearby. Dalkhan agreed and said he would talk to our commanders before we left the village. The following day we were on our way again.

The lads were given a horse by the owner of the house where we spent the night. He also gave us a guide to escort us to Shaami-Yurt. The route proved very difficult and we had twice to cross rivers. The first time there was a log bridge and the lads carried me. The second time we had no choice but to wade across. It was a frosty night. The fighters took off their shoes and outer clothing. The water was shoulder-high and I was carried across on their raised hands. At this point, a helicopter came and hovered above us. The fighters opened fire with rifles and light machine guns from all directions and it quickly flew off, not even returning fire. Soon, however, we were subjected to Russian artillery fire.

After crossing the river our route took us through dense forest and undergrowth. My horse-drawn sledge kept snagging on the scrub and soon fell apart. One of my assistants had presciently put a stretcher on the sledge. The lads freed the horse, put me on the stretcher, and carried me on to Shaami-Yurt. That was a considerable distance, so several times those travelling with us took over from the lads in my security detail. Seeing how tired they were,

I felt very guilty. They tried to lighten the atmosphere by telling jokes and funny stories about their lives. I am profoundly grateful to them. They risked their lives to save mine.

When we got to Shaami-Yurt, people started distributing us to different houses. We were taken to a house and spent the daylight hours there. The lads gave me a painkilling injection and I slept the whole time. In the evening we moved on. The next village on our way was Valerik. We rejoined the general column. When we approached the village, we found a great many people waiting and were approached by a man called Ali. I remember his name because it was the same as my brother's. Ali talked to me as if we were great friends, although I had no recollection of him. However, I made no comment and my bodyguards decided we must know each other well. He invited us to his home, a car stopped beside us, and Ali suggested my lads put me in the back seat. I transferred to the car and Shaaman and Anzor came with me. We were driven to the far end of the village.

As we passed through, I saw a small group of soldiers marching in threes. I found this very odd, because Chechen fighters usually only marched formally when on parade. As we overtook the marchers, I recognized Magomed Khambiev, striding out in the lead wearing his invariable general's peaked cap and I realized this was our celebrated 'National Guard,' also known as Khambiev's Guard. Seeing these youths marching along, I could see why Khambiev had been lying low in his basement. They were no more than children, and Khambiev could not possibly have taken up a fighting position with them without causing completely pointless loss of life. When a young person the age of Khambiev's soldiers was among adults, it was not so obvious, but when three dozen children were gathered together and dressed in military uniforms they looked like a unit of the Hitler Youth. It was just as well they never got caught by a news cameraman, or Putin's propagandists could have accused Aslan Maskhadov of recruiting child soldiers. It turned out that there was an unwritten rule that nobody in the 'National Guard' could be taller than its commander, and given Khambiev's modest stature, his soldiers really did look like children. These were the sons of Khambiev's friends and relatives in Nozhai-Yurt whom he had recruited as his 'Guards' because, between the wars, service in this unit was paid. Naturally, Magomed bore sole responsibility for these youngsters in the eyes of their parents and relatives, and that was why he spent all the time there was fighting in Grozny in his basement, keeping them safe.

Soon we arrived at our destination. The driver took us to a newly built house which was not fully finished inside. It was, however, very warm. Ali, the owner of the house, and Ibrakhim arrived but, after spending just a short time with us, Ali left, saying he would be back in a little while. Ibrakhim inspected the house and found that only the room where we were staying had a door or glass in the windows. In all the other rooms, the doorways and window openings were empty. After inspecting the interior, Ibrakhim and Anzor looked round outside and, when they came back, asked me how well I knew our host. I told them I did not know him at all or, if I did, I really could not remember him. Ibrakhim said the house was right on the edge of the village and he wanted to know which houses the other members of our brigade were staying in. I was given another painkilling injection and dozed off. When I woke, I listened in on the radio to what our fighters were saying. Almost until daylight they had been moving along the already prescribed route. People in the villages through which the column passed fed our men and found a warm place for them to rest. The Russian Command knew what was happening and began bombing the villages, mostly after our men had already left. This was done to punish the villagers for giving shelter to our volunteers. News of casualties spread through the republic, and there were people to be found among the Chechens who tried to persuade others that 'the Wahhabis and the Russian Army are in cahoots against the people, and that is why the Russians bomb villages only after the Wahhabis have left them.' (Russian and pro-Russian propaganda called anyone who resisted the invaders 'Wahhabis'.) Alas, some people believed that.

During the day, Russian planes carried out air strikes on Katar-Yurt, a village to the west of Valerik, and that morning, several Russian aircraft fired missiles in the outskirts of Valerik, several of them exploding near where we were staying. Anzor and Shaaman were with me at the time. After the explosions we heard rifle and heavy machine gun fire near our house. Anzor rushed outside, and Shaaman stayed with me. The shooting intensified, and we heard shouts of 'Allahu Akbar!' Several shots were fired from an anti-tank grenade launcher, and real fighting broke out. Shaaman went over to the window and said Russian troops were entering the village. He saw armour accompanied by infantry and told me the invaders were coming in our direction. At this moment, Ibrakhim and Sulambek dashed in, grabbed me, put me on a blanket, carried me through to another room, and dropped me through a window opening on the other side of the house. I fell on builder's rubble and felt a sharp pain shoot through the whole of my body, but it passed quickly. Ibrakhim and Sulambek put me back on the blanket, lifted the ends, and carried me away from the house into the recesses of the village. Nobody panicked.

We passed through several courtyards and found ourselves on a street. I asked them if they knew where they were going and Ibrakhim said they did. The night before, they had become suspicious when our host disappeared and had made themselves familiar with the surrounding area. Ilias, a unit commander in our brigade, was a native of Valerik and they moved our fighters to neighbouring houses and posted sentries. The fighting I heard was men from our brigade taking on the enemy. Dalkhan was now in the house next door and, I learned later, was wounded in the arm during the battle. A Lada stopped next to us in the street. Shaaman and Anzor jumped out. Ilias was at the wheel. They put me in the back and, as we drove away, Ilias told me the enemy had entered the village from every direction and all the roads were blocked, so that for the time being it was impossible to leave. We turned on to a street only to find a column of Russian armoured vehicles ahead. Ilias made no attempt to stop and reverse, but accelerated and turned into another street. Ahead of us we saw a large crowd. Sulambek asked Ilias, 'What's going on?' He replied, 'It must be a funeral.' Sulambek said, 'Turn into the courtyard.'

In accordance with Chechen custom, the gate to the yard was wide open. Ilias drove in and stopped in the middle of the courtyard. They pulled me out of the car. Sulambek greeted the people there, expressed his condolences. and asked where they could put me. Some young people immediately came forward to carry me, but Sulambek asked them just to show him where I could lie. We were taken into the house, down a hallway, and came to the room they had set aside. I was laid on a bed and all except Shaaman left, saying they would be out in the courtyard. Sulambek and Ilias were in civilian clothing but Ibrakhim, Anzor, Shaaman and I were in army uniform. We also had bushy beards. Ilias said he would get Ibrakhim and Anzor to change into civilian clothes, and they left.

The room had two windows, but both looked out into the street. We could hear voices there clearly and see the silhouettes of people through the white cotton curtains, which did a good job of concealing the room from outside view. Shaaman stood by the window and shortly afterwards we saw the outline of Sulambek. He was talking loudly to someone so that we could hear. Almost immediately we heard the roar of armoured vehicles and Russian voices. A Russian army officer shouted that they were checking passports and everyone should go back to their homes. Someone rushed into the yard and said a Russian convoy was approaching. The wailing of the women in the yard intensified. The elders tend to disapprove of women weeping and wailing at a funeral, and usually during the ceremonies they are assigned a separate place.

Today, however, after my arrival, the mourning women were deliberately brought into the courtyard and, as the invaders approached, their lamentation grew all the louder. Shaaman and I could clearly see the Russian special operations forces through the window curtain. He took a hand grenade, removed the safety catch and asked, 'Are you ready?' I replied affirmatively. Shaaman recited the shahada and I repeated it after him. We heard one of the special operations troops say they had information that militants had entered the village, and their orders were to check every courtyard and every house. One of the men told him they were in mourning. Someone had died, they were preparing to bury him, and they had no militants in their house. Their voices were drowned out by the wailing and lamentation of the women. The special forces, at the urging of the Chechen elders, left the courtyard where the Tezet was in progress and, a couple of hours later, left the village.

I always had complete faith in the lads at my side, in their courage, greatness of spirit and readiness to sacrifice their lives for their ideals. Shaaman's actions testified to that. We were in a situation where we appeared to have no choice but to die or surrender ignominiously. We had weapons but could not use them without condemning to death those magnanimous people who were not members of our families, with whom we were not even acquainted but who had, nevertheless, given us refuge and risked their lives to save us.

For me, the most trying aspect of this situation was that all these people were being put at risk because of me. I was immensely touched that Shaaman, by asking if I was prepared for death, was trying to stop me feeling responsible for having landed him in this situation. The trouble was that, when we left Zakan-Yurt, they had suggested moving me to Ingushetia. I had flatly refused, arguing that leaving Chechnya would be tantamount to betrayal on my part. I misjudged the situation. The painkiller with which I was continually being injected prevented me from forming a reasoned judgement. Under the influence of the injections, it never occurred to me that I was placing at risk the lives of everyone in my vicinity. I was a useless burden, as the incident in Valerik made very clear. It was only as a result of the courageous decisions of the Chechen volunteers, as well as the cool thinking and resourcefulness of local people mourning the death of a young man in their family, that the episode did not end in tragedy.

After this, I was moved to a different house. Ilias and Sulambek came in to see me several times during the day and said they were negotiating with Gantemirovite policemen to get them to smuggle me through the Russian checkpoints to Urus-Martan. Knowing Dalkhan had been wounded, I told him via Sulambek to order the brigade to break away from the general column of the withdrawing Chechen forces. I asked Ilias to meet the commanders of detachments in the village and suggest they should collect the fighters' weapons for safekeeping, so that they could return to their homes through checkpoints unhindered. We needed time. We needed to sit out the winter. That did not mean we were giving up, just that there would have to be an interval before we could continue organized resistance with a central Command, given that so many commanders had been killed. New appointments would be needed, new operations planned in the light of the changed situation. In any case, during this period while we were taking a break, I was sure the Redskins would continue to harass the army of occupation. The Redskin groups devised their own operations and chose their own targets, usually command posts or army columns on the move. Ilias came back after a while to say that several detachments had agreed to hand over their weapons to him. That was to prove the final order I issued to my brigade. I was never to see my commanders on the territory of Chechnya again.

When it was dark, I was carried out to the courtyard where an off-roader was waiting. I was put in the back with Shaaman and Sulambek and the Gantemirovite police officers sat in front. They were worried about my long beard and bandaged head and suggested I should shave off the beard and remove the head bandage. I refused, unreasonably, to part with my beard, but agreed to take off the bandage. With that settled, we drove out of the yard to the street where a car with Ibrakhim and Anzor was waiting. They were in civilian clothes but armed and followed behind us.

I forget just how many checkpoints we passed through, but the procedure was invariable. Russian soldiers stopped our car, the Gantemirovite police showed their ID, the soldiers said they needed to report to their commander. After a short time, an officer appeared, greeted the bearers of the ID, and was handed a package. The commander then ordered the soldiers to let us pass, and they raised the barrier.

When we entered Urus-Martan, Sulambek asked me where to go. I gave him the name of my mother's brother, Mokhaddin. Sulambek was from Urus-Martan himself and knew not only Mokhaddin but almost all my other relatives. We drove up to his gate, Sulambek opened it, and the two cars drove into the yard. My companions carried me into the house, and then Sulambek and the Gantemirovites left. Anzor and Ibrakhim went to warn my elder brother, Ali, that I was in Urus-Martan and to tell him where I was staying. He came early in the morning to see me and told Mokhaddin that during the day he would find somewhere for me to move to. Mokhaddin replied that he would take me nowhere because there was plenty of room in his house for me and my bodyguards. Neither he nor I knew that the occupying forces had already embarked on a determined manhunt to track me down. We soon found out. That same morning, the Gantemirov policemen returned and asked my uncle to move me immediately, because they had information that the Russian Command knew I was in Urus-Martan and might well come today to search the house. 'We do not want to go down in history as traitors,' they added. Hearing that the occupying forces were planning to search my relatives' houses, and afraid people might think they were the informants, they had found Sulambek and came back with him to my uncle. This intelligence caused Mokhaddin to soften his stance, and Ali had me carried out to the car in which he had come to visit me. Khalid, a close relative, was at the wheel. Ali told him where to take me.

We soon reached our destination and stopped at the gates of a large brick house. Khalid got out, went into the courtyard, and a few minutes later the gates were opened. He drove us into the yard, I was taken from the car and carried into the house. The owner was called Khasan and, although I did not know him, he clearly knew me. He told us to make ourselves at home. Soon my brother Ali appeared with a doctor from the Urus-Martan hospital, who examined and questioned me and said I needed inpatient treatment. The priority was to scan my spine because I had acute back pain. Ali said that about an hour after we left with Khalid, Russian troops had cordoned off the whole district and searched Mokhaddin's house and the houses of my mother's three other brothers. They said openly that they had intelligence I was hiding at the house of one of my mother's brothers. Khasan looked disconcerted. Ali left, saying we would probably not be able to see each other for a while, because he was sure the FSB would soon be following him.

I have to say that the only place I stayed after arriving in Urus-Martan which was not raided by Russian troops was Khasan's house, although I lived there longer than anywhere else and even, after a short break, for a second time. In fact, I convened a meeting there of the heads of departments of the Ministry of Culture. This was the last time I saw my deputy, Makkala Sabdullaev. After that meeting, we moved elsewhere. The next day Khasan came to see my brother, Ali, and told him that he was no longer worried; even if there was a change of regime, he was in good standing with the government of Ichkeria. At the same time as giving me refuge, Khasan was working for the occupying forces as director of the market.

After I left Khasan's house, I played a deadly game of hide-and-seek with the Russian Army. We could not stay for even a day in the same place, and on one occasion left right under the noses of the Russian special operations forces. We drove out when they were within 50 metres of cordoning off the place where we were staying. My home, where Ali lived with his family, was raided several times. As expected, he and my sisters were being followed and for the rest of my time in Chechnya I was unable to see any of them. My movements were taken care of by those same lads: Shaaman, Ibrakhim, Anzor and Muslim. There were invariably two of them with me around the clock. Khalid brought me news of my relatives, who supported me and worked to ensure my safety. Wherever I was, they would be on the lookout and give timely warning to my bodyguards to move me on to a new place. When Russian troops arrived to search a place I had stayed overnight, they were always thirty minutes or an hour too late. We decided on my next sanctuary as we drove along.

It became increasingly obvious to me and my companions that it was impractical for me to stay any longer in Urus-Martan, or even in Chechnya, because sooner or later the occupation forces would stumble upon us. Ibrakhim got in touch with Alik, the chief of our brigade's Special Department. As a former officer of the Soviet Ministry of the Interior, he had many friends and acquaintances in the occupying regime's newly formed institutions. Alik arranged for his former colleagues to move me from Urus-Martan to nearby Goyty. Before leaving the city, I asked them to drive me past my father's house. Deep down, I had a sense that I would not be returning to the haunts of my youth for a long time, although I never imagined how abruptly my life was changing at that moment. At my request, they stopped the vehicle some way before reaching my home. I saw my sister-in-law, Raisa, talking in the street to Markha, her neighbour from across the road. I could not speak to them, because those transporting me did not want the women to see me in their company, so we drove slowly past the house where I had spent my childhood. There was a time when those gates had enclosed the safest place in the world for me, but today when I so needed a place of safety, the occupying regime had turned my home into a deadly trap.

In the course of those two weeks, they sealed off our entire district twice, rushing into the house, forcing everyone to lie face down on the ground and ordering them to say where they were hiding me. They threw a cordon right round the district, and a circle of troops round the house. During the second raid they nearly killed my nephew, eleven-year-old Adlan, who was in the back yard. The special operations agents skulking there opened fire and it was by the purest fluke they did not hit the boy. Frightened by the shooting, Adlan cried out, and it was only then the soldiers realized they were shooting at a child. One of the bastards came over, pointed his rifle at the boy's head, and ordered him to say where his uncle Akhmed was. Many, many Chechen children have been traumatized by the invaders in the course of those two wars, made to feel insecure in their own family homes, and I have no doubt these hundreds of thousands of children will never forgive or forget what was done to them. My home remains in my memory exactly as I last saw it that day as I drove past on the way to Goyty.

Alik's friends transferred me to the care of a colleague who worked for the occupying regime and we stayed with him for three days. Alik said it would be best to get me right out of the Urus-Martan region. I had many friends in Atagi and we decided to move there.

We reached Atagi without incident and spent almost three weeks there. One night was spent with a friend of Alik's, and the rest of the time with the family of one of the members of our government. In the course of those two weeks, Alik and one of my relatives agreed with an FSB officer who was Chechen by nationality that, in return for US$ 5,000, he would transport me to Ingushetia. I had become reconciled to the fact that I would have to leave the republic, and only regretted not having accepted the offer of the lads back in Zakan-Yurt to move me to Ingushetia.

In early March, Alik and my relative came to collect me. Shaaman and Anzor were with me that day and carried me out to the car. Sitting in the front were two people I did not know, whom I took to be FSB. That day I bade farewell to Shaaman and Anzor and have not seen them since. One now lives in Europe and the other in Chechnya. I think of them and will always remember them with deep gratitude.

Within a few hours we arrived at the notorious Kavkaz–1 checkpoint. The FSB agent told his driver to stop the car before we reached it. Yunus, as the agent was called, walked to the checkpoint, came back, and we drove on. As we were driving through the zigzag of concrete blocks I saw very solidly reinforced bunkers and, despite the fact that there was almost no traffic, there were large numbers of soldiers in full combat readiness at the checkpoint. The blocks were laid fairly wide apart on the road and did not greatly impede the traffic, but for me the time passed very slowly as we negotiated those obstacles. Alik and my relative told me they had taken robust precautions again treachery, but while I trusted them implicitly, I did not entirely trust those they trusted.

At the checkout we were stopped by a Russian officer who greeted Yunus and asked, 'What's this, your usual cargo of villains?' I was sitting in the back seat between Alik and my relative. The officer did not even glance in and we drove on. When we were well past the checkpoint, Yunus told us he gave all the money he collected for transporting people as bribes to the Russians, and was doing it without any ulterior motive. He just wanted to save as many Chechens as possible from harm. Later I learned that he was associated with Arbi Baraev, who came from his village, and personally arranged all Arbi's movements around the republic.

We encountered no more checkpoints on the road, but met several columns of armour moving towards Chechnya. Soon we reached Nazran, where a car was waiting. Yunus said he could take us on to where we were staying, but my cousin said we were not stopping in Ingushetia but heading on. Alik sat down beside me and said he would go back to Chechnya with Yunus to make sure he could not follow us and find out where we were staying. We drove off in different directions, but stopped almost immediately and drove into a courtyard. There I was transferred to another car occupied by local policemen. They took me to their colleague, and I spent my first night in Ingushetia at his house. The next day, I asked the house-owner to phone my friend, Akhmed Kodzoev. Akhmed arrived after lunch and insisted I was moved to his home. I confess, I had been hoping he would, because staying with him would be much more agreeable than staying with strangers. Akhmed and I had been fellow students at the Arts Institute in Voronezh, although his father later moved him to the Law Faculty in Vladikavkaz, or Ordzhonikidze as it was called back then. Nevertheless, all these years Akhmed and I had remained good friends. After the First War he often came to see me and Said-Khusein Tazbaev. I knew all the members of his family, and his parents treated me with great respect. One of Akhmed's brothers was working in Ruslan Aushev's government. Akhmed first took me to see his father and, late at night, I was taken to a ground floor apartment. From that time, Akhmed Kodzoev and his family assumed responsibility for my safety, and they took very good care of me. I had complete confidence in them and felt safe. Akhmed made me break off all contact with Chechnya, except for a few very close friends.

X
A New President for Russia

From Ingushetia Zakaev is moved, with highly placed help, to Ossetia and Georgia. A battle between those in the retreating Chechen column and a Russian paratroop brigade is demythologized. Retreating Chechen troops are not well protected by their commanders, and a massacre occurs at Saadi-Kotar (Komsomolskoye). A stage-managed 'capture' of Salman Raduev, in fact handed over by Kadyrov, boosts Putin's ratings and, on 26 March 2000, he is elected president of Russia.

During my stay in Ingushetia, a number of events radically changed the situation in Putin's favour. The first was the battle at Komsomolskoye, where the Chechens suffered huge losses. Many of the units which had withdrawn from Grozny had reached Shatoy and there was a great concentration of our forces there. The commanders of these units chose Ruslan Gelaev as their leader. An exception was Hattab, who also arrived in Shatoy with a small group to move Shamil Basaev to his base in the vicinity of Vedeno. Khusein Isabaev and the fighters of our brigade who had gone on to Shatoy with the main column also declined to place themselves under Gelaev's command, as did Ramzan Akhmadov and his detachment. Khusein Isabaev, Ramzan Akhmadov and their men decided to throw in their lot with Hattab and Shamil Basaev, and they left Shatoy together, moving towards Dargo. Some 1,200 Chechen fighters in all left for Vedeno.

This was the occasion of a clash which to this day is described in Russia as 'the Heroic Sacrifice of the Paratroopers of Pskov.' In fact there was no heroic sacrifice and the paratroopers did not, as claimed, deliberately put themselves in the line of fire. I know this for a fact from what I have been told by fighters who took part in this battle, and in particular by Khusein Isabaev. Khusein told me that the first to come across the paratroopers was a group led by Abudar of Goyty. A skirmish began in the afternoon. The paratroopers were in well fortified trenches on a hill on the route of the advancing column of Chechen fighters. Abudar was wounded, and saw his reconnaissance group would not be able to cope with the enemy. He asked for support. Shamil Basaev called for volunteers to dislodge the paratroopers and enable the main force to pass. There were many volunteers, but just 40 fighters were chosen to storm the height. Apti Akhmadov negotiated with the paratroopers, inviting them to surrender and promising on behalf of the Command that their lives would be spared. They opened negotiations, called Apti into the open, and a sniper shot him in the head. At that, Rezvan Akhmadov rushed the enemy trenches, followed by the other fighters, and annihilated the paratroopers. According to the official Russian version of the battle, 84 paratroopers were killed. The actual losses on the Chechen side were about 20 killed. Khusein Isabaev said that during the march they buried the dead in shallow graves so that they could easily be reburied later. I spoke to other participants in this battle and the highest estimate of the number of Chechen fighters killed at that time was 25. I spoke also to residents of Makhkety who reburied the Chechens and they testified that they had found a total of 42 bodies in temporary graves. I can safely say, therefore, that tales of 470 Chechens killed in the battle, as well as the claim that the paratroopers 'drew fire on themselves,' are untrue and just another fiction devised by Putin's propagandists.

If we move on from poppycock to reality, Russian forces did achieve success in the Argun Gorge. Not long before, they had succeeded in dislodging Hattab's fighters from Duba-Yurt and, after heavy fighting, gained control of the Gorge. At the same time, the invaders began making their way from the Dzheirakh Gorge in Ingushetia to Itum-Kale and, occupied this regional centre. They gained control of the road to Shatili in Georgia and were able to advance on Shatoy in a pincer movement, from the southwest from the direction of the Georgian border, and from the northeast, from the Argun Gorge. Gelaev, situated in Shatoy with the combined forces, convened a meeting of the commanders and proposed that they should descend to the plains of Chechnya to take Urus-Martan and adjacent villages. Not all the commanders agreed with this. Daud Akhmadov and Baudin Bakuev, for example, left with their detachments, the former to Zums in Itum-Kale region and the latter to Nizhal in Cheberloy region. Additionally, Arbi Baraev took his men to their village of Yermolovka. As was later related by men who had been in Saadi-Kotar (Komsomolskoye), many of those with Gelaev had been weakened by days of trekking in the mountains and lack of food. They were counting on being able to restore their strength in the lowlands and not expecting to engage in military operations.

Slightly more than 1,000 men moved from Shatoy towards Saadi-Kotar in a single overnight march. Gelaev proposed that they should not go into his village but instead move on. The exhausted fighters refused to obey him, and some accused him of not wanting to expose his home village to the risk of damage during possible fighting. Be that as it may, the fighters entered Saadi-Kotar, and that night Ruslan Gelaev left the village with his family and some 40 men who were directly under his command. Before departing, Gelaev delegated command over the fighters remaining in the village to his deputy, Vakhid Bamatgireyev. Gelaev told him he would return in three days. Those three days were to prove fateful for those who stayed in Saadi-Kotar. According to Visami, one of those caught up in these events, they could have escaped from the village during that period, but Bamatgireyev failed to give the command, saying Ruslan Gelaev had only gone away for a short time and they could decide what to do next when he returned. After three days, Vahid told the commanders that, as Gelaev had not returned as promised, he no longer wished to be responsible for the consequences and each of them was free to take his own decision on how to proceed. By this time, however, Russian troops had surrounded Saadi-Kotar and had effectively taken hostage villagers who came to them to ask to be allowed to leave. Throughout the days of the ensuing battle for Saadi-Kotar, the occupying army kept these people out in the open, using them as human shields. This monstrous crime was documented by the Memorial Human Rights Centre. The Russian troops at Saadi-Kotar were under the command of Major General Valeriy Vasilievich Gerasimov, and overall command was exercised by Colonel General Mikhail Ivanovich Labunets.

It was during the battle at Saadi-Kotar that Russian troops first used the TOS–1 Heavy Flame Thrower System of Buratino ('Pinocchio') multiple rocket launchers mounted on a T–72 tank chassis. The system had previously been used in Afghanistan. Data from the manual states, 'The TOS–1 is designed to engage lightly armoured vehicles and transport, setting fire to and destroying fortifications and buildings, engaging military personnel in open countryside and in fortifications by means of shrapnel, shock waves produced in the target area by massive use of unguided missiles and incendiary and thermobaric warheads.'

From what survivors tell us, there was no fighting in Saadi-Kotar except for one skirmish. Early in the morning of 6 March, Russian troops entered the village and, within a few hours, Chechen fighters had destroyed almost all the enemy's armoured vehicles. The invaders themselves say that their casualties that day were 50 killed and more than 300 wounded. Thereafter, the invader blockaded the village and bombarded it with long-range artillery. In these battles the Chechens suffered their heaviest casualties ever. According to those who buried Chechens killed in the village, they interred 750 people in a common grave. That number includes only those buried in the cemetery between Goyskoye and Saadi-Kotar. In addition to those, relatives collected the bodies of several hundred more fighters and buried them back in their own villages. There were fighters from all over the republic in Saadi-Kotar at that time, and although the Russian Command contended that in 'Komsomolskoye' (Saadi-Kotar) 'the detachment of Ruslan Gelaev has been destroyed,' this was completely untrue. On the first night Gelaev had left the village with his unit. Those who were in Saadi-Kotar were detachments under the command of Tavus Boguraev of Naur, the unit of Badruddin Ganatov from a detachment subordinate to Vakha Arsanov, detachments of Visami of Nadterechny, Vakhid Bamatgireyev of Sernovodsk, as well as many smaller independent groups.

Another supposed feature of these events was that, for the first time in both wars, Chechen fighters were shown surrendering. There were 70 or so of them. There is, however, evidence that the horrific video footage of tortured and beaten Chechen prisoners was stage managed and timed to ensure Putin's election. The video shows people, most of them wounded and swathed in bandages, barely able to move and, in all probability, unconscious when they were taken prisoner. This footage, and the report put out over all the Russian media that Salman Raduev had been detained in Chechnya, contributed to a surge in the popularity rating of Presidential Candidate Vladimir Putin in a Russia thirsting for revenge. Putin himself constantly commented on all this, making it clear that he was the man in charge. After Yeltsin's resignation, the Russian Federation Council declared a presidential election on 26 March 2000. The events described above occurred just two weeks before that date. They had an impact on the outcome.

I watched all this on television in Ingushetia. On 13 March 2000, all Russian TV channels broadcast the message that 'as the result of a Special Operation, the Chechen terrorist commander of "General Dudaev's Army," Salman Raduev, has been arrested.' He was supposedly in command of almost 3,000 fighters. In fact, at the outbreak of the Second Russo-Chechen War, Raduev disbanded his group and disappeared off the radar. Even his group members had no idea where he was. Needless to say, even at the peak of his popularity, Raduev never had anything like 3,000 men under his command as the Russian media so insistently claimed. It was, incidentally, only due to the Russian media that he became so high-profile after the First War. Raduev was hyped in Russia for the simple reason that he was prepared to 'claim responsibility' for every attack that took place in the post-Soviet territories.

The Kremlin found it advantageous in propaganda terms to make him the 'face' of independent Chechnya. Aware of the simple rules, Raduev enthusiastically gave interviews to Russian reporters, filling the air with empty threats and boasting of attacks wholly unrelated to him or any other Chechen. This did not prevent his arrest from being trumpeted in Russia as a spectacular success of the Russian intelligence agencies. In reality, Raduev never posed any threat to Russia. Indeed, in the almost three years between the wars he did everything in his power to discredit the government of the independent Chechen Republic. It was he who initiated political sabotage against the Chechen state and, together with the Udugov brothers and Shamil Basaev, helped Russia start the Second Russo-Chechen War. When it began, Raduev and his scary, self-proclaimed 'Army of General Dudaev' vanished in a puff of smoke.

According to information we received later, Salman Raduev was handed over to the Russians by Akhmad-haddzhi Kadyrov. Salman had agreed with him to dissolve his band and offer no resistance to Russian troops. In return, Kadyrov was supposed to help him leave Chechnya via Baku and move to Turkey and the Middle East, where he would spearhead a campaign to discredit Aslan Maskhadov and deny the Chechen president political and financial support. As agreed with Kadyrov, Raduev was sitting in the village of Novogrozny near Gudermes, having shaved off his beard and even dismissed his personal bodyguard. All his closest associates, headed by Adam Dimelkhanov, transferred their allegiance to Kadyrov. Raduev sat at the rendezvous waiting for Kadyrov's people to spirit him off to Baku. Early one morning in March they duly arrived, only they spirited him off to Moscow and straight into the Lubyanka headquarters of the FSB. Putin himself commented on the arrest, calling Raduev an 'animal.' When Kadyrov had discussed his plan to send Raduev to Turkey with Moscow, it was decided that the sensational arrest and trial of 'Chechen Terrorist and Russia's Enemy No. 1' would bring greater political rewards than anything Raduev might do to discredit President Maskhadov abroad. The more so because that was already being done in a highly competent manner by the Udugov brothers on behalf of Shamil Basaev, who had considerably more influence in the Islamic world than Raduev.

At that moment I knew nothing of all this and, despite the fact that Raduev had done so much harm to a cause for which thousands of Chechens had sacrificed their lives, I felt sorry for a man who was plainly deranged. I saw him as another victim of a war Yeltsin began in 1994 in order to boost his political standing in Russia. Now Yeltsin and Putin had again played 'the

Chechen card' immediately before a presidential election with the aim of ensuring 'continuity' of government in Russia. Raduev, putting his trust in Akhmad-haddzhi Kadyrov, did them a favour. I really do not believe that Raduev had been recruited as an agent of Russian intelligence, although many Chechens believe that was the case. The truth is, however, that if he had been a Russian agent, he would have behaved in precisely the way he did. By arresting Salman Raduev, Putin gained a huge electoral propaganda advantage.

An early Russian presidential election was held on 26 March and, to the surprise of many, Acting President Putin won it in the first round. Why was that unexpected? The opinion polls and analyses showed Putin in the lead, but it was generally assumed he would win only in the second round. I little doubt that the reason he won in the first round, with almost 53% of the vote, was the events described above.

The military campaign in Chechnya and its successful prosecution laid the foundation of Putin's political career, because the average Russian citizen following the war on television believed everything going on there was the doing of Putin personally. The defeat of Ruslan Gelaev's units, hyped and demonized in the Russian media no less than Raduev, as well as the arrest of the latter, was represented by the Russian media as great victories notched up by Putin himself. Despite my negative attitude to the man, I have to admit that Putin was not just lucky, but very skilful in exploiting our failures during the Second War, and in playing on the baser instincts of ordinary members of the Russian public whose national pride had been so bruised by defeat in the First War.

Shortly afterwards, another event occurred which merits mention. There were some 200,000 Chechen refugees in Ingushetia at this time, many of them living in tents in temporary camps or, if they could afford it, in rented accommodation. Not a few were offered shelter and hospitality in Ingush homes. Among the refugees were active members of Chechen society who supported the Resistance, and members of the Resistance themselves who had decided to sit out the winter in Ingushetia. I had many friends and relatives among them, but could stay in touch with only a very limited number of people. One was Musa Khaddzhimuradov, my trusted friend and comrade-in-arms, who had come to Ingushetia for medical treatment. His leg had healed, although he was still limping, but I persuaded him to remain in Ingushetia as someone through whom I could have contact with the outside world. Musa knew where I was, and if anyone wanting to meet me appeared in Ingushetia, he would let me know and leave me to decide for myself whether or not to meet them. One day Musa came to say that Apti Batalov, the head of President Maskhadov's Administration, was looking for me. I imagined he had been sent by Aslan and asked Musa to bring him to see me. I was staying at the time with Akhmed Kodzoev. When we met, however, I discovered that Apti knew nothing about Aslan Maskhadov, had not seen him for almost six months, and had, as he said, fallen out with him. This, of course, greatly perplexed me because, if I had known that, I would never have agreed to meet Batalov or let him know where I was.

I told him he had chosen an odd time to fall out with Maskhadov. He should have done so a year and a half earlier when he was the president's confidant with a very important position in the government. Apti began by saying we needed to do everything possible to stop the war, and that the way to do so was for all 'healthy forces' to unite around Akhmad-haddzhi Kadyrov. Apti undertook to arrange for me to meet Kazbek Makhashev, who he understood was also in Ingushetia at this time. According to Apti, we all needed to rally round Kadyrov because we still enjoyed the respect of the people and needed to warn them that this war would not end like the last one. We must convince all Chechens to cease resistance in order to avoid unnecessary casualties. Apti tried to persuade me that the Russians would not retreat this time but would see matters through to the end. He had brought someonea n we both knew to the meeting. As I listened to Apti, I realized it had been a big mistake to see him.

I did not argue any more and, just pointing to my injuries, said I could no longer be of use to anyone. Apti continued trying to persuade me that Kazbek and I should support Kadyrov, and said he would shortly find Kazbek through Movlen Salamov, the former head of President Dudaev's Administration, and arrange for us to meet. I did not argue. I just wanted him to leave with the belief that he had completed his mission of encouraging me to cooperate with Kadyrov Senior, in other words, with Russia. Apti and his companion departed, and I told Akhmed Kodzoev I needed to move somewhere else immediately. Akhmed arranged it, and literally within fifteen minutes of Batalov's departure I was out of a house where, until then, I had felt completely safe.

Through Akhmed's brother who worked in the government, that same night I met one of the Ingush president's aides whom I knew well. I was taken to a village where Ingush officials lived and settled in the house of a senior Ministry of the Interior official, where I spent exactly one week. He insisted that for that week I broke off contact with everyone other than Ruslan Aushev's aide, and I was left in the house with only one of my relatives. His elderly mother was living there and took care of us. I remember her very warmly, because the old lady was kindness personified. The master of the house returned each evening, and during the daytime I and my relative did not go out, not even venturing into the courtyard. A week later, Ruslan Aushev's aide moved me to the home of another member of the Ministry of the Interior who lived in the same village. It was a large house with an enclosed courtyard, and while there I re-established contact, through Akhmed Kodzoev, with Musa Khaddzhimuradov and a few of my relatives.

In my new home I heard the news on Russian television that 'Apti Batalov, head of Aslan Maskhadov's Administration, has been arrested in a Special Operation.' It later became clear that this 'special operation' had been necessary only to legitimize his treachery and launch him on a career of blatant cooperation with the occupying forces and their collaborators. For a while he was in Moscow, making political statements on Russian television. On NTV there was a broadcast in which he participated. Apti told reporters by phone that he was in the toilet in some apartment in Moscow and that people were trying to kill him. He begged for help. This was followed by a replay of Putin's September speech in which he threatened to 'pulp the Chechen terrorists in the latrines.' All the Russian media wrote about what an influential person Apti Batalov was in President Maskhadov's team and how highly esteemed he was among the Chechens, and this was followed by a television broadcast featuring the voice of a man pleading for help from the toilet. This kind of derisive propaganda showed the true attitude of Putin and his FSB colleagues towards traitors, notwithstanding the fact that they needed their services. They could not resist the temptation to amuse themselves and their revanchist Russian dullards by poking fun at a defeated and humiliated enemy. It was Putin's way of saying thank you to those who elected him, mainly a bloc of voters who, in autumn 1996, had been 'ashamed for our great nation,' in the words of a popular film character. Putin rose to power by pandering to the chauvinistic instincts of this bloc. The Batalov episode seemed to be demonstrating that Russia's new leader meant what he said. He had promised to 'pulp them in the latrines,' and here he was literally doing just that. Ordinary Chechens found all this farcical nonsense, first with Salman Raduev and then with Apti Batalov, profoundly shaming. Chechens are extremely sensitive, I would even say unforgiving, in matters of honour and personal dignity. They took the view that the likes of Raduev and Batalov should have preferred death to allowing the Russians to show them so humiliated.

In short, Apti Batalov ended up, as Maskhadov had predicted, by dishonouring himself. In May 2000, the Chechen president stripped him of all state awards and military rank, but even this Apti tried to turn to his advantage. On the day he returned to Chechnya from Moscow, another episode with his participation was shown on television. The commentary announced that 'Apti Batalov emerges from Lefortovo Prison under amnesty' to be met by Bislan Gantemirov. In fact, Batalov had never been held in Lefortovo. The presenter told viewers this was 'a highly significant moment,' because the two men meeting outside the gates of the FSB's prison had been on opposite sides of the front line in the Chechen campaign. Apti Batalov then said, literally, 'In the course of the investigation, as far as I know, no aggravating circumstances of my participation in illegal armed groups were found and that is why I have been released. I qualify under the terms of the amnesty.' Next, referring to Maskhadov's decree stripping him of his CRI awards and titles, Apti said, 'I heard that Maskhadov has cashiered me, declared me an enemy of the people, and sentenced me to death.' In fact the Chechen president's decree contained no mention of capital punishment for him or the other traitors and Apti just threw this in to explain why he would be under FSB protection in his village in Chechnya. He added that, in spite of everything, he was returning to Chechnya, and that he and Gantemirov agreed on the need to 'rally all the healthy forces, roll up our sleeves, and work for the good of the people and for peace in the land of Chechnya.' Apti was repeating almost word for word what he had said to me in Ingushetia, only then his ignominious 'healthy forces' had needed to rally round Kadyrov.

The fact that Apti was shown in the company of Gantemirov indicated that there were still some in the FSB promoting the latter as their main puppet in Chechnya. For all that, it was Akhmad-haddzhi Kadyrov who took Apti Batalov back to Chechnya. He came to collect him from the apartment where he was being held by the FSB. Emerging with him, Kadyrov told journalists, 'We look after our own.' It confirmed what Aslan Maskhadov told me later. He said Apti Batalov had betrayed him and the cause of Chechen independence long before the staging of his 'arrest' and subsequent 'amnesty.' After his television appearances, Apti Batalov lived at home in Naur until 2002, under FSB protection. The Russian intelligence agencies got their money's worth out of him in every respect. As one of my friends said, the FSB do not put all their eggs in one basket, and this was not the end of the story of Apti Batalov. His next appearance in the political and news arena came in a different era and in different circumstances, but that is a story for later.

Shortly after the stage-managed detention and release of Apti Batalov, Khozh-Akhmed Yarikhanov came to see me. He gave me money from Aslan Maskhadov and his instruction that I should try to move to Georgia. Maskhadov warned that he had information from Ruslan Aushev that the Russian intelligence agencies knew I was in Ingushetia, and Ruslan was very concerned. It was not only a matter of the friendly relations I enjoyed with him, but also that, if anything were to happen to me in Ingushetia, it could cast a shadow on relations between our two fraternal Vainakh peoples, and be used by Russian agents provocateurs to drive a wedge between the Chechens and Ingush. For me it was a sign that we should not abuse Ingush hospitality. As it was no longer safe for me to remain in Ingushetia, my family and friends decided to move me to North Ossetia. In the period between the wars I had often gone there to meet President Alexander Dzasokhov and had developed a very friendly relationship with the Ossetian leadership. My good relations with Dzasokhov began, paradoxically, with the speech I gave at his inauguration, which concerned the plight of Ingush refugees from the Prigorodny region of North Ossetia. I drew attention to the unresolved Ossetian-Ingush conflict, and said that for Chechens this was a very painful issue, as the Chechens and Ingush are brothers and we see their misfortunes as our own. I urged that the Ossetians should resolve these problems on our own level, in the best traditions of the Caucasus, without looking to Moscow. This would ensure friendship and stability in the North Caucasus. The speech, I later discovered, had made me very popular with the Ingush. Although I did not know it at the time, the inauguration ceremony was being broadcast live in Ingushetia too.

When Alexander Dzasokhov took up his duties as president, he formed a committee to provide material and legal assistance to Ingush refugees wishing to return to homes they had been forced to abandon during the 1992 conflict. This was a major breakthrough in resolving the conflict. While Galazov, Dzasokhov's predecessor, was in office nothing of the sort was possible. On Dzasokhov's instructions, the committee regularly sent reports to us in Chechnya on how work was proceeding on enabling the Ingush refugees to return to their homes. After that, Kazbek Makhashev and I went on several occasions to North Ossetia, met Dzasokhov and members of the Refugee Commission, and talked to the Ingush returning to their abandoned homes. The process moved slowly, but it did move.

At the beginning of the Second War against Chechnya, a checkpoint was established on the border between Ingushetia and North Ossetia, at the so-called Chermen Circle. The crossing was staffed exclusively by FSB officers from Moscow and no vehicle passed through without being checked. Over 200,000 Chechen refugees were officially living in Ingushetia, 140,000 of them in temporary tented camps. I suspect there were an equal number of unregistered refugees renting accommodation or staying with family members and friends. Most were active supporters of our independence, forced to leave Chechnya because extrajudicial executions had already begun of anyone opposed to the occupation. In the interwar period, the Russian intelligence agencies collected personal information on all adult residents of Chechnya, and knew about people's politics. From the very beginning of the occupation of Chechnya, Russian 'death squads' used this information to murder not only members of the Resistance, but anyone who was an active or potential supporter of our armed forces. The Russian killers took to heart Putin's call to 'destroy the very environment of terrorism,' by which he meant a merciless campaign of terror against individuals or entire families who actively supported the sovereign independence of the Chechen Republic of Ichkeria. Chechen political activists were forced to flee to Ingushetia to avoid certain death.

People in immediate danger of being seized by the Russian intelligence agencies or killers from the death squads were unaware that they could find political asylum in European countries. The first to take advantage of this right were Chechens living in Moscow, as well as people completely unconnected with Chechnya. In the early years, according to the immigration services of European countries, there was an influx of some 4 million refugees from Chechnya and Ingushetia. This despite the fact that even in the most peaceful times the combined population of Chechens and Ingush never exceeded 1.5 million people. I offer this statistic so that Europeans uninitiated in these matters should have a realistic picture of what was going on in those days. The main flow of refugees from Chechnya and Ingushetia to Europe started only in 2003 and 2004, when the Chechen refugee camps in Ingushetia began being closed down. The stream continues to this day.

Ruslan Aushev did not, of course, allow the Russian intelligence agencies to commit the atrocities and extrajudicial executions they routinely carried out with impunity in Chechnya. Accordingly, the agencies focused the whole power of their propaganda machine on seeking to discredit the government of Ingushetia. This was done primarily by using the First and Second channels of Russian television, which accused Ruslan Aushev and members of his government of supporting President Aslan Maskhadov and of 'aiding and abetting Chechen terrorists.' The Kremlin's main mouthpiece, Mikhail Leontiev, in his television programme *However*, called Ingushetia 'a springboard for outlaws.' The FSB agents stationed at the Chermen checkpoint naturally inspected and scrutinized every vehicle, even those of the most senior officials from Ingushetia. Given that situation, the Ingush government was unable at that time to take responsibility for spiriting me through this checkpoint to North Ossetia, so I had to negotiate my move with the Ossetian government, and my good relations at the highest level came in very useful. The Ministry of the Interior of Ingushetia passed me over to officers of the North Ossetian Ministry of the Interior, where I spent over two weeks. I lived on the border with South Ossetia in the family of a friend of Alik. After that I was collected by the South Ossetian Ministry of the Interior, escorted across the Russo-Georgian border, and delivered to officers of Georgia's State Security who met me in South Ossetia.

Over the past several centuries, Russia has done everything in its power to divide the peoples of the Caucasus and to sow enmity between them. This was done cynically and efficiently: the imperial centre arranged the administrative boundaries in the North Caucasus in such a way that each nation should have territorial claims against its neighbour. For example, after Moscow deported the Vainakhs to Central Asia in 1944, the Checheno-Ingush Autonomous Republic was abolished and its land apportioned between Dagestan, Georgia, and North Ossetia. The main part of Checheno-Ingushetia became the Grozny region, which was settled by colonists brought in from different parts of Russia. When the Checheno-Ingush Autonomous Republic was restored in 1957 during the 'Khrushchev Thaw,' part of the territory of Chechnya was left in Dagestan, and one of the regions of Ingushetia, Prigorodny, was left within the administrative borders of North Ossetia. This was done deliberately by Moscow to ensure that no anti-imperial solidarity should develop between the peoples of the North Caucasus, despite their shared history, culture and traditions. It was a textbook example of the old imperial principle of 'divide and rule.' This misanthropic policy led to armed conflict, provoked by Moscow, in autumn 1992 between Ossetians and Ingush which resulted in heavy casualties, mainly among the Ingush because the Russian Army sided with North Ossetia. However, despite the fact that since then there has been hostility between the Ingush and the Ossetians, some of them united in solidarity with the Chechen war of liberation against the Russian Empire. I mention this because Ingush, Ossetians, Georgians, Dagestanis, and other Caucasian peoples helped many Chechens who had taken up arms against the Russian invaders to escape from mortal danger. Including me.

Nothing is ever simple, however. The help extended to Chechens by other Caucasian peoples was paradoxically combined with a desire on the part of many of their representatives to see us defeated in the struggle against Russia. This was true of the political, business and, to a large extent, the intellectual elite of our neighbours, the most influential strata of the peoples of the Caucasus who generate the ideology and political attitudes of the rest of the population. To illustrate this, let me quote the view expressed on Radio Liberty on 10 March 2003 by Sergey Arutyunov, Corresponding Member of the Russian Academy of Sciences, an ethnographer who heads the Caucasian Department at the Institute of Ethnology of the Russian Academy of Sciences:

If I were a member of the Armenian government, I would of course be apprehensive of self-determination for Chechnya. If somehow the Chechen, Ichkerian insurgents were to become established, maintain and develop some sort of force, it is entirely possible that a volunteer Chechen detachment might intervene in the conflict on the borders of Karabakh. One well-armed Armenian regiment can defeat an Azerbaijani army, but even an indifferently armed Chechen regiment will defeat an Armenian army. It is just a matter of a genetically inherited ability to wage war, a talent for war. Armenians have it to a moderate but sufficient degree; in Azeris it is very low; but the Chechens! The only people in the world who can be compared with the Chechens are the Nepalese Gurkhas who provided the elite units of the British colonial army. They are super-soldiers.

Few people can imagine what it meant psychologically for a one million strong people to have been victorious in the 1994-6 War over a 150 million strong hypermilitarized superpower. If the Chechens themselves attributed their success to the help of the Almighty, who always aids those with truth on their side, our Caucasian neighbours saw the success as a direct threat. Needless to say, this concern was actively promoted by Russian chauvinist propaganda, which wrote and spoke openly of the 'imperial ambitions' of the Chechens. There were claims that the Chechens intended to oust Russia from the Caucasus and take its place, creating a regional empire of their own. This fantasy figured not only in journalistic offerings in publications like Alexander Prokhanov's newspaper *Zavtra* (*Tomorrow*), but even in literary writings. A Russian writer called Mikhail Orlitsyn wrote a whole fantasy narrative titled *The Trap of Freedom* which describes not merely a Caucasian but a global empire created by the Chechens. If regional elites in the Caucasus had learned over the centuries to cooperate with

Moscow and find a common language on many issues, the Chechen leaders' aspiration to national independence was something they found completely baffling. The values to which we aspired were far outside the rules they were used to living by. The sheer numerousness of the Vainakhs and their passionate temperament told the Caucasian elites that, without Russia's military patronage, they would have to return to the Chechens and Ingush the territories taken from them by Stalin. Defeat for the Chechens in a war against Russia would reassure the Caucasian elites that nothing needed to change.

In reality, of course, the Chechens harbour no imperial ambitions. Our neighbours need only turn to past history to understand that. The Chechens simply believed, and still believe, that the peoples of the Caucasus, who have a shared mentality, a shared past, shared traditions and etiquette, should come together in solidarity and steadfastness in the face of a shared external threat. That threat, for as far back as we can remember, proceeded and continues to proceed from the Russian Empire. The Chechens fought, and continue to fight, against that empire, not in order to replace it, earning the hatred and contempt of their neighbours, but in order to free themselves from that yoke and help liberate other peoples of the Caucasus from it. Perhaps with time our Caucasian brothers will understand these obvious truths, and our struggle and our freedom will become a shared cause.

For almost three months, as I moved from one place to another, I was never parted from my pistol and a hand grenade. It was only in Tbilisi that I handed them over to those who met me. I have to admit that I really felt secure only in Georgia. I was not to know how drastically my life would change from then on, or that I was destined to spend the years to come far from my homeland, from my father's house, from my family and friends. But that is another story.